Essays in
The theory and measurement of consumer behaviour

Essays in
The theory and measurement of
consumer behaviour
in honour of
Sir Richard Stone

Edited by
ANGUS DEATON

CAMBRIDGE UNIVERSITY PRESS

Cambridge
London   New York   New Rochelle
Melbourne   Sydney

Published by the Press Syndicate of the University of Cambridge
The Pitt Building, Trumpington Street, Cambridge CB2 1RP
32 East 57th Street, New York, NY 10022, USA
296 Beaconsfield Parade, Middle Park, Melbourne 3206, Australia

First published 1981

Printed in the United States of America

British Library Cataloguing in Publication Data
Essays in the theory and measurement of consumer
behaviour.
1. Consumption (Economics) – Addresses, essays,
lectures
I. Stone, *Sir* Richard
II. Deaton, Angus
339.4'7   HB801   80-40903
ISBN 0 521 22565 5

Contents

v

Foreword

Sir Richard Stone retired from his chair in Cambridge in September 1980. To mark the occasion, this volume has been written in his honour. It is not a *festschrift* after the usual mould, where friends and colleagues contribute a diverse collection of papers. Sir Richard's achievements have been too broad and his disciples too many to permit a single collection along such lines. Instead, I have taken one single field in which Sir Richard has been preeminent, and attempted to bring together a first-rate collection of papers in that field. Many of the authors are close friends or ex-colleagues of Sir Richard's, but several have had little more than professional contact. However, all are indebted to him through his scientific work, and in contributing to this volume are united in their wish to honour him and to acknowledge their indebtedness. In editing the volume it is my hope that the best way of honouring Sir Richard and commemorating his retirement is the preparation of a volume of the best current work in the economics of consumer behaviour. The papers published here are representative of a wide range of contemporary research in the field and only a few important topics are not covered at some point. They provide a good indication not only of the state of the art but also of the extraordinary area over which Sir Richard's own work has been an influence.

ANGUS DEATON

Princeton, October 1979

Contributors

S. N. AFRIAT	University of Ottawa
A. B. ATKINSON	London School of Economics
A. S. DEATON	University of Bristol and Princeton University
W. E. DIEWERT	University of British Columbia
N. P. FEDORENKO	Central Institute for Mathematical Economics, Moscow
W. M. GORMAN	London School of Economics and Johns Hopkins University
D. F. HENDRY	London School of Economics
L. JOHANSEN	Institute of Economics, University of Oslo
K. LAITINEN	University of Chicago
J. MUELLBAUER	Birkbeck College, London
M. NERLOVE	Northwestern University
A. RAZIN	University of Tel-Aviv
N. J. RIMASHEVSKAYA	Central Institute for Mathematical Economics, Moscow
N. H. STERN	University of Warwick
H. THEIL	University of Chicago
THOMAS VON UNGERN-STERNBERG	University of Bonn

PART ONE

The analysis of commodity demands

Introduction to part one

In a volume dedicated to Sir Richard Stone, it is appropriate that first consideration should be given to the theory and measurement of commodity demands. Sir Richard's own great monograph, *The Measurement of Consumers' Expenditure and Behaviour in the United Kingdom* [51]* retains its classic status in applied econometrics to this day. The research programme established there and in the 1954 *Economic Journal* article [48] on the linear expenditure system is still flourishing and the five papers in part one represent several aspects of it.

The first set of topics concern the appropriate choice of functional form for empirical demand equations. In [51], Sir Richard and his coworkers adopted a largely pragmatic approach using a loglinear constant elasticity form. This has great advantages in computation and allows a much more flexible research strategy than is possible with more complex non-linear equations in which all commodities are dealt with simultaneously. However, as has been known for a long time, loglinear demand functions for all commodities are inconsistent with utility theory in that they cannot permit the predicted demands to add up to the predetermined sum of expenditures. This reflects a quite general problem: how do we choose functional forms which are convenient to work with, which allow the easy incorporation of such information as we possess about the nature of individual demands, and which are consistent with the theory? The first two papers in this section are addressed to that question.

The paper by Terence Gorman investigates a generalization of perhaps the most obvious type of functional form for Engel curves, a polynominal structure with expenditures related to powers of income. Important examples of this are well-known: linear Engel curves, characterized by the so-called 'Gorman polar form', (Gorman, 1961) – the class to which the linear expenditure system belongs, as well as the quadratic expenditure system more recently described and estimated in Pollak and Wales (1978) and Howe, Pollak and Wales (1980). In his paper, Gorman proves a remarkable result: essentially, the quadratic case is as general as we can go. Demand equations with more than three terms in income (e.g.

---

* References given by numbers in brackets are to Sir Richard's own publications which are contained in a separate bibliography at the end of the book. Other citations are given by author and date, e.g., Gorman (1961).

a constant, linear and quadratic terms) are degenerate in the sense that the matrix of coefficients linking each demand to each power of income cannot be of rank greater than three. On the other hand, useful functional forms such as

$$w_i = \alpha_i + \beta_i \log m + \gamma_i (\log m)^2$$

or

$$w_i = a_i + b_i m + c_i m^2$$

for budget shares w_i and income m, are allowed without restrictions on the coefficients. In recent years, more and more large samples of data on individual households are being analysed at the microeconomic level, so that such flexible Engel curves will be increasingly required while, at the same time, the rank restriction ought to be testable in practice.

An alternative approach to the specification of demands is to assume a particular utility function and to derive demands from it, the linear expenditure system being the classic example. Such an approach has two main drawbacks. First, it is rarely straightforward to derive demand functions explicitly and second, it is extremely difficult to choose a utility function which will guarantee some desirable empirical feature in the demands. For example, the estimated functions often embody strong *prior* restrictions on the quantities which are being estimated, often precluding genuine measurement at all; for the case of the linear expenditure system see Deaton (1974b; 1975). Both these difficulties have largely been overcome by two recent developments: first, the use of duality methods and, second, the invention and widespread use of what are known as 'flexible functional forms'. Through duality, preferences are described indirectly through the indirect utility function or cost (expenditure) function and these representations are connected very simply, by differentiation or integration, to the commodity demands. (For descriptions of this theory see, for example, Diewert (1974; 1981), McFadden (1978), or, at a simpler level, Deaton and Muellbauer (1980a, chapters 2 and 3).) The closer relationship between demands and preferences makes it possible to choose preference orderings which are tailored to specific applications. Particularly useful are the flexible functional forms which are general enough and contain sufficiently many parameters to guarantee an arbitrarily close local approximation (usually second order) to any general utility function. Such a choice guarantees that the demand functions have enough free parameters to prevent any possibility of prior restrictions between income and price elasticities other than those generally required by utility theory.

A complementary strategy is advocated in the second paper, that by Leif Johansen. He suggests that separability theory be used to break up the overall utility function into branches, each of which can be given a different functional form tailored to the group of goods being modelled. Within such a scheme, we might have the linear expenditure system for allocating to broad groups, say food, leisure and services, while the subutility function for food could be such as to permit quadratic Engel curves for bread, cereals, meat and so forth as functions of total food expenditure. Different structures could then be chosen for leisure goods and for services as the circumstances and the data dictate. How all this can be fitted together is the subject of the paper.

The two empirical papers which follow cover two topics in which there have been major developments in recent years. That by Angus Deaton discusses some of the theoretical and practical problems which arise if we wish to estimate demand functions when some of the consumption levels are determined outside the consumer's control. This is the area of rationing theory and here again we have a topic in which much of the seminal work was done in Cambridge by the group around Sir Richard Stone in the early days of the Department of Applied Economics: see particularly the papers by Rothbarth (1941), Tobin and Houthakker (1951) and the survey by Tobin (1952) which virtually closed the subject for nearly twenty years. If we are to construct tests for the presence of rationing (for example of whether individuals are voluntarily or involuntarily unemployed), it is necessary to be able to compare rationed and unrationed demands for the goods which can be freely chosen. Deaton presents a technique for linking constrained and unconstrained cost functions and applies it to a model which is a generalization of the linear expenditure system. On annual British data, housing expenditure is treated as a predetermined commitment and the results suggest that this may be a more appropriate assumption than its opposite, that such expenditures are always at their optimal levels. At the same time, the treatment through rationing resolves at least some of the apparent conflict between the evidence and the homogeneity requirement of utility theory.

The paper by Henri Theil and Kenneth Laitinen surveys a recent development not tied to but usually associated with empirical and theoretical work using the Rotterdam model. In the earliest days of utility theory, pioneers such as Gossen, Jevons, Edgeworth, Marshall and Pigou typically assumed that wants were 'independent' of one another so that preferences could be represented as the sum of specific satisfactions from each good. Such an assumption simplifies the analysis of demand but unfortunately imposes restrictions which are typically rejected by the evidence: see, among others, the studies by Barten (1969) and Deaton (1974a). What Theil and Laitinen do, however, is to define new goods or commodities as linear combinations of the original goods, with respect to which an additive structure of preferences can be maintained. This technique, the 'independence transformation', is surveyed in the paper together with a number of empirical applications including the demand for meats and the demand for leisure, its complements and substitutes.

The final paper in the section is about demand analysis as a tool of economic policy and planning. Sir Richard Stone has always seen the ultimate aim of his own work as being economic policy-making and successive versions of the linear expenditure system have been incorporated in the Cambridge growth model over the years: see Cambridge, Department of Applied Economics (1962–74) and Deaton (1975). The paper presented here, by Academicians Fedorenko and Rimashevskaya of the Central Institute for Mathematical Economics in Moscow, surveys the techniques used for projecting consumers' demands in Russia in a situation where such projection is of more than academic interest. The approach, as befits policy-making, is an eclectic one but, almost inevitably, the linear expenditure system has a central role. It must be very rare in economics for one specific model and one specific paper to exert such an ubiquitous influence in both theoretical and policy-related discussions.

References

Barten, A. P. (1969), 'Maximum likelihood estimation of a complete system of demand equations', *European Economic Review*, **1**, pp. 7–73.

Cambridge, Department of Applied Economics (1962–74), *A programme for growth*, Vols. I–XII, Chapman and Hall, London.

Deaton, A. S. (1974a), 'The analysis of consumer demand in the United Kingdom 1900–1970', *Econometrica*, **42**, pp. 341–67.

(1974b), 'A reconsideration of the empirical implications of additive preferences', *Economic Journal*, **84**, pp. 338–48.

(1975), *Models and projections of demand in post-war Britain*, Chapman and Hall, London.

Deaton, A. S. and J. Muellbauer (1980), *Economics and consumer behavior*, Cambridge University Press, New York.

Diewert, W. E. (1974), 'Applications of duality theory', Chapter 3 in Intriligator, M. D. and D. A. Kendrick (eds.), *Frontiers of quantitative economics*, Vol. II, North-Holland, Amsterdam.

(1981), 'Duality approaches to microeconomic theory', in Arrow, K. J. and M. Intriligator (eds.), *Handbook of Mathematical Economics*, North-Holland, Amsterdam.

Gorman, W. M. (1961), 'On a class of preference fields', *Metroeconomica*, **13**, pp. 53–6.

Howe, H., R. A. Pollak, and T. J. Wales (1980), 'Theory and time series estimation of the quadratic expenditure system', *Econometrica*, **48**, pp. 1231–47.

McFadden, D. (1978), 'Cost, revenue and profit functions', in Fuss, M. and D. McFadden (eds.), *Production economics: a dual approach to theory and applications*, North-Holland, Amsterdam.

Pollak, R. A. and T. J. Wales (1978), 'Estimation of complete demand systems from household budget data', *American Economic Review*, **68**, pp. 348–59.

Rothbarth, E. (1941), 'The measurement of change in real income under conditions of rationing', *Review of Economic Studies*, **8**, pp. 100–7.

Tobin, J. (1952), 'A survey of the theory of rationing', *Econometrica*, **20**, pp. 512–53.

Tobin, J. and H. S. Houthakker (1951), 'The effects of rationing on demand elasticities', *Review of Economic Studies*, **18**, pp. 140–53.

1 Some Engel curves[1]

W. M. GORMAN

0 Introduction

In this paper I investigate the conditions under which rational[2] individuals have Engel curves of the type

$$x_i = \sum_{r \in R} b^{ri}(p)\psi^r(m) \quad \text{for each good } i \tag{1}$$

in the usual notation, where R is a finite set. They are of interest for three, related, uses:

(i) for fitting to surveys;
(ii) as a generalisation of linear Engel curves, which have turned out to be useful in several contexts, particularly as the solution of the aggregation problem

$$x_i = f^i(p, \phi(m)) \quad \text{for each } i, \ m = (m_1, m_2, \ldots, m_T) \tag{2}$$

where m_t is the income of the tth household, x_i, the market demand for good i, and $\phi(.)$ a scalar aggregate;
(iii) as the solution of the more general version of (2) in which $\phi(.)$ is a vector of aggregates.
   Incidentally, the $\psi(.)$ may contain equivalent adult and other corrections.
   On the other hand, they are rendered less interesting by the fact that m in (1), and each m_t in (2), stands for *money* income.
   If the Engel curves in (1) represent well-behaved preferences, we find that
(i) The rank $R(B(p))$ of the coefficient matrix $B(p) = [b^{ri}(p)]$ is at most 3.
(ii) When $R(B(p)) = 3$,[3] either (a) each $\psi^r(m) = m(\log m)^r$, and each $r \in R$ is an integer, or (b) each $\psi^r(m) = m^{r+1}$, or (c) each $\psi^r(m) = m \sin(r \log m)$ or $m \cos(r \log m)$, for each $r \geq 0$,[4] with $0 \in R$ in each case. In section 4 I conjecture that $R = \{-m\omega, -(m-1)\omega, \ldots, 0, \omega, \ldots, n\omega\}$ with a few gaps sometimes.
(iii) When $R(B(p)) = 3$ the cost function underlying (1) may be written

$$m = \phi(\alpha(p), \beta(p), \gamma(p), u) \tag{3}$$

7

where $\alpha(.)$, $\beta(.)$, $\gamma(.)$ are unit cost functions, which may be thought of as corresponding to baskets of commodities. It is tempting to rewrite (3) in primal form as

$$u = f(x) = \max\{F(a(y), b(z), c(w))|y + z + w \le x\} \qquad (4)$$

where $a(.)$, $b(.)$, $c(.)$ are the corresponding *conical*[5] production functions, in which case $\phi(., u)$ in (3) would be the cost function corresponding to $u = F(.)$. Unfortunately $\phi(., u)$, though conical, is not necessarily concave, so that this interpretation is not strictly justified. When it is, we may say that the various goods affect our welfare through the basic wants a, b, c – an interpretation which remains enlightening even when not strictly justified.

(iv) (iib) clearly includes the polynomials. When $R(B(p)) = 3$, then $\phi(., u)$ in (3) is additively homogeneous, as well as conical – that is, multiplicatively homogeneous. That is,

$$\phi(\lambda\theta, u) = \lambda\phi(\theta, u); \quad \phi(\theta + \mu e, u) = \phi(\theta, u) + \mu \qquad (5)$$

so that

$$\phi(\lambda\theta + \mu e, u) = \lambda\phi(\theta, u) + \mu$$

$$\phi(\alpha, \beta, \gamma, u) = \alpha + (\beta - \alpha)\psi((\gamma - \alpha)/(\beta - \alpha), u)^6 \text{ say} \qquad (6)$$

where $e = (1, 1, ..., 1)$, $\lambda \ge 0$, so that, where justified, (4) may be rewritten

$$u = f(x) = \max\{\bar{F}(a(y), b(z))|c(x - y - z) \ge 1\} \text{ say} \qquad (7)$$

so that $c = 1$ may be thought of as the satisfaction of a basic 'need', or, if you like, an overhead of existence.

These results are extended to a wider class of Engel curves at the end of section 3.

(v) Since $R(B) \le 3$, quadratics are particularly interesting. The cost function is then

$$m = \alpha(p) + \delta(p)/(1 - u\varepsilon(p)) \qquad (8)$$

where

$$\delta = \beta - \alpha, \ \varepsilon = (\gamma - \beta)/(\beta - \alpha) \qquad (9)$$

(vi) When $R(B(p)) = 2$, the cost function may be written

$$m = \phi(\alpha(p), \beta(p), u) \qquad (10)$$

where $\alpha(.)$, $\beta(.)$ are once more unit cost functions and $\phi(., u)$ is conical but not necessarily either concave or additively homogeneous.

Iff it is closed concave, the corresponding primal may be written

$$u = f(x) = \max\{F(a(y), b(z))|y + z \le x\} \tag{11}$$

where $u = F(.)$ is the dual of $\phi(., u)$, $a(.)$, $b(.)$ of $\alpha(.)$, $\beta(.)$. When $\phi(., u)$ is additively homogeneous, (10) may be written

$$m = \alpha(p) + u\delta(p), \quad \delta = \beta - \alpha \tag{12}$$

so that the Engel curves are straight lines, as in the standard case referred to in the opening paragraph.

(vii) When $R(B(p)) = 1$, $u = f(x)$ is homothetic, and the Engel curves straight lines radiating from the origin.

1 Preliminaries

It will be convenient to write the equations of the Engel curves in terms of the budget shares $w_j = p_j x_j / m$, and accordingly to use the logarithmic cost function

$$h(q, u) = \log g(p, u) = \log m; \; q_j = \log p_j, \text{ for each } j \tag{1}$$

since

$$w_j = h_j(q, u), \text{ for each } j \tag{2}$$

where I use suffixes to function names to denote differentiation.

Consider complete systems of Engel curves of the type

$$h_j(q, u) = \sum_{r \in R} a(r, j; q)\phi(r; h(q, u)); \text{ for each good } j \tag{3}$$

where R is a finite set.

This is a curious notation. One would expect the labels r, j to appear as subscripts, as in $a_{rj}(q)$, or superscripts as in $a^{rj}(q)$, rather than as arguments, as in $a(r, j; q)$. However, I will be using subscripts to denote derivatives, and powers will come into the analysis so often that I cannot use the superscript notation either. To distinguish between the discrete labels such as r, j and the continuous variables such as q, m, I will put the labels before, and the variables after, the ';' in each case. It will frequently be convenient not to mention the latter explicitly, writing $a(r, j)$ for $a(r, j; q)$, for instance.

Assume without loss of generality that this representation is unique so that

$$\sum_{r \in R} c_r \phi(r; .) = 0 \quad \text{implies each } c_r = 0$$

$$\sum_{r \in R} c_r a(r, .; .) = 0 \quad \text{implies each } c_r = 0 \tag{4}$$

the former since we would otherwise have

$$\sum_{r \in R} a(r, j; q)\phi(r; h) = \sum_{r \in R} \left\{ a(r, j; q) \right.$$

$$\left. + c_r \sum_{s \in R} d_s a(s, j; q) \right\} \phi(r; h) \tag{5}$$

the latter since we would otherwise have

$$\sum_{r \in R} a(r, j; q)\phi(r; h) = \sum_{r \in R} \left\{ a(r, j; q) \right.$$

$$\left. + d_r \sum c_s\, a(s, j; q) \right\} \phi(r; h) \tag{6}$$

for any $d_R = (d_r)_{r \in R}$, so that (3) would not be unique as required in either case.

What else can we say about

$$\phi(R; .) = \{\phi(r; .) | r \in R\} \tag{7}$$

and the space $\Phi(R)$ it spans?

In the first place

$$\sum_{r \in R} \left\{ \sum_j a(r, j; q) \right\} \phi(r; h) = \sum_j h_j(q, u) = \sum w_j = 1 \tag{8}$$

so that $1 \in \Phi(R)$ and we can, and do, take

$$\phi(0; h) = 1 \tag{9}$$

without loss of generality, so that (8) yields

$$\sum_j a(0, j; q) = 1; \quad \sum_j a(r, j; q) = 0, \quad r \neq 0 \in R \tag{10}$$

Now look at the linear space, $\mathscr{A}(q)$, spanned by the vectors

$$a(r; q) = (a(r, 1; q), a(r, 2; q), ...), \quad \text{for each } r \in R \tag{11}$$

We will see in the next section that its dimension $N(q) \leq 3$, for each q, so that the $a(r; q)$, $r \in R$, will typically be linearly dependent. However,

$$\sum_{r \in R} c(r; q)a(r; q) = 0 \quad \text{implies} \quad c(0; q) = 0 \tag{12}$$

because of (10), so that $a(0; q)$ is linearly independent of the other $a(r; q)$, $r \in R$.

So much for the condition that the budget shares add up to one. I will now turn to the more powerful Slutsky or integrability conditions $h_{jk}(q, u) = h_{kj}(q, u)$. These will allow me to specify the admissible $\phi(r; h)$ completely.

Now

$$h_{jk} = \sum_{r \in R} a_k(r, j)\phi(r) + \sum_{r \in R} a(r, j)\phi'(r) \cdot \sum_{s \in R} a(s, k)\phi(s),$$

$$\text{for each } j, k \quad (13)$$

where I have dropped the explicit reference to the variables q, h, as will frequently be convenient, and where $a_k(r, j) = \partial a(r, j; q)/\partial q_k$, $\phi'(r) = d\phi(r; h)/dh$.

Consider any $\phi'(r)\phi(s)$, $r, s \in R$. It may or may not belong to $\Phi(R)$. If not, add it to the basis $\phi(R; .)$ to get $\phi(R^*; .)$ say, spanning $\Phi(R^*)$. Next take any other $\phi'(r)\phi(s)$, $r, s \in R$. It may or may not belong to $\Phi(R^*)$, ...; since there are only a finite number of such products, we ultimately end up with a linear space $\Phi(T) \supseteq \Phi(R)$, with a basis $\phi(T; .)$, $T \supseteq R$. Clearly, then

$$\phi'(r)\phi(s) = \sum_{t \in T} c_{rst}\phi(t), \text{ for each } r, s \in R \quad (14)$$

and, in particular,

$$\phi'(r) = \phi'(r)\phi(0) = \sum_{t \in T} c_{r0t}\phi(t), \text{ for each } r \in R \quad (15)$$

and

$$\text{each } c_{0st} = 0 \quad (16)$$

since $\Sigma_{t \in T}\, c_{0st}\phi(t) = \phi'(0)\phi(s) = 0$, and $\phi(T; .)$ is linearly independent.

Substitute from (14) into (13), and use the fact that $h_{jk} = h_{kj}$, to get

$$\sum_{r \in R} \sum_{s \in R} c_{rst}\{a(r, j)a(s, k) - a(r, k)a(s, j)\}$$

$$= a_j(t, k) - a_k(t, j), \text{ for each } t \in T \quad (17)$$

$$= 0, \text{ for each } t \notin R \quad (18)$$

since $\phi(T; .)$ is linearly independent, where we define

$$a(t, j; q) = 0, \quad t \notin R \quad (19)$$

Sum (18) over j, and use (10) and (16) to get

$$\sum_{r \in R} c_{r0t}a(r; q) = 0, \text{ for each } t \notin R, \quad \text{each } k \quad (20)$$

since $a(r; q) = (a(r, 1; q), a(r, 2; q), ...)$, and hence

$$c_{r0t} = 0 \text{ for each } r \in R, t \notin R \quad (21)$$

by (4), so that (14) becomes

$$\phi'(r) = \sum_{s \in R} c_{ros}\phi(s) \tag{22}$$

or, equivalently,

$$\phi'(R) = C\phi(R) \tag{23}$$

where C is a square matrix.

I will now show that we may take each

$$\phi(r; h) = \phi(\lambda, m; h) = h^m e^{\lambda h}, \text{ say}, \quad m = 0, 1, ..., M(\lambda) \tag{24}$$

where λ is a latent root of C with multiplicity $M(\lambda) + 1$.

To see this, let

$$D = LCL^{-1} \tag{25}$$

be the canonical form of D, block diagonal, a typical block being

$$D(\lambda) = \begin{bmatrix} \lambda, 0, 0, & ... & 0, 0 \\ 1, \lambda, 0, & ... & 0, 0 \\ 0, 1, \lambda, & ... & . \ . \\ . \ . \ . & ... & . \ . \\ 0, 0, 0, & ... & 1, \lambda \end{bmatrix} \tag{26}$$

and write $\psi(r) = L\phi(R)$ to get

$$\psi'(R) = D\psi(R) \tag{27}$$

Set now $r = (\lambda, m)$ where r corresponds to the $(m + 1)$th row of $D(\lambda)$. (27) then reads

$$\psi'(\lambda, 0; h) = \lambda\psi(\lambda, 0; h)$$

$$\psi'(\lambda, m; h) = \lambda\psi(\lambda, m; h) + \psi(\lambda, m - 1; h); \quad 0 < m \leq \bar{m}(\lambda) \tag{28}$$

where $\bar{m}(\lambda) + 1$ is the order of $D(\lambda)$. This set of differential equations is easily seen to have the general solution

$$\psi(\lambda, m; h) = \sum_{n \leq m} b_{m-n} h^n e^{\lambda h}/n!, \quad 0 \leq m \leq \bar{m}(\lambda) \tag{29}$$

so that

$$\theta(\lambda, m; h) = h^m e^{\lambda h}, \quad 0 \leq m \leq \bar{m}(\lambda) \tag{30}$$

is a basis for the ψs associated with the block $D(\lambda)$ of D. Going through the different blocks in turn we generate a basis $\theta(R; .)$ for $\psi(R; .)$, and hence for $\phi(R; .)$. Should any λ have more than one such block $D(\lambda)$ corresponding to it, $\theta(R; .)$ would have fewer elements than $\phi(R; .)$, which is impossible since the latter is linearly independent. Hence there is only one such, $\bar{m}(\lambda) = M(\lambda)$ in (28), (29) and (30), and we may take $\theta(R; .)$ as the new $\phi(R; .)$ to get (24) as required.

(3) now becomes

$$h_j(q, u) = \sum_{\lambda \in L} \sum_{m=0}^{M(\lambda)} a(\lambda, m, j; q)h^m e^{\lambda h} \tag{31}$$

in an obvious notation, and (17)–(18),

$$\sum m\{a(\lambda, m, j)a(\mu - \lambda, n - m + 1, k)$$
$$- a(\lambda, m, k)a(\mu - \lambda, n - m + 1, j)\}$$
$$+ \sum \lambda\{a(\lambda, m, j)a(\mu - \lambda, n - m, k)$$
$$- a(\lambda, m, k)a(\mu - \lambda, n - m, j)\}$$
$$= a_j(\mu, n, k) - a_k(\mu, n, j), \quad \text{in general,}$$
$$= 0, \quad \text{when} \tag{32}$$

$$\mu \notin L \text{ or } \mu \in L, n > M(\mu); \quad \text{or equivalently}$$
$$s = (\mu, n) \notin R \tag{33}$$

where we take

$$a(\theta, m, j) = 0, \quad \theta \notin L, \text{ or } \theta \in L, \quad m \notin \{0, 1, ..., M(\theta)\} \tag{34}$$

as in (19).

(32)–(33) is the basic result on which the argument in the next section will turn. It will be slightly more convenient to use it in the form

$$\sum_{m>n/2} (2m - n - 1)\{a(\lambda, m, j)a(\mu - \lambda, n - m + 1, k)$$

$$- a(\lambda, m, k)a(\mu - \lambda, n - m + 1, j)\}$$
$$+ \sum_{\lambda>\mu/2} (2\lambda - \mu)\{a(\lambda, m, j)a(\mu - \lambda, n - m, k)$$

$$- a(\lambda, m, k)a(\mu - \lambda, n - m, j)\} = 0 \tag{35}$$

when (33) holds. To derive this one brings together the terms corresponding to λ, m and $\bar{\lambda} = \mu - \lambda$, $\bar{m} = n - m + 1$ in the first summation, and to λ, m and $\bar{\lambda} = \mu - \lambda$, $\bar{m} = n - m$ in the second.

(35) states a series of bilinear relations between the coefficient vectors $a(\lambda, m; q)$. In the next section, I will use them to show that the rank of the coefficient matrix $A(q)$, or equivalently the dimension $N(q)$ of $\mathcal{A}(q)$, is at most three. I will devote most of my attention to the case where $N(q) = 3$. This is because, in a certain sense, 'there is no integrability problem when $N(q) = 2$'.

To see why, consider the case $N(q) = N$ and write

$$a(r, j; q) = \sum_{n=1}^{N} b(r, n; q)c(n, j; q) \tag{36}$$

to get

$$h_j(q, u) = \sum_{n=1}^{N} \left\{ \sum_{r \in R} b(r, n; q)\phi(r; h(q, u)) \right\} c(n, j; q) \qquad (37)$$

Define the gradient of $h(., u)$ by

$$h'(q, u) = (h_1(q, u), h_2(q, u), ...) \qquad (38)$$

and choose $u_1 < u_2 < ... < u_N$ such that $h'(q, u_1), h'(q, u_2), ... \, h'(q, u_N)$ span $\mathscr{A}(q)$. Define

$$\theta(n; q) = h(q, u_n), \, c(n; q) = (c(n, 1; q), c(n, 2; q), ...),$$
$$n = 1, 2, ..., N \quad (39)$$

The θs are functionally independent and

$$\theta'(m; q) = \sum_{n=1}^{N} \left\{ \sum_{r \in R} b(r, n; q)\phi(r; \theta(m; q)) \right\} c(n; q),$$
$$n = 1, 2, ..., N \quad (40)$$

Solving this for the $c(n; q)$ in terms of the $\theta'(m; q)$ and substituting into (37), we get

$$h_j(q, u) = \sum_{n=1}^{N} \left\{ \sum_{r \in R} d(r, n; q)\phi(r; h(q, u)) \right\} \theta_j(n, q),$$
$$\text{say, for each } j \quad (41)$$

so that

$$h(q, u) = H(\theta(1, q), \theta(2, q), ..., \theta(N, q), u) \qquad (42)$$

given the necessary smoothness and connectivity.

Now $\theta(n, q) = h(q, u_n)$ is a logarithmic cost function, each n, and may without loss of generality be taken to be the logarithmic *unit* cost function for a fictitious intermediate good, or composite commodity, produced under constant returns – that is, they may be taken to be the logarithmic prices of those intermediate goods. Now there is no integrability problem when there are only two goods, and it is the integrability conditions which I will be examining in section 2. Hence my concentration on the case where $N > 2$.

So far I have not used the fact that the consumer's behaviour, and hence the budget shares, is unaffected when prices and income all change in the same proportion. It is easiest to approach this matter indirectly. Take any 'logarithmic price index' $\alpha(q)$ such that

$$\sum_{j} \alpha_j(q) = 1 \qquad (43)$$

so that exp $\alpha(q)$ is homogeneous of degree one in the prices $p_j = \exp q_j$, and write

$$k(q, u) = h(q, u) - \alpha(q) \qquad (44)$$

which may be thought of as a 'real' logarithmic expenditure function. Clearly

$$\sum_j k_j(q, u) = 0 \qquad (45)$$

Now substitute $h = k + \alpha$ into (31) to get

$$k_j = \sum_{\lambda \in L} \sum_{m=0}^{M(\lambda)} b(\lambda, m, j) k^m \, e^{\lambda k} \qquad (46)$$

where

$$b(\lambda, n, j) = e^{\lambda \alpha} \sum_{m=n}^{M(\lambda)} \binom{m}{n} \alpha^{m-n} a(\lambda, m, j) \quad \text{unless } n = \lambda = 0 \qquad (47)$$

$$b(0, 0, j) = \sum_{n=0}^{M(0)} \alpha^m a(0, m, j) - \alpha_j \qquad (48)$$

or, equivalently,[7]

$$a(\lambda, n, j) = e^{-\lambda \alpha} \sum_{m=n}^{M(\lambda)} \binom{m}{n} (-\alpha)^{m-n} b(\lambda, m, j) \quad \text{unless } n = \lambda = 0 \qquad (49)$$

$$a(0, 0, j) = \sum_{m=0}^{M(0)} (-\alpha)^m b(0, m, j) + \alpha_j \qquad (50)$$

Multiplying each price p_j and income m by θ is the same as adding $\mu = \log \theta$ to each q, h and α. Doing this in (46) and equating coefficients of k^n $e^{\lambda k}$ we get

$$b(\lambda, n, j; q + \mu e) = b(\lambda, n, j; q), \text{ for each } \lambda, n, j, q, \mu \qquad (51)$$

where

$$e = (1, 1, ..., 1) \qquad (52)$$

which is clearly sufficient as well as necessary for homogeneity. That the *a*s should be generated by *b*s, satisfying (51)–(52), as in (49)–(50), is therefore both necessary and sufficient for the homogeneity of the Engel system (31).

Finally a little more notation. Since the λs are the latent roots of a general square matrix C, they may be complex. If so, they come in conjugate pairs. Write

$$\lambda = \sigma + i\tau = (\sigma, \tau), \quad r = (\lambda, m) = (\sigma + i\tau, m) = (\sigma, \tau, m) \tag{53}$$

$$R = \{(\lambda, m) | \lambda \in L, \quad m = 0, 1, \ldots, M(\lambda)\} \tag{54}$$

$$S = \{\sigma | \sigma + i\tau \in L, \text{ some } \tau\}, \quad T = \{\tau | \sigma + i\tau \in L, \text{ some } \sigma\} \tag{55}$$

Note by the way that

$$0 \in R, \quad \text{and hence } 0 \in L, 0 \in S, 0 \in T \tag{56}$$

because $c_{00t} = 0$, for each t, since $\phi'(0; h) = 0$ and $\phi(T; .)$ is linearly independent. It would be surprising were this not so!

2 The main theorem

Theorem 1(a): If the complete Engel system (1.3) reflects well-behaved preferences, the rank $N(q)$ of its coefficient matrix is at most 3.

Theorem 1(b): When $N(q) = 3$, (1.3) takes one of the forms

$$h_j(q, u) = a(j; q) + b(j; q)h + c(j; q) \sum_{m=1}^{M} C(m; q)h^m \tag{1}$$

$$h_j(q, u) = a(j; q) + b(j; q) \sum_{\sigma \in S}^{\sigma < 0} B(\sigma; q) \, e^{\sigma h}$$

$$+ c(j; q) \sum_{\sigma \in S}^{\sigma > 0} C(\sigma; q) e^{\sigma h} \tag{2}$$

$$h_j(q, u) = a(j; q) + b(j; q) \sum_{\tau \in T}^{\tau > 0} B(\tau; q) \cos \tau h$$

$$+ c(j; q) \sum_{\tau \in T}^{\tau > 0} C(\tau; q) \sin \tau h \tag{3}$$

Proof: Equation (1.35) will be used repeatedly, so I will record it here:

$$\sum_{m > n/2} (2m - n - 1)\{a(\lambda, m, j)a(\mu - \lambda, n - m + 1, k)$$

$$- a(\lambda, m, k)a(\mu - \lambda, n - m + 1, j)\}$$

$$+ \sum_{\lambda > \mu/2} (2\lambda - \mu)\{a(\lambda, m, j)a(\mu - \lambda, n - m, k)$$

$$- a(\lambda, m, k)a(\mu - \lambda, n - m, j)\} = 0 \tag{4}$$

when

$$\mu \notin L \quad \text{or} \quad \mu \in L, m > M(\mu) \tag{5}$$

I will proceed in a series of lemmas.

Lemma 1: Suppose S contains a positive element. Then

$$a(r, j) = C(r)c(j), \text{ say, } \quad \text{when } \sigma \geq 0, \quad \text{unless } \sigma = \tau = m = 0 \qquad (6)$$

Proof: Set

$$\sigma^* = \max\{\sigma \in S\} > 0, \quad \tau^* = \max\{\tau|(\sigma^*, \tau) \in L\} \geq 0 \qquad (7)$$

$$\lambda^* = \sigma^* + i\tau^*, \quad M(\lambda^*) = m^*, \quad r^* = (\lambda^*, m^*) \qquad (8)$$

and define the lexicographic ordering

$$r > r' \text{ if } \sigma > \sigma', \quad \text{or } \sigma = \sigma', \tau > \tau', \quad \text{or } \sigma = \sigma', \tau = \tau', \quad m > m' \qquad (9)$$

Set

$$c(j) = a(r^*, j), \text{ for each } j \qquad (10)$$

and erect the inductive hypothesis

$$a(r, j) = C(r)c(j), \text{ say, for each } j \qquad (11)$$

when

$$r > \bar{r} > 0 \qquad (12)$$

I will show that this implies that (11) holds for $\bar{r}$ too. Since it certainly holds for r^*, it will hold for each $r > 0$.

Take then $r^* > \bar{r} > 0$

(i) If $\bar{\lambda} = \lambda^*, \bar{m} < m^*$, write down (4) with $\mu = 2\lambda^* \notin L, n = \bar{m} + m^* - 1$, to get

$$(m^* - \bar{m})\{c(j)a(\bar{\lambda}, \bar{m}, k) - c(k)a(\bar{\lambda}, \bar{m}, j)\} = 0 \qquad (13)$$

all the other terms vanishing by the inductive hypothesis (11)–(12). Hence (11) holds for $r = \bar{r} = (\bar{\lambda}, \bar{m})$ too.

(ii) If $\bar{\lambda} \neq \lambda^*$ write down (4) with $\mu = \lambda^* + \bar{\lambda}, n = m^* + \bar{m}$, to get

$$(\lambda^* - \bar{\lambda})\{c(j)a(\bar{\lambda}, \bar{m}, k) - c(k)a(\bar{\lambda}, \bar{m}, j)\} = 0 \qquad (14)$$

so that (11) holds for $r = \bar{r} = (\bar{\lambda}, \bar{m})$ too.

This leaves us with the cases where $\bar{\sigma} = 0, \bar{\tau} < 0$. For them we merely replace the ordering (9) by one in which we put τ first at the second stage when $\sigma = 0$.

This completes the proof of Lemma 1.

Remark: when $\bar{r} = 0, r^* + \bar{r} \in R$ so that (5) does not hold.

Lemma 2: If S has a negative element

$$a(r, j) = B(r)b(j), \text{ say, } \quad \text{when } \sigma \leq 0, \quad \text{unless } r = 0 \qquad (15)$$

Corollary: If $S \neq \{0\}$ and

$$N(q) \geq 3 \qquad (16)$$

S has both positive and negative elements.

Lemma 3: If $T \neq \{0\}$,[8]
then unless $r = (\sigma, \tau, m) = 0$,

$$a(\sigma, \tau, m, j) = D(\sigma, \tau, m)d(j) \tag{17}$$

$$a(\sigma, -\tau, m, j) = \bar{a}(\sigma, \tau, m, j) = \bar{D}(\sigma, \tau, m)\,\bar{d}(j) \tag{18}$$

where we take $\tau \geq 0$ without loss of generality and $\bar{\cdot}$ denotes the complex conjugate.

Proofs: These lemmas are proved in the same way as Lemma 1. Remember that T is symmetric about the origin.

Lemma 4: When $N(q) \geq 3$, either $S = \{0\}$ or $T = \{0\}$.

Proof: Suppose neither is $\{0\}$. If $\tau^* \in T$, so does $-\tau^*$, because complex latent roots come in conjugate pairs. Suppose without loss of generality that $\lambda^* = \sigma^* + i\tau^* \in L$, with $\sigma^* \geq 0$. The Lemmas 1 and 3 imply that

$$D(\sigma^*, \tau^*, 0)d_j = C(\sigma^*, \tau^*, 0)c_j; \quad \bar{D}(\sigma^*, \tau^*, 0)\bar{d}_j$$
$$= C(\sigma^*, -\tau^*, 0)c_j, \text{ for each } j \tag{19}$$

so that $\bar{d}_j = Ed_j$, each j, say, so that $N \leq 2$ by Lemma 3, and we have a contradiction.

Lemma 5: When $N(q) \geq 3$, $M(0) = 0$ unless $S = T = \{0\}$.

Proof: Suppose $S \neq \{0\}$. The corollary to Lemma 2 implies that it has both positive and negative elements, and Lemmas 1 and 2 that $B(0, 1)b_j = C(0, 1)c_j$ if $M(0) > 1$.

The proof for $T \neq \{0\}$ is similar.

Lemma 6: When $N(q) \geq 3$ and $L \neq \{0\}$, $M(\lambda) = 0$, for each $\lambda \in L$.

Proof: $L \neq \{0\}$ iff either $S \neq \{0\}$, or $T \neq \{0\}$. Let $S \neq \{0\}$. According to the corollary to Lemma 2 it has both positive and negative elements. Define

$$m^+ = \max\{M(\sigma)|\sigma > 0, \sigma \in S\}, \quad \sigma^+ = \max\{\sigma \in S|M(\sigma) = m^+\}$$

$$m^- = \max\{M(\sigma)|\sigma < 0, \sigma \in S\},$$
$$\sigma^- = \max\{\sigma \in S|\sigma < 0, M(\sigma) = m^-\} \tag{20}$$

If $m^+, m^- > 0$, $m^+ + m^- > M(\sigma^+ + \sigma^-)$ when $\sigma^+ + \sigma^- \in S$. Hence we can apply (4) with $n = m^+ + m^-$, $\mu = \sigma^+ + \sigma^-$, to get

$$(\sigma^+ - \sigma^-)C(\sigma^+, m^+)B(\sigma^-, m^-)\{b(j)c(k) - b(k)c(j)\} = 0 \tag{21}$$

so that $N(q) < 3$, contradicting our assumption.

If $m^+ > 0$, $m^- = 0$, define

$$\sigma^\pm = \min\{\sigma \in S|M(\sigma) = m^+\}; \quad \sigma^= = \min\{\sigma \in S\} < 0^{[9]} \tag{22}$$

Consider $\mu = \sigma^\pm + \sigma^= < \sigma^\pm$, $n = m^+ > M(\sigma^\pm + \sigma^=)$ when $\sigma^\pm$

$+ \ \sigma^= \in S$. Hence we may apply (4) to this (μ, n) to get:

$$(\sigma^\pm - \sigma^=)C(\sigma^\pm, m^+)B(\sigma^=, 0)\{b(j)c(k) - b(k)c(j)\} = 0,^{10} \text{ say} \quad (23)$$

so that $N(q) \le 3$ again.

A similar proof holds for $m^+ = 0$, $m^- > 0$. Hence $m^+ = m^- = 0$, so that $M(\sigma) = 0$, for each $\sigma \in S$ as required.

A similar proof holds for $T \ne \{0\}$. It is rather simpler because $m^+ = m^-$ in that case.

Lemma 7: When $N(q) \ge 3$ and $M(0) = M \ne 0$,

$$a(0, m, j) = A(m)c(j), \text{ say, each } j, \text{ for each } m \ge 2 \quad (24)$$

Proof: Since $L = \{0\}$, I will drop the 0 in $a(0, m, j)$ for simplicity. Clearly $M \ge 2$.

Define

$$a(M, j) = c(j), \text{ for each } j \quad (25)$$

and erect the inductive hypothesis

$$a(m, j) = A(m)c(j), \text{ say, for each } j \quad (26)$$

for each $m > \bar{m} \ge 2$. Then $M + \bar{m} - 1 > M = M(0)$, so that we can apply (4) with $n = M + \bar{m} - 1$, $\mu = 0$ to get

$$(M - \bar{m} + 1)\{c(j)a(\bar{m}, k) - c(k)a(\bar{m}, j)\} = 0 \quad (27)$$

the other terms vanishing by the inductive hypothesis. Hence (26) holds for $m = \bar{m}$, too. Since it holds for $m = M$, it holds for all $m \ge 2$.

This completes the proof of the theorem. (1), (2) and (3) correspond to the cases in which $M(0) \ne 0$, $S \ne \{0\}$, $T \ne \{0\}$ respectively.

Corollary 1: If S has just one negative element $-\omega$,

$$h_j = a(j) + b(j) \ e^{-\omega h} + c(j) \sum_{r=1}^{r^*} C(r) \ e^{r\omega h}, \text{ say, } \Pi C(r) \ne 0 \quad (28)$$

Proof: Arrange the positive elements $\sigma_1 < \sigma_2 < ... < \sigma_{r^*}$ in increasing sequence and define $\sigma_0 = 0$.

Erect the inductive hypothesis

$$\sigma_r = r\omega, \quad r = 0, 1, ..., \bar{r} - 1 \quad (29)$$

It certainly holds for $r = 0$. If, therefore, (29) implies that it holds for $\bar{r}$, it will hold for $r = 0, 1, ..., r^*$. Now $\sigma_{\bar{r}} > (\bar{r} - 1)\omega$. Hence $\sigma_r > \sigma_r - \omega > (\bar{r} - 2)\omega$, so that,

$$\sigma_{\bar{r}} - \omega = (\bar{r} - 1)\omega \quad (30)$$

if it is in S. If it is not in S, apply (4) with $\mu = \sigma_r - \omega$, to get

$$(\sigma_{\bar{r}} + \omega)C(\sigma_{\bar{r}})\{c(j)b(k) - c(k)b(j)\} = 0 \quad (31)$$

in the notation of Lemmas 1 and 2, the other terms vanishing by Lemma 1, so that $N(q) < 3$. Hence $\sigma_{\bar{r}} - \omega = (\bar{r} - 1)\omega$, and (29) holds for $r = \bar{r}$, completing the proof of the lemma.

Corollary 2: If S has just one positive element,

$$h_j = a(j) + b(j) \sum_{r=1}^{r^o} B(r)\, e^{-r\omega h} + c(j)\, e^{\omega h}, \quad \Pi B(r) \neq 0 \tag{32}$$

by an exactly similar argument.

Remark 1: (32) may be written

$$k_j = b(j) + a(j)k + c(j) \sum_{r=2}^{r^o+1} C(r - 1)k^r \tag{33}$$

with a trivial change in notation, where

$$k(q, u) = e^{\omega h} = g(p, u)^\omega; \quad q_j = \log p_j \text{ for each } j \tag{34}$$

$g(p, u)$ being the cost function. In particular this represents a complete system of polynomial Engel curves when $\omega = 1$. It is clearly the most general case.

Remark 2: The point to note is that none of the Bs or Cs vanish.

Remark 3: Unfortunately (4) does not imply this in general.

$$\begin{aligned} h_j(q, u) = {}& a(j; q) + b(j; q)(e^{-2h} + B(q)\, e^{-h}) \\ & + c(j; q)(e^{3h} - 5\, e^{2h}/3B(q)) \end{aligned} \tag{35}$$

is a counter-example for $S \neq \{0\}$, because the coefficient of e^h vanishes,

$$\begin{aligned} h_j(q, u) = {}& a(j; q) + d(j; q)\{e^{-4ih} - A(q)\, e^{-iB(q)}\, e^{-3ih} \\ & - 1.4\, e^{2iB(q)}\, e^{-2ih}\} + \bar{d}(j; q)\{e^{4ih} - A(q)\, e^{iB(q)}\, e^{3ih} \\ & - 1.4\, e^{-2iB(q)}\, e^{2ih}\} \end{aligned} \tag{36}$$

a counter-example for $T \neq \{0\}$, because those of e^{ih} and e^{-ih} do. Each is the most general for the particular L used. No such gaps can occur when S has less than 6 elements or T less than 7.

I imagine that we can restrict ourselves to S, T of the form $\{n\omega | n \in N\}$, where N is a set of positive and negative integers with a few gaps permitted in general, symmetric when T is being represented. I have not seriously attempted the combinatorial feat required to settle the matter, but mention a few relevant considerations in section 4.

Theorem 2: When $N(q) = 2$,

$$h_j = a(j) + b(j) \sum_{\lambda \in L} \sum_{m=0}^{M(\lambda)} B(\lambda, m)h^m\, e^{\lambda h}, \text{ say} \tag{37}$$

where

$$B(\bar{\lambda}, m) = \bar{B}(\lambda, m); \quad B(0, 0) = 0; \quad \sum_j b(j) = 0; \quad \sum_j a(j) = 1 \tag{38}$$

or, to be more precise

$$h_j(q, u) = \alpha_j(q) + \beta_j(q) \sum_{\lambda \in L} \sum_{m=0}^{M(\lambda)} D(\lambda, m; \beta(q))\{h(q, u)$$
$$- \alpha(q)\}^m \; e^{\lambda(h(q,u)-\alpha(q))} \quad (39)$$

where[11]

$$\alpha(q) = h(q, u_1); \quad \alpha(q) + \beta(q) = h(q, u_2), \text{ say} \quad u_2 > u_1, \text{ say} \quad (40)$$

(a) $\displaystyle\sum_{\lambda \in L} \sum_{m=0}^{M(\lambda)} D(\lambda, m; \beta)\beta^m \; e^{\lambda\beta} = 1;$

(b) $\displaystyle\sum_{\lambda \in L} D(\lambda, 0; \beta) = 0;$

(c) $D(\bar{\lambda}, m; \beta) = \hat{D}(\lambda, m; \beta);$

(d) $\left\{\displaystyle\sum_{\lambda \in L} \sum_{m=0}^{M(\lambda)} D(\lambda, m; \beta)k^m \; e^{\lambda k}\right\}$

$$\cdot \left\{\sum_{\lambda \in L} \sum_{m=0}^{M(\lambda)} D(\lambda, m; k)\beta^m \; e^{\lambda\beta}\right\} = 1 \quad (41)$$

Proof: For (37) all we need is the fact that $a(0, 0; q)$ is linearly independent of the other $a(\lambda, m; q)$ because $\Sigma_j \, a(0, 0; q) = 1$, $\Sigma_j \, a(\lambda, m, j; q) = 0$ when $(\lambda, m) \neq (0, 0)$. This is repeated in the last two equations in (38). $B(0, 0) = 0$ is just a convenient normalization. $B(\bar{\lambda}, m) = \bar{B}(\lambda, m)$ is the sort of condition we always have with complex conjugates in the analysis of real systems.

To derive (39) we write down (37) with $u = u_1$, and put

$$k(q, u) = h(q, u) - \alpha(q) \quad (42)$$

to get

$$k_j = b(j) \sum_{\lambda} \sum_{0}^{M(\lambda)} C(\lambda, m; q)k^m \; e^{\lambda k} \quad (43)$$

as in section 1, where

$$\sum_{\lambda} C(\lambda, 0; q) = 0 \quad (44)$$

because $k(q, u_1) = h(q, u_1) - h(q, u_1) \equiv 0$. Writing (43) down for $u = u_2$ and dividing into (43) we get

$$k_j \Big/ \sum_{\lambda} \sum_{0}^{M(\lambda)} C(\lambda, m; q) \, k^m \, e^{\lambda k} = \beta_j \Big/ \sum_{\lambda} \sum_{0}^{M(\lambda)} C(\lambda, m; q)\beta^m \, e^{\lambda\beta} \quad (45)$$

so that

$$k = K(\beta, u) \quad (46)$$

with

$$\partial k/\partial \beta = \sum_{\lambda, m} D(\lambda, m; \beta)k^m e^{\lambda k} \equiv \psi(k, \beta), \text{ say} \tag{47}$$

with the Ds satisfying (41). This is in principle integrable when the functions are reasonably well-behaved, and leads immediately to (39) which is in principle always integrable, too, when the functions are reasonably well-behaved.

(41c) merely says that we are interested in 'real' solutions. The other three parts may be written

$$\text{(a)} \ \psi(\beta, \beta) = 1; \quad \text{(b)} \ \psi(0, \beta) = 0; \quad \text{(c)} \ \psi(k, \beta)\psi(\beta, k) = 1 \tag{48}$$

To derive (a), put $u = u_2$ in (46), to get $k \equiv \beta$ so that $\partial k/\partial \beta = 1$. For (b) put $u = u_1$, to get $k \equiv 0$, and $\partial k/\partial \beta = 0$. (c) is a little more difficult. Fix u_1, but think of $v = u_2$ as potentially variable. (46) then becomes

$$k(q, u) = K^*(k(q, v), u, v), \text{ say} \tag{49}$$

or, equivalently

$$k(q, v) = K^*(k(q, u), v, u) \tag{50}$$

(c) merely states that $\partial k(q, v)/\partial k(q, u)$ is the inverse of $\partial k(q, u)/\partial k(q, v)$, u and v being held constant during both differentiations.

3 Polynomial Engel curves

As we saw at the end of the previous section,[12] complete systems of polynomial Engel curves can always be written as

$$x_j = a(j; p) + b(j; p)m + c(j; p) \sum_{2}^{R} A(r; p)m^r, \text{ say} \tag{1}$$

In terms of the cost function

$$g(p, u) = \min\{p.x|f(x) \geq u\}, \text{ say} \tag{2}$$

this becomes

$$g_j(p, u) = a(j; p) + b(j; p)g(p, u) + c(j; p) \sum_{2}^{R} A(r; p)g(p, u)^r \tag{3}$$

To proceed further, assume first that $a(p) = (a(1; p), a(2; p), \dots)$, $b(p)$ and $c(p)$ are linearly independent, and write

$$\theta(r; p) = g(p, u_r), \quad r = 1, 2, 3; \quad u_1 < u_2 < u_3 \tag{4}$$

as in section 1, and substitute into (3). Now write

$$\alpha(p) = \theta(1; p) \tag{5}$$

$$h(p, u) = g(p, u) - g(p, u_1) = g(p, u) - \alpha(p) \tag{6}$$

to get

$$h_j(p, u) = b(j; p)h(p, u) + c(j; p) \sum_{r=1}^{R} B(r; p)h^r(p, u), \text{ say} \tag{7}$$

Set now

$$\beta(p) = h(p, u_2) = \theta(2; p) - \theta(1; p) \tag{8}$$

$$k(p, u) = h(p, u)/\beta(p) = [g(p, u) - \alpha(p)]/\beta(p) \tag{9}$$

in (7) to get

$$k_j(p, u) = c(j; p) \sum_{r=1}^{R} C(r; p)k^r(p; u), \text{ say} \tag{10}$$

where[13]

$$\sum_{r=1}^{R} C(r; p) = 0 \tag{11}$$

Finally set

$$\gamma(p) = k(p, u_3) = h(p, u_3)/h(p, u_2)$$
$$= (\theta(3; p) - \theta(1; p))/(\theta(2; p) - \theta(1; p))$$
$$= [\theta(3; p) - \alpha(p)]/\beta(p) \tag{12}$$

to get

$$k_j(p, u) \Big/ \sum_{1}^{R} C(r; p)k^r = \gamma_j(p) \Big/ \sum_{1}^{R} C(r; p)\gamma^r \tag{13}$$

so that

$$k(p, u) = K(\gamma(p), u), \text{ say} \tag{14}$$

and (13) becomes

$$\partial k/\partial\gamma = K'(\gamma, u) = \sum_{1}^{R} D(r; \gamma)k^r, \text{ say} \tag{15}$$

so that we have reduced the problem to the integration of an ordinary first order differential equation which can always be done in principle for sufficiently well-behaved functions. Putting $u = u_3; u_2$ in (15) we have

$$\sum_{1}^{R} D(r; \gamma)\gamma^r = 1; \quad \sum D(r, \gamma) = 0 \tag{16}$$

the former reflecting the fact that $\partial K(\gamma, u_3)/\partial\gamma = \partial\gamma/\partial\gamma = 1$, the latter that $\partial K(\gamma, u_2)/\partial\gamma = \partial 1/\partial\gamma = 0$. Setting $u = u_1$ confirms that $D(0; \gamma) = 0$.

Finally

$$\left(\sum_{1}^{R} D(r; \gamma)k^r\right)\left(\sum_{1}^{R} D(r; k)\gamma^r\right) = 1 \tag{17}$$

as in the proof of section 2 (48(c)).

According to (6), (9) and (14)

$$\begin{aligned} g(p, u) &= \alpha(p) + \beta(p)k(p, u) \\ &= \alpha(p) + \beta(p)K(\gamma(p), u) \\ &= G(\theta(p), u), \text{ say} \end{aligned} \tag{18}$$

where

$$\theta(p) = (\theta(1; p), \theta(2; p), \theta(3; p)) \tag{19}$$

and

$$K(\gamma, u) = G(0, 1, \gamma, u) \tag{20}$$

so that

$$G(\lambda e + \mu\theta, u) = \lambda + \mu G(\theta, u); \quad \mu \geq 0, \quad e = (1, 1, ..., 1) \tag{21}$$

Differentiating (18) by p_j, using (15), and writing $g_j = x_j$, $g = m$, we have the general equation

$$\begin{aligned} x_j = \alpha_j(p) + \beta_j(p)(m - \alpha(p))/\beta(p) \\ + \beta(p)\gamma_j(p) \sum_{1}^{R} D(r; \gamma)\{(m - \alpha(p))/\beta(p)\}^r \end{aligned} \tag{22}$$

α, β, γ are defined in (5), (8) and (12) in terms of the cost functions $\theta(1; p)$, $\theta(2; p)$, $\theta(3; p)$ and the Ds satisfy (16) and (17).

Let us now look at the quadratic case – in a reasonable sense the most general nondegenerate polynomial system. (16) implies that $D(2) = -D(1) = 1/\gamma(\gamma - 1)$, so that

$$\begin{aligned} x_j = \alpha_j(p) + \beta_j(p)(m - \alpha(p))/\beta(p) + \beta(p)\gamma_j(p)[(m - \alpha(p))/\beta(p) \\ - \{(m - \alpha(p))/\beta(p)\}^2]/\gamma(1 - \gamma) \end{aligned} \tag{23}$$

and, in (15),

$$\partial k/\partial \gamma = K' = k(k - 1)/\gamma(\gamma - 1) \tag{24}$$

Now $dz/z(z - 1) = dz/(z - 1) - dz/z = d \log\{(z - 1)/z\}$, so that (24) yields

$$(k - 1)/k = u(\gamma - 1)/\gamma \tag{25}$$

in an obvious normalisation. Hence

$$\begin{aligned} g(p, u) &= \alpha(p) + \beta(p)k(p, u) \\ &= \alpha(p) + \beta(p)/(1 - u\delta(p)) \end{aligned} \tag{26}$$

where

$$\delta(p) = (\gamma(p) - 1)/\gamma(p) = (\theta(3; p) - \theta(2; p))/(\theta(3; p) - \theta(1; p)) \tag{27}$$

is the cost function corresponding to a complete quadratic system of Engel curves.

So much for the quadratic case. What made it relatively straightforward was the fact that

$$D(1; \gamma) : D(2; \gamma) = -1 : 1 \tag{28}$$

Consider now the more general case with $R > 2$ and

$$D(1; \gamma) : D(2; \gamma) : \dots : D(R; \gamma) = a_1 : a_2 : \dots : a_R \tag{29}$$

where the a_r are constants and, of course,

$$\sum a_r = 0; \quad a_R = 1, \text{ without loss of generality} \tag{30}$$

by (16). (15) then becomes

$$\partial k / \partial \gamma = \sum a_r k^r \bigg/ \sum a_r \gamma^r \tag{31}$$

I will confine my attention to the case where the zeros, $b_1 = 0$, $b_2 = 1$, $b_3 \dots b_R$ of $\Sigma a_r z^r$ are real and distinct, though a similar treatment works when they are not. We then have

$$1 \bigg/ \sum a_r z^r = \sum_r c_r/(z - b_r), \text{ say; } \quad c_r = 1 \bigg/ \prod_{s \neq r} (b_r - b_s) \tag{32}$$

so that

$$dz \bigg/ \sum a_r z^r = \sum c_r dz/(z - b_r) = d \log \prod (z - b_r)^{c_r} \tag{33}$$

(31) therefore yields

$$\prod (k - b_r)^{c_r} = u \prod (\gamma - b_r)^{c_r} \tag{34}$$

in an appropriate normalisation. Moreover

$$\sum c_r = 0 \tag{35}$$

as can be seen by equating coefficients of z^r in $\Sigma c_r \, \Pi_{s \neq r} (z - b_s) = 1$, derived from (32). Since $m = g = \alpha + \beta k$ by (18), we may therefore rewrite (34) in the form

$$u = \Pi\{(m - \alpha(p) - b_r \beta(p))/(\gamma(p) - b_r)\}^{c_r}; \quad \sum c_r = 0$$
$$= \Pi\{[(m - \alpha)/\beta - b_r)]/(1 - b_r)\}^{c_r} \tag{36}$$

or, if you prefer,

$$u = \Pi \frac{b_r(m - \theta(2; p)) + (1 - b_r)(m - \theta(1; p))}{b_r(\theta(3; p) - \theta(2; p)) + (1 - b_r)(\theta(3; p) - \theta(1; p))} \tag{37}$$

Drop (29) and turn to the *fully degenerate* case in which

$$\lambda(p)a(j; p) + \mu(p)b(j; p) + \nu(p)c(j; p) = 0 \tag{38}$$

where it is not true that $\lambda(p) = \mu(p) = \gamma(p) = 0$. Since $\Sigma p_j x_j = m$, $\mu(p) = 0$. Hence either

$$c(j; p) = 0 \tag{39}$$

yielding the familiar linear Engel system with

$$g(p, u) = \alpha(p) + \beta(p)u \tag{40}$$

in the obvious normalisation, or

$$a(j; p) = \rho(p)c(j; p), \text{ say} \tag{41}$$

so that

$$x_j = b(j; p)m + c(j; p) \sum_{r \neq 1} A(r; p)m^r, \text{ say} \tag{42}$$

A simplified version of the proof leading up to (22) yields (15)–(17), (22), with

$$\alpha(p) = \theta(1; p) = 0 \tag{43}$$

The polynomial Engel curves were generated by putting $\omega = 1$ in section 2(32). According to section 2(32) a similar analysis applies for g^ω in the general case discussed there. We can analyse it exactly as we have just done the polynomial case. The results are so similar that I will not spell them out here.

Replacing $g(.)$ by $h(.)$ in the discussion one can apply the same analysis to section 2(1). Note that the polynomial form is guaranteed here, not a further assumption.

4 Concluding remarks

In order to keep this article to a reasonable length, the following remarks have been kept to a perhaps undesirable brevity. The discussion in sections 2 and 3 was entirely local, asking, if you like, when is

$$x_i = \sum_{r \in R} a(r, i; p)\phi(r; m) \tag{1}$$

to the second order nearer $\bar{p}$, $\bar{m}$? If so, it will clearly still be so near $\lambda\bar{p}$, $\lambda\bar{m}$, and I will normalise to take $\bar{m} = 1$ for simplicity. The main condition was then that the rank $N(\bar{p})$ of $A(\bar{p}) = [a(r, i; \bar{p})]$ is ≤ 3.

Let us now assume that representations similar to (1) are possible throughout an open set Ω in p space. Then $N(\bar{p}) \leq 3$ throughout Ω. Suppose that $N(\bar{p}) = 3$, some $\bar{p} \in \Omega$. Then it will be so throughout a maximal neighbourhood $\Omega(\bar{p}) \subseteq \Omega$ of $\bar{p}$. There may be many such disjoint neighbourhoods. They will commonly be divided by $\bar{n} - 1$ dimensional surfaces on which $N(p) = 2$, and these by $\bar{n} - 2$ dimensional surfaces when $N(p) = 1$, when $\bar{n}$ is the number of goods. Clearly one cannot move in just any direction and stay in one of these surfaces, as my calculus arguments require. I do not believe that this is a genuine problem, at least if there are sufficient goods, but have not verified this. If you like, apply the arguments for $N(p) = 1, 2$, only in cases where this region is solid. $N(p) = 3$ is, of course, the important case. A similar argument may be applied when max $\{N(p)|p \in \Omega\} = 2$, for instance. There the neighbourhoods $\Omega(p)$ are those in which $N(p) = 2$, rather than 3.

Look again at the main theorem as stated at the beginning of section 2. If $N = 3$, it states, we are in one of the cases (i), (ii), (iii). Of these, (iii) differs from (ii) only in having purely imaginary exponents, rather than purely real, while (i) is the usual logarithmic limiting case of an expression like (ii). We may therefore concentrate on (ii) as a representative case. It may be written

$$h_j(q, u) = a(j; q) + b(j; q) \sum_{b \in B} B(b; q)e^{-bh} + c(j; q) \sum_{c \in C} C(c; q)e^{ch} \qquad (2)$$

where $B = \{b > 0 : -b \subseteq S\}, C = \{c > 0 : c \in S\}$. This equation may be treated like (3.1). We set $u = u_1, u_2, u_3$ in turn, $\theta(r; q) = h(q, u_r)$ to get

$$\begin{aligned}
h(q, u) &= H(\theta(1), \theta(2), \theta(3), u) \\
&= \theta(1) + \tilde{H}(\theta(2) - \theta(1), \theta(3) - \theta(1), u) \\
&= \alpha + \tilde{H}(\beta, \varepsilon, u), \text{ say}
\end{aligned} \qquad (3)$$

when the second representation is possible because the coefficient of $a(i)$ is 1.

The bother about this is that $\tilde{H}(., ., u)$ has two arguments, and so that there is an integrability problem. One can say a good deal about the nature of a complete solution, but not find it explicitly as one can in the cases discussed in section 3.

B and C have each at least one element. What made a complete solution possible in section 3 was the assumption that one or other had just one. Let it be B and set $B = \{\omega\}$. Then

$$h_j(q, u) = a(j; q) + b(j; q)e^{-\omega h} + C(j; q) \sum_{m=1}^{n} c(r, q) e^{r\omega h} \qquad (4)$$

Because the coefficients of $a(j; q)$ and $b(j; q)$ both depend only on h, it is possible to reduce the 3 variables in (3) to 1, not just 2. Because they are 1, $e^{\omega h}$ this takes the form

$$h(q, u) = \alpha + \beta K(\gamma, u), \quad \gamma = \varepsilon/\beta \qquad (5)$$

since $K(., u)$ has only one argument, there is no integrability condition to be solved.

$B = \{1\}$ is the polynomial case, $B = C = \{1\}$ the quadratic,

given $\omega = 1$.

Turn now to the purely imaginary case (iii). $B = \{\omega\}$ then corresponds to $T = \{-\omega, 0, \omega\}$ so that we get a direct analogue of the quadratic of the form.

$$h_j = a(j) + b(j) \cos \omega h + c(j) \sin \omega h \qquad (6)$$

When $B = \{\omega\}$, $C = \{\omega, 2\omega, ..., n\omega\}$ say so that $S = \{-\omega, 0, \omega, 2\omega, ..., n\omega\}$. It is *not* true that $S = \{-m\omega, -m - 1\omega, ..., 0, \omega, ..., n\omega\}$ in general – section 2(35) and section 2(36) are counter-examples. However, it can[14] be shown that this will be so in a 'generic' sense in what I think is a reasonable use of the word; and I suspect that S is always of this form, wherever $N = 3$, if we allow a few gaps.

Notes

1 I had planned a contribution worthier of Sir Richard Stone, in which the results would have been related to more general ideas. Unfortunately, I miscalculated the time available and this paper is the rather incomplete result.

   The ideas in this paper were first presented to the Quantitative Economics Workshop at the London School of Economics in January 1977 and January 1978. I am grateful to John Wise, who, for the special case of polynomial Engel curves, suggested the probable importance of the rank of the coefficient matrix. I am also grateful to John Muellbauer and my colleagues at the LSE for their comments. I thank the SSRC for its funding and the LSE for my colleagues.

2 Having smooth strictly quasi-concave preferences, and being greedy.

3 Of course the rank of $B(p)$ depends on p in general. It is ≤ 3 everywhere. If it equals 3 at a point, it will in an open neighbourhood of it. The analysis of $R(B(p)) = 3$, which takes up most of the paper, may be thought of as carried out in such a neighbourhood. Presumably regions in which it takes lower values commonly divide those in which it takes higher. See section 4.

4 Both terms will normally occur.

5 That is, positively homogeneous of degree one. The term is Sydney Afriat's.

6 $\psi(\delta, u) = \phi(0, 1, \delta, u)$.

7 Since $h = k + \alpha$ is equivalent to $k = h - \alpha$, one merely replaces α in (47)–(48) by $-\alpha$ to get (49)–(50).

8 One can obviously apply the same arguments to T as S, remembering only that the final results have to be real, in particular T symmetric.

9 S has both positive and negative elements by the corollary to Lemma 2.

10 We sum over (σ, m), $(\sigma', m') \in S$ such that $\sigma + \sigma' = \mu = \sigma^\pm + \sigma^=$, $m + m' = n = m^+$. When $\sigma\sigma' \geq 0$ the term vanishes. When $\sigma\sigma' < 0$, take $\sigma >$

0, $\sigma' < 0$. Then $0 \leq m' \leq m^- = 0$. Hence $m' = 0$, $m = m^+$. Hence $(\sigma^\pm, m^+)$, $(\sigma^=, 0)$ are the only such pair in S.

11 Put $u = u_1$, u_2 in (39), and eliminate $a(j)$, $b(j)$ from it and the resulting equations.

12 Put $\omega = 1$ in section 2(34).

13 To derive (11) : set $u = u_2$ to get $k(p, u_2) = 1$, and $0 = \partial 1/\partial p_j = c(j; p) \Sigma_r C(r; p)$. Remember that $c(p) = (c(1; p), c(2; p), ...) \neq 0$ since $N = 3$.

14 *Added in proof:* Consider this as a conjecture. I have lost my notes on the point, and do not even remember the meaning I gave to generic, let alone the proof.

2 Suggestions towards freeing systems of demand functions from a strait-jacket

LEIF JOHANSEN[1]

1 Introduction

The development of complete systems of demand functions has been one of the most important trends in research on consumer demand in the last couple of decades. Richard Stone's Linear Expenditure System and the theoretical approach which he used in establishing this system have been instrumental in this development. The LES system has been widely used both in its original form and in forms modified and generalized in various directions. Several other systems have also appeared. There is no doubt that great advances have been achieved. It seems to me, however, that research in this field has, voluntarily, put on a strait-jacket. I have in mind the requirement that all demand functions constituting the system shall be 'of the same form', differing only in the values of the parameters. The purpose of the present paper is to suggest approaches which may help to free theory and applied work from this strait-jacket.

The idea that it would be sound and useful to abandon the requirement that all functions in the system should be of the same form is not entirely uncontroversial. L. J. Lau has argued that such uniformity 'is desirable because it allows all commodities to be treated symmetrically'. This kind of symmetry does of course possess a sort of aesthetic value, and it is also convenient from a mathematical and computational point of view. Furthermore, one might feel that an element of arbitrariness is introduced if the researcher decides to treat different commodities in formally different ways. Nevertheless, although these arguments are attractive, I do not find them compelling.

Now, if one has some ideas about different behaviour of different commodities in the demand system, then one could of course try to establish a system which is sufficiently general so as to encompass all the forms which one feels are relevant, thus avoiding an a priori association of particular commodities with particular forms. This approach, however, would easily involve too many parameters.

31

It is now quite common to combine information from different sources in establishing systems of demand functions. In particular, it is quite common to establish some properties of the Engel functions (demand as a function of income or total expenditure) on the basis of cross-section information, and next estimate coefficients representing the effects of prices by means of time-series data. In cross-section studies of consumer demand where the intention is not to proceed to the construction of complete systems including prices, there is more freedom to choose functional forms, and then forms have often been used successfully which are not compatible with any of the well known complete systems which include prices. Among functional forms which have been used successfully for Engel functions, without involving too many parameters, are the Törnqvist functions. (See particularly H. Wold, 1952, pp. 3–4, 107–8 and 271–7. See also P. R. Fisk, 1958–59.) By using different functional forms they are able to describe the behaviour of 'necessities', 'relative luxuries', and 'luxuries', and by variations of parameter values also inferior commodities. An example of the use of these functions is given by J. G. van Beeck and H. den Hartog (1964) for the Netherlands. (It has also been reported that the functions have been found useful for some groups of commodities in the USSR, see A. Keck, 1968, p. 176.) Another type of Engel curves which has been used successfully is the lognormal probability function as proposed by J. Aitchison and J. A. C. Brown (1954). In this case the same functional form is able to cover qualitatively different cases because of the inflection of the curve and the possibility to use different parts of it for the relevant range by stretching and compressing it.

For systems of Engel curves where the functional form is different as between groups of commodities, two different approaches are conceivable at the empirical stage. (1) One may try the different functional forms for each commodity and choose the one which fits best according to some statistical criterion. (2) One may choose the functional form for each commodity on a priori grounds. In the latter case the 'a priori' reasons may not necessarily be of a purely intuitive or introspective type. 'Objective needs' might be measured for certain commodities, and the results used as a basis for choosing among the functional forms and for specification of values of certain parameters, for instance saturation levels. Such an objective needs approach is used to some extent in connection with long-term projections and planning in the USSR. See for instance K. K. Valtukh (1975), who argues that the usual demand theory is rather empty unless one introduces some sort of objective information about needs. Such an approach, using investigations of objective needs, ought not to be absolutely alien to neoclassical theory. It was K. Wicksell who wrote: 'Perhaps some day the physiologists will succeed in isolating and evaluating the various human needs for bodily warmth, nourishment, variety, recreation, stimulation, ornament, harmony etc., and thereby lay a really rational foundation for the theory of consumption.' (The quotation is taken from Å. E. Andersson (1977), who discusses the implications of this view in specific contexts.)

It might be tempting to start out from such rather satisfactory Engel curve systems and construct complete systems of demand functions on this basis. However, this is not easy. In the first place, the Törnqvist functions and the Aitchison–Brown type of functions do not satisfy the adding-up condition, except for special cases of the Törnqvist functions. They therefore need some amendment on this point. (See especially J. G. van Beeck and H. den Hartog (1964).) In the second place, and more importantly, it is not easy to find a simple way of introducing price effects so as to comply with the requirements of demand theory based on utility maximization. For instance, it might be tempting to supplement the Engel functions by price effects by writing a demand function as a product of a function of prices and the function of (real) income corresponding to the Engel curve, as was suggested by Aitchison and Brown. However, it has been shown recently by H. R. Varian (1978) that this procedure is compatible with the requirements of standard demand theory only if the Engel function exhibits constant income elasticity.

Now there are of course in the literature some systems of demand functions which have somewhat flexible Engel function properties so that they are able to represent the structure over more than local ranges. The LES system in its original form displays linear Engel curves, but it has been modified by L. Solari (1971), F. Carlevaro and others so as to acquire better Engel function properties. Some studies indicate reasonably good Engel function properties for the Fourgeaud–Nataf system and for the Houthakker system based on indirect addilog utility functions. There are also other variants too numerous to be detailed here. However, they are rather complicated when the number of commodities is not fairly small. Furthermore, their properties are usually not very transparent. They may therefore easily lead to unsatisfactory results over wider ranges even if they fit data quite well over the observed ranges. I think, therefore, that explorations and investigations of possible benefits from abandoning the requirement that all functions should be of the same form may be worth undertaking.

2 The main idea: combination of functional forms

The main idea to be explored in the remainder of this paper is the possibility of elaborating manageable systems by combining well known simpler systems. For instance, the LES system has perfectly satisfactory properties for some commodities, but not for commodities for which the consumer has a saturation level. On the other hand, a system based on a quadratic utility function implies such saturation levels, but is obviously not good for *all* commodities. Perhaps a useful system could be obtained by combining these systems so as to use the LES functions for some commodities and functions derived from quadratic utilities for other commodities. Obviously one cannot combine the functions without some adaptations if the usual constraints implied by utility maximization and the budget constraint are to be satisfied. The question then is whether some of the simplicity of the two separate systems will survive the combination. The systems mentioned are just examples; corresponding problems arise in connection with any combination of systems.

In the paper already referred to, L. J. Lau (1977) mentions that one can always relax the uniformity requirement for the functional forms by defining the demand function for the nth commodity as a residual from the budget constraint when the functional forms of the $n - 1$ other commodities have been specified, but he considers this to involve an arbitrary element. This is certainly true. This is not the kind of relaxation of the uniformity requirement which I have in mind here. It is, however, of some interest to observe that at least in one particular case this procedure can be made to conform with utility maximization. H. Wold (1952, pp. 106–7) and O. Hoflund (1954) have considered the case of two commodities of which one has a demand function depending on income and own price with constant elasticities and the other has a function determined as a residual, and they derive the corresponding utility function by integration. (The function will in general be meaningful only over a limited region in the commodity space, but this may be perfectly plausible.) Interestingly enough, according to H. Wold the problems as to whether such a system is compatible with utility maximization had already been posed by V. Pareto.

As already suggested, the idea to be discussed further in this paper is the use of different forms of demand functions for different commodities. It may be in order to mention that there is another type of combination which has already been suggested in the literature. This consists in deriving demand functions from utility functions of different forms which have been spliced together, i.e. different functional forms are assumed to be valid over different regions in the commodity space. For instance, M. B. McElroy (1975) spliced a constant elasticity of substitution (CES) utility function over one region with a quadratic utility function over another region. This produces some interesting results. It does not satisfy the needs which I have pointed out above, and the spliced utility function tends to create some rather artificial kinks in the demand functions. However, the empirical results are quite interesting and show clearly the need for a framework which permits different forms of Engel curves for different commodities.

For a representation of the combination of systems to be studied here, let the complete vector of quantities demanded be

$$x = (x_I, x_{II}) = (x_1, \ldots, x_n, x_{n+1}, \ldots, x_{n+m}) \tag{2.1}$$

where x_I is the vector of quantities of the first n commodities, and x_{II} is the vector of quantities demanded of the remaining m commodities. We shall, for convenience, distinguish only two groups, but most of the ideas can be extended in a similar way to the more general case.

For the full set of commodities we have a price vector p which can be partitioned in the same way as x:

$$p = (p_I, p_{II}) = (p_1, \ldots, p_n, p_{n+1}, \ldots, p_{n+m}) \tag{2.2}$$

Total expenditure y can be divided into expenditure on commodities in group I, y_I, and expenditure on commodities in group II, y_{II}:

$$y_I = \sum_I p_i x_i, \quad y_{II} = \sum_{II} p_i x_i, \quad y = y_I + y_{II} \tag{2.3}$$

The idea now is to use different functional forms for the demand for commodities in group I and commodities in group II. A natural way of doing this is to consider a two-step procedure as considered in the theory of utility trees or separable utility functions. Let the utility function be

$$\Omega = \Omega(U(x_I), V(x_{II})) \tag{2.4}$$

U and V are 'partial' utility functions for the two groups, and Ω is the total utility function (non-decreasing in each of the arguments).

For the utility functions introduced, we use the following notations for the derivatives:

$$\frac{\partial \Omega}{\partial U} = \omega_I = \omega_I(x), \quad \frac{\partial \Omega}{\partial V} = \omega_{II} = \omega_{II}(x)$$

$$\frac{\partial U(x_I)}{\partial x_i} = u_i = u_i(x_I) \quad (i \in I) \tag{2.5}$$

$$\frac{\partial V(x_{II})}{\partial x_i} = v_i = v_i(x_{II}) \quad (i \in II)$$

The derivatives ω_I and ω_{II} introduced on the first line are in general functions of the full vector x via $U(x_I)$ and $V(x_{II})$, but, when Ω is additive in U and V, ω_I will depend only on x_I and ω_{II} only on x_{II}.

Solving now the problem of maximizing the total utility function subject to the budget constraint we obtain conditions which can be written in the following way:

$$\frac{u_i(x_{\mathrm{I}})}{p_i} = \lambda_{\mathrm{I}} \quad (i \in \mathrm{I}) \tag{2.6}$$

$$\frac{v_i(x_{\mathrm{II}})}{p_i} = \lambda_{\mathrm{II}} \quad (i \in \mathrm{II}) \tag{2.7}$$

$$\lambda_{\mathrm{I}}\omega_{\mathrm{I}}(x) = \lambda_{\mathrm{II}}\omega_{\mathrm{II}}(x) \tag{2.8}$$

These equations together with the budget constraint determine the ordinary demand functions. The common value λ_{I} of the proportions in (2.6) could be called the marginal U-utility of expenditure on commodities in group I, and similarly λ_{II} could be called the marginal V-utility. The terms $\lambda_{\mathrm{I}}\omega_{\mathrm{I}}$ and $\lambda_{\mathrm{II}}\omega_{\mathrm{II}}$ in (2.8) are equal to the overall marginal utility of expenditure.

Now we can also see these conditions as derived by the following two steps: first maximize $U(x_{\mathrm{I}})$ subject to $\Sigma_{\mathrm{I}} p_i x_i = y_{\mathrm{I}}$ and similarly $V(x_{\mathrm{II}})$ subject to $\Sigma_{\mathrm{II}} p_i x_i = y_{\mathrm{II}}$, as if y_{I} and y_{II} were given. Next, adjust y_{I} and y_{II} subject to $y_{\mathrm{I}} + y_{\mathrm{II}} = y$ so that the total utility function Ω is maximized.

The first of these steps gives what we might call partial demand functions. We write them in the following way for the two groups:

$$x_i = \varphi_i(p_{\mathrm{I}}, y_{\mathrm{I}}) \quad (i \in \mathrm{I}) \tag{2.9}$$

$$x_i = \psi_i(p_{\mathrm{II}}, y_{\mathrm{II}}) \quad (i \in \mathrm{II}) \tag{2.10}$$

The functions in (2.9) are based upon (2.6) and the budget equation for group I, and the demand functions in (2.10) are based on (2.7) and the budget equation for the second group. Each of these sets of demand functions is an ordinary system of demand functions, only limited to a group of commodities and depending on expenditure on that group of commodities instead of total expenditure. Due to the separability assumption in (2.4) the demand functions for commodities in group I depend only on prices for that group, and correspondingly for group II.

The overall utility maximization is achieved by determining y_{I} and y_{II} so as to maximize Ω. By inserting from (2.9) and (2.10) into (2.4) we get total utility as a function of y_{I} and y_{II} (and given prices). We write this as

$$\Omega = \Omega(U(\varphi(p_{\mathrm{I}}, y_{\mathrm{I}})), V(\psi(p_{\mathrm{II}}, y_{\mathrm{II}}))$$

$$= \Omega(U^*(p_{\mathrm{I}}, y_{\mathrm{I}}), V^*(p_{\mathrm{II}}, y_{\mathrm{II}})) \tag{2.11}$$

Here $\varphi(p_{\mathrm{I}}, y_{\mathrm{I}})$ and $\psi(p_{\mathrm{II}}, y_{\mathrm{II}})$ are the vectors of demand functions (2.9) and (2.10), and $U^*(p_{\mathrm{I}}, y_{\mathrm{I}})$ and $V^*(p_{\mathrm{II}}, y_{\mathrm{II}})$ are indirect utility functions for the partial systems. Maximizing this with respect to y_I and y_{II} subject to $y_I + y_{II} = y$ we obtain

$$\omega_I \frac{\partial U^*}{\partial y_I} = \omega_{II} \frac{\partial V^*}{\partial y_{II}} \qquad (2.12)$$

In this condition ω_I and ω_{II} are, in general, functions of both p_I, y_I and p_{II}, y_{II}, via U and V. The terms $\partial U^*/\partial y_I$ and $\partial V^*/\partial y_{II}$ are, of course, the same as the marginal U-utility λ_I and the marginal V-utility λ_{II} in (2.8).

Equation (2.12) together with $y_I + y_{II} = y$ will now determine the allocation of y to the two groups. It may not necessarily be possible to solve the equations explicitly, but at least implicitly they define y_I and y_{II} as functions of total expenditure and prices:

$$\begin{aligned} y_I &= y_I(p_I, p_{II}, y) \\ y_{II} &= y_{II}(p_I, p_{II}, y) \end{aligned} \qquad (2.13)$$

Since they determine how the total expenditure y will be allocated to the two groups of commodities we shall call them 'allocation functions'.

The complete demand functions will now be obtained by inserting from (2.13) into (2.9) and (2.10), i.e. we have

$$x_i = \varphi_i(p_I, y_I(p_I, p_{II}, y)) \equiv f_i(p, y) \quad (i \in I) \qquad (2.14)$$

$$x_i = \psi_i(p_{II}, y_{II}(p_I, p_{II}, y)) \equiv g_i(p, y) \quad (i \in II) \qquad (2.15)$$

Here f_i and g_i are the final forms of the demand functions for the two groups, depending in general on all prices and total expenditure.

One might now use well known and relatively simple demand functions for the partial functions (2.9) and (2.10), chosen so that the forms φ_i are suitable for commodities in group I and ψ_i are suitable for commodities in group II. These functions may be derived from direct utility functions U and V respectively, or from the corresponding indirect utility functions U^* and V^*. The total system as represented by (2.14) and (2.15) requires some more information about preferences, here represented by the utility function Ω which combines U and V. How simple the resulting system will be depends upon the functions in (2.13), which again depend upon the condition (2.12). One might hope that this condition takes a simple form so that the functions (2.13) are also simple; then the system (2.14–15) would be a manageable system. However, even if the functions in (2.13) are not very simple, the overall system may still be manageable since φ_i and ψ_i are manageable functions and the complexities of the overall system enter only through the functions y_I and y_{II}. Instead of viewing the complete system as a system of $n + m$ complicated functions f_i and g_i, one could view it as a system of $n + m$ simple functions φ_i and ψ_i plus 2 more complicated functions determining y_I and y_{II}. Also, for estimation purposes this way of looking at the system may be practical and convenient.

The approach taken here to establishing demand functions bears some relationship to R. A. Pollak's 'conditional demand functions' (1969). However, the aims of his study are different. His conditional demand functions for commodities in one group are conditional upon given amounts of commodities in another group. In our context we might try to utilize some of the ideas of Pollak's conditional demand functions for a more general case by abandoning the separability assumption for the utility function (2.4) and formulating our partial demand functions for commodities in group I, i.e. φ_i, as conditional upon given amounts of the commodities in group II, and similarly for the functions ψ_i for group II. In establishing the final form of the complete system, corresponding to (2.14) and (2.15), we must then require consistency between the 'given' quantities entering as conditions in one set of functions and the decisions about these quantities represented by the other set of functions. This would give a more general approach, but would yield little hope of simple results. I shall therefore retain the assumption of some sort of separability. For this case there is a close connection between the formulas of the following section and formulas in R. A. Pollak (1971a).

3 The derivatives of the complete demand functions

The derivatives of the demand functions f_i and g_i established by (2.14–15) can be decomposed into derivatives characterizing the simpler systems consisting of φ_i and ψ_i, and the derivatives of the allocation functions (2.13). The formulas are simple enough, but we put them down for completeness since we need them later on.

For the derivatives with respect to total expenditure we have:

$$\frac{\partial f_i}{\partial y} = \frac{\partial \varphi_i}{\partial y_I} \frac{\partial y_I}{\partial y} \quad (i \in I) \tag{3.1}$$

$$\frac{\partial g_i}{\partial y} = \frac{\partial \psi_i}{\partial y_{II}} \frac{\partial y_{II}}{\partial y} \quad (i \in II) \tag{3.2}$$

These formulas show how the Engel curves of the partial systems φ_i and ψ_i are modified in the final form of the system through the way in which y_I and y_{II} depend upon total expenditure y. Even if the partial systems have unsatisfactory properties taken by themselves, the total system may be satisfactory. For instance, if one of the partial systems is an LES system, with constant derivatives with respect to the allocation y_I or y_{II} to that group, the complete system may be able to capture more sophisticated forms. But, since all demand functions in one group are modified in the same way, all commodities in one group should in a way have the same basic character, for instance all commodities in one group being 'necessities', or all being 'luxuries'.

The derivatives with respect to prices in the own group are given by

$$\frac{\partial f_i}{\partial p_j} = \frac{\partial \varphi_i}{\partial p_j} + \frac{\partial \varphi_i}{\partial y_I} \frac{\partial y_I}{\partial p_j} \quad (i, j \in \mathrm{I}) \tag{3.3}$$

$$\frac{\partial g_i}{\partial p_j} = \frac{\partial \psi_i}{\partial p_j} + \frac{\partial \psi_i}{\partial y_{II}} \frac{\partial y_{II}}{\partial p_j} \quad (i, j \in \mathrm{II}) \tag{3.4}$$

The price derivatives of the partial systems are modified by price effects via the allocation functions. These modifications can go in either direction and can make the price derivatives depend in interesting ways upon total income even if the partial systems are too rigid in this sense taken by themselves.

For the price derivatives across groups we have

$$\frac{\partial f_i}{\partial p_j} = \frac{\partial \varphi_i}{\partial y_I} \frac{\partial y_I}{\partial p_j} \quad (i \in \mathrm{I}, j \in \mathrm{II}) \tag{3.5}$$

$$\frac{\partial g_i}{\partial p_j} = \frac{\partial \psi_i}{\partial y_{II}} \frac{\partial y_{II}}{\partial p_j} \quad (i \in \mathrm{II}, j \in \mathrm{I}) \tag{3.6}$$

These effects assert themselves only through the effects of the price on the total allocation to the group to which the commodity belongs. It appears that the complete system can exhibit both complementarity and alternativity in demand even if the partial systems are too simple to do so. However, if inferiority is ruled out in the partial systems, then all commodities in one group show the same sort of relation to a particular commodity in the other group.

4 Additive separability

Let us consider the case where the separability assumption in (2.4) is strengthened to additive separability, i.e.

$$\Omega = U(x_I) + V(x_{II}) \tag{4.1}$$

Then the terms ω_I and ω_{II} in the formulations in section 2 are both equal to unity. The condition determining the allocation functions (2.13) is then

$$\frac{\partial U^*(p_I, y_I)}{\partial y_I} = \frac{\partial V^*(p_{II}, y_{II})}{\partial y_{II}} \tag{4.2}$$

The derivatives entering this condition are the same as λ_I and λ_{II} entering the formulation (2.6–8) of the conditions for utility maximization. Condition (4.2) can therefore also be written

$$\frac{u_i(\varphi(p_I, y_I))}{p_i} = \frac{v_j(\psi(p_{II}, y_{II}))}{p_j} \quad (i \in I, j \in II) \tag{4.3}$$

Conditions (4.2) or (4.3) are somewhat simpler than the conditions in the general case, in that we have avoided the appearance of all p_I, p_{II}, y_I, y_{II} on both sides of the equations. However, the allocation functions will still tend to be rather cumbersome.

Let us explore the working of the system by considering one group of commodities which, within the group, obey the linear expenditure system, and another group which corresponds to a quadratic utility function. We might consider the latter group as a group of necessities, with quadratic utility functions formulated so as to imply a saturation point for each commodity in the group. For the commodities in the group corresponding to the linear expenditure system, we should stipulate minimum quantities. For simplicity we omit these parameters; they could easily be introduced afterwards if we so wish. The total utility function can then be written as

$$\Omega = \sum_I \alpha_i \ln x_i - \frac{1}{2} \sum_{II} \frac{1}{k_i} (c_i - x_i)^2 \tag{4.4}$$

In the second group c_i are the saturation quantities. The utility functions in this group are meant to follow the quadratic curve up to this point, and to be flat from there on. Since the marginal utility is always positive for commodities in the first group, it is clear that a meaningful maximization takes place so that we have $x_i < c_i$ for all commodities in the second group. (We assume all $\alpha_i > 0$, all $k_i > 0$, and $\Sigma \alpha_i = 1$.)

The partial system for the first group is now simply

$$x_i = \varphi_i(p_I, y_I) = \alpha_i \frac{y_I}{p_i} \quad (i \in I) \tag{4.5}$$

The functions for the second group can be written as

$$x_i = \psi_i(p_{II}, y_{II}) = c_i - k_i p_i \frac{\sum_{II} p_h c_h - y_{II}}{\sum_{II} k_h p_h^2} \quad (i \in II) \tag{4.6}$$

It should be observed that the Engel functions for both systems are linear.

A more general system based on a quadratic utility function, allowing for interaction terms which we have neglected here, has been studied by A. S. Goldberger (1967), and in a dynamic context by H. S. Houthakker and L. D. Taylor (1970). The system has also been studied by L. Wegge (1968), following up earlier work by H. Houthakker. Houthakker and

Wegge take into account the non-negativity condition $x_i \geqq 0$ and permit boundary solutions, using a quadratic programming approach. The Engel curves are then kinked linear. We shall neglect this possibility and assume interior solutions. Then (4.6) is valid.

It remains to find the allocation functions. We may proceed according to (4.3). This yields

$$\frac{1}{y_I} = \frac{\sum_{II} p_h c_h - y_{II}}{\sum_{II} k_h p_h^2} = \frac{A - y_{II}}{B} \tag{4.7}$$

where we have introduced, for convenience, A and B for the sums entering the numerator and the denominator in the middle expression. Combining now this with the budget constraint $y_I + y_{II} = y$ we obtain an equation for y_I which can be solved to give

$$y_I = \frac{1}{2} \{(y - A) + [(y - A)^2 + 4B]^{1/2}\} \tag{4.8}$$

Mathematically there is also a solution with a minus before the square root, but this solution is irrelevant.

When we have the allocation function (4.8) for y_I it follows that the allocation to group II will be

$$y_{II} = \frac{1}{2} \{y + A - [(y - A)^2 + 4B]^{1/2}\} \tag{4.9}$$

For very small values of y, (4.9) will give $y_{II} < 0$, which is not meaningful. It is necessary that $y > \dfrac{B}{A}$. If we had retained the 'minimum quantities' in the LES system for group I this could have turned out differently, especially if we had permitted them to take negative values.

From these allocation functions it follows that total expenditure on each of the two groups will now increase in a non-linear fashion with total expenditure y. It is seen that if y increases beyond all limits, then y_I will take a dominating part of y, while y_{II} will take an insignificant share. In fact, we have

$$\frac{y_I}{y} \to 1 \quad \text{and} \quad \frac{y_{II}}{y} \to 0 \quad \text{when } y \to \infty \tag{4.10}$$

In absolute terms $y_{II} \to A$ when $y \to \infty$, which agrees with the interpretation of A as the amount necessary to buy the saturation quantities c_i for $i \in II$. We might say that group II as a whole (for y above some limit) behaves as a necessity, while group I behaves as the remainder must behave according to the budget constraint. This is plausible in view of the fact that we introduced saturation limits for the commodities in group II, while there were no such limits for the commodities in group I. Representative curves for y_I and y_{II} as functions of y corresponding to (4.8) and (4.9) are shown in figure 1 (together with curves for examples to be discussed further on).

From the non-linearities of the allocation functions it follows by insertion into (4.5) and (4.6) that the complete demand functions will now also imply Engel curves which show similar non-linear characteristics.

The system investigated above can be seen as a generalization of a two-commodity system used by A. Brown and A. Deaton (1972) to illustrate the concept of 'absolute saturation'.

For the allocation function, it is of special interest to compare (4.8) with Engel curve forms proposed by D. G. Champernowne for luxuries. In fact, (4.8) is precisely one of the forms proposed by Champernowne if our A and B, which are functions of prices, are interpreted as constants in Champernowne's formula. This is natural, since Champernowne was only considering Engel curves in connection with household budget data. Champernowne's form is somewhat richer in that he has one additional

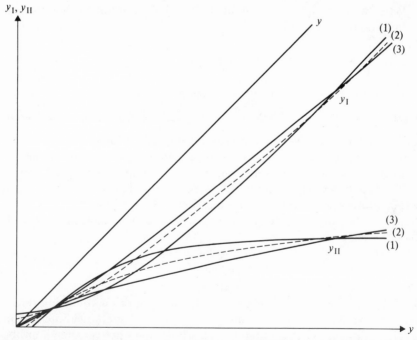

Figure 1. Allocation functions: y_I and y_{II} as functions of y. (1) Based on the logarithmic/quadratic utility function (4.4). (2) Based on the logarithmic/negative exponential utility function (4.13). (3) Based on the combined LES systems, see (5.3) and (5.6–7).

coefficient which would, in our notations, appear as a coefficient in front of y on the right hand side of (4.8). Such a free coefficient is not generated by our specification. Champernowne apparently constructed the function for a curve-fitting purpose, and applied it to several groups of commodities. Together with the Törnqvist forms, Champernowne's forms have been described as 'entirely pragmatic' and have been considered to be without theoretical basis. (See for instance L. Phlips, 1974, p. 112.) It is therefore interesting to observe that the form is generated by utility maximization according to a quite natural specification once we abandon the requirement that all demand functions should be of the same mathematical form.

Before leaving this combined system a remark on the specification and estimation of the parameters may be in order. A natural procedure would be to estimate the parameters of the partial systems by studies for each group of commodities separately, and next determine the remaining parameter(s) by studying the allocation functions. (I shall not go into the econometric aspects of this two-step procedure. Many issues of relevance to such methods are treated in Theil (1975, 1976).) In the present case the parameters α_i would be determined by the analysis for the first group of commodities. They are uniquely determined since we have introduced the normalization $\Sigma_I \alpha_i = 1$. For the second group of commodities the analysis will determine all parameters c_i uniquely. However, the parameters k_i will be determined only up to a proportionality factor. This is seen from (4.6), where a proportional change in all k_i would leave the demand functions ψ_i unaffected. We might have introduced

$$k_i = k k_i^*, \quad \sum_{II} k_i^* = 1 \tag{4.11}$$

so that the parameters k_i^* are normalized so as to sum to unity. Then these parameters would be determined by the study of the second group of commodities, and the demand functions given in (4.6) could be written with k_i^* instead of k_i. Consider next the allocation function (4.8). In the expression for this function A depends on prices through $A = \Sigma_{II} p_h c_h$, where the c_hs have already been determined. B depends on prices through $B = \Sigma_{II} k_h p_h^2$. This can be written as

$$B = k B^*, \quad B^* = \sum_{II} k_h^* p_h^2 \tag{4.12}$$

where the parameters k_h^* have already been determined. The only remaining parameter to be determined by studying the allocation functions will then be k. (If we had also normalized the parameters k_i in (4.4) directly, then we would have predetermined the allocation between the two groups of commodities on the basis of the parameters of the partial demand systems, which would be very artificial.)

From the allocation functions it is seen that, the larger the value of the parameter k, the larger will be the share of total expenditure allocated to group I of commodities, which is of course natural from the formulation (4.4) of the total utility function.

In the system expounded above we used a quadratic function for the utility of the 'necessities'. One might feel that the saturation points implied by this system are too rigidly determined. An alternative would be to try to use (negative) exponential functions, i.e. to replace the utility function (4.4) by

$$\Omega = \sum_I \alpha_i \ln x_i - \sum_{II} \gamma_i \exp(-x_i/\beta_i) \tag{4.13}$$

In this combination the utility function for the second group will be bounded above without reaching an absolute saturation point (whereas the utility function for the first group is not bounded).

Again we may normalize the parameters in the first group by $\Sigma_I \alpha_i = 1$, while for the same reason as above we do not normalize the parameters γ_i for group II in this way. (The negative exponential utility function and the corresponding demand functions have been studied by R. A. Pollak (1971b).)

The partial system of demand functions ψ_i, for group II, will now be

$$x_i = \beta_i \left[\ln \left(\frac{\gamma_i}{\beta_i p_i} \right) + \frac{1}{A} (y_{II} - B) \right] \quad (i \in II) \tag{4.14}$$

where

$$A = \sum_{II} \beta_h p_h, \quad B = \sum_{II} \beta_h p_h \ln \left(\frac{\gamma_h}{\beta_h p_h} \right) \tag{4.15}$$

Again it is seen that the Engel curves of the partial system are linear.

Proceeding in a similar way as for the logarithmic-quadratic system above, we now obtain the following equation for determining the allocation functions:

$$\frac{1}{y_I} = e^{(B-y_{II})/A} \tag{4.16}$$

Using $y_I + y_{II} = y$ we get

$$y_I + A \ln y_I = y - B \tag{4.17}$$

Although this does not permit an explicit expression for y_I, it is simple enough. The coefficient A, defined by (4.15), is positive. It follows that y_I increases with y. We have

$$\frac{\partial y_I}{\partial y} = \frac{y_I}{y_I + A} \tag{4.18}$$

It is seen that group I at the margin takes a proportion of total expenditure which is less than unity, but increases towards unity with y (since y_I increases with y). It follows that the allocation to group II takes a marginal share which approaches zero. In this sense group II behaves as a group of 'necessities'. However, in the present case, in contrast to the logarithmic-quadratic case, there is no finite upper limit to the absolute level of y_{II}.

Representative allocation functions based on (4.13–18) are also shown in figure 1.

If the partial demand systems have been estimated by studies for each group separately, then the parameters β_i will be known from group II. For the parameters γ_i there will be a level factor which is not determined from the partial system, but which remains to be determined in connection with the allocation functions similarly to the parameter k introduced in connection with (4.11–12).

In both the cases studied above it appears that, apart from total income, the allocation functions for y_I and y_{II} depend only upon prices of commodities in group II. In particular, in the set (4.8–9) the parameters A and B are defined in (4.7), and in connection with (4.16) they are defined in (4.15); in both cases they depend only upon p_{II}. This is due to the form of the marginal utility function corresponding to the logarithmic utility function which we have used for group I. This is simply y_I^{-1}. If, instead of simply writing $\ln x_i$ in the utility function, we had written $\ln(x_i - c_i)$ as we should do for the full LES system, then this would not be so. The marginal utility of expenditure in group I would then also depend upon p_I, and so also would the allocation functions for y_I and y_{II}. It is a simple matter to introduce this in the formulas above; it is only for convenience that we have omitted these parameters.

5 Partial utility transformations

An increasing transformation of the total utility function Ω will not alter the demand functions. In a utility tree formulation like (2.4) an increasing transformation of U or V will also not alter the demand functions if the function Ω is adjusted so as to offset the transformation of U or V. However, if we subject U and/or V to an increasing transformation without changing Ω in this way, then the demand functions in the complete set will change. It is clear, however, that such transformations will not alter the partial demand systems φ and ψ. They will only change the complete demand functions by changing the allocation functions.

These general considerations imply that we can construct new complete demand functions not only by combining different forms of partial demand systems, but also by combining similar types of demand functions for both groups. For instance, consider again the simplified linear expenditure system. We now assume this system to be valid for both groups. If we have a utility function

$$\Omega = \sum_I \alpha_i \ln x_i + \sum_{II} \alpha_i \ln x_i \tag{5.1}$$

then both the partial systems as well as the complete system would be LES systems. However, if we subject one or both parts of the total utility function to increasing transformations by

$$\Omega = F_I \left(\sum_I \alpha_i \ln x_i \right) + F_{II} \left(\sum_{II} \alpha_i \ln x_i \right) \tag{5.2}$$

where F_I and F_{II} (or at least one of them) are increasing, non-linear functions, then both the partial systems will still be LES systems, while the complete system will be of a different form. In particular, the Engel curves will no longer be linear. Since the LES system is so convenient to handle and in some respects also empirically successful, but at the same time not quite satisfactory especially with regard to the Engel curve aspects, a formulation like (5.2) may give rise to an extended range of applicability of demand analysis on the basis of LES functions.

As an example of (5.2) one might use the antilogarithm for the transformation F_I. This gives

$$\Omega = k \prod_{i=1}^{n} x_i^{\alpha_i} + \sum_{II} \alpha_i \ln x_i \tag{5.3}$$

The first part of this formula also corresponds to a usual way of writing the utility function underlying the LES system. In this formulation we may have the normalizations $\Sigma_I \alpha_i = 1$ and $\Sigma_{II} \alpha_i = 1$.

We now have

$$x_i = \varphi_i(p_I, y_I) = \alpha_i \frac{y_I}{p_i} \quad (i \in I) \tag{5.4}$$

$$x_i = \psi_i(p_{II}, y_{II}) = \alpha_i \frac{y_{II}}{p_i} \quad (i \in II)$$

Using these as in connection with (4.1–3), with U corresponding to the first part of (5.3) and V corresponding to the second part, we obtain an equation for the allocation functions which gives the following value for y_{II}:

$$y_{II} = k^{-1} \prod_{j=1}^{n} \left(\frac{p_j}{\alpha_j} \right)^{\alpha_j} \tag{5.5}$$

y_I is then y minus the expression (5.5) for y_{II}. This is a rather strange case, with y_{II} independent of total expenditure y, but depending upon the prices of commodities in the first group. The reason for this peculiar case is that there is, for given prices, a constant marginal utility of expenditure in group I. For changes in total expenditure y we accordingly have to keep the allocation to group II at such a level that the marginal utility there is the same as the constant marginal utility for group I, and accordingly transfer all variation in total expenditure to group I. This system seems to have no special merit; it only serves to illustrate how a combination of partial systems of the same form can have quite dramatic consequences.

A more reasonable case would emerge if, instead of normalizing the coefficients in the first group by $\Sigma_I \alpha_i = 1$, we had, say, $\Sigma_I \alpha_i = \alpha_I < 1$. Then the demand functions for the first group should be written as

$$x_i = \frac{\alpha_i}{\alpha_I} \frac{y_I}{p_i} \quad (i \in I) \tag{5.6}$$

The equation determining the allocation functions would now be

$$y_{II} = k^{-1} \left[\prod_{j=1}^{n} \left(\frac{p_j}{\alpha_j} \right)^{\alpha_j} \right] \left(\frac{y_I}{\alpha_I} \right)^{1-\alpha_I} \tag{5.7}$$

We can get the allocation functions for y_I and y_{II} explicitly only for special values of the parameter α_I, but the system could of course be used with the implicit formulation. This system is also illustrated in figure 1 (for $\alpha_I = 0.4$).

In general, the formulation (5.2) of the utility function gives rise to the following type of relationship determining the allocation between the two groups of commodities:

$$\frac{1}{y_I} F_I' \left(\sum_I \alpha_i \ln \frac{\alpha_i}{p_i} + \ln y_I \right) = \frac{1}{y_{II}} F_{II}' \left(\sum_{II} \alpha_i \ln \frac{\alpha_i}{p_i} + \ln y_{II} \right) \tag{5.8}$$

where F_I' and F_{II}' are the derivatives of the transformation functions F_I and F_{II}, each being a function of *one* argument (and where both $\Sigma_I \alpha_i = 1$ and $\Sigma_{II} \alpha_i = 1$). If F_I and F_{II} are linear so that F_I' and F_{II}' are constant, then this reduces to the ordinary LES system, implying a constant proportion between y_{II} and y_I (when we have, for simplicity, omitted the fixed minimum quantities). Otherwise it is seen that the proportion between y_{II} and y_I increases or decreases with y according to how the derivatives F_I' and F_{II}' change with their arguments.

In the case studied on the basis of the utility function (4.4) we introduced saturation quantities for each commodity in group II separately. When we use linear expenditure functions for both groups of commodities, as in the present section, this cannot be done. However, we can introduce a sort of saturation point for the commodities in a group, say group II, taken together, by letting F_{II} be a function which increases only up to a certain value of its argument, and then remains constant, for instance by letting F_{II} be quadratic up to a value of its argument where it becomes horizontal. For given prices p_{II} there will then be a limit to how much y_{II} will increase even if y increases beyond all limits. Nevertheless, within this limit there will be considerable scope for substitution between the commodities entering group II, there being no *specific* limit to the consumption of each commodity. This type of formulation may be relevant for some groups of food. The fact just mentioned is related to the fact that formulation (5.2) may introduce alternativity or complementarity between the commodities in a group.

6 Some further observations on the general case. Admissible combinations of LES systems

In sections 4 and 5 we assumed some special forms of combinations represented by the utility functions (4.1) and (5.2). The approaches illustrated in these sections are probably most convenient when the partial utility functions underlying the partial demand systems are known explicitly, either in direct form or in indirect form. However, some systems of demand functions have been proposed that are such that the utility function is not known, or is known but cannot be written in explicit form. Then the approaches illustrated in sections 4 and 5 are not so immediately applicable. For the more general case we may pose the following problem.

Suppose that the two partial demand systems $x_i = \varphi_i(p_I, y_I)$ for $i \in I$ and $x_i = \psi_i(p_{II}, y_{II})$ for $i \in II$ are known and we know that each of them satisfies the usual requirements implied by utility maximization (but we do not necessarily know the utility functions explicitly). Suppose that we form a complete system of demand functions by introducing the allocation functions $y_I = y_I(p_I, p_{II}, y)$ and $y_{II} = y_{II}(p_I, p_{II}, y)$, satisfying $y_I(.) + y_{II}(.) \equiv y$, and combining them with φ_i and ψ_i so as to form a complete set of demand functions as represented by (2.14–15). The question now is whether we can say anything about the class of allocation functions $y_I(.)$ and $y_{II}(.)$ which are admissible if the total demand system is to satisfy the requirements implied by utility maximization.

It is obvious that the functions $y_I(.)$ and $y_{II}(.)$ must be homogeneous of degree 1 in all prices and total expenditure.

The more interesting requirement is the symmetry requirement. We can study this on the basis of the formulas given in section 3, given that the functions φ_i and ψ_i satisfy internal symmetry requirements for each partial system.

First consider the symmetry requirements for $i, j \in I$. The requirement then is

$$\frac{\partial f_i}{\partial p_j} + x_j \frac{\partial f_i}{\partial y} = \frac{\partial f_j}{\partial p_i} + x_i \frac{\partial f_j}{\partial y} \quad (i, j \in I) \tag{6.1}$$

Using equations (3.1) and (3.3) this can be written as

$$\frac{\partial \varphi_i}{\partial p_j} + \frac{\partial \varphi_i}{\partial y_I} \frac{\partial y_I}{\partial p_j} + x_j \frac{\partial \varphi_i}{\partial y_I} \frac{\partial y_I}{\partial y} = \frac{\partial \varphi_j}{\partial p_i} + \frac{\partial \varphi_j}{\partial y_I} \frac{\partial y_I}{\partial p_i} + x_i \frac{\partial \varphi_j}{\partial y_I} \frac{\partial y_I}{\partial y} \quad (i, j \in \mathrm{I}) \quad (6.2)$$

We know that the partial system satisfies the symmetry condition so that we have

$$\frac{\partial \varphi_i}{\partial p_j} + x_j \frac{\partial \varphi_i}{\partial y_I} = \frac{\partial \varphi_j}{\partial p_i} + x_i \frac{\partial \varphi_j}{\partial y_I} \quad (i, j \in \mathrm{I}) \tag{6.3}$$

Combining this with (6.2) we obtain a condition which can be written as

$$\left[\left(1 - \frac{\partial y_I}{\partial y} \right) x_j - \frac{\partial y_I}{\partial p_j} \right] \frac{\partial \varphi_i}{\partial y_I} = \left[\left(1 - \frac{\partial y_I}{\partial y} \right) x_i - \frac{\partial y_I}{\partial p_i} \right] \frac{\partial \varphi_j}{\partial y_I} \quad (i, j \in \mathrm{I}) \tag{6.4}$$

A similar condition will hold for $i, j \in \mathrm{II}$. In view of the fact that $y_I(.) + y_{II}(.) \equiv y$ this can be written as

$$\left[\frac{\partial y_I}{\partial y} x_j + \frac{\partial y_I}{\partial p_j} \right] \frac{\partial \psi_i}{\partial y_{II}} = \left[\frac{\partial y_I}{\partial y} x_i + \frac{\partial y_I}{\partial p_i} \right] \frac{\partial \psi_j}{\partial y_{II}} \quad (i, j \in \mathrm{II}) \tag{6.5}$$

For $i \in \mathrm{I}$ and $j \in \mathrm{II}$ we have instead of (6.1)

$$\frac{\partial f_i}{\partial p_j} + x_j \frac{\partial f_i}{\partial y} = \frac{\partial g_j}{\partial p_i} + x_i \frac{\partial g_j}{\partial y} \quad (i \in \mathrm{I}, j \in \mathrm{II}) \tag{6.6}$$

Using again the equations from section 3 this can be written as

$$\left[\frac{\partial y_I}{\partial p_j} + \frac{\partial y_I}{\partial y} x_j \right] \frac{\partial \varphi_i}{\partial y_I} = \left[\frac{\partial y_{II}}{\partial p_i} + \frac{\partial y_{II}}{\partial y} x_i \right] \frac{\partial \psi_j}{\partial y_{II}} \quad (i \in \mathrm{I}, j \in \mathrm{II}) \tag{6.7}$$

where again $y_I(.) + y_{II}(.) \equiv y$ could be used to express the condition in terms only of $y_I(.)$.

Admissible allocation functions $y_I(.)$ and $y_{II}(.)$ are now functions homogeneous of degree 1 which satisfy the requirements (6.4), (6.5) and (6.7). In these conditions $x_i = \varphi_i(p_I, y_I(p_I, p_{II}, y))$ for $i \in \mathrm{I}$ and $x_i = \psi_i(p_{II}, y_{II}(p_I, p_{II}, y))$ for $i \in \mathrm{II}$. The functions φ_i and ψ_i are known functions. The conditions above then constitute a system of (quasi-linear) differential equations. It can, of course, be shown, by somewhat laborious calculations, that all the allocation functions used as illustrations in sections 4 and 5 satisfy these requirements. However, I have not managed to give a useful general characterization of the class of admissible functions on this basis, and the conditions given above are offered only tentatively as a possible starting point for further explorations.

A sufficient condition for (6.4) to be satisfied is, of course, that the terms in brackets in (6.4) are zero, and correspondingly for (6.5). Then the terms in brackets in (6.7) will also vanish so that all the symmetry conditions hold. However, these conditions seem to be too stringent. For instance, they fail to be satisfied by the systems studied in sections 4 and 5 where y_I depends only on total expenditure y and prices in group II.

Although a simple general characterization of admissible allocation functions cannot be given, the equations may be manageable in specific cases with regard to the forms φ_i and ψ_i. For instance, we may consider the case where both φ_i and ψ_i, as partial systems, are linear expenditure systems, i.e.

$$\varphi_i = \frac{\alpha_i y_I}{p_i} \text{ for } i \in I, \quad \psi_i = \frac{\alpha_i y_{II}}{p_i} \text{ for } i \in II$$

Then conditions (6.4) reduce to

$$\frac{\partial y_I}{\partial p_j} \frac{\alpha_i}{p_i} = \frac{\partial y_I}{\partial p_i} \frac{\alpha_j}{p_j} \quad (i, j \in I)$$

which can be written as

$$\frac{\partial y_I}{\partial p_i} \frac{p_i}{\alpha_i} = R_I(p_I, p_{II}, y) \quad (i \in I) \tag{6.8}$$

where R_I is some function independent of i for $i \in I$. In the same way the conditions in (6.5) reduce to

$$\frac{\partial y_I}{\partial p_i} \frac{p_i}{\alpha_i} = R_{II}(p_I, p_{II}, y) \quad (i \in II) \tag{6.9}$$

where R_{II} is some function independent of i for $i \in II$. Conditions (6.7) reduce to a form, which we, when we use (6.8–9), can write as

$$y_I = R_I(p_I, p_{II}, y) + R_{II}(p_I, p_{II}, y) + \frac{\partial y_I}{\partial y} y \tag{6.10}$$

One could now proceed by solving the system of partial differential equations by some standard method. However, we have a clue in the form in which the prices enter the indirect utility function. Considering the general formulation (2.11–12) defining the allocation functions we know that, in the case of two LES systems for the partial systems, the indirect utility functions U^* and V^* are such that the prices enter only through such combinations as

$$\sum_I \alpha_i \ln \frac{\alpha_i}{p_i}, \quad \sum_{II} \alpha_i \ln \frac{\alpha_i}{p_i}$$

or transformations of these expressions. By analogy with the forms (5.5) and (5.7) we may use the forms

$$P_I(p_I) = \prod_{i=1}^{n} \left(\frac{p_i}{\alpha_i}\right)^{\alpha_i}, \quad P_{II}(p_{II}) = \prod_{i=n+1}^{n+m} \left(\frac{p_i}{\alpha_i}\right)^{\alpha_i} \tag{6.11}$$

We then know that the allocation function $y_I = y_I(p_I, p_{II}, y)$ must be of the form

$$y_I = T(P_I(p_I), P_{II}(p_{II}), y) \tag{6.12}$$

The question is then reduced to the following: What is the class of functions $T(.)$ of three arguments which are such that the allocation function defined by (6.12) will satisfy the conditions (6.8), (6.9) and (6.10)? The answer is: all functions T which are homogeneous of degree one (limiting, of course, considerations to continuous and differentiable functions).

Consider first condition (6.8). From (6.11) and (6.12) we get

$$\frac{\partial y_I}{\partial p_i} \frac{p_i}{\alpha_i} = P_I(p_I) \frac{\partial T}{\partial P_I} = R_I(p_I, p_{II}, y) \quad (i \in I) \tag{6.13}$$

The expression obtained is independent of the particular i for $i \in I$, as required. In the same way we get

$$\frac{\partial y_I}{\partial p_i} \frac{p_i}{\alpha_i} = P_{II}(p_{II}) \frac{\partial T}{\partial P_{II}} = R_{II}(p_I, p_{II}, y) \quad (i \in II) \tag{6.14}$$

confirming (6.9).

There remains condition (6.10). Using R_I and R_{II} from (6.13) and (6.14) this condition takes the following form:

$$y_I = P_I(p_I) \frac{\partial T}{\partial P_I} + P_{II}(p_{II}) \frac{\partial T}{\partial P_{II}} + y \frac{\partial T}{\partial y} \tag{6.15}$$

By Euler's theorem this is fulfilled if $T(.)$ is homogeneous of degree one. This must clearly be the case. In (6.12) P_I and P_{II} are homogeneous of degree one, and then $T(.)$ must also be homogeneous of degree one if y_I, as a function of p_I, p_{II} and y, is to be homogeneous of degree one as required.

The examples (5.5) and (5.7) are special cases of the general form now obtained. In (5.7) we could not always write y_I and y_{II} as explicit functions. This does not contradict the present general result, since there is no requirement involved which implies that the function $T(.)$ in (6.12) can be written in explicit form.

The present result has quite specific implications for the way in which prices, in combination for each of the two groups, enter the allocation functions, and thereby also the complete demand functions for the individual commodities. But otherwise it shows that partial LES systems can be combined in very flexible ways without contradicting the symmetry (or integrability) condition of general demand theory.

Taking also into account the sign condition for the direct substitution effects we may have some further restrictions on the class of admissible T-functions. This point will not be pursued here.

7 Summary and conclusion

The purpose of this paper has been to explore the possibilities which are opened up for constructing useful systems of demand functions by abandoning the requirement that the functions for all commodities should be of the same mathematical form. We can then use relatively simple well-known systems for groups of commodities, and use 'allocation functions' for allocating expenditure between the groups of commodities so that overall utility maximization is achieved. The examples developed in sections 4 and 5 show that the approach is feasible and able to yield Engel curves which are more flexible and satisfactory than the Engel curve properties of the partial systems taken each by itself. (Other examples can easily be constructed by combining the various partial systems in different ways from those used in sections 4 and 5.) I have concentrated on the Engel curve aspects because the Engel curve properties of many of the relatively simple usual systems are known, from empirical studies, to be unsatisfactory. I have used the LES system as a standard example because this system is so convenient and successful in some respects. It is therefore a very attractive candidate for partial systems to be used in the combined total systems, and I think the examples illustrate that this can be a fruitful direction of development and lead to a valuable extension of the scope of application for this system. The results in the last part of section 6 are especially important in this respect.

Although I have concentrated on the Engel curve properties of the systems, the combinations do, of course, also have implications for the price elasticities. The examples in section 5 show how simple combinations can introduce non-additivity in the overall system although each partial system is based on an additive utility function. It would be interesting to explore to what extent such simple extensions help to overcome the rather rigid connections between price and income elasticities which have been studied (and criticized) by A. Deaton (1974).

There are now available several empirical studies which compare the performance of various systems of demand functions. Some of them are rather inconclusive, while others are more or less contradictory. One reason for this may be that none of the systems is good for all commodities. Summarizing one such study A. P. Barten (1977) comments as follows: 'For all groups together, the Rotterdam system is superior to the indirect addilog model, which does better than the LES. The picture is mixed for individual groups, however. For food and beverages and tobacco, the Rotterdam model is better; for durables, the indirect addilog system dominates the Rotterdam system slightly; while the LES is clearly outstanding for the remainder.' Such results seem to call for combined systems and lend empirical support to the approach taken in the present paper.

Note

1 I am grateful to Karl Moene for his very valuable assistance in the preparation of this paper, and to Knut Sydsæter for useful discussions on special points.

References

Aitchison, J. and Brown, J. A. C. (1954), 'A Synthesis of Engel Curve Theory', *Review of Economic Studies*, **22**, pp. 35–46.
    (1963), *The Lognormal Distribution*, Cambridge University Press, Cambridge.
Andersson, Å. E. (1977), 'Merit Goods and Micro-Economic Dependence', in A. J. Culyer and V. Halberstadt (eds.), *Public Economics and Human Resources*, Editions Cujas, Paris, pp. 215–36.
Barten, A. P. (1977), 'The Systems of Consumer Demand Functions Approach: A Review', *Econometrica*, **45**, pp. 23–51.
van Beeck, J. G. and den Hartog, H. (1964), 'Consumption Forecasts for the Netherlands', in J. Sandee (ed.), *Europe's Future Consumption*, North-Holland, Amsterdam.
Brown, A. and Deaton, A. (1972), 'Surveys in Applied Economics: Models of Consumer Behaviour', *The Economic Journal*, **82**, pp. 1145–1236.
Carlevaro, F. (1974), *Sur la comparaison et la généralisation de certains systèmes des fonctions de consommation semi-agrégées*, Herbert Lang, Berne.
    (1976), 'A Generalization of the Linear Expenditure System', in *Private and Enlarged Consumption* (edited by L. Solari and J.-N. Pasquier), North-Holland, Amsterdam.
Champernowne, D. G. (1969), *Uncertainty and Estimation in Economics*. Volume 2, Oliver and Boyd, Edinburgh.
Deaton, A. (1974), 'A Reconsideration of the Empirical Implications of Additive Preferences', *The Economic Journal*, **84**, pp. 338–48.
Fisk, P. R. (1958–59), 'Maximum Likelihood Estimation of Törnqvist Demand Equations', *Review of Economic Studies*, **26**, pp. 33–50.
Goldberger, A. S. (1967), *Functional Form and Utility: A Review of Consumer Demand Theory*, Social Systems Research Institute, University of Wisconsin.
Hoflund, O. (1954), 'On the Geometric Structure of Indifference Maps', Paper presented at the European Meeting of the Econometric Society, Uppsala.
Houthakker, H. S. and Taylor, L. D. (1970), *Consumer Demand in the United States: Analysis and Projections*, Harvard University Press, Cambridge (Mass.). Second edition.
Keck, A. (1968), *Nationaleinkommen-Konsumption*, Verlag die Wirtschaft, Berlin (GDR).
Lau, L. J. (1977), 'Complete Systems of Consumer Demand Functions through Duality', in M. C. Intriligator (ed.), *Frontiers of Quantitative Economics*, Vol. III A, North-Holland, Amsterdam.
McElroy, M. B. (1975), 'A Spliced CES Expenditure System', *International Economic Review*, pp. 765–78.
Phlips, L. (1974), *Applied Consumption Analysis*, North-Holland, Amsterdam.
Pollak, R. A. (1969), 'Conditional Demand Functions and Consumption Theory', *Quarterly Journal of Economics*, **83**, pp. 70–8.
    (1971a), 'Conditional Demand Functions and the Implications of Separable Utility', *Southern Economic Journal*, **37**, pp. 423–33.
    (1971b), 'Additive Utility Functions and Linear Engel Curves', *Review of Economic Studies*, **38**, pp. 401–13.

Solari, L. (1971), *Théorie des choix et fonctions de consommation semi-agrégées – Modèles Statiques*, Librarie Droz, Geneva and Paris.

Somermeyer, W. H. and Langhout, A. (1972), 'Shapes of Engel Curves and Demand Curves: Implications of the Expenditure Allocation Model, Applied to Dutch Data', *European Economic Review*, pp. 351–86.

Stone, J. R. N. (1954), 'Linear Expenditure Systems and Demand Analysis: An Application to the Pattern of British Demand', *The Economic Journal*, **64**, pp. 511–27.

Theil, H. (1975, 1976) *Theory and Measurement of Consumer Demand*, two volumes, North-Holland.

Valtukh, K. K. (1975), 'A Theoretical Model of Mass Consumer Behavior and some Methodological Problems of Social Studies', *Quantity and Quality*.

Varian, H. R. (1978), 'A Note on Locally Constant Income Elasticities', *Economics Letters*, pp. 9–13.

Wegge, L. L. (1968), 'The Demand Curves from a Quadratic Utility Indicator', *Review of Economic Studies*, **35**, pp. 209–24.

Wold, H. (1952), in association with L. Juréen, *Demand Analysis*, Almquist and Wiksell, Stockholm, and Wiley, New York.

3 Theoretical and empirical approaches to consumer demand under rationing[1]

ANGUS DEATON

It is a matter of common observation that the quantities consumed of many goods and services are not directly under the control of those who consume them. The level of provision of public goods cannot be varied to taste by any single consumer: shortages or formal rationing of market goods may place an upper limit on consumption: transactions costs or market imperfections, particularly in asset markets, may prevent the short-run adjustment of stocks to their optimum levels so that consumers may have to consume too much as well as too little. Perhaps most importantly, involuntary unemployment in the labour market can be thought of as an enforced consumption of an undesirably large amount of leisure. All these situations involve *quantity constraints* on consumer behaviour, and although rationing is only one possibility, we shall use the term to deal with all, including those situations where more is consumed than would be freely bought.

As one might expect, much of the early work on rationing was done during and immediately after the second world war. This work is surveyed in the classic paper by Tobin (1952). For a considerable period subsequently, there appeared to be little interest in the subject and little was published, although see the two papers by Pollak (1969; 1971). In the last few years, however, rationing has once again become a major focus of attention. On this occasion the impetus has come, not from the policy issues raised by actual rationing, but from theorists constructing general equilibrium models in which markets are not assumed to clear. In such a world, some buyers and sellers will go short or long and these quantity constraints will have repercussions in other markets. The analysis of these interactions is an exercise in rationing theory and the properties of such equilibria depend upon the properties of demand and supply functions under rationing. For further discussions of this literature, see Barro and Grossman (1976), Malinvaud (1977) or Muellbauer and Portes (1978).

In this paper, I shall be concerned with alternative approaches to deriving rationed demand functions which are suitable for empirical im-

55

56   A. S. DEATON

plementation. In particular, I wish to illustrate how duality theory can be used to generate empirically estimable demand functions under rationing in the same way that it can do so in the unrationed case and with the same benefits (see Deaton, 1978). I also deal with the practically important case where one needs a 'matched' pair of demand functions, one rationed and one unrationed, each deriving from the same preferences. Such functions are necessary if we wish to predict behaviour under rationing when we have only observations on free demand (e.g. if an unprecedented shortage occurs) and can sometimes even be used in the converse situation, of predicting unrationed from rationed demands. Similarly, we may wish to estimate a system of consumer demand and labour supply functions on a cross-section of households, some of which are rationed (e.g. in the labour market) and some of which are not. Such functions can only be estimated efficiently if common preferences with common parameters are assumed for all households so that the same parameters appear in both sets of demand functions corresponding to the two 'regimes'. The theory of this construction is discussed in section 1; it is a fuller version of the results sketched in chapter 4, section 3 of Deaton and Muellbauer (1980a), results independently derived by Neary and Roberts (1980). Section 2 presents a simple empirical example in which it is assumed that consumers' expenditure on housing in Britain is predetermined in the short run and a model embodying this assumption is contrasted with a more conventional specification in which housing and other expenditures are simultaneously determined. Section 3 discusses the specification of 'flexible functional form' models under rationing. For many purposes, empirical models with matched rationed and unrationed demands will yield functional forms which are too restrictive. It is thus important to have general models to incorporate rationing and I discuss a modification to the AIDS (Almost Ideal Demand System) of Deaton and Muellbauer (1980b) which permits ration levels to appear in a simple, theoretically satisfactory, and empirically tractable manner. Such a formulation also offers an elegant choice-theoretic foundation for the introduction of stocks into demand functions. Finally, the extended AIDS is applied to the housing example considered in section 2. Section 4 is a summary with conclusions.

1 The specification of rationed and unrationed demands

In order to keep the exposition as simple as possible, I shall consider only the case of a single rationed good (at least until section 3 below). The results can straightforwardly be extended to the case of multiple constraints while the analysis for a single good does not require the use of matrix algebra. Let q_0, good zero, be the good to be constrained, while q_1, q_2,

$\ldots$, q_n, or q, is the vector of unconstrained goods. Hence, if z is the level to which q_0 is constrained, the two problems, rationed and unrationed, are given by

$$\max u = v(q_0, q) \quad \text{s.t.} \quad p_0 q_0 + p.q = x \tag{1}$$

$$\left.\begin{array}{l}\max u = v(q_0, q) \quad \text{s.t.} \quad p_0 q_0 + p.q = x \\ \qquad\qquad\qquad \text{and} \quad q_0 = z\end{array}\right\} \tag{2}$$

where p_0 and p are the prices of q_0 and q, x is total outlay, u is the utility level, and $v(q_0, q)$ is the utility function. To save complications, I assume that this latter has all the standard properties, i.e. it is a strictly quasi-concave, differentiable and increasing function of its arguments. Problem (1) has solutions in the normal way, for $i = 0, \ldots, n$,

$$q_i = g_i(x, p_0, p) \tag{3}$$

while for (2), we write, for $i = 1, \ldots, n$

$$q_i = g_i^*(x, z, p_0, p) \tag{4}$$

The questions to be discussed are (a) the relationship between (3) and (4), (b) the properties of (4), (c) suitable functional forms for (4).

Consider first the important special case where preferences are weakly separable between q_0 and q – see Pollak (1971). Under separability, $v(q_0, q)$ can be written in the form $v^*(q_0, \phi(q))$ say, so that (2) can be written, after substitution of z for q_0 as

$$\max u = v^*\{z, \phi(q)\} \quad \text{s.t.} \quad p.q = x - p_0 z \tag{5}$$

The z in $v^*(\ )$ is essentially irrelevant; problem (5) is clearly identical to the maximization of $\phi(q)$ subject to total outlay corrected for the cost of the ration. The rationed demand functions (4) are thus, $i = 1, \ldots, n$

$$q_i = g_i^*(x, z, p_0, p) = f_i(x - p_0 z, p) \tag{6}$$

for suitable functions $f_i(\ )$ satisfying all the usual properties of demand functions. Hence, under weak separability, the ration level has income effects only and, provided income is corrected for the cost of the ration, the demands for unrationed goods can be dealt with in the usual way. For many goods, particularly public goods, this will provide a satisfactory solution. Once I have paid my taxes for my share of the defence budget, that is the end of the matter and I am unlikely to attempt to make up for a cut in the national defence budget by substituting guns for butter in my private consumption pattern.

In general, however, we cannot suppose that preferences are weakly separable between rationed and unrationed goods. In particular, if leisure is being rationed, there are clearly a number of goods and services the demand for which cannot be explained in terms of income alone without reference to the number of hours worked. In principle, problem (2) can be solved for any specification of $v(q_0, q)$ and the demand functions (4) estimated. However, just as in the unrationed case (see Deaton (1978) for a full discussion), such problems rarely have explicit solutions in interesting cases and, even when they do, empirical analysis is hampered by the lack of a clear relationship between the demands and the direct representation of preferences. It is also difficult to characterize the rationed demands in relation to the unrationed demands from consideration of the direct utility function. The classic treatment is that of Tobin and Houthakker (1951) who manipulate the first-order conditions for (2) to obtain properties of the *derivatives* of the rationed demands (4). Similarly, they obtain *locally* valid relationships between the derivatives of the rationed and unrationed functions, for example, the Le Chatelier result – see Samuelson (1947) – that, *at the point where the ration would have been bought anyway,* compensated price rises cause no greater falls in demand under rationing than without it. Such results are of great importance but are insufficient if we require characterizations of the demands themselves rather than only their derivatives. These problems can be solved by following a dual approach.

Begin by defining, for unrationed demands, the consumer's cost function

$$c(u, p_0, p) = \min_{q_0, q} \{p_0 q_0 + p.q; \quad v(q_0, q) \geq u\} \tag{7}$$

The cost-minimizing q_0 and q in (7) give the Hicksian demand functions corresponding to the Marshallian demands (4). For the rationed situation, exactly analogously, define the rationed cost function

$$c^*(u, p_0, p, z) = \min_q \{p_0 z + p.q; \quad v(z, q) \geq u\} \tag{8}$$

so that $c^*(u, p_0, p, z)$ is the minimum cost of reaching u at p_0 and p, given that z of good 0 must be bought. Since the only function of z in (8) is to restrict choice compared with (7), we have at once

$$c(u, p_0, p) = \min_z c^*(u, p_0, p, z) \tag{9}$$

This equation is the envelope property illustrated in figure 1; the unrestricted cost function is the inner envelope of the four restricted cost functions, each indexed on a particular value of z. Note that since the degree of concavity of the cost function gives the size of the own-price substitution effect, figure 1 is the basis for the Le Chatelier principle.

It is clear that (8) may be rewritten

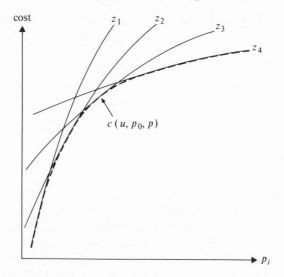

Figure 1. Rationed and unrationed cost functions

$$c^*(u, p_0, p, z) = p_0 z + \min_q \{p.q; \quad v(z, q) \geq u\}$$
$$= p_0 z + \gamma(u, z, p), \text{ say} \tag{10}$$

where the function $\gamma(u, z, p)$ is independent of p_0, the price of the rationed good. To link the rationed and unrationed costs, we define p_0^* as that price for good 0 which, at utility u and prices p, would induce the consumer to buy the ration z. Hence, p_0^* is a function of u, p and z and we write it

$$p_0^* = \xi_0(u, z, p) \tag{11}$$

This price can be thought of as the shadow or 'virtual' – Rothbarth (1941) – price of z; such a price will always exist if preferences are convex and our supplementary assumptions guarantee its uniqueness. The function $\xi_0(u, z, p)$ can be derived from the unrationed cost function by setting p_0 such that the derivative with respect to p_0, i.e. the unrationed demand for good 0, is equal to z. Formally, p_0^* is the solution to

$$\frac{\partial c(u, p_0^*, p)}{\partial p_0} = z \tag{12}$$

so that (11) and (12) are equivalent and the properties of $\xi_0(u, z, p)$ can be deduced from the latter.

Now if $p_0 = p_0^*$, the ration z will be freely chosen by an unrationed consumer so that, at this price, the minimum cost of reaching u at p must be the same whether or not the ration is imposed, i.e. $c^*(u, p_0^*, p, z) = c(u,$

p_0^*, p). Hence, from (10) and (11), as an identity in u, p and z,

$$c\{u, \xi_0(u, z, p), p\} = z.\xi_0(u, z, p) + \gamma(u, z, p) \tag{13}$$

Finally, $\gamma(u, z, p)$ can be eliminated between (10) and (13) to give the desired relationship between rationed and unrationed cost functions,

$$c^*(u, p_0, p, z) = \{p_0 - \xi_0(u, z, p)\}z + c\{u, \xi_0(u, z, p), p\} \tag{14}$$

where, rewriting (11) and (12), ξ_0 is implicitly defined by

$$\frac{\partial c\{u, \xi_0(u, z, p), p\}}{\partial p_0} = z \tag{15}$$

Equations (14) and (15) are the central results of the theory of demand under quantity restrictions and the other results I shall need follow directly from them. By differentiating (14) singly and doubly with respect to p and z, rationed and unrationed demands can be compared globally and the effects of ration levels on unrationed demands traced. I shall not discuss these results here, partly because an excellent presentation is already available in Neary and Roberts (1980), but principally because my main purpose here is to show by illustration how (14) and (15) may be used in practice to provide empirically estimable rationed and unrationed demand functions. Two different approaches are followed in the next two sections.

2 A matched pair of rationed and unrationed demands

The implementation of the foregoing theory requires selection of a specific cost function. The main consideration in making a choice in the present context is to ensure that equation (15), defining the virtual price of the ration, should have a specific solution. Consider the class of cost functions defined by Muellbauer (1981) in the context of labour supply. This may be written

$$c(u, p_0, p) = u\, p_0^\delta \{a(p)\}^{1-\delta} + b(p)\, p_0 + d(p) \tag{16}$$

where $a(p)$ and $d(p)$ are linearly homogeneous functions of p, $b(p)$ is a zero-degree homogeneous function of p and $\delta \in (0, 1)$ is a parameter. The cost minimizing consumer will equate total expenditure x to $c(u, p_0, p)$ so that

$$x = u\, p_0^\delta \{a(p)\}^{1-\delta} + b(p)\, p_0 + d(p) \tag{17}$$

can be used to give the indirect utility function, i.e. u as a function of x, p_0 and p. In the labour supply context as discussed by Muellbauer, p_0 is the wage rate and x must be interpreted as 'full' income, i.e. unearned income plus the value of the time endowment. For a fuller analysis of this and similar models in the rationing context see Deaton and Muellbauer (1981). For the present there is no need to tie the interpretation of (16) and (17) to this particular case although note that, if good 0 is on a par with the other goods in the unrationed case, the cost function treats it asymmetrically (although this depends on the choice of the functions $a(p)$, $b(p)$ and $d(p)$).

The unrationed demand functions can be derived by differentiating (16) with respect to p_0 and p_i in turn, using (17) to substitute for u. The results are

$$p_0 q_0 = \delta\{x - d(p)\} + (1 - \delta)p_0 b(p) \tag{18}$$

$$q_i = \{a(p)\}^{-1} a_i(p)(1 - \delta)\{x - p_0 b(p) - d(p)\} + p_0 b_i(p) + d_i(p) \tag{19}$$

where $a_i(p)$, $b_i(p)$ and $d_i(p)$ are the ith partial derivatives of $a(p)$, $b(p)$ and $d(p)$. In the labour supply context, these functions are particularly attractive because, in a cross-section of households, $a_i(p)$, $b_i(p)$, $d_i(p)$, $a(p)$, $b(p)$ and $d(p)$ are constant, so that both $p_0 q_0$ and q_i are modelled as linear functions of x and p_0. To derive the rationed demands, we first equate $\partial c / \partial p_0$ to z to derive the virtual price function $\xi_0(u, p_0, p)$. Hence,

$$z = \delta u p_0^{\delta - 1} \{a(p)\}^{1 - \delta} + b(p) \tag{20}$$

so that (11) becomes

$$p_0^* = a(p)\{\delta u / (z - b(p))\}^{1/(1 - \delta)} \tag{21}$$

Note that p_0^* is linear homogeneous in p and non-increasing in z; a check with (15) shows these to be quite general properties of $\xi_0(u, p_0, p)$. Substitution of (21) and (16) for the general expressions in (14) yields the rationed cost function $c^*(u, p_0, p, z)$, i.e.

$$c^*(u, p_0, p, z) = p_0 z + d(p) \\ + (\delta^{-1} - 1)(\delta u)^{1/(1 - \delta)}(z - b(p))^{-\delta/(1 - \delta)} a(p) \tag{22}$$

or, more compactly, writing $u^* = (\delta^{-1} - 1)(\delta u)^{1/(1 - \delta)}$, and $\rho = \delta/(1 - \delta)$

$$c^*(u, p_0, p, z) = p_0 z + d(p) + a(p)u^*(z - b)^{-\rho} \tag{23}$$

These two equations, (22) and (23), are thus the exact representations of preferences under rationing when (16) is the representation without it. Note that, since $\rho > 0$, $c^*(u, p_0, p, z)$ is *convex* in z, a result which follows quite generally from the quasi-concavity of the direct utility function $v(q_0, q)$, see section 3 below.

The rationed demand functions for q can be derived from (22) or (23) in the usual way. Hence, with q_0 set to z, we have, for $i = 1, ..., n$,

$$q_i^* = d_i(p) + \left\{\frac{a_i(p)}{a(p)} + \frac{\rho b_i(p)}{z - b(p)}\right\}\{x - p_0 z - d(p)\} \tag{24}$$

The comparison between (19) and (24) is instructive. The ration quantity z modifies the original demands in two ways. In the first, x is reduced by $p_0 z$ to take account of the cost of the ration; this adjustment would take place even if preferences were separable between rationed and unrationed goods. The second modification is to the marginal propensity to consume of each good. In (19), $\partial(p_i q_i)/\partial x$ is $(1 - \delta) . \partial \log a/\partial \log p_i$. However, in (24), the $(1 - \delta)$ becomes unity (since good 0 is now replaced by z) and there is the additional term $\rho p_i b_i(p)/\{z - b(p)\}$. This latter shows how changes in z affect the marginal propensity to spend on the other goods. In this particular case $b_i(p) > 0$ implies that increases in z *decrease* the marginal propensity to spend on good i, with the reverse if $b_i(p) < 0$ (recall that $\Sigma p_k b_k(p) = 0$ by homogeneity). These effects are the additional effects of the ration on the pattern of commodity demands given that preferences are *not* separable. It is easily shown that a necessary and sufficient condition for (16) to represent separable preferences is that $b_i(p) = 0$ for all i, so that the additional effects of the ration on the marginal propensities to spend vanish if and only if preferences are weakly separable between q_0 and q.

The most obvious application of the matched rationed and unrationed demands (18), (19) and (24) is to cross-section data where, for example, some households are free to vary their hours of work while others are either involuntarily unemployed or must work fixed hours. Since the same parameters appear in both rationed and unrationed regimes, fully efficient estimation is possible while, on the other hand, suitable data would allow a test of the theory of rationing as incorporated in the three equations. For the present, I take a more straightforward example based on time-series data. In a world in which there are imperfect secondhand markets for durable goods, so that there are differences between buying and selling prices or there are major transactions costs, the stocks of durable goods inherited from the past are effectively fixed in the short run, at least for many households. This is particularly true for the stock of housing and, although a minority of consumers can and do adjust their housing in any one year, the majority remain in houses which are too small or too large relative to their current needs and circumstances rather than face the heavy transactions costs and disturbance of moving. If housing expenditure were fixed for all households, the rationed model would be the appropriate one and in the experiments which follow I compare this extreme position with that usually adopted, which treats housing expenditure as a category of consumers' expenditure subject to the same laws as, say, food or services.

As a measure of the ration level for housing, I adopt the definition of current expenditure on housing given in the National Income and Expenditure Blue Books. This includes three principal elements: rents, both actual and imputed, which are ideally the flows corresponding to the actual stocks; rates and water charges, which are essentially taxes over which the consumer has no control but which yield local services; and household maintenance and repairs, again a largely necessary payment, given the stock in existence. Over none of these elements do consumers have direct short-run control, while together they yield a flow of services which will be substitutable or complementary to other consumption flows. In principle, the stock of any durable could be treated as the ration level itself, and this offers a theoretically satisfactory way of introducing the influence of such stocks into demand functions. However, given the availability of flow data in the current instance, it seems appropriate to use it.

To apply the models based on (16) to time-series data where the prices of the non-rationed goods vary, it is necessary to give specific functional forms to the three functions $a(p)$, $b(p)$ and $d(p)$. Consider the following:

$$a(p) = \alpha_0 \Pi p_k^{\alpha_k}; \quad \sum_1^n \alpha_k = 1$$

$$b(p) = \gamma_0 + \beta_0 \Pi p_k^{\beta_k}; \quad \sum_1^n \beta_k = 0 \tag{25}$$

$$d(p) = \sum_1^n \gamma_k p_k$$

where $\alpha_0, ..., \alpha_n, \beta_0, ..., \beta_n$ and $\gamma_0, ..., \gamma_n$ are parameters to be estimated. It may easily be checked that, as required, $a(p)$ and $d(p)$ are homogeneous of degree one and $b(p)$ of degree zero. The unrationed and rationed demands (18), (19) and (24) can now be derived; these give

$$p_0 q_0 = p_0 \gamma_0 + p_0 \beta_0 \Pi p_k^{\beta_k} + \delta(x - \gamma_0 p_0 - \gamma.p - p_0 \beta_0 \Pi p_k^{\beta_k}) \tag{26}$$

$$p_i q_i = p_i \gamma_i + \beta_i p_0 \beta_0 \Pi p_k^{\beta_k} + (1 - \delta)\alpha_i(x - \gamma_0 p_0 - \gamma.p - p_0 \beta_0 \Pi p_k^{\beta_k}) \tag{27}$$

for the unrationed demands for housing and for other goods, while, in the rationed case, the functions for the unrationed goods are

$$p_i q_i^* = p_i \gamma_i + \left(\alpha_i + \frac{\beta_i \rho \beta_0 \Pi_k^{\beta_k}}{z - \gamma_0 - \beta_0 \Pi p_k^{\beta_k}}\right)(x - \gamma.p - z p_0) \tag{28}$$

where $\rho = \delta/(1 - \delta)$. Note that when β_0 or all of the β_is are zero, (26) and (27) reduce to Stone's (1954) linear expenditure system. To the extent that the βs are important, housing occupies a special place in the free demands while under rationing, the value of z influences the marginal propensities to consume in (28). Once again, when $\beta = 0$, the separable linear expenditure system guarantees that the only effect of z in (28) is the income effect $-z p_0$.

To estimate equations (26) to (28), I have used post-war annual British data from 1954 to 1974 on seven non-durable expenditure categories plus housing: food; clothing; fuel; drink and tobacco; transport and communication; other goods; services. This means there are 27 parameters in (26) and (27), 25 of which can be freely determined. All of these parameters also appear in (28) and, given sufficient variation in the data, all can in principle be identified. Note, in particular that δ, the marginal propensity to spend on housing in the free regime, can be estimated when housing is quantity-constrained. The practical situation is somewhat different, especially if we try to estimate by Full Information Maximum Likelihood (FIML). Consider the attempt to estimate (26) and (27) as a set under the (realistic) assumption of no prior knowledge about the variance–covariance matrix of cross-equation errors. Looking first at (26) alone, the equation contains a total of 17 parameters $(\gamma_0, \beta_0, \beta_1, ..., \beta_7, \gamma_1, ..., \gamma_7, \delta)$. There are only 21 observations and, although these parameters appear in other equations, it will be possible, at the price of a very poor fit elsewhere, to obtain an almost perfect fit for (26) alone, or indeed for any other single equation. In FIML estimation, where the determinant of the estimated variance–covariance matrix is being minimized, a perfect fit for one equation guarantees a zero determinant and an infinite log likelihood. Hence, for the data at hand, it is not sensible to try to estimate these models by FIML techniques.

An alternative procedure is to impose prior restrictions on the variance–covariance matrix. For example, if we write ω_{ij} for $E(u_{ti}u_{tj})$ where u_{ti} and u_{tj} are the errors at time t in equations i and j, then one possibility is to write $\omega_{ij} = \sigma^2(\delta_{ij} - n^{-1})$ where δ_{ij} is the Kronecker delta. This leads to estimation by minimizing the total residual sum of squares over all equations (see Deaton, 1975, p. 39). A number of equations were estimated in this way but it became clear that the zero degree price function $\beta_0\Pi p_k^{\beta_k}$ was always close to being constant over the sample. This is to be expected given the collinearity of the prices, but means that, in (26) and (27), it is not possible to identify both β_0 and γ_0 while, in (28), in addition, ρ cannot be identified. It is thus best in practice to accept the approximation and rewrite the three equations as

$$w_0 = r_0\gamma_0^* + \delta(1 - \gamma_0^*r_0 - \gamma.r) \tag{26'}$$

$$w_i = r_i\gamma_i + \beta_i^*r_0 + (1 - \delta)\alpha_i(1 - \gamma_0^*r_0 - \gamma.r) \tag{27'}$$

and

$$w_i^* = r_i\gamma_i + \left(\alpha_i + \frac{\beta_i^{**}}{z - \gamma_0^*}\right)(1 - \gamma.r - z.r_0) \tag{28'}$$

where $\gamma_0^* = \gamma_0 + \beta_0\Pi p_k^{\beta_k}$, $\beta_i^* = \beta_i\beta_0\Pi p_k^{\beta_k}$, $\beta_i^{**} = \beta_i^*\rho$, $w_i = p_iq_i/x$ (the budget share of good i) and $r_i = p_i/x$. (The division by x is likely to reduce heteroscedasticity and render the constant variance stochastic specification more plausible.) These revised equations are now clearer to interpret since, by (26′), housing follows the LES in the long run with, by (27′), the price of housing modifying the committed quantities of other goods. (n.b. $\Sigma\beta_i^* = \Sigma\beta_i^{**} = \Sigma\beta_i = 0$.) In (28′) the zs still affect the marginal budget shares provided $\beta_i^{**} \neq 0$; for $\beta_i^{**} > 0$ increases in z *decrease* the marginal budget share of good i and conversely for $\beta_i^{**} < 0$. Note finally that, with the removal of $\Pi p_k^{\beta_k}$, equations (26′) to (28′) can now straightforwardly be estimated by FIML.

The FIML estimates for (26′), (27′) and (28′) are given in table 1, the unrestricted model on the left-hand side and those for the rationed model on the right. Note first that the likelihood values given at the foot of the table cannot be compared; the free model explains one more variable than does the rationed model and this automatically leads to the higher likelihood in this case. However, note that the budget share for each of the non-rationed commodities is better explained by the rationed than by the free model. This gain is due to two quite separate effects. The first is that, in the rationed model, it is $x - p_0 z$ rather than x itself which is the total expenditure variable. The second is the explicit rationing effect which operates through the non-zero β^{**} parameters. Both these differences

Table 1. *FIML parameter estimates of free and rationed models*

	Free model				Rationed model			
	γ	α	β^*	R^2	γ	α	β^{**}	R^2
1. Food	88.8	−0.040	34.3	0.988	79.9	0.045	5.2	0.995
	(2.5)	(0.026)	(7.8)		(4.9)	(0.012)	(1.5)	
2. Clothing	23.7	0.118	0.7	0.827	9.9	0.082	4.2	0.972
	(1.6)	(0.020)	(5.7)		(2.1)	(0.007)	(0.7)	
3. Fuel	11.8	0.059	2.5	0.626	14.9	0.070	−1.1	0.655
	(2.7)	(0.018)	(6.1)		(2.7)	(0.005)	(0.6)	
4. Drink and	43.9	0.189	−11.0	0.852	36.5	0.163	−0.8	0.904
tobacco	(2.4)	(0.020)	(6.2)		(2.0)	(0.004)	(0.5)	
5. Transport and	21.5	0.420	−47.2	0.958	30.1	0.307	−9.1	0.995
communication	(3.3)	(0.018)	(6.3)		(3.2)	(0.016)	(1.3)	
6. Other goods	22.6	0.142	2.9	0.568	15.5	0.156	0.4	0.671
	(1.8)	(0.015)	(4.8)		(2.9)	(0.004)	(0.5)	
7. Other services	37.5	0.112	17.8	0.014	29.7	0.177	1.2	0.561
	(3.6)	(—)	(—)		(4.5)	(—)	(—)	
0. Housing	−8.3	0.280	—	0.958	—	—	—	—
	(3.1)	(—)						
	2 log L = 1563.1				2 log L = 1382.8			
	$TLES_6$ = 52.3				$TLES_6$ = 73.6			

Note: Estimated standard errors in brackets. Coefficients without standard errors are either imposed or derived from homogeneity or adding-up constraints.

make a contribution. If free and rationed LES models are estimated, i.e. by setting β_i^* to zero for (27') and β_i^{**} to zero for (28'), the rationed model fits better to the unrationed commodities. The effect of introducing the β^* and β^{**} is then assessed by a χ^2-test on the joint significance of these parameters in each of the models. These tests are the $TLES_6$ figures given in table 1 which, in both cases, indicate the importance of the β-parameters. For both models, the parameters for food and for transport and communication are highly significant with that for clothing also so in the rationed model. Hence, if we believe the latter, an increase in housing services (e.g. by an unwanted increase in education raised by higher local rates) causes (*apart* from income effects) a cut in consumption of food and clothing and an increase in the consumption of transport and communication.

Although I believe these results to be promising, I must conclude this section with some caveats, both theoretical and econometric. First, although the unrationed model (26') aggregates perfectly over consumers, so justifying an aggregate approach on *per capita* data, this is *not* true of the rationed model (28') if the ration levels z vary over households. Secondly, there is a good deal of inconsistency between the two sets of parameter estimates in table 1. Of course, since each model implies the incorrectness of the other, inconsistencies are to be expected. If the rationed model is true, the explanation of housing in the free model is quite incorrect while the other equations are mis-specified by the omission of z. Conversely, if the free model is correct, the rationed model will suffer from simultaneity bias since z is jointly determined with the other quantities. It is thus not clear without a good deal more analysis whether the inconsistencies can be explained by these factors. In any case, the β^* and β^{**} parameters (n.b. in theory $\beta^{**} \simeq \frac{1}{3}\beta^*$) are not all well determined and are rather sensitive to the stochastic specification. They should not therefore be taken too seriously at this stage. Thirdly, and finally, the LES (and even the minor extension embodied in (26') and (27')) is a highly restrictive model which undoubtedly omits or biases important determinants of behaviour, see e.g. Deaton (1974). Hence, it is not difficult to find essentially spurious correlations by introducing new variables into the model which are correlated with omitted effects. I turn to this in detail in the next section where a much more general model is analysed.

3 A general model for rationed demands

The restrictiveness of the model analysed in the previous section was a consequence of the need to select a functional form for the cost function which permitted an explicit solution of the equations leading to the matched pair of rationed and unrationed demands. If general functional forms are assumed for the unrationed cost function, it is rarely possible to solve equation (15) for the function $\xi_0(u, z, p)$. For specific examples, solutions could be generated numerically and a rationed system of demand functions estimated with knowledge of only the unrestricted cost function. However, in many situations, matched demand functions are unnecessary and all that is required is a general procedure for producing utility-consistent rationed demand functions. This will be the case, for example, in the analysis of public goods where we are interested not in how consumers would provide such goods for themselves, but rather in how the public goods levels affect the structure of private consumption. Now, in the unrationed case, the fundamental theorem of duality tells us that, given a cost function with all the correct properties (positive linear homogeneous, concave, etc.), preferences can always be recovered from it, so that, instead of starting from the specification of a utility function, it is equally valid to start from the cost function. Similarly, given knowledge of its properties, the restricted cost function can be used in exactly the same way.

Recall equation (10) and the definition of $\gamma(u, z, p)$, i.e.

$$\gamma(u, z, p) = \min_q \{p \cdot q; v(z, q) \geq u\} \tag{29}$$

where we now allow z to be a vector of ration levels. The function $\gamma(u, z, p)$ is simply the rationed cost function $c^*(u, p_0, p, z)$ less the cost of the ration $p_0 z$. Note first that, regarded as a function of u and p, $\gamma(u, z, p)$ has all the conventional properties of a cost function, including the derivative property for the unrationed demands, i.e. $\partial\gamma(u, z, p)/\partial p_i = q_i$. It thus only remains to categorize the properties with respect to z. The function $\gamma(u, z, p)$ is a special case of a *restricted profit function* (see McFadden, 1978), and a full treatment can be found in that reference. For the following discussion, I wish to focus on only two properties, that $\gamma(u, z, p)$ is *decreasing* and *convex* in z.

Both propositions can be established directly from (29). Let z^0 be some arbitrary z, with q^0 the cost minimizing selection of q given u and z^0. For any $z^1 \geq z^0$, $v(z^1, q^0) \geq v(z^0, q^0) = u$, so that u can be reached or improved upon at q^0 for u and z^1. But this is not necessarily the best way of doing so. Hence, $\gamma(u, z^1, p) \leq \gamma(u, z^0, p)$ for all $z^1 \geq z^0$. The inequality is clearly strict if non-satiation is also assumed. Note that if, in addition, $\gamma(u, z, p)$ is differentiable in z, then, from (13)

$$\frac{\partial\gamma(u, z, p)}{\partial z} = -\xi_0(u, z, p) \tag{30}$$

so that $\xi_0(u, z, p)$ is positive given non-satiation. Convexity of $\gamma(u, z, p)$ in z follows from the convexity of preferences as we now demonstrate. Let

z^1 and z^2 be two vectors of rations and let q^1 and q^2 be the corresponding optimal choices for unrationed goods at utility u and prices p. Hence $\gamma(u, z^1, p) = p \cdot q^1$ and $\gamma(u, z^2, p) = p \cdot q^2$ while, since utility is the same in both situations,

$$v(q^1, z^1) = v(q^2, z^2) = u \tag{31}$$

Hence, by the quasi-concavity of $v(\ )$, for $0 \le \lambda \le 1$,

$$v(\lambda q^1 + (1 - \lambda)q^2, \lambda z^1 + (1 - \lambda)z^2) \ge u \tag{32}$$

Hence, $\lambda q^1 + (1 - \lambda)q^2$ is one way of attaining at least u given $\lambda z^1 + (1 - \lambda)z^2$ and prices p, but not necessarily the cheapest. In other words

$$\gamma(u, \lambda z^1 + (1 - \lambda)z^2, p) \le \lambda p.q^1 + (1 - \lambda)p.q^2$$

so that

$$\gamma(u, \lambda z^1 + (1 - \lambda)z^2, p) \le \lambda\gamma(u, z^1, p) + (1 - \lambda)\gamma(u, z^2, p) \tag{33}$$

which establishes the convexity of the function.

Given these results, the analysis of rationed behaviour can proceed from the specification of a suitable function for $\gamma(u, z, p)$ possessed of the properties discussed above. In Deaton and Muellbauer (1980b) a flexible functional form for an unrestricted cost function was proposed which led to the Almost Ideal Demand System (AIDS) in which the budget shares of each commodity are linearly related to the logarithms of prices and price-deflated total expenditure. To define an analogous model which allows for a single ration z, define

$$\begin{aligned}
\log \gamma(u, z, p) = {} & \alpha_0 + \sum \{\alpha_k + \eta_k z\} \log p_k \\
& + \frac{1}{2} \sum_k \sum_j \gamma_{kj}^* \log p_k \log p_j \\
& + \beta_0 \Pi p_k^{\beta_k} \left\{ u + \theta_0 z + \frac{1}{2} \theta_1 z^2 + \frac{1}{2} \theta_2 u z \right\}
\end{aligned} \tag{34}$$

(The extension to a vector of zs is straightforward.) The demand functions can be derived from $w_i = \partial \log \gamma / \partial \log p_i$ giving budget shares as a proportion of total non-rationed expenditure. Hence,

$$w_i = \alpha_i + \eta_i z + \sum_j \gamma_{ij} \log p_j + \beta_i \log \left(\frac{x - p_0 z}{P} \right) \tag{35}$$

where

$$\log P = \alpha_0 + \sum_k \{\alpha_k + \eta_k z\} \log p_k + \frac{1}{2} \sum\sum \gamma_{kj} \log p_k \log p_j \tag{36}$$

and

$$\gamma_{ij} = \frac{1}{2} (\gamma_{ij}^* + \gamma_{ji}^*)$$

and we have the parameter restrictions: for *adding-up*,

$$\sum_i \alpha_i = 1, \quad \sum_i \eta_i = 0, \quad \sum_i \gamma_{ij} = 0, \quad \sum_i \beta_i = 0 \qquad (37)$$

for *homogeneity*,

$$\sum_j \gamma_{ij} = 0 \qquad (38)$$

and for *symmetry*,

$$\gamma_{ij} = \gamma_{ji} \qquad (39)$$

Note carefully that this system, (35)–(36), is *not* the model which would result from restricting one good within a free AIDS. (The unrestricted cost function from (34) is quite different from the AIDS cost function given by Deaton and Muellbauer (1980b).)

The ration level z appears through its income effect $(x - p_0 z)$ as usual but also enters the value shares linearly with coefficients η_i adding to zero. An additional complication is introduced by the presence of z in log P from (36), but in many practical applications it will be possible to approximate log P by some parameter-independent price index so that (35) can be estimated as a linear system of equations. The conditions on $\gamma(u, z, p)$ as a function of z can be investigated by deriving the shadow price function from $p_0^*/(x - p_0 z) = - \partial \log \gamma(u, z, p)/\partial z$. Hence,

$$\frac{p_0^*}{(x - p_0 z)} = - \sum \eta_k \log p_k - \beta_0 \Pi p_k^{\beta_k} \left\{ \theta_0 + \theta_1 z + \frac{1}{2} \theta_2 u \right\} \qquad (40)$$

This will be positive for an appropriate choice of parameters θ_0, θ_1 and θ_2 and a suitably restricted range for the independent variables. Similar restrictions guarantee convexity of $\gamma(u, z, p)$ in z, at least locally.

In the earlier work with the AIDS in Deaton and Muellbauer (1980b), in which no ration effects were allowed, one of the most important findings was the decisive rejection of the homogeneity restriction (38). Hence, an interesting use of the current model is to investigate whether the presence of the zs can modify this conclusion. The range of possible ration variables is large, including many items of government expenditure. However, stocks of durable goods are again likely to be important and I conclude by repeating the experiments with housing of section 2, but now using the rationed AIDS (or RAIDS) given by (35). The equation was estimated for each of the seven unrationed commodities; in each case the homogeneity restriction (38) was tested by estimating with and without the restriction and calculating an F-ratio. These are given in table 2 together with the F-ratios for the similar tests without z and including housing as one of the commodities (these are calculated from table 1 of Deaton and Muellbauer (1980b)). Note first that in the AIDS, housing itself is strongly inhomogeneous as one would expect it to be if the rationed model were true. More importantly, the rejection of homogeneity in the food and clothing categories is now no longer encountered, while that for transport and communication, although still present, has a greatly reduced F-ratio. In the unrestricted RAIDS regressions, only in transport and communication does z have a significant effect, and the coefficient is positive. In the restricted homogeneous regressions, this positive effect is much more pronounced (t-value of 14.3), and in addition there are now significant negative coefficients in the food and clothing regressions. These sign patterns are identical to those revealed in table 1, with increases in z depressing food and clothing expenditure and increasing transport and communication. Since the two models are very different, this suggests that the effects are more than chance correlations. Even so, the z variable is only significant in all three categories *after* the absolute price level is suppressed and it is clearly possible that z is standing proxy for another variable, or for a combination of variables, for example stocks of other durable goods. Further, homogeneity is still rejected overall as a result of inhomogeneity of transport and communication, although the χ^2-likelihood ratio test is now only some twice its critical value rather than ten times. Hence, while it is clear that the rationed model performs a good deal better than the unrationed version so that the stock of housing interpreted as a ration can explain a good deal of the inhomogeneity of demands, it is not clear that the housing stock is the only or most appropriate such variable.

Table 2. *Tests of homogeneity for AIDS with and without rationing effects* (5% critical value: $F_{1,11} = 4.84$)

	AIDS	RAIDS
1. Food	19.4	0.1
2. Clothing	20.3	2.1
3. Housing	82.8	—
4. Fuel	1.2	0.4
5. Drink and tobacco	0.0	0.8
6. Transport and communication	171.6	15.5
7. Other goods	0.5	0.6
8. Other services	4.0	0.3
$2(\log L_{\text{free}} - \log . L_{\text{hom}})$	143	28

4 Conclusions

In this paper, I have discussed the theory of rationed demand functions and presented a method for generating rationed from unrationed demands. The technique was applied to an extended version of the linear expenditure system and the resulting model used to investigate the effects of treating the housing stock as a ration level. The empirical results suggested the existence of effects running from an increase in housing to compensating decreases in food and clothing expenditure and compensating increases in transport and communication. Finally, a methodology for generating flexible functional forms for rationed demands was presented. This was used to generate an 'almost ideal demand system' with rationing which, when applied to the same data, produced results consistent in direction with the first rationed model. Furthermore, the treatment of housing as a ration helped to explain much of the apparent inhomogeneity in the demand functions. These results suggest that the role of stocks treated as rations is a topic worthy of a good deal more investigation.

Notes

1 I am grateful to John Muellbauer for helpful comments.

References

Barro, R. and Grossman, H. (1976), *Money, Employment and Inflation*, Cambridge University Press.

Deaton, A. S. (1974), 'A reconsideration of the empirical implications of additive preferences', *Economic Journal*, **84**, pp. 338–48.

(1975), *Models and Projections of Demand in Post-war Britain*, Chapman and Hall, London.

(1978), 'Specification and testing in applied demand analysis', *Economic Journal*, **88**, pp. 524–36.

Deaton, A. S. and Muellbauer, J. (1980a), *Economics and Consumer Behaviour*, Cambridge University Press.

(1980b), 'An almost ideal demand system', *American Economic Review* **70**, pp. 312–26

Deaton, A. S. and Muellbauer, J. (1981), 'Functional forms for labour supply and commodity demands with and without quantity constraints', *Econometrica*, **49**, forthcoming.

McFadden, D. (1978), 'Cost, revenue and profit functions', in Fuss, M. and D. McFadden (eds.), *Production Economics: a dual approach to theory and applications*, North-Holland.

Malinvaud, E. (1977), *The Theory of Unemployment Reconsidered*, Oxford, Basil Blackwell.

Muellbauer, J. (1981), 'Linear aggregation in neoclassical labour supply', *Review of Economic Studies*, **48**, pp. 21–36.

Muellbauer, J. and Portes, R. (1978), 'Macroeconomic models with quantity rationing', *Economic Journal,* **88,** pp. 788–821.

Neary, J. P. and Roberts, K. W. S. (1980), 'The theory of household behaviour under rationing', *European Economic Review,* **13,** pp. 25–42.

Pollak, R. A. (1969), 'Conditional demand functions and consumption theory', *Quarterly Journal of Economics,* **83,** pp. 70–8.

(1971), 'Conditional demand functions and the implications of separable utility', *Southern Economic Journal,* **37,** pp. 423–33.

Rothbarth, E. (1941), 'The measurement of change in real income under conditions of rationing', *Review of Economic Studies,* **8,** pp. 100–7.

Samuelson, P. A. (1947), *Foundations of Economic Analysis,* Cambridge, Massachusetts: Harvard University Press.

Stone, J. R. N. (1954), 'Linear expenditure systems and demand analysis: an application to the pattern of British demand', *Economic Journal,* **64,** pp. 511–27.

Tobin, J. (1952), 'A survey of the theory of rationing', *Econometrica,* **20,** pp. 512–53.

Tobin, J. and Houthakker, H. S. (1951), 'The effects of rationing on demand elasticities', *Review of Economic Studies,* **18,** pp. 140–53.

4 The independence transformation: a review and some further explorations[1]

HENRI THEIL
AND KENNETH LAITINEN

1 Introduction

The objective of this chapter is to discuss the relationship between the technique of principal components, first applied to economic data in the pioneering paper by Stone (1947), and the analysis of consumer demand.

The purpose of principal component analysis in statistics is to formulate a set of variables that are in some way 'more basic' than the observed variables. Factor analysis has a similar objective. Starting in 1956, Gorman and his associates (Boyle *et al.*, 1977; Gorman, 1956; 1959; 1976b) applied these statistical techniques to consumer demand in order to assess the consumer's basic wants, while Lancaster (1966, 1971) and Becker (1965) pursued similar goals by extending the economic theory of the consumer rather than using statistical tools. The independence transformation, which originated with Theil (1967; 1975–76; 1977), Brooks (1970), and Laitinen and Theil (1978), is related to both approaches and is in fact 'between' them. The transformation requires no extension of the theory of the utility-maximizing consumer, although it can handle such extensions without difficulty (see the example on leisure in section 2). At the same time, the transformation has a simple statistical interpretation, viz., that of a constrained principal component transformation.

To provide adequate motivation, we discuss some examples in section 2. Sections 3 and 4 describe the preference independence transformation and the underlying differential approach to consumption theory. Section 5 gives a brief discussion of similar results in the theory of the firm. A comparison with principal components follows in section 6, after which the article concludes with two sections (7 and 8) on strong and weak separability. To simplify the exposition, the more complicated mathematics has been put into the appendix. The account which follows is largely expository, but there are some new results, in particular on the independence

73

transformation under weak separability (section 8) and the case in which the consumer's utility function has a Hessian matrix that is not definite (appendix B).

2 Three examples

Transformed meats

The consumer is assumed to maximize a utility function $u(q)$ subject to the budget constraint $p'q = M$, where $p = [p_i]$ and $q = [q_i]$ are n-element price and quantity vectors and M is total expenditure (or, for short, income). One specification of the utility function, known as the Klein–Rubin (1948) or the Stone (1954)–Geary (1950) utility function, is

$$u(q) = \sum_{i=1}^{n} \theta_i \log (q_i - c_i) \tag{2.1}$$

where the c_is are constants and the θ_is positive constants with unit sum. Note that (2.1) implies that the marginal utility of each good is independent of the consumption of every other good. More generally, if the consumer's preferences can be represented by an additive utility function,

$$u(q) = \sum_{i=1}^{n} u_i(q_i) \tag{2.2}$$

then the marginal utility of the ith good equals du_i/dq_i, which is independent of all q_js with $j \neq i$. We shall refer to the preference structure (2.2) as preference independence.

It is unlikely that preference independence is realistic for narrowly defined goods. Indeed, when we analyze the demand for beef, pork, and chicken in the United States from 1950 to 1972, we find that the data contradict the additive structure (2.2).[2] But we can ask whether it is possible to transform these three observed meats so that each transformed meat has a marginal utility that is independent of the consumption of the other transformed meats. The answer is affirmative: the procedure to be used is the preference independence transformation. A major tool is the composition matrix which describes the expenditure on each transformed meat in terms of the expenditures on all observed meats and vice versa. The following is a bordered composition matrix for these meats:

$$
\begin{array}{ccc|cc}
0.148 & 0.383 & 0.202 & 0.734 & (T_1) \\
0.296 & -0.092 & 0.000 & 0.204 & (T_2) \\
0.037 & 0.095 & -0.070 & 0.063 & (T_3) \\
\hline
0.481 & 0.387 & 0.133 & 1 & \\
\text{(beef)} & \text{(pork)} & \text{(chicken)} & &
\end{array}
\tag{2.3}
$$

The composition matrix consists of the nine figures above the horizontal line and to the left of the vertical line. The last row contains the column sums of this matrix. The figures in this row are the expenditures on the observed meats measured as fractions of the expenditure on the three-meat group. Thus, 48.1 per cent of this total expenditure is allocated to beef, 38.7 per cent to pork, and 13.3 per cent to chicken. These percentages obviously change as time proceeds. This means that, in general, the results of the preference independence transformation are time-dependent. The composition matrix (2.3) is based on data for the mid 1950s.

The row sums in the last column of (2.3) are the expenditure shares of the transformed meats, each of which has (by construction) a marginal utility that is independent of the consumption of the other transformed meats. One of these, labelled T_1, accounts for 73.4 per cent of the expenditure on the three-meat group. The positive sign of the elements in the first row of the composition matrix implies that the three observed meats all contribute positively to T_1, suggesting that this transformed meat corresponds to the consumer's basic want for meat. However, it will appear that T_1 has the smallest income elasticity of the three transformed meats; these elasticities provide information on transformed goods beyond that provided by the composition matrix (see sections 4 and 7). Since a small income elasticity is indicative of modest quality, we conclude that T_1 corresponds to the consumer's basic want for affordable meat.

The transformed meats in the second and third rows of (2.3) are both contrasts between observed meats. Thus, T_2 is a contrast between beef and pork, every two dollars' worth of T_2 consisting of (approximately) three dollars' worth of beef minus one dollar's worth of pork which is given up. The associated basic want is the consumer's desire to eat beef rather than pork; it is the most luxurious want (see section 7). The third transformed meat, finally, is a contrast between beef and pork on one hand and chicken on the other.

Transformed goods involving leisure

The occurrence of contrasts is a standard feature of the independence transformation. We shall illustrate this with some results obtained by Flinn (1978) for a demand system that includes the demand for leisure; this system was derived from Barnett's study (1974) and is based on US data for the period 1890–1955. Taking leisure into account implies that M must be interpreted as full income, including the market value of the household's time. As before, there are three goods which are relevant for the independence transformation: semi-durables, durables, and leisure in this case. The bordered composition matrix for the early 1950s is as follows:

0.082	0.117	0.795	0.994	(T_1)
0.018	0.016	-0.028	0.006	(T_2)
0.004	-0.005	0.002	0.000	(T_3)	(2.4)
0.104	0.127	0.769	1	
(semi-durables)	(durables)	(leisure)		

A comparison of (2.3) and (2.4) reveals a similar numerical structure except that (2.4) is more extreme. In the case of (2.4), T_2 and T_3 are contrasts, but they account for only a very small fraction of the expenditure on the group. As we shall see in section 7, the income elasticities (with respect to full income) of T_2 and T_3 are substantially larger than that of T_1. Given that all three observed goods including leisure are positively represented in the first row of (2.4), and that many durables are time-saving goods, it seems reasonable to conclude that T_1 corresponds to the household's basic want for affordable free time. About 99 per cent of the expenditure on the three-good group is allocated to this want. The negative contribution of leisure to T_2 means that household members give up leisure (and hence go to work) when they buy this transformed good.

Transformed inputs

The preference independence transformation changes observed consumer goods into transformed goods so that the marginal utility of each is independent of the consumption of all other transformed goods. The input independence transformation in the theory of the firm is similar in that it changes observed inputs into transformed inputs so that the elasticity of output with respect to each transformed input is independent of the quantities of all other transformed inputs.

We shall illustrate the input independence transformation for a translog production function,

$$\log z = \text{constant} + \alpha \log K + \beta \log L + \xi(\alpha\beta)^{1/2} \log K \log L \quad (2.5)$$

where z is output, K is capital, L is labour, and α, β, and ξ are constants $(\alpha, \beta > 0)$. The elasticities of output with respect to the two inputs are

$$\frac{\partial \log z}{\partial \log K} = \alpha + \xi(\alpha\beta)^{1/2} \log L \quad (2.6)$$

$$\frac{\partial \log z}{\partial \log L} = \beta + \xi(\alpha\beta)^{1/2} \log K \quad (2.7)$$

If $\xi = 0$, the elasticity of output with respect to each input is independent of the other input; the technology (2.5) is then said to be input independent. If $\xi \neq 0$, (2.5) is not input independent, in which case we apply the input independence transformation.

This transformation takes a simple form when we select units so that $K = L = 1$ holds at the point of the firm's optimum. We write f_K and f_L for the factor shares of capital and labour: the expenditures on these inputs measured as fractions of total input expenditure ($f_K + f_L = 1$). The following is the composition matrix of the input independence transformation for the technology (2.5):

$$\begin{bmatrix} \frac{1}{2}(f_K + (f_K f_L)^{1/2}) & \frac{1}{2}(f_L + (f_K f_L)^{1/2}) \\ \frac{1}{2}(f_K - (f_K f_L)^{1/2}) & \frac{1}{2}(f_L - (f_K f_L)^{1/2}) \end{bmatrix} \tag{2.8}$$

The sums of the elements in the two columns are the factor shares f_K and f_L of the two observed inputs. These should be compared with the expenditure shares 0.481, 0.387, and 0.133 of the observed meats in (2.3). The row sums of (2.8) are the factor shares of the transformed inputs: $\frac{1}{2} + (f_K f_L)^{1/2}$ and $\frac{1}{2} - (f_K f_L)^{1/2}$. For example, when we specify $f_K = 0.2$ and $f_L = 0.8$ and indicate the transformed inputs by T_1 and T_2, (2.8) yields the following bordered composition matrix:

$$
\begin{array}{cc|cc}
0.3 & 0.6 & 0.9 & (T_1) \\
-0.1 & 0.2 & 0.1 & (T_2) \\
\hline
0.2 & 0.8 & 1 & \\
\text{(capital)} & \text{(labour)} & &
\end{array}
\tag{2.9}
$$

Both observed inputs are positively represented in T_1, whereas T_2 is a contrast between labour and capital. Buying more T_2 means that the firm's operation becomes more labour-intensive, each dollar spent on T_2 being equivalent to two dollars' worth of labour compensated by one dollar's worth of capital services which is given up.

3 The differential approach to consumption theory

A demand equation system in differential form

The simplest formulation of the preference independence transformation is in terms of the differential approach to the theory of the consumer. This approach should be contrasted with that which postulates a particular algebraic form of the utility function such as (2.1). When we maximize (2.1) subject to the budget constraint, we obtain (after minor rearrangements) demand equations of the following form:

$$p_i q_i = p_i c_i + \theta_i \left(M - \sum_{j=1}^{n} p_j c_j \right) \tag{3.1}$$

This is the linear expenditure system, which is probably the most popular demand system since Stone (1954) introduced it in 1954. Differentiation of (3.1) with respect to M shows that θ_i can be interpreted as the marginal expenditure share of the ith good:

$$\theta_i = \frac{\partial(p_i q_i)}{\partial M}, \quad \sum_{i=1}^{n} \theta_i = 1 \tag{3.2}$$

These marginal shares should be contrasted with the 'average' expenditure shares or budget shares:

$$w_i = \frac{p_i q_i}{M}, \quad \sum_{i=1}^{n} w_i = 1 \tag{3.3}$$

The differential approach to consumption theory considers infinitesimal displacements and does not restrict itself to a particular algebraic form of the utility function. Divisia indexes (1925) play an important role in this approach. We write the differential of the budget constraint as $dM = \Sigma_i q_i dp_i + \Sigma_i p_i dq_i$. Division by M and use of (3.3) give

$$d(\log M) = d(\log P) + d(\log Q) \tag{3.4}$$

where log stands for natural logarithm (here and elsewhere) and $d(\log P)$ and $d(\log Q)$ are the consumer's Divisia price and volume indexes in differential form:

$$d(\log P) = \sum_{i=1}^{n} w_i d(\log p_i) \tag{3.5}$$

$$d(\log Q) = \sum_{i=1}^{n} w_i d(\log q_i) \tag{3.6}$$

We shall find it advantageous to write (3.4) in the equivalent form

$$d(\log Q) = d \left(\log \frac{M}{P} \right) \tag{3.7}$$

with the expression on the right interpreted as $d(\log M) - d(\log P)$. Equation (3.7) states that the Divisia volume index is equal to the logarithmic change in money income deflated by the Divisia price index.

We assume that the consumer's utility function is appropriately differentiable and that the Hessian matrix of this function, $U = [\partial^2 u / \partial q_i \partial q_j]$, is symmetric negative definite.[3] The equilibrium conditions consist of the budget constraint and the proportionality of marginal utilities and prices.

Since these conditions hold identically in income and prices, we can differentiate them with respect to the latter variables, the result of which can be written in the form of Barten's (1964) fundamental matrix equation. By solving this equation we obtain

$$\frac{\partial q_i}{\partial p_j} = \lambda u^{ij} - \frac{\lambda}{\partial \lambda / \partial M} \frac{\partial q_i}{\partial M} \frac{\partial q_j}{\partial M} - \frac{\partial q_i}{\partial M} q_j \tag{3.8}$$

where λ is the marginal utility of income and u^{ij} is the (i, j)th element of U^{-1}. The last term in (3.8) represents the income effect of the change in p_j on q_i, while the two preceding terms jointly represent the substitution effect. The firm term (λu^{ij}) describes the specific substitution effect and the second the general substitution effect. The latter effect deals with the general competition of all goods for an extra dollar of the consumer's income, whereas the former is concerned with the utility interaction of the ith and jth goods. The distinction between these two components of the substitution effect is from Houthakker (1960).

The differential approach uses (3.8) to describe the change in the demand for the ith good in terms of the changes in income and all prices. A convenient result is obtained when we specify the left-hand variable as $w_i d(\log q_i)$, which is the contribution of the ith good to the Divisia volume index [see (3.6)]. The result is then

$$w_i d(\log q_i) = \theta_i d \left(\log \frac{M}{P} \right) + \phi \sum_{j=1}^{n} \theta_{ij} d \left(\log \frac{p_j}{P'} \right) \tag{3.9}$$

which is the ith equation of the differential demand system. It should be contrasted with the linear expenditure system (3.1) that is obtained from the utility function (2.1).

Discussion of the differential demand system

Before explaining the various symbols in (3.9) we note that the deflator which transforms money income into real income is not the same as the deflator which transforms absolute prices into relative prices. Income is deflated by the income effect of the price changes; this is equivalent to the use of the Divisia price index as deflator [see (3.5) and (3.7)]. In the substitution term of (3.9) it is the specific substitution effect of the price changes which is deflated by the general substitution effect. The deflator involved is the Frisch price index (1932, pp. 74–82),

$$d(\log P') = \sum_{i=1}^{n} \theta_i d(\log p_i) \tag{3.10}$$

which uses marginal rather than budget shares as weights.

It is readily verified from (3.2) and (3.3) that the ratio of a marginal share to the corresponding budget share is the income elasticity:

$$\frac{\theta_i}{w_i} = \frac{\partial \log q_i}{\partial \log M} \tag{3.11}$$

A comparison of (3.10) and (3.5) shows that luxuries (goods with income elasticities larger than 1) have a larger weight in the Frisch price index than in the Divisia price index, whereas the opposite is true for necessities (with income elasticities smaller than 1). If a good is inferior ($\theta_i < 0$), an increase in its price has a downward effect on the Frisch price index.

We proceed to discuss (3.9) term by term. The expression on the left is not only the contribution of good i to the Divisia volume index (3.6) but also the quantity component of the change in its budget share. This may be verified by taking the differential of $w_i = p_i q_i / M$:

$$dw_i = w_i d(\log p_i) + w_i d(\log q_i) - w_i d(\log M) \tag{3.12}$$

Hence the change in a budget share consists of a price, a quantity, and an income component. Using the *quantity component* of this change as the left-hand variable of a demand equation emphasizes the fact that the quantities bought are the consumer's decision variables. Using a component of the change in a *budget share* emphasizes the fact that consumption theory is basically an allocation theory; it is concerned with the allocation of the fixed amount of total expenditure to the individual goods, given this amount and the prices of these goods. Equation (3.9) emphasizes the allocation character of consumer demand, which may be clarified when we use (3.7) to write the equation as

$$w_i d(\log q_i) = \theta_i d(\log Q) + \phi \sum_{j=1}^{n} \theta_{ij} d\left(\log \frac{p_j}{P'}\right) \tag{3.13}$$

This equation describes the contribution of good i to the Divisia volume index in terms of this index and relative price changes. When we sum (3.13) over i, we obtain $d(\log Q) = d(\log Q)$ in view of $\Sigma_i \theta_i = 1$ [see (3.2)] and the zero sum of the substitution term of (3.13).[4]

The first term on the right in (3.13) is the real-income component of the change in the demand for the ith good, with real income measured by the Divisia volume index. This index is multiplied by the marginal share θ_i which also occurs in the linear expenditure system (3.1). However, there is an important difference in that θ_i is a constant in the linear expenditure system, whereas the differential approach postulates no constancy. This approach allows all coefficients [θ_i, ϕ, and θ_{ij} in (3.13)] to depend on the levels of income and prices.

The coefficient ϕ in the substitution term of (3.13) is defined as the reciprocal of the income elasticity of the marginal utility of income:

$$\frac{1}{\phi} = \frac{\partial \log \lambda}{\partial \log M} \tag{3.14}$$

We shall refer to ϕ as the income flexibility; it is negative because of the negative definiteness of U.[5] The coefficient θ_{ij} in (3.13) is

$$\theta_{ij} = \frac{\lambda}{\phi M} p_i u^{ij} p_j \tag{3.15}$$

where u^{ij}, as in (3.8), is the (i, j)th element of U^{-1}. It follows from $\phi < 0$ and the symmetric negative definiteness of U that θ_{ij} is an element of a symmetric positive definite matrix $[\theta_{ij}]$. Also, the θ_{ij}s in each equation add up to the corresponding marginal share,[6]

$$\sum_{j=1}^{n} \theta_{ij} = \theta_i \tag{3.16}$$

When we sum both sides of (3.16) over i and use $\Sigma_i \theta_i = 1$, we find that the sum of all θ_{ij}s equals 1. Thus, we shall refer to the θ_{ij}s as the *normalized price coefficients* of (3.13). Each θ_{ij} is the coefficient of the logarithmic change in a relative price.

When we write (3.15) in $n \times n$ matrix form and invert both sides, we obtain

$$\theta^{ij} = \frac{\phi M}{\lambda} \frac{\partial^2 u}{\partial(p_i q_i)\partial(p_j q_j)} \tag{3.17}$$

where θ_{ij} is the (i, j)th element of $[\theta_{ij}]^{-1}$. The derivative on the right describes the change in the marginal utility of a dollar spent on the ith good which is caused by an extra dollar spent on the jth. So we may conclude from (3.17) that the normalized price coefficient matrix of the differential demand system (3.13) is inversely proportional to the Hessian matrix of the utility function in expenditure terms.

Preference independence and specific substitutes and complements

Under the preference independence condition (2.2) the Hessian U is diagonal. Its inverse is then also diagonal, so that $\theta_{ij} = 0$ whenever $i \neq j$ in view of (3.15), while (3.16) is simplified to $\theta_{ii} = \theta_i$. Therefore, under preference independence (3.13) becomes

$$w_i d(\log q_i) = \theta_i d(\log Q) + \phi \theta_i d \left(\log \frac{p_i}{P'} \right) \tag{3.18}$$

which contains only one relative price. Inferior goods cannot occur under preference independence because $\theta_i = \theta_{ii} > 0$, the $>$ sign being based on the positive definiteness of the matrix $[\theta_{ij}]$. Inferior goods are also excluded by the linear expenditure system (3.1).

Following Houthakker (1960), we call the ith and jth goods specific substitutes (complements) when θ_{ij} is negative (positive).[7] We conclude from (3.13) and $\phi < 0$ that an increase in the jth relative price raises (lowers) the demand for the ith good when the two goods are specific substitutes (complements). Also, (3.18) shows that under preference independence no good is a specific substitute or complement of any other. The preference independence transformation may be viewed as an annihilator of all specific substitution and complementarity relations so that demand equations of the form (3.18) emerge, each containing one relative price.

4 The preference independence transformation

The main results of the transformation

The preference independence transformation diagonalizes the Hessian matrix U (and hence also the normalized price coefficient matrix $[\theta_{ij}]$) subject to the constraint that the consumer's income and the associated Divisia indexes (3.5) and (3.6) are invariant. The main results are stated below. An outline of the derivations is given in appendix A.

We write Θ for the matrix $[\theta_{ij}]$ and W for the $n \times n$ diagonal matrix with the budget shares on the diagonal. The transformation involves a diagonalization of Θ relative to W,

$$(\Theta - \lambda_i W)x_i = 0 \qquad (4.1)$$

where $i = 1, ..., n$. The λ_is are latent roots and the x_is are characteristic vectors normalized so that $x_i' W x_j = 0$ for $i \neq j$ and $x_i' W x_i = 1$. We can implement (4.1) in the more convenient form

$$(D^{-1}\Theta D^{-1} - \lambda_i I)Dx_i = 0 \qquad (4.2)$$

where D is the diagonal matrix with the square roots of the budget shares on the diagonal. Both diagonalizations, (4.1) and (4.2), are unique when the roots $\lambda_1, ..., \lambda_n$ are all distinct. These roots are all real and positive because $D^{-1}\Theta D^{-1}$ in (4.2) is symmetric positive definite.

A third equivalent diagonalization is also useful. We introduce the $n \times n$ matrix X whose ith column is the characteristic vector x_i and the $n \times n$ diagonal matrix Λ whose ith diagonal element is the latent root λ_i. Then the normalization rules $x_i' W x_j = 0$ for $i \neq j$ and $x_i' W x_i = 1$ can be written as $X'WX = I$, while (4.1) for all i can be written in the form $\Theta X = WX\Lambda$. On premultiplying by X' we obtain $X'\Theta X = X'WX\Lambda$, or $X'\Theta X = \Lambda$ because $X'WX = I$. Therefore,

$$X'\Theta X = \Lambda, \quad X'WX = I \qquad (4.3)$$

which shows that (4.1) combined with the normalization rule on the characteristic vectors can be viewed as a simultaneous diagonalization of Θ and W, Θ being transformed into Λ and W into I.

The λ_is are the income elasticities of the transformed goods, i.e. the transformed versions of θ_i/w_i [see (3.11)]. Thus, the fact that the transformation is unique when the λ_is are distinct is equivalent to the proposition that *transformed goods are identified by their income elasticities*. Later we shall explore what happens when two λ_is are equal or almost equal. The fact that the λ_is are all positive implies that transformed goods can never be inferior goods. The income elasticities of the transformed meats described in section 2 are directly related to these λ_is, but a more complete discussion is postponed until section 7 because this application is confined to the expenditure on meat rather than consumption as a whole.

The composition matrix of the transformation takes the form

$$T = (X^{-1}\iota)_{\Delta} X^{-1} \tag{4.4}$$

where ι is a column vector consisting of n unit elements and $(X^{-1}\iota)_{\Delta}$ stands for the vector $X^{-1}\iota$ written in the form of a diagonal matrix. The column sums of T are the budget shares of the observed goods and the row sums are the budget shares of the transformed goods. We cannot exclude the possibility that the vector $X^{-1}\iota$ contains a zero element. If this happens, $(X^{-1}\iota)_{\Delta}$ contains a zero row and so does the composition matrix in view of (4.4). This means that there is a transformed good which receives no contribution from any observed good so that nothing is spent on that transformed good. It is shown in appendix A how this can be explained in terms of the consumer's preferences.

The invariance of total expenditure and its Divisia indexes is imposed, but several other coefficients and variables can also be shown to be invariant, including the income flexibility ϕ and the Frisch index (3.10). Also, when the prices (quantities) of all observed goods change proportionately, the price (quantity) of each transformed good changes in the same proportion, which is a desirable property.

The transformation under changing budget shares

Even when Θ is a matrix of constant elements (which need not be the case), the diagonalization (4.1) will yield results that vary over time because the budget shares in the diagonal of W will typically change. The analysis of such variations is frequently interesting. For example, the composition matrix for meats [see (2.3)] changed from the early 1950s until the early 1970s in several respects, one of which was the fact that T_1 (affordable meat) was gradually 'beefed up' in the sense that the contribution of beef to T_1 increased by more than 100 per cent. Since beef has the largest income elasticity of the three observed meats, this also raised the income elasticity of T_1 relative to those of the other transformed meats. Suppose that during this process two such income elasticities become equal. It is then no longer possible to separate the associated transformed goods because these are identified by their income elasticities. But is it possible to trace the transformed goods during that process? We shall answer this question for

$$\Theta = 10^{-10} \begin{bmatrix} 6553660128 & -57241262 & -433379614 \\ -57241262 & 3594930590 & -38381041 \\ -433379614 & -38381041 & 909413116 \end{bmatrix} \quad (4.5)$$

When we specify the budget shares of the observed goods as

$$[w_1 \quad w_2 \quad w_3] = [0.6 \quad 0.3 + \varepsilon \quad 0.1 - \varepsilon] \quad (4.6)$$

we obtain $\lambda_1 = \lambda_2 = 1.2$ and $\lambda_3 = 0.8$ for $\varepsilon = 0$. The upper part of table 1 shows the bordered composition matrices and λ_is for $\varepsilon = -10^{-5}$, $\varepsilon = 0$, and $\varepsilon = 10^{-5}$. The results show that the changes are very gradual and that there is no difficulty in tracing the behaviour of the first and second transformed goods in spite of the multiple root problem.

Next, for the same Θ, consider

$$[w_1 \quad w_2 \quad w_3] = [0.6 + 2\varepsilon \quad 0.3 - \varepsilon \quad 0.1 - \varepsilon] \quad (4.7)$$

Again there is no difficulty in tracing the behaviour of the transformed goods when ε takes the values -10^{-5}, 0, and 10^{-5} (see the lower part of table 1), but note that (4.6) and (4.7) are identical for $\varepsilon = 0$ and that the associated second and fifth composition matrices in the table are not identical at all except for the last row. This illustrates the indeterminancy caused by the multiple roots. Also, the different behaviour of the first two transformed goods in the upper and lower half of the table illustrates that this behaviour depends on the path of the budget shares of the observed goods. In the case of (4.6) and (4.7) this path is linear, but there are more complicated cases (see appendix A).

5 Extensions to the theory of the firm

Although this volume deals with the consumer, it is appropriate to pay some attention to the firm also. One reason is the increased awareness of the role of duality theory in these areas; see Deaton (1979), Diewert (1974), Gorman (1976a), and McFadden (1978). An even more important reason in the present context is the fact that the differential approach to the demand and supply side of the firm yields interesting extensions of the results obtained for the consumer. For an integrated treatment see Theil (1980); the remarks which follow summarize the highlights.

Table 1. *Multiple roots*

Bordered composition matrix				λ_i	θ_{Ti}
First perturbation					
0.343530	0.013652	−0.085974	0.271218	1.199967	0.325452
−0.027698	0.261164	−0.004612	0.228854	1.200040	0.274634
0.284168	0.025164	0.190596	0.499928	0.799942	0.399913
0.600000	0.299990	0.100010	1		
0.343465	0.013664	−0.085975	0.271153	1.200000	0.325384
−0.027705	0.261164	−0.004612	0.228847	1.200000	0.274616
0.284240	0.025173	0.190587	0.500000	0.800000	0.400000
0.600000	0.300000	0.100000	1		
0.343401	0.013665	−0.085976	0.271089	1.200033	0.325316
−0.027713	0.261163	−0.004611	0.228839	1.999960	0.274598
0.284312	0.025182	0.190578	0.500072	0.800058	0.400087
0.600000	0.300010	0.099990	1		
Second perturbation					
0.030777	0.303726	−0.021018	0.313485	1.199959	0.376169
0.285064	−0.028885	−0.069567	0.186612	1.199997	0.223934
0.284139	0.025169	0.190595	0.499903	0.799949	0.399897
0.599980	0.300010	0.100010	1		
0.030796	0.303721	−0.021027	0.313490	1.200000	0.376188
0.284964	−0.028894	−0.069560	0.181510	1.200000	0.223811
0.284240	0.025173	0.190587	0.500000	0.800000	0.400000
0.600000	0.300000	0.100000	1		
0.030815	0.303716	−0.021035	0.313496	1.200041	0.376208
0.284863	−0.028903	−0.069553	0.186407	1.200003	0.223689
0.284342	0.025177	0.190579	0.500097	0.800051	0.400103
0.600020	0.299990	0.099990	1		

(1) Consider a single-product firm whose objective is to minimize the total expenditure on n inputs by varying these inputs subject to a technology constraint for given input prices and output. This objective implies (under appropriate regularity conditions) a system of n equations, each describing the demand for an input in terms of input prices and output. Theil (1977) formulated a differential version of this input demand system which is similar but not identical to the demand system (3.13) for the consumer. The difference results from the fact that the firm's problem is not an allocation problem [see the discussion preceding (3.13)]. The firm

does not take the total amount of input expenditure as given; it wants to minimize this amount.

(2) The gap between the firm and the consumer can be eliminated by summing the input demand equations over all inputs. This yields a proportionality between the Divisia input volume index and the change in output which describes the aggregate input change needed to produce the given output change. Then, by substituting this proportionality into the ith input demand equation, we obtain

$$f_i d(\log q_i) = \theta_i d(\log Q) - \psi \sum_{j=1}^{n} \theta_{ij} d \left(\log \frac{p_j}{P'} \right) \tag{5.1}$$

This is the input allocation decision for input i, which should be compared with (3.13). On the left, $f_i = p_i q_i / C$ is the factor share of input i (C = total cost). On the right, $d(\log Q)$ is the Divisia input volume index [equal to $\Sigma_i f_i d(\log q_i)$] and θ_i is the share of input i in marginal cost.[8] The marginal shares $\theta_1, ..., \theta_n$ are the weights of the logarithmic input price changes in the Frisch price index which occurs as a deflator in the last term [compare (3.10)].

(3) The θ_{ij}s in (5.1) are normalized price coefficients which form a symmetric positive definite matrix. We extend the definitions given at the end of section 3 by calling inputs i and j specific substitutes (complements) when θ_{ij} is negative (positive). For (2.5), $[\theta_{ij}]$ is a positive scalar multiple of

$$\begin{bmatrix} f_K & \xi(f_K f_L)^{1/2} \\ \xi(f_K f_L)^{1/2} & f_L \end{bmatrix} \begin{matrix} \text{(capital)} \\ \text{(labour)} \end{matrix} \tag{5.2}$$

which shows that capital and labour are specific substitutes (complements) when the elasticity of output with respect to either input is a decreasing (increasing) function of the other input [see (2.6) and (2.7)].

(4) The input independence transformation changes observed inputs into transformed inputs as stated in the paragraph preceding (2.5). This transformation diagonalizes $[\theta_{ij}]$ relative to the diagonal factor share matrix, which means that total cost and its Divisia indexes are invariant. The composition matrix (2.8) is obtained from (4.3) and (4.4) after appropriate reinterpretations. By dividing (5.1) by f_i we find that θ_i / f_i is the ith Divisia elasticity, i.e. the elasticity of q_i with respect to the Divisia input volume index, which is the input version of an income elasticity. The diagonal of Λ in (4.3) contains here the Divisia elasticities of the transformed inputs.

(5) Laitinen and Theil (1978) extended the above results for a firm which makes m products. They also formulated profit maximizing supply equations in differential form under the condition that the firm takes the product prices as given. These equations describe the change in supply in

terms of the changes in the m product prices, each deflated by a Frisch input price index. Output independence is the case in which the firm's cost function is additive in the m outputs; in that case the change in the supply of each product does not involve the price of any other product.[9] The output independence transformation changes observed products into transformed products so that the firm's cost function is additive in the latter products. The mathematics of this transformation are identical to those of its two predecessors.

6 Constrained principal components

A comparison of principal components with the independence transformation is appropriate for several reasons, one of which is that both techniques diagonalize a square matrix. The principal component transformation changes a set of n correlated variables into a set of n uncorrelated variables. This transformation is not unique because it depends on the units of measurement of the former variables.[10] To make it unique statisticians frequently standardize these variables so that they all have unit variance. Let V be the covariance matrix prior to the standardization and $\hat{V}$ the diagonal matrix whose diagonal is identical to that of V so that $\hat{V}^{-1/2}V\hat{V}^{-1/2}$ is the covariance matrix after the standardization. The principal component technique involves the derivation of latent roots (λ_i) from the determinantal equation

$$\left|\hat{V}^{-1/2}V\hat{V}^{-1/2} - \lambda_i I\right| = 0 \tag{6.1}$$

for $i = 1, ..., n$. Having obtained these λ_is, we can derive the principal components and various weight vectors directly, but these are irrelevant for our present purposes.

In (6.1) we pre- and post-multiply V by $\hat{V}^{-1/2}$, $\hat{V}$ being the diagonal matrix whose diagonal is identical to that of V. In (4.2) we pre- and post-multiply Θ by D^{-1} and D is also a diagonal matrix, but its diagonal has nothing to do with the diagonal of Θ. The diagonal elements of V and $\hat{V}$ are variances. The diagonal of D consists of square roots of budget shares, whereas the diagonal elements of Θ are the θ_{ii}s which describe the change in the demand for a good caused by a change in its own relative price [see (3.13)]. Both D and Θ occur in (4.2) because Θ is diagonalized relative to W in (4.1). The presence of W results from the budget constraint that is imposed on the transformed goods. This constraint takes the form of an invariance constraint on M and its Divisia indexes via the logarithmic change in M [see (3.4)]. Thus, the preference independence transformation may be viewed as an income-constrained principal component transformation; the input independence transformation of the firm is a cost-constrained and the output independence transformation is a revenue-constrained principal component transformation. Such constraints are more natural than the rather arbitrary standardization convention.

A second reason why a comparison of principal components and the independence transformation is appropriate is that it is not difficult to introduce randomness into demand and supply systems. Imagine that we add a random disturbance ε_i to the right-hand sides of (3.13) and (5.1). Does the independence transformation yield uncorrelated disturbances? The answer is yes under the theory of rational random behaviour, provided that account is taken of the fact that both demand equations are obtained by optimization subject to a constraint. The theory of rational random behaviour is beyond the scope of this article (see Theil, 1980, chapters 7 and 8).

Although a comparison with principal components is illuminating, we should not conclude that the usual interpretations of such components are applicable to the independence transformation. It is common among statisticians to arrange the λ_is of (6.1) in descending order and to use the first $r < n$ principal components as an approximate description of the behaviour of the variables. We could follow this practice by considering only the transformed goods with the largest income or Divisia elasticities, but we do not recommend this. If we applied this idea to the meats of section 2 with $r = 2$, we would miss T_1, which accounts for over 70 per cent of the expenditure on the three-meat group [see (2.3)]. If we followed the same procedure for (2.4), we would miss even more. The objective of the independence transformation is not a reduction of the number of dimensions. Its objective is to present the consumer's preferences and the firm's technology in the simplest form. The preference independence transformation makes utility additive around the point of maximum utility. The output independence transformation makes the cost function additive in the outputs around the point of maximum profit. The input independence transformation makes the logarithm of output additive in the inputs around the point of minimum input expenditure.

7 Groups of goods and strong separability

The independence transformation for strongly separable groups

Let there be G groups of goods, $S_1, \ldots, S_G$, so that each good falls under exactly one group. Let the consumer's utility function be the sum of G functions, one for each group,

$$u(q) = u_1(q_A) + u_2(q_B) + \ldots \tag{7.1}$$

where q_A, q_B, ... are subvectors of q, q_A containing the q_is of S_1, q_B those of S_2, and so on. The utility structure of (7.1) is known as strong separability or as block-independence; the marginal utility of each good is then independent of all goods that belong to different groups. When the goods are appropriately numbered, the Hessian matrix U and its inverse are block-diagonal, and so is $[\theta_{ij}]$ in view of (3.15). Therefore, if the ith good belongs to S_g, (3.13) becomes

$$w_i d(\log q_i) = \theta_i d(\log Q) + \phi \sum_{j \in S_g} \theta_{ij} d\left(\log \frac{p_j}{P'}\right) \tag{7.2}$$

where the summation in the substitution term is confined to $j \in S_g$. We conclude that under (7.1) no good is a specific substitute or complement of any good that belongs to a different group. Preference independence is a special case of (7.1) with all groups consisting of one good.

If (7.1) holds, can we apply the preference independence transformation to each group of goods separately? The answer is yes, which we shall illustrate for the case of two groups. We write (4.3) in partitioned form as

$$\begin{bmatrix} X_A' & 0 \\ 0 & X_B' \end{bmatrix} \begin{bmatrix} \Theta_A & 0 \\ 0 & \Theta_B \end{bmatrix} \begin{bmatrix} X_A & 0 \\ 0 & X_B \end{bmatrix} = \begin{bmatrix} \Lambda_A & 0 \\ 0 & \Lambda_B \end{bmatrix} \tag{7.3}$$

$$\begin{bmatrix} X_A' & 0 \\ 0 & X_B' \end{bmatrix} \begin{bmatrix} W_A & 0 \\ 0 & W_B \end{bmatrix} \begin{bmatrix} X_A & 0 \\ 0 & X_B \end{bmatrix} = \begin{bmatrix} I & 0 \\ 0 & I \end{bmatrix} \tag{7.4}$$

where Θ_A and Θ_B are the principal submatrices of Θ which correspond to the two groups, Λ_A and Λ_B are the principal submatrices of Λ (both Λ_A and Λ_B are diagonal), and W_A and W_B are principal submatrices (both diagonal) of W. Clearly, (7.3) and (7.4) are satisfied by $X_A'\Theta_A X_A = \Lambda_A$, $X_A'W_A X_A = I$, and by a similar equation pair with subscript B. A comparison with (4.3) shows that the independence transformation can be applied to each group separately.

The demand for groups and conditional demand

For the developments which will follow in section 8 it is useful to explore the implications of (7.1) further. We write W_g for the combined budget share of the goods of group S_g and $d(\log Q_g)$ for the Divisia volume index of this group:

$$W_g = \sum_{i \in S_g} w_i, \quad d(\log Q_g) = \sum_{i \in S_g} \frac{w_i}{W_g} d(\log q_i) \tag{7.5}$$

The ratio w_i/W_g is the expenditure of the ith good measured as a fraction of the total expenditure on the group to which this good belongs. We shall refer to this ratio as the ith conditional budget share.

We write Θ_g for the combined marginal share of the goods of S_g and $d(\log P'_g)$ for the Frisch price index of this group,

$$\Theta_g = \sum_{i \in S_g} \theta_i, \quad d(\log P'_g) = \sum_{i \in S_g} \frac{\theta_i}{\Theta_g} d(\log p_i) \tag{7.6}$$

where θ_i/Θ_g is the conditional marginal share of good i. Note that this share exists because Θ_g is positive under (7.1). To prove this we use the block-diagonal structure of $[\theta_{ij}]$ to write (3.16) as

$$\sum_{j \in S_g} \theta_{ij} = \theta_i \quad \text{if} \quad i \in S_g \tag{7.7}$$

By summing (7.7) over $i \in S_g$ we obtain Θ_g on the right and the double sum of θ_{ij} over $i, j \in S_g$ on the left. This double sum is positive because of the positive definiteness of $[\theta_{ij}]$.[11]

Summation of (7.2) over $i \in S_g$ yields, after minor rearrangements,

$$W_g d(\log Q_g) = \Theta_g d(\log Q) + \phi \Theta_g d \left(\log \frac{P'_g}{P'} \right) \tag{7.8}$$

which is a composite demand equation for S_g as a group. Next we multiply (7.8) by θ_i/Θ_g and subtract the result from (7.2), so that $d(\log Q)$ disappears. After rearrangements we obtain

$$w_i d(\log q_i) = \frac{\theta_i}{\Theta_g} W_g d(\log Q_g) + \phi \sum_{j \in S_g} \theta_{ij} d \left(\log \frac{p_j}{P'_g} \right) \tag{7.9}$$

which is a conditional demand equation for the ith good within its group. By dividing (7.9) by W_g we find

$$\frac{w_i}{W_g} d(\log q_i) = \frac{\theta_i}{\Theta_g} d(\log Q_g) + \frac{\phi}{W_g} \sum_{j \in S_g} \theta_{ij} d \left(\log \frac{p_j}{P'_g} \right) \tag{7.10}$$

which is the within-group version of (7.2).

The expression on the left in (7.10) is the quantity component of $d(w_i/W_g)$, i.e. of the change in the conditional budget share of the ith good,[12] and it is also the contribution of this good to the Divisia volume index of the group [see (7.5)]. The first term on the right in (7.10) is the volume component and the second is the substitution component. The normalized price coefficients in the latter component are identical to those of (7.2), but the price deflator in (7.10) is the Frisch price index of the group. Similarly, the volume component in (7.10) takes the form of the Divisia volume index of the group multiplied by the ith conditional marginal share, whereas the corresponding term in (7.2) is the Divisia volume index of the consumer's total expenditure multiplied by the (unconditional) marginal share θ_i. A further discussion of (7.8) to (7.10) is postponed until section 8, where we will discuss more general results under a condition weaker than (7.1).

Meats and leisure revisited

The implementation of (7.10) does not require any data on goods outside S_g.[13] Since the preference independence transformation can be directly applied to such a group, the procedure is straightforward. For example, take the meats of section 2 and recall from the discussion following (7.7) that the θ_{ij}s of S_g have a sum equal to Θ_g. Hence the price coefficients of the goods of S_g normalized within the group are of the form θ_{ij}/Θ_g. The maximum-likelihood estimate of the matrix of these coefficients is

$$\begin{bmatrix} 0.863 & -0.131 & -0.018 \\ -0.131 & 0.396 & -0.046 \\ -0.018 & -0.046 & 0.131 \end{bmatrix} \begin{matrix} \text{(beef)} \\ \text{(pork)} \\ \text{(chicken)} \end{matrix} \qquad (7.11)$$

The negative off-diagonal elements in (7.11) indicate that the three meats are specific substitutes of each other. The simultaneous diagonalization (4.3) can then be applied with Θ specified as the matrix (7.11), but note that W has now the conditional budget shares on the diagonal. Also, given that the matrix (7.11) is normalized within the group, its row and column sums are conditional marginal shares. Therefore, the income elasticity shown in (3.11) is now replaced by

$$\frac{\theta_i/\Theta_g}{w_i/W_g} = \frac{\theta_i/w_i}{\Theta_g/W_g} \qquad (7.12)$$

which is the conditional income elasticity of good i within its group. By dividing (7.8) by W_g we find that Θ_g/W_g is the income elasticity of the demand for the group S_g. Hence (7.12) implies that the conditional income elasticity of a good is equal to its unconditional income elasticity θ_i/w_i divided by the group income elasticity.

The application of (4.3) to (7.11) also involves the interpretation of the diagonal elements of Λ as the conditional income elasticities of the transformed goods. In the case of meats these are the income elasticities of the three transformed meats divided by the income elasticity of the demand for the three-meat group. The λ_is associated with the composition matrix (2.3) are $\lambda_1 = 0.74$, $\lambda_2 = 1.90$, and $\lambda_3 = 1.17$. This confirms that T_1 (affordable meat) has the smallest and T_2 (the beef–pork contrast) the largest income elasticity.

Using conditional demand equations is one procedure for the implementation of the independence transformation, but it is not the only one.

Barnett (1974) considered the system (3.13) for all n goods including leisure and specified $n = 5$: services, perishables, semi-durables, durables, and leisure. He then simplified his system as far as his data permitted and concluded that the additive specification (7.1) is acceptable for three groups. Two groups consist of one good each (services and perishables) and the third group consists of three goods: semi-durables, durables, and leisure. Flinn's (1978) maximum-likelihood estimate of the matrix of price coefficients of the last group (normalized within the group) is

$$\begin{bmatrix} 0.501 & 0.042 & -0.342 \\ 0.042 & 0.560 & -0.419 \\ -0.342 & -0.419 & 1.378 \end{bmatrix} \begin{matrix} \text{(semi-durables)} \\ \text{(durables)} \\ \text{(leisure)} \end{matrix} \qquad (7.13)$$

The off-diagonal elements indicate that semi-durables and durables are both specific substitutes of leisure and that the two former goods are specific complements of each other. Application of (4.3) to (7.13) is straightforward, but the interpretation of the λ_is as conditional income elasticities must be amended; they are conditional full income elasticities because of the inclusion of leisure. Below the composition matrix (2.4) we mentioned that the full income elasticities of T_2 and T_3 are substantially larger than that of T_1. This is confirmed by the λ_is associated with (2.4): $\lambda_1 = 0.97$, $\lambda_2 = 5.8$, $\lambda_3 = 4.2$. The unconditional full income elasticities of the three transformed goods are much smaller because the full income elasticity of the group is well below 1.

8 Weak separability

Differential demand equations under weak separability

An assumption which is weaker than (7.1) is that the utility function is some function $f(\ )$, rather than the sum, of G group utility functions:

$$u(q) = f(u_1(q_A), u_2(q_B), \ldots) \qquad (8.1)$$

To clarify this utility structure we consider $\partial u / \partial(p_i q_i)$, the marginal utility of a dollar spent on the ith good, and $\partial^2 u / \partial(p_i q_i)\partial(p_j q_j)$, the change in this marginal utility caused by an additional dollar spent on the jth good. This second derivative vanishes under (7.1) when i and j belong to different groups, but it does not vanish under (8.1). However, it can be shown that at the point of maximum utility this second derivative takes the same value for all i and j in two different groups and that this value depends only on these groups. Thus, if food and clothing are two such groups, an extra dollar spent on either bread or butter has the same effect on the marginal utility of a dollar spent on any good of the clothing group. This means that the utility interaction of goods belonging to different groups is a matter of the groups rather than the individual goods. Accordingly, we can refer to the utility structure (8.1) as 'blockwise dependence', although 'weak separability' is used more often.[14]

It should be clear that the Hessian U is no longer block-diagonal. Hence $[\theta_{ij}]$ is not block-diagonal either, which means that the ith demand equation differs from (7.2) in that it contains changes in relative prices of goods that do not belong to S_g. However, it contains such prices only in the form of Frisch price indexes of groups, thus illustrating blockwise dependence at the level of differential demand equations.

To clarify this further we must note that under (8.1) Frisch price indexes cannot be defined as shown in (7.6). The reason is that if (7.1) is replaced by (8.1), the ratio θ_i/Θ_g need not exist because Θ_g may vanish. But if Θ_g vanishes, so does θ_i for each $i \in S_g$ and the conditional marginal share θ_i^g exists for each $i \in S_g$. Accordingly, we define the Frisch price index of S_g as

$$d(\log P_g') = \sum_{i \in S_g} \theta_i^g d(\log p_i) \tag{8.2}$$

The ith demand equation ($i \in S_g$) under (8.1) can now be written in the form (7.2) except that

$$\phi\theta_i^g \sum_{h \neq g} \Theta_{gh} d\left(\log \frac{P_h'}{P'}\right) \tag{8.3}$$

must be added on the right, where

$$\Theta_{gh} = \sum_{i \in S_g} \sum_{j \in S_h} \theta_{ij} \quad g, h = 1, \ldots, G \tag{8.4}$$

We conclude that under (8.1) the substitution term is the sum of two terms, one containing the prices of the individual goods of the same group and the other the Frisch price indexes of all other groups.

Additional insight is obtained when we sum the demand equation over $i \in S_g$, which yields a composite demand equation for the group:

$$W_g d(\log Q_g) = \Theta_g d(\log Q) + \phi \sum_{h=1}^{G} \Theta_{gh} d\left(\log \frac{P_h'}{P'}\right) \tag{8.5}$$

This is a generalization of (7.8) because we have

$$\sum_{h=1}^{G} \Theta_{gh} = \Theta_g \tag{8.6}$$

which becomes $\Theta_{gg} = \Theta_g$ when the $G \times G$ matrix $[\Theta_{gh}]$ is diagonal, as is the case under (7.1). Note that (7.8), (8.5), and (8.6) are simply 'uppercase versions' of (3.18), (3.13), and (3.16) respectively. Thus, under (8.1) we obtain composite demand equations for groups of goods that take the general form (3.13) of differential demand equations, while under (7.1) such composite equations take the form (3.18) of preference independence.[15]

We obtained the conditional demand equation (7.9) by multiplying the equation for the group by θ_i/Θ_g and subtracting the result from the ith unconditional equation. When we proceed similarly here, replacing θ_i/Θ_g by θ_i^g, we find

$$w_i d(\log q_i) = \theta_i^g W_g d(\log Q_g) + \phi \sum_{j \in S_g} \theta_{ij} d \left(\log \frac{p_j}{P_g'} \right) \tag{8.7}$$

and, after dividing both sides by W_g,

$$\frac{w_i}{W_g} d(\log q_i) = \theta_i^g d(\log Q_g) + \frac{\phi}{W_g} \sum_{j \in S_g} \theta_{ij} d \left(\log \frac{p_j}{P_g'} \right) \tag{8.8}$$

These two equations are identical to (7.9) and (7.10) except for the different notations of the conditional marginal shares.

The composite demand equations for groups and the conditional demand equations for goods within their groups enable the consumer to apply a two-stage budgeting procedure. First, he uses (8.5) for the change in the allocation of total expenditure to the G groups, which requires knowledge of the volume index $d(\log Q)$ and the price indexes of the groups.[16] Second, he uses (8.7) or (8.8) for the change in the allocation of the amount available for each group to the goods of this group. This requires knowledge of the volume index $d(\log Q_g)$ which is available from the first step, and of the price changes of the individual goods.[17] It is easy to visualize a more extensive hierarchy, groups being divided into subgroups and these into goods, but we shall not pursue this matter here.

The independence transformation under weak separability

We know from section 7 that under condition (7.1) the preference independence transformation can be applied to each group separately. The question arises whether a similar result holds for the weaker condition (8.1). It is obviously not sufficient to apply the transformation to the θ_{ij}s of each group, because such a procedure would not eliminate the p_js that are represented by the Frisch price indexes of groups in (8.3). But these indexes are multiplied by Θ_{gh}s, the normalized price coefficients of the composite demand equations for groups [see (8.5)], which suggests that the independence transformation under (8.1) might be implemented as some combination of a transformation for groups (based on the Θ_{gh}s) and G transformations for goods within their groups, one for each group. This problem has been the subject of numerous blackboard discussions in Chicago during many years.

Before proceeding we should mention that there is no problem at all in applying the independence transformation; the question to be considered is whether we can *simplify* this transformation by means of transformations between and within groups. It follows from (8.2) that the normalized price coefficient for the jth relative price ($j \in S_h$, $h \neq g$) in (8.3) is of the form $\Theta_{gh}\theta_i^g\theta_j^h$. This is an element of the matrix $\Theta_{gh}\bar{\theta}_g\bar{\theta}_h'$, where $\bar{\theta}_g$ is the vector of conditional marginal shares of the goods of S_g. Thus, the $n \times n$ normalized price coefficient matrix for $i \in S_g$ and $g = 1, \dots, G$ can be written as

$$
\Theta = \begin{bmatrix}
A_1 & \Theta_{12}\bar{\theta}_1\bar{\theta}_2' & \dots & \Theta_{1G}\bar{\theta}_1\bar{\theta}_G' \\
\Theta_{21}\bar{\theta}_2\bar{\theta}_1' & A_2 & \dots & \Theta_{2G}\bar{\theta}_2\bar{\theta}_G' \\
\cdot & \cdot & & \cdot \\
\cdot & \cdot & & \cdot \\
\cdot & \cdot & & \cdot \\
\Theta_{G1}\bar{\theta}_G\bar{\theta}_1' & \Theta_{G2}\bar{\theta}_G\bar{\theta}_2' & \dots & A_G
\end{bmatrix}
\tag{8.9}
$$

where $A_1, \dots, A_G$ are the principal submatrices of Θ which contain the θ_{ij}s with $i, j \in S_g$ for $g = 1, \dots, G$. Note that the submatrices in (8.9) outside the diagonal blocks all have unit rank. This has led to the conjecture that the composition matrix under (8.1) might also have off-diagonal submatrices of unit rank, which would mean that the transformation treats observed goods of different groups in a 'blockwise' manner.

Suppose that we apply the independence transformation to (8.7) or (8.8) for each S_g. This is always possible and it amounts to a transformation of the matrix (8.9) so that $A_1, \dots, A_G$ are changed into diagonal matrices. Since the sum of the elements of A_g equals Θ_{gg} [see (8.4)] and since the row and column sums of A_g are proportional to the marginal shares of the goods of S_g, A_g thus becomes $\Theta_{gg}(\bar{\theta}_g)_\Delta$, where $(\bar{\theta}_g)_\Delta$ stands for the conditional marginal share vector $\bar{\theta}_g$ written in the form of a diagonal matrix.[18] Hence (8.9) now takes the following form:

$$
\Theta = \begin{bmatrix}
\Theta_{11}(\bar{\theta}_1)_\Delta & \Theta_{12}\bar{\theta}_1\bar{\theta}_2' & \dots & \Theta_{1G}\bar{\theta}_1\bar{\theta}_G' \\
\Theta_{21}\bar{\theta}_2\bar{\theta}_1' & \Theta_{22}(\bar{\theta}_2)_\Delta & \dots & \Theta_{2G}\bar{\theta}_2\bar{\theta}_G' \\
\cdot & \cdot & & \cdot \\
\cdot & \cdot & & \cdot \\
\cdot & \cdot & & \cdot \\
\Theta_{G1}\bar{\theta}_G\bar{\theta}_1' & \Theta_{G2}\bar{\theta}_G\bar{\theta}_2' & \dots & \Theta_{GG}(\bar{\theta}_G)_\Delta
\end{bmatrix}
\tag{8.10}
$$

Is it possible to apply a second transformation, based on the diagonalization of the $G \times G$ price coefficient matrix $[\Theta_{gh}]$ of the groups, so that (8.10) is changed into a diagonal matrix?

To answer this question we should recognize that it involves observed and transformed groups because the preference independence transformation applied to $[\Theta_{gh}]$ changes observed groups into transformed groups. In the case of (7.3) and (7.4) this is trivial; the transformation for groups is the identity transformation and each transformed good is associated with one observed group. But it is not trivial for (8.9) and (8.10). When we apply the independence transformation to either matrix, the computer provides us with transformed goods arranged in the order of increasing or decreasing income elasticities. How can we decide whether a particular transformed good is associated with a particular observed group? This is possible when the transformed goods of a group have certain character-istics in common. One conjecture, based on the proposition that trans-formed goods are identified by their income elasticities, is that when the transformation is applied to (8.10), the conditional income elasticities of the transformed goods of each group are invariant; that is, if i and j belong to the same group, λ_i/λ_j equals the ratio of some θ_i/w_i to some θ_j/w_j. This would enable us to relate each transformed good to one of the goods re-presented by a row and a column of the matrix (8.10).

Numerical explorations

We are not ashamed to admit that the uncertainty as to the exis-tence of transformed groups that can be related to the observed groups has induced us to proceed numerically. We start with a case of two groups consisting of two goods each. The conditional budget shares of the first group are 0.4 and 0.6 and the conditional marginal shares are 0.34 and 0.66 so that the conditional income elasticities are 0.85 and 1.1. The condi-tional budget shares of the second group are 0.9 and 0.1, the conditional marginal shares are 0.81 and 0.19, and hence the conditional income elas-ticities are 0.9 and 1.9. The budget and marginal shares of the first group are $W_1 = 0.8$ and $\Theta_1 = 0.6$ and those of the second $W_2 = 0.2$ and $\Theta_2 = 0.4$. Hence the income elasticities of the groups are $\Theta_1/W_1 = 0.75$ and $\Theta_2/W_2 = 2$, while those of the four goods are 0.6375, 0.825, 1.8, and 3.8. These elasticities are in ascending order and also in the order in which we introduced the goods, which is convenient. The normalized price coef-ficient matrix is as shown in (8.10) for $G = 2$ with the Θ_{gh}s specified as

$$[\Theta_{gh}] = \begin{bmatrix} 0.6 + \varepsilon & -\varepsilon \\ -\varepsilon & 0.4 + \varepsilon \end{bmatrix} \tag{8.11}$$

When ε vanishes, $[\Theta_{gh}]$ is diagonal and so is Θ of (8.10). When we put ε equal to a value close to zero, we should be able to relate the transformed goods to the observed goods if such a relation exists. For $\varepsilon = 10^{-5}$ we ob-tain the following composition matrix:

$$T = 10^{-8} \begin{bmatrix} 32000257 & 0 & 237 & 20 \\ 0 & 48000590 & 548 & 42 \\ -237 & -548 & 17999215 & 0 \\ -20 & -42 & 0 & 1999937 \end{bmatrix} \tag{8.12}$$

This matrix is skew-symmetric as far as the off-diagonal elements are concerned and its 2×2 principal submatrices upper left and lower right are both diagonal. Clearly, in the case of (8.12) the transformed good of row i corresponds to the observed good of column i.

To verify that we are not caught by the special numerical structure of one example we shall consider a second with three groups, the first consisting of two goods, the second of three, and the third of four.[19] The price coefficient matrix of the groups is now of order 3×3 and is specified as

$$[\Theta_{gh}] = \begin{bmatrix} 0.24 - \varepsilon & 3\varepsilon & -2\varepsilon \\ 3\varepsilon & 0.36 - 2\varepsilon & -\varepsilon \\ -2\varepsilon & -\varepsilon & 0.40 + 3\varepsilon \end{bmatrix} \qquad (8.13)$$

The bordered composition matrix is shown in the upper half of table 2 for $\varepsilon = 10^{-5}$ and in the lower half for $\varepsilon = -10^{-5}$. Both matrices reveal the same regularity as (8.12) does. The change in the sign of ε causes the off-diagonal elements to change in sign also. The diagonal elements are all virtually identical to the geometric mean of the corresponding row and column sums, which is the maximum value that any element of a composition matrix can take.[20]

The regularities described above indicate that groups continue to exist after the independence transformation as long as the utility structure (8.1) is sufficiently close to the additive specification (7.1). Also, the conditional income elasticities appear to be invariant under that condition. For example, consider (8.13) for $\varepsilon = 0$ so that the observed and transformed goods are identical. The income elasticities of the two goods of the first group are then 0.36 and 0.76. Next take $\varepsilon = 10^{-5}$, which yields the composition matrix in the upper half of table 2. The income elasticities of the transformed goods corresponding to the first two rows of this matrix are 0.35998499 and 0.75996833, both of which are 0.00417 percent below the corresponding value for $\varepsilon = 0$. For the three goods of the second group the percentage reductions are all equal to 0.00556. For the four goods of the third group the income elasticities at $\varepsilon = 10^{-5}$ exceed those at $\varepsilon = 0$ and the percentage excess is 0.00750 for each of the four. The uniform changes of the unconditional income elasticities of the goods of each group imply that the conditional elasticities remain unchanged.[21]

The changes in the unconditional elasticities appear to be identical to those of the groups. For example, the income elasticities of the three groups are 0.4, 1.2, and 4 in the three-group case. When we select $\varepsilon = 10^{-5}$ and apply the independence transformation to the groups (rather than the individual goods), we obtain the following income elasticities of the transformed groups: 0.39998333, 1.19993334, and 4.00030000. These figures imply percentage deviations from the values 0.4, 1.2, and 4 equal to -0.00417, -0.00556, and 0.00750, respectively. The latter figures are identical to the percentage deviations discussed in the previous para-

Table 2. *Two composition matrices under weak separability*

Composition matrix for $\epsilon = 10^{-5}$

53997511	0	−1822	−868	−249	95	160	132	64	53995023
0	5998692	−962	−389	−79	28	44	34	16	5997385
1823	962	18002982	0	0	49	71	54	24	18005964
868	389	0	9001373	0	30	42	31	14	9002747
249	79	0	0	3000432	40	35	21	8	3000865
−95	−28	−49	−30	−40	1999758	0	0	0	1999516
−160	−44	−71	−42	−35	0	3499648	0	0	3499297
−132	−34	−54	−31	−21	0	0	2999727	0	2999455
−64	−16	−24	−13	−8	0	0	0	1499875	1499749
54000000	6000000	18000000	9000000	3000000	2000000	3500000	3000000	1500000	100000000

Composition matrix for $\epsilon = -10^{-5}$

54002488	0	1823	868	249	−95	−160	−132	−64	54004976
0	6001307	962	389	79	−28	−44	−34	−16	6002614
−1822	−962	17997017	0	0	−49	−71	−54	−24	17994035
−868	−389	0	8998627	0	−30	−42	−31	−13	8997255
−249	−79	0	0	2999568	−40	−35	−21	−8	2999135
95	28	49	30	40	2000242	0	0	0	2000484
160	44	71	42	35	0	3500352	0	0	3500703
132	34	54	31	21	0	0	3000273	0	3000545
64	16	24	14	8	0	0	0	1500125	1500251
54000000	6000000	18000000	9000000	3000000	2000000	3500000	3000000	1500000	100000000

Note: All entries are to be multiplied by 10^{-8}.

graph, which suggests that the income elasticities of the transformation for the groups can be used to obtain the (unconditional) income elasticities of the individual transformed goods.

Also, the composition matrix of the independence transformation for groups is similar to that of the individual goods in that it is skew-symmetric with respect to the off-diagonal elements. For example, when we select $\varepsilon = 10^{-5}$ in (8.13), we obtain the following bordered composition matrix (multiplied by 10^8) of the three groups:

59996805	−3750	555		59993610
3751	30004107	357		30008215
−555	−357	9999087		9998175
60000000	30000000	10000000		100000000

Unfortunately, this composition matrix does not agree with the matrix of the individual goods. When we sum the elements of each submatrix of the composition matrix in the upper part of table 2, we obtain

59996203	−4369	573		59992408
4370	30004787	419		30009576
−573	−419	9999008		9998017
60000000	30000000	10000000		100000000

The row sums of this array are not equal to the budget shares of the transformed groups. Also, it is not true that the off-diagonal submatrices of the composition matrix for the individual goods have unit rank. A visual inspection of (8.12) and table 2 is sufficient to verify this.

Until now we have discussed the case in which the off-diagonal elements of $[\Theta_{gh}]$ are close to zero. Table 3, which is based on the two-group example, provides some information on what happens when ε in (8.11) moves away from zero. The composition matrices on the left show that the 2×2 principal submatrices corresponding to the two groups cease to be diagonal when ε takes increasing positive values, but that the diagonal elements of these submatrices continue to dominate the off-diagonal elements. The skew-symmetry displayed by the off-diagonal submatrices continues in approximate form until $\varepsilon = 0.01$, but it is much less noticeable at $\varepsilon = 0.1$ and even less so at $\varepsilon = 0.2$.

The εs in the right half of the table are all negative and show a more substantial impact, particularly the larger negative εs. This is not surprising because the matrix (8.11) becomes singular at $\varepsilon = -0.24$ but remains pos-

Table 3. *Bordered composition matrices and income elasticities of transformed goods under weak separability*

Bordered composition matrix					λ_i	Bordered composition matrix					λ_i
ε = 0.001						*ε = −0.001*					
32026	0	24	2	32052	0.639	31975	0	−24	−2	31949	0.636
−1	48058	55	4	48117	0.826	−1	47940	−55	−4	47880	0.824
−24	−54	17922	0	17844	1.805	24	55	18079	0	18158	1.796
−2	−4	0	1994	1988	3.810	2	4	0	2006	2013	3.791
32000	48000	18000	2000	100000		32000	48000	18000	2000	100000	
ε = 0.01						*ε = −0.01*					
32290	43	233	20	32585	0.648	31777	46	−243	−21	31560	0.627
−50	48505	536	41	49033	0.838	−54	47318	−558	−43	46664	0.811
−220	−508	17231	−1	16502	1.845	255	591	18800	−1	19645	1.755
−19	−40	0	1939	1881	3.895	22	45	0	2065	2131	3.705
32000	48000	18000	2000	100000		32000	48000	18000	2000	100000	
ε = 0.1						*ε = −0.01*					
36833	3601	2353	208	42995	0.732	33007	8747	−4523	−382	36849	0.507
−3539	47301	3774	305	47841	0.935	−5872	27882	−3673	−276	18061	0.642
−1170	−2648	11858	−38	8001	2.283	4455	10520	26110	−253	40832	1.410
−123	−253	15	1524	1163	4.756	409	852	86	2911	4259	2.860
32000	48000	18000	2000	100000		32000	48000	18000	2000	100000	
ε = 0.2						*ε = −0.2*					
42217	12745	5330	484	60776	0.804	17513	22225	−11203	−1092	27444	0.189
−8755	38480	4214	354	34293	1.023	2281	−2301	277	20	277	0.468
−1297	−2886	8422	−70	4169	2.803	9749	22888	27452	−2110	57978	1.147
−166	−339	34	1232	762	5.720	2457	5188	1473	5183	14300	1.971
32000	48000	18000	2000	100000		32000	48000	18000	2000	100000	

Note: All elements of the bordered composition matrices (not the λ_is) are to be multiplied by 10^{-5}.

100

itive definite at $\varepsilon = 0.24$. The composition matrix for $\varepsilon = -0.2$ contains a negative diagonal element and the smallest root ($\lambda_1 = 0.189$) is much smaller than that at $\varepsilon = -0.1$. The behaviour of the λ_is as functions of ε is otherwise very smooth. When ε moves toward -0.24, λ_1 converges to zero, which implies that the conditional income elasticities cannot be invariant when ε is not close to zero.

The numerical evidence discussed above suggests that when weak separability is treated by means of a Taylor expansion from the point of strong separability, the leading term (but not the next terms) of this expansion has a blockwise structure. The mathematical form of this structure merits a further investigation.

APPENDIX

A Derivations for the preference independence transformation

Invariance constraints

Let each dollar spent on the jth observed good imply r_{ij} dollars spent on the ith transformed good, where r_{ij} is to be determined but is not yet defined. When p_jq_j dollars are spent on the jth observed good, the expenditure on the ith transformed good is thus $r_{ij}p_jq_j$ dollars insofar as this expenditure originates with the jth observed good. Summation over j yields $\Sigma_j \, r_{ij}p_jq_j$, which is the total amount spent on the ith transformed good. Next, by summing this over i, we obtain $\Sigma_j \, (\Sigma_i \, r_{ij})p_jq_j$, the total amount spent on all n transformed goods. We require the total amount spent to be invariant (equal to $M = \Sigma_j \, p_jq_j$), which implies $\Sigma_i \, r_{ij} = 1$ for each j or

$$\iota'R = \iota' \tag{A.1}$$

where $\iota' = [1 \ ... \ 1]$ and R is the $n \times n$ matrix $[r_{ij}]$.

Since the amount spent on the ith transformed good is $\Sigma_j \, r_{ij}p_jq_j$, its budget share equals $\Sigma_j \, r_{ij}p_jq_j/M = \Sigma_j \, r_{ij}w_j$. We write this as

$$W_T\iota = RW\iota \tag{A.2}$$

where W_T is the diagonal matrix with the budget shares $w_{T1}, \, ..., \, w_{Tn}$ of the transformed goods on the diagonal.

We write π and κ for the n-element column vectors whose ith elements are $d(\log p_i)$ and $d(\log q_i)$, respectively. Let the logarithmic price and quantity changes of the transformed goods be linear transformations of their observed counterparts,

$$\pi_T = S\pi, \quad \kappa_T = S\kappa \tag{A.3}$$

in such a way that the Divisia indexes (3.5) and (3.6) are invariant.[22] The index (3.5) equals $\iota'W\pi$ and its transformed counterpart is $\iota'W_T\pi_T = \iota'W_TS\pi$, which is equal to $\iota'WR'S\pi$ in view of (A.2). The invariance of this index thus amounts to

$$R'S = I \tag{A.4}$$

which implies $R' = S^{-1}$. Since $R'\iota = \iota$ follows from (A.1), this yields $S^{-1}\iota = \iota$ and hence, after premultiplication by S,[23]

$$S\iota = \iota \tag{A.5}$$

Note that (A.4) requires R to be nonsingular. The singular case will be considered at the end of this section.

The diagonalization

We write (3.16) as $\Theta\iota = \theta$, where $\theta = [\theta_i]$ is the marginal share vector. The Frisch price index (3.10) can then be written as $\theta'\pi = \iota'\Theta\pi$ and the demand system (3.13) for $i = 1, \ldots, n$ as

$$W\kappa = (\iota'W\kappa)\Theta\iota + \phi\Theta(I - \iota'\Theta)\pi \tag{A.6}$$

where $\iota'W\kappa = d(\log Q)$. We premultiply (A.6) by R:

$$RW\kappa = (\iota'W\kappa)R\Theta\iota + \phi R\Theta(I - \iota'\Theta)\pi$$

The left-hand side equals $RWR'S\kappa = RWR'\kappa_T$ [see (A.3) and (A.4)]. When we proceed similarly on the right, using (A.1) also, we obtain

$$RWR'\kappa_T = (\iota'W\kappa)(R\Theta R')\iota + \phi R\Theta R'[I - \iota'(R\Theta R')]\pi_T \tag{A.7}$$

Since the Divisia volume index is invariant by construction ($\iota'W\kappa = \iota'W_T\kappa_T$), (A.7) is a demand system of the same form as (A.6), with price and quantity changes π_T and κ_T, provided RWR' on the left can be identified with the diagonal budget share matrix W_T. The new normalized price coefficent matrix is $R\Theta R'$,[24] which occurs in the same three places in (A.7) as Θ does in (A.6). Therefore, two conditions are required in order that (A.7) be a differential demand system in preference independent form:

$$RWR' = W_T, \quad R\Theta R' = \text{diagonal} \tag{A.8}$$

These are two conditions on R, which must satisfy (A.1) also.

We proceed to prove that these three conditions are satisfied by

$$R = (X^{-1}\iota)_\Delta X' \tag{A.9}$$

where X and $(X^{-1}\iota)_\Delta$ are defined as in the first subsection of section 4. Condition (A.1) in the form $R'\iota = \iota$ is satisfied by (A.9) because $X(X^{-1}\iota)_\Delta\iota = XX^{-1}\iota = \iota$. Also, $RWR' = (X^{-1}\iota)_\Delta X'WX(X^{-1}\iota)_\Delta = (X^{-1}\iota)_\Delta^2$, where the last step is based on (4.3). Therefore, the first condition in (A.8) is satisfied in the following form:

$$RWR' = W_T = (X^{-1}\iota)^2_\Delta = \text{diagonal} \tag{A.10}$$

The second condition is satisfied in the form

$$R\Theta R' = (X^{-1}\iota)^2_\Delta \Lambda = \text{diagonal} \tag{A.11}$$

which follows from (A.9) and $\Theta = (X')^{-1}\Lambda X^{-1}$ [see (4.3)]. The first term on the right in (A.7) shows that $(R\Theta R')\iota$ is the marginal share vector of the transformed goods; hence the diagonal elements of the matrix product (A.11) are these marginal shares.

To verify the composition matrix (4.4) we recall from the discussion preceding (A.1) that the expenditure on the ith transformed good is $r_{ij}p_jq_j$ dollars insofar as it originates with the jth observed good. By dividing this by M we obtain $r_{ij}w_j$, which is the budget share of the ith transformed good insofar as it originates with the jth observed good. This $r_{ij}w_j$ is the (i, j)th element of the composition matrix T and obviously also the (i, j)th element of RW, so that $T = RW$. We then obtain (4.4) from $RW = (X^{-1}\iota)_\Delta X'(X')^{-1}X^{-1} = (X^{-1}\iota)_\Delta X^{-1}$, where use is made of (A.9) and $W = (X')^{-1}X^{-1}$ [see (4.3)]. Post-multiplication of $T = RW$ by ι gives $T\iota = RW\iota = W_T\iota$ [see (A.2)]; hence the row sums of T are the budget shares of the transformed goods. Also, $\iota'T = \iota'RW = \iota'W$, which proves that the column sums of T are the budget shares of the observed goods.

Multiple roots and near-multiple roots

The solution (A.9) is unique when there are no multiple roots [i.e. no equal diagonal elements in Λ in (4.3)].[25] We proceed to consider a pair of multiple roots, $\lambda_1 = \lambda_2 \neq \lambda_i$ for $i > 2$. The characteristic vectors x_1 and x_2 associated with the multiple root are not uniquely determined; we may post-multiply $[x_1 \quad x_2]$ by an arbitrary 2×2 orthogonal matrix and the two vectors which emerge satisfy (4.1) and the normalization rules. This indeterminacy of x_1 and x_2 implies a similar indeterminacy of the budget and marginal shares of the two transformed goods. If $\lambda_3, ..., \lambda_n$ are distinct, the budget and marginal shares of the last $n - 2$ transformed goods are well defined, so that the combined budget share and the combined marginal share of the first two are also well defined. Also, the first two rows of the composition matrix are indeterminate, although constrained by the fact that their sum is determinate. This means that the two transformed goods with equal income elasticities are identical or, equivalently, that they behave like one good so that there are only $n - 1$ transformed goods.

We proceed to discuss the perturbations of table 1, the last column of which contains the marginal shares of the transformed goods. We perturb

W by a diagonal matrix dW; this matrix must satisfy $\iota'(dW)\iota = 0$ because the budget shares add up to 1. The perturbed version of (4.1) is

$$[\Theta - (\lambda_i + d\lambda_i)(W + dW)](x_i + dx_i) = 0 \qquad (A.12)$$

Using (4.1) and ignoring products of differentials, we obtain

$$(\Theta - \lambda_i W)dx_i = (d\lambda_i)Wx_i + \lambda_i(dW)x_i \qquad (A.13)$$

which we premultiply by x_i' to obtain

$$d\lambda_i = -\lambda_i x_i'(dW)x_i \qquad (A.14)$$

If dW_i is multiplied by -1, so is $d\lambda_i$ in view of (A.14) and so is dx_i in view of (A.13). This explains why the two perturbations of table 1 have an approximately linear effect on the λ_is, θ_{Ti}s, and the elements of the bordered composition matrix.

The nature of this effect can be conveniently illustrated geometrically (Figure 1) for $n = 3$. Point W in the triangle below corresponds to $w_1 = 0.6$, $w_2 = 0.3$, $w_3 = 0.1$, which is the point at which $\lambda_1 = \lambda_2$ in table 1. The first perturbation keeps w_1 at 0.6 but lets w_2 increase at the expense of w_3. This path is indicated by the horizontal arrow through W. The second perturbation is orthogonal to the first and raises w_1 while reducing w_2 and w_3 equally. This path corresponds to the vertical arrow through W. Any other linear path through W would have the same general characteristics as the two displayed in table 1, but the path need not be linear. A nonlinear path is shown in the lower part of the triangle with W' the point at which $\lambda_1 = \lambda_2$. In this case θ_{T1} and θ_{T2} and the first two rows of the bordered composition matrix will change quickly; how quickly depends on the degree of curvature of the path. Tracing the behaviour of the trans-

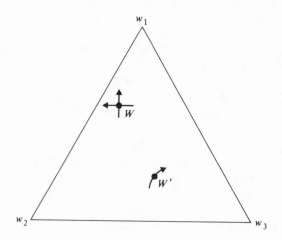

Figure 1

formed goods as a function of the budget shares of the observed goods will now be much more difficult.

The transformation in the singular case

We write $\pi_T = S\pi$ [see (A.3)] in scalar form as

$$d(\log p_{Ti}) = \sum_{j=1}^{n} s_{ij} d(\log p_j) \tag{A.15}$$

where $d(\log p_{Ti})$ is the ith element of π_T and s_{ij} is the (i,j)th element of S. It follows from (A.4) and (A.9) that

$$S = (X^{-1}\iota)_{\Delta}^{-1} X^{-1} \tag{A.16}$$

but this solution does not apply when $(X^{-1}\iota)_{\Delta}$ is singular. This occurs when $X^{-1}\iota$ contains a zero element so that R is singular and no S exists which satisfies (A.4).

To interpret this we start with the case in which all elements of $X^{-1}\iota$ are non-zero. Hence (A.15) applies with $[s_{ij}] = S$ defined as in (A.16). Next we consider a perturbation of the consumer's preferences so that the ith element of $X^{-1}\iota$ moves toward zero.[26] It follows from (A.16) that the ith row of S will consist of elements that increase beyond bounds, so that (A.15) implies that the logarithmic price change of the ith transformed good moves toward $\pm\infty$. If the move is toward ∞, this good is priced out of the market and nothing is spent on it in the limit. If the move is toward $-\infty$, the good becomes free and, again, nothing is spent on it in the limit. Thus, a transformed good on which nothing is spent can be viewed as a limiting case with either zero or infinite price that results from the consumer's preferences. The presence of such a good implies that there are effectively only $n - 1$ transformed goods. This is similar to the case of a multiple root [see the paragraph preceding (A.12)], but note the difference. In the latter case we have two transformed goods which are indistinguishable and behave like one good because they have the same income elasticity and it is impossible to separate their compositions in terms of the observed goods. In the present case there is no identification problem; there is simply one good on which nothing is spent.

B Barten's matrix equation and the case in which the Hessian of the utility function is not definite

A matrix equation and its solution

By differentiating the budget constraint $p'q = M$ with respect to M and p' we obtain

$$p' \frac{\partial q}{\partial M} = 1, \quad p' \frac{\partial q}{\partial p'} = -q' \tag{B.1}$$

where $\partial q/\partial p'$ is the $n \times n$ matrix $[\partial q_i/\partial p_j]$. Next, by differentiating the proportionality of marginal utilities and prices, $\partial u/\partial q_i = \lambda p_i$ where λ is the marginal utility of income, with respect to M and p' we find

$$U \frac{\partial q}{\partial M} = \frac{\partial \lambda}{\partial M} p, \quad U \frac{\partial q}{\partial p'} = \lambda I + p \frac{\partial \lambda}{\partial p'} \tag{B.2}$$

We can combine (B.1) and (B.2) in partitioned matrix form,

$$\begin{bmatrix} U & p \\ p' & 0 \end{bmatrix} \begin{bmatrix} \partial q/\partial M & \partial q/\partial p' \\ -\partial \lambda/\partial M & -\partial \lambda/\partial p' \end{bmatrix} = \begin{bmatrix} 0 & \lambda I \\ 1 & -q' \end{bmatrix} \tag{B.3}$$

which is Barten's fundamental matrix equation.

If U is negative definite, the inverse of the bordered Hessian on the far left in (B.3) can be written as

$$\frac{1}{p'U^{-1}p} \begin{bmatrix} (p'U^{-1}p)U^{-1} - U^{-1}p(U^{-1}p)' & U^{-1}p \\ (U^{-1}p)' & -1 \end{bmatrix} \tag{B.4}$$

Pre-multiplication of (B.3) by the matrix (B.4) yields

$$\frac{\partial \lambda}{\partial M} = \frac{1}{p'U^{-1}p}, \quad \frac{\partial q}{\partial M} = \frac{1}{p'U^{-1}p} U^{-1}p \tag{B.5}$$

$$\frac{\partial q}{\partial p'} = \lambda U^{-1} - \frac{\lambda}{p'U^{-1}p} U^{-1}p(U^{-1}p)' - \frac{1}{p'U^{-1}p} U^{-1}pq' \tag{B.6}$$

after which (3.8) follows from (B.6) and some rearrangements based on (B.5).

What happens if the Hessian is not definite?

The assumption of a negative definite U guarantees that utility is maximized subject to the budget constraint, but this assumption is stronger than necessary. A sufficient condition is

$$x'Ux < 0 \quad \text{for all} \quad x \neq 0 \quad \text{satisfying} \quad x'p = 0 \tag{B.7}$$

which is constrained negative definiteness.[27] We define

$$A = -P^{-1}UP^{-1} \tag{B.8}$$

where P is the diagonal matrix with $p_1, ..., p_n$ on the diagonal. For $y = Px$ we have $x'p = y'P^{-1}p = y'\iota$, so that (B.7) is equivalent to

$$y'Ay > 0 \quad \text{for all} \quad y \neq 0 \quad \text{satisfying} \quad y'\iota = 0 \tag{B.9}$$

It follows from (3.17) and (B.8) that if U and hence Θ are nonsingular,

$$A = k\Theta^{-1} \tag{B.10}$$

where $k = -\phi M/\lambda$. However, U and A may be singular semi-definite or indefinite under (B.7) and (B.9). Examples of a semi-definite A_1 and an indefinite A_2 satisfying (B.9) are

$$A_1 = \begin{bmatrix} 0.8 & 0.4 \\ 0.4 & 0.2 \end{bmatrix}, \quad A_2 = \begin{bmatrix} 0.8 & 0.45 \\ 0.45 & 0.2 \end{bmatrix} \tag{B.11}$$

which may be verified from the fact that (B.9) for $n = 2$ implies a y vector of the form $[y_1 \ -y_1]'$ for some non-zero scalar y_1.

The possible nonexistence of Θ (due to the singularity of U) does not by itself exclude the preference independence transformation. The objective of this transformation is to make utility additive; this requires a diagonalization of U, which can be performed even if U is singular. It will be convenient to proceed under the temporary assumption that U is non-singular so that Θ exists. We premultiply (4.1) by Θ^{-1}, which yields $(I - \lambda_i \Theta^{-1} W)x_i = 0$. This can be written as

$$\left(\Theta^{-1} - \frac{1}{\lambda_i} W^{-1} \right) Wx_i = 0 \tag{B.12}$$

which shows that $1/\lambda_i$ is a latent root, and Wx_i a characteristic vector associated with this root, of the diagonalization of Θ^{-1} relative to W^{-1}. When we normalize according to $(Wx_i)'W^{-1}(Wx_j) = 0$ for $i \neq j$ and $(Wx_i)'W^{-1}(Wx_i) = 1$, we obtain $X'WX = I$ as before.

Since (B.10) shows that A is inversely proportional to Θ if Θ exists, (B.12) suggests a diagonalization of A relative to W^{-1}:

$$(A - \delta_i W^{-1})Wx_i = 0 \tag{B.13}$$

If A is singular, one δ_i, say δ_1, will be zero. If A is indefinite, δ_1 will be negative. The former case could be viewed as a limiting case in which one transformed good has an income elasticity that increases beyond bounds $(\lambda_1 \to \infty)$. In the latter case there would be an inferior transformed good $(\lambda_1 < 0)$. Such goods could be considered acceptable if nothing were spent on them. Unfortunately, this is not true.

To prove this we define Δ as the diagonal matrix with $\delta_1, ..., \delta_n$ on the diagonal. We can then write (B.13) for $i = 1, ..., n$ in the form $AWX = X\Delta$. We postmultiply this by X', $AWXX' = X\Delta X'$, implying

$$A = X\Delta X' \tag{B.14}$$

because $WX = (X')^{-1}$ follows from $X'WX = I$. On combining (B.14) with (B.9) we obtain $y'X\Delta X'y > 0$ for any $y \neq 0$ satisfying $y'\iota = 0$. We define $z = X'y$ and conclude that $z'\Delta z > 0$ holds for any $z \neq 0$ which satisfies $z'X^{-1}\iota = 0$. This is equivalent to the proposition that if $z \neq 0$ and $z'\Delta z \leq 0$, then $z'X^{-1}\iota \neq 0$. We specify z as the first column of the $n \times n$ unit matrix; then $z'\Delta z \leq 0$ becomes $\delta_1 \leq 0$ and $z'X^{-1}\iota \neq 0$ becomes the statement that the top element of $X^{-1}\iota$ is non-zero. But this element is a square root of w_{T1} in view of (A.10), so that a positive amount is spent on the transformed good with $\delta_1 \leq 0$. Ironically, the *only* good for which it is possible to prove that a positive amount is spent is that which we would like to have zero expenditure!

This result suggests that a replacement of the negative definiteness of U by the weaker assumption (B.7) is unsatisfactory from the viewpoint of the preference independence transformation. It is appropriate to add that (B.7) is not very much weaker when we require it to be satisfied for *any* price vector p. This stronger version of (B.7) is still somewhat weaker than unconstrained negative definiteness, because all elements of p must be positive. The issue is probably of minor importance, since the application of the transformation to statistical data typically involves groups of goods under the assumption of strong separability and this assumption involves unconstrained negative definiteness.

C Finite change parametrizations

The application of differential consumer demand systems to data requires a finite change parametrization. We define $Dx_t = \log(x_t/x_{t-1})$ as the log-change in any positive variable x from $t - 1$ to t. The most popular finite-change version of (3.13) is

$$\bar{w}_{it}Dq_{it} = \theta_i DQ_t + \sum_{j=1}^{n} \nu_{ij}\left(Dp_{jt} - \sum_{k=1}^{n}\theta_k Dp_{kt}\right) + \varepsilon_{it} \qquad (C.1)$$

where $\bar{w}_{it} = (w_{i,t-1} + w_{it})/2$, $DQ_t = \Sigma_i\, \bar{w}_{it}Dq_{it}$, $\nu_{ij} = \phi\theta_{ij}$, and ε_{it} is a random disturbance. The ν_{ij}s are not identifiable without additional restrictions; this problem is related to their lack of invariance under monotone transformations of the utility function (see Theil, 1975–76, section 2.5). One way of solving this problem consists of writing the substitution term of (C.1) as $\Sigma_j\, \pi_{ij}Dp_{jt}$, where $\pi_{ij} = \nu_{ij} - \phi\theta_i\theta_j$ is the (i, j)th Slutsky coefficient, which is invariant. The next step is to simplify the model in the direction of preference independence as much as the data permit. See also Barnett (1979) for an interesting contribution to the aggregated (per capita) version of this model.

In the case of conditional systems, (C.1) can be implemented in two alternative forms, one based on (7.9) and the other on (7.10). Both versions were applied to meats and (7.10) was used because of its better fit. Details can be found in Theil (1975–76, chapter 7).

Notes

1 Research supported in part by NSF Grant SOC 76–82718.
2 The numerical results in the discussion which follows are from chapters 7 and 13 of Theil (1975–76).
3 The negative definiteness of U guarantees the existence of a budget-constrained utility maximum, but a weaker condition is sufficient for this exis-

tence. In appendix B we analyse some implications of this weaker condition.

4 This may be verified by writing the substitution term of (3.13) as a multiple ϕ of $\Sigma_j \theta_{ij} d(\log p_j) - \theta_i d(\log P')$ [see (3.16)]. Summation of this expression over i yields zero because of the symmetry of $[\theta_{ij}]$, (3.16), and $\Sigma_i \theta_i = 1$.

5 The derivative $\partial \lambda / \partial M$ equals the reciprocal of $p' U^{-1} p$, which is obtained by solving Barten's fundamental matrix equation. This matrix equation and its solution are given in appendix B.

6 Equation (3.16) follows from (3.15) and $\theta_i = (\lambda / \phi M) p_i \Sigma_j u^{ij} p_j$, which is obtained by solving Barten's fundamental matrix equation.

7 This definition differs from Hicks' which is based on the total substitution effect. Houthakker's definition is more useful for our present purposes.

8 That is, θ_i equals the ratio of $\partial(p_i q_i)/\partial z$ to $\partial C/\partial z$, where z = output. If the firm maximizes profit under competitive conditions on the supply side, θ_i equals the additional expenditure on input i caused by an extra dollar of output revenue, which is more directly comparable to (3.2). The ψ in (5.1) is a curvature measure of the logarithmic cost function; it is positive, implying $-\psi < 0$ in (5.1), to be compared with $\phi < 0$ in (3.13).

9 Hall (1973) has shown that under output independence the multi-product firm can be split up into m single-product firms, each making one of the products of the multi-product firm, in such a way that when the single-product firms independently maximize profits, they supply the same rate of output and use the same total quantity of each input as the multi-product firm.

10 This problem does not arise when all variables are expressed in the same unit. (This applies to Stone's (1947) application in which all variables are in dollars per year.) However, even in that case we obtain different results when we measure the variables from their natural zeros or from their means.

11 Also note that when the group indexes in (7.5) and (7.6) are weighted with the group budget and marginal shares W_g and Θ_g, respectively, we obtain the indexes (3.6) and (3.10) which refer to the budget as a whole.

12 The other components are $(w_i/W_g)d(\log p_i)$ and $-(w_i/W_g)d(\log W_g M)$. The first of these is the price component of the change in the conditional budget share and the second is the component which is attributable to the change in the amount spent on the group. This result should be viewed as a within-group version of (3.12).

13 The implementation does require a parametrization; see appendix C for this matter.

14 The analogous constraint on the input structure of a firm was considered by MaCurdy (1975).

15 Additional 'uppercase extensions' can be formulated. We may define S_g and S_h as specific substitutes (complements) when Θ_{gh} in (8.5) is negative (positive). Under (7.1) no group is a specific substitute or complement of any other group. Also, no group can be inferior under (7.1) because $\Theta_g > 0$, but inferior groups can exist under (8.1).

16 The required price indexes of the groups include both Divisia and Frisch price indexes. The reason is that the logarithmic change in the amount spent on S_g equals $d(\log P_g) + d(\log Q_g)$, where $d(\log P_g)$ (no prime!) is the Divisia price index of S_g. This index is obtained by substituting p_i for q_i in (7.5).

17 When random disturbances are added to the demand equations, the separation of the allocation into two steps requires the disturbances of the composite demand equations for groups to be uncorrelated with those of the conditional equations. It can be shown that this is indeed the case under rational random behaviour; this theory implies that disturbances of conditional demand equations of different groups are also uncorrelated.

18 Strictly speaking, we should use a notation indicating that these conditional

marginal shares refer to goods obtained from the independence transformation applied to the group, but we prefer not to do so to simplify the notation. It is, of course, possible that the G group utility functions (8.1) are additive in their arguments, in which case (8.9) takes the form (8.10) without any intermediate transformation. This special case was considered particularly by Pearce (1961; 1964). In the discussion later in this section we shall proceed as if (8.10) refers to observed goods.

19 The budget shares of the groups are specified as 0.6, 0.3, and 0.1; the marginal shares implied by (8.13) are 0.24, 0.36, and 0.40 for any value of ε, so that the income elasticities are 0.4, 1.2, and 4. The conditional budget shares are specified as 0.9 and 0.1 for the first group; 0.6, 0.3, and 0.1 for the second; and 0.20, 0.35, 0.30, and 0.15 for the third. The conditional marginal shares are 0.81 and 0.19 for the first group; 0.54, 0.30, and 0.16 for the second; and 0.12, 0.28, 0.33, and 0.27 for the third. The unconditional income elasticities are 0.36, 0.76, 1.08, 1.20, 1.92, 2.4, 3.2, 4.4, and 7.2. As in the earlier example, these elasticities are in ascending order and also in the order in which the goods are introduced.

20 When we divide each element of the composition matrix by the geometric mean of the corresponding row and column sums, an orthogonal matrix emerges. The elements of such a matrix are all between -1 and 1. See Theil (1975–76, section 12.3).

21 The conditional budget and marginal shares are not invariant. One might surmise that these shares are invariant, given that the conditional demand equations take the same form under weak and strong separability, but this conjecture is not correct. For example, when we change ε from zero to 10^{-5} in (8.13), the unconditional budget share of the first transformed good declines by 0.0092 per cent and that of the second (which belongs to the same group) by 0.0436 per cent. The invariance of the conditional budget shares would require these two percentage changes to be equal.

22 It is possible to proceed under the weaker condition that the two transformations may be different: $\pi_T = S_1\pi$ and $\kappa_T = S_2\kappa$. However, when both Divisia indexes are constrained to be invariant, both S_1 and S_2 must be equal to the inverse of R' and, hence, equal to each other.

23 When the prices of all observed goods change proportionately, π is a scalar multiple of ι so that (A.3) and (A.5) imply that π_T is equal to the same scalar multiple of ι. This proves the statement on proportionate price changes at the end of the first subsection of section 4.

24 This matrix is indeed normalized because $\iota'R\Theta R'\iota = \iota'\Theta\iota = 1$.

25 This statement is subject to the qualification that the right-hand side of (A.9) may be pre-multiplied by an arbitrary permutation matrix. The only effect of such a multiplication is a change in the order in which the transformed goods are listed.

26 The simplest way to visualize such a perturbation is in terms of the Hessian matrix of the utility function. A change in this Hessian affects the matrix $[\theta_{ij}]$ in view of (3.15) and hence also X [see (4.3)].

27 It was shown by Barten, Kloek, and Lempers (1969) that the bordered Hessian matrix on the far left in (B.3) continues to be non-singular under this weaker condition so that (B.3) can still be solved.

References

Barnett, W. A. (1974) *Labor Supply and the Allocation of Consumption Expendi-*

ture. Doctoral dissertation, Carnegie-Mellon University.

(1979) 'Theoretical Foundations for the Rotterdam Model'. *Review of Economic Studies*.

Barten, A. P. (1964) 'Consumer Demand Functions Under Conditions of Almost Additive Preferences'. *Econometrica*, **32**, pp. 1–38.

Barten, A. P., Kloek, T, and Lempers, F. B. (1969) 'A Note on a Class of Utility and Production Functions Yielding Everywhere Differentiable Demand Functions'. *Review of Economic Studies*, **36**, pp. 109–11.

Becker, G. S. (1965) 'A Theory of the Allocation of Time'. *Economic Journal*, **75**, pp. 493–517.

Boyle, J. R., Gorman, W. M., and Pudney, S. E. (1977) 'Demand for Related Goods: A Progress Report'. *Frontiers of Quantitative Economics*, Vol. IIIA (M. D. Intriligator, ed.), pp. 87–101. Amsterdam: North-Holland Publishing Company.

Brooks, R. B. (1970) *Diagonalizing the Hessian Matrix of the Consumer's Utility Function*. Doctoral dissertation, The University of Chicago.

Deaton, A. S. (1979) 'The Distance Function and Consumer Behaviour with Applications to Index Numbers and Optimal Taxation'. *Review of Economic Studies*, **46**, pp. 391–405.

Diewert, W. E. (1974) 'Applications of Duality Theory'. *Frontiers of Quantitative Economics*, Vol. II (M. D. Intriligator and D. A. Kendrick, eds.), pp. 106–71. Amsterdam: North-Holland Publishing Company, 1974.

Divisia, F. (1925) 'L'indice monétaire et la théorie de la monnaie'. *Revue d'Economie Politique*, **39**, pp. 980–1008.

Flinn, C. (1978) 'A Preference Independence Transformation Involving Leisure'. Report 7847 of the Center for Mathematical Studies in Business and Economics, The University of Chicago.

Frisch, R. (1932) *New Methods of Measuring Marginal Utility*. Tübingen: J. C. B. Mohr.

Geary, R. C. (1950) 'A Note on "A Constant Utility Index of the Cost of Living"'. *Review of Economic Studies*, **18**, pp. 65–6.

Gorman, W. M. (1956) 'Demand for Related Goods'. Journal Paper J3129, Iowa Agricultural Experiment Station.

(1959) 'Demand for Fish: An Application of Factor Analysis'. Birmingham Discussion Paper A6.

(1976a) 'Tricks with Utility Functions'. *Essays in Economic Analysis* (M. J. Artis and A. R. Nobay, eds.), pp. 211–43. Cambridge University Press.

(1976b) 'A Possible Procedure for Analysing Quality Differentials in the Egg Market'. Discussion Paper No. B4 of the London School of Economics and Political Science.

Hall, R. E. (1973) 'The Specification of Technology with Several Kinds of Output'. *Journal of Political Economy*, **81**, pp. 878–92.

Houthakker, H. S. (1960) 'Additive Preferences'. *Econometrica*, **28**, pp. 244–57; errata, **30** (1962), p. 633.

Klein, L. R., and Rubin, H. (1948) 'A Constant-Utility Index of the Cost of Living'. *Review of Economic Studies*, **15**, pp. 84–7.

Laitinen, K., and Theil, H. (1978) 'Supply and Demand of the Multiproduct Firm'. *European Economic Review*, **11**, pp. 107–54.

Lancaster, K. J. (1966) 'A New Approach to Consumer Theory'. *Journal of Political Economy*, **74**, pp. 132–57.

(1971) *Consumer Demand: A New Approach*. New York: Columbia University Press.

MaCurdy, T. (1975) 'The Firm's Demand for Inputs When These Inputs Are Blockwise Dependent'. Report 7539 of the Center for Mathematical Studies in Business and Economics, The University of Chicago.

McFadden, D. (1978) 'Cost, Revenue, and Profit Functions'. *Production Economics: A Dual Approach to Theory and Applications* (M. Fuss and D. McFadden, eds.). Amsterdam: North-Holland Publishing Company.

Pearce, I. F. (1961) 'An Exact Method of Consumer Demand Analysis'. *Econometrica,* **29,** pp. 499–516.

(1964) *A Contribution to Demand Analysis.* Oxford University Press.

Stone, R. (1947) 'On the Interdependence of Blocks of Transactions'. Supplement, *Journal of the Royal Statistical Society,* **9,** pp. 1–45.

(1954) 'Linear Expenditure Systems and Demand Analysis: An Application to the Pattern of British Demand'. *Economic Journal,* **64,** pp. 511–27.

Theil, H. (1967) *Economics and Information Theory.* Amsterdam: North-Holland Publishing Company.

(1975–76) *Theory and Measurement of Consumer Demand.* Two volumes. Amsterdam: North-Holland Publishing Company.

(1977) 'The Independent Inputs of Production'. *Econometrica,* **45,** pp. 1303–27.

(1980) *The System-Wide Approach to Microeconomics.* University of Chicago Press.

Note added in proof: Several theoretical and empirical developments have occurred since this article was written in 1978. Rossi (1979) proved that when all n observed goods are specific substitutes (complements), the independence transformation yields one transformed good in which all observed goods are positively represented, viz., the transformed good with the smallest (largest) income or Divisia elasticity, all $n - 1$ other transformed goods being contrasts between observed goods. Chang (1980) derived an interesting result for the *maximal* degree of dependence among observed consumer goods, inputs or outputs. Theil (1979) introduced the notion of equicorrelated substitutes and a similar concept for Nasse's (1970) extension of the linear expenditure system. The independence transformation based on this extension takes a particularly simple form; it was applied by Meisner and Clements (1979) to Australian data. Offenbacher (1980) applied the input independence transformation to the demand for money by US firms. Theil (1980) proved that when the consumer's tastes are close to preference independence, each transformed good is uniquely associated with one observed good. Also, corresponding off-diagonal elements of the composition matrix are then equal apart from sign and are inversely proportional to the difference between the income elasticities of the two associated observed goods. A blockwise extension of this result (see Section 8 above) would be appropriate.

Chang, F.-R. (1980) "The Maximal Degree of Dependence Among Inputs, Outputs, and Consumer Goods." *Economics Letters,* 5, pp. 93–96.

Meisner, J. F., and Clements, K. W. (1979) "Specific Complements and the Demand for Money in Australia." *Economics Letters,* 3, pp. 207–210.

Nasse, P. (1970) "Analyse des effets de substitution dans un système complet de fonctions de demande." *Annales de l'Insée,* 5, pp. 81–110.

Offenbacher, E. K. (1980) "The Basic Functions of Money: An Application of the Input Independence Transformation." *Economics Letters,* forthcoming.

Rossi, P. E. (1979) "The Independence Transformation of Specific Substitutes and Specific Complements." *Economics Letters,* 2, pp. 299–301.

Theil, H. (1979) "Equicorrelated Substitutes and Nasse's Extension of the Linear Expenditure System." *Economics Letters,* 3, pp. 81–4.

Theil, H. (1980) "The Independence Transformation under Almost Additivity." *Economics Letters,* forthcoming.

5 The analysis of consumption and demand in the USSR

N. P. FEDORENKO
AND N. M. RIMASHEVSKAYA

In the USSR, consumption and demand undergo both constant growth in volume and qualitative structural change. The total growth of consumption and demand may be illustrated by the data on retail sales which by 1978 had increased 2.4-fold over the 1965 level. In addition, consumption and demand patterns constantly undergo considerable qualitative changes due to increases in the consumption of, and demand for, high-calorific food, for non-foods that satisfy developing needs, and for products that make house-keeping easier and save time. Thus the total sale of meat and meat products increased 2.1 times between 1965 and 1977. For the same period the corresponding figure for milk and milk products was 2.1, for eggs 3.7, and for fruit 2.2. At the same time, the consumption of bread and potatoes *per capita* has decreased and the level of sugar and vegetable oil consumption has been constant, in accordance with physiological standards.

Among non-foods the demand for knitted garments and carpets had the highest rate of growth during this period (i.e. 1965–77) increasing 3.3-fold and 5.7 respectively. Furniture sales increased 2.3-fold, articles for cultural and domestic needs 2.4-fold and so on. The provision of most durable goods has also been improved. Thus the supply of TV sets increased 3.3 times during the period, refrigerators by 6.5 times, washing machines by 3.3 times, vacuum cleaners by 3.1 times and so on.

These figures testify to a high rate of growth of current demand and consumption in the USSR which is the result of improved welfare, the acceleration of scientific and technological progress and its effect on the life-style of the Soviet people. Nonetheless, it is necessary to note that demand and consumption growth is rather uncertain, since it depends on many different factors. Some of them are of a social and psychological nature and are extremely difficult to deal with. This makes the study of consumption and demand complex, though at the same time it stimulates investigations in the area and promotes the improvement of existing analytical techniques and the invention of new ones.

113

The needs of planning and management in the socialist economies also stimulate work in this area. Consumption and demand forecasts influence long-term, medium-term, and short-term plans for industrial development, welfare improvements and other social and economic problems of primary importance. The analysis of consumption and demand is also essential for routine planning and management. Its results are used by industries at the stage of the elaboration of their current production programmes and by trading organizations deciding upon their orders for consumer goods. They are also taken into account for the allocation of production resources in order to provide the population of the various regions with goods in the best possible way.

All these inspire the study of consumption and demand and provide the challenge for finding new techniques in analysis and forecasting which combine mathematics with informal analytical approaches towards the solution of all types of problems in economic planning. Nowadays the study of consumption and demand in the USSR is considered to be one of the most important branches of mathematical economics. This tendency has become increasingly important in our country since the end of the fifties and the beginning of the sixties although several papers of interest in this area were published as early as the twenties, in particular, by S. G. Strumilin (1965) and V. A. Bazarov (1927).

Currently, we have several mathematical economic models in the USSR and these constitute the basis for computer forecasts of consumption and demand for various time horizons. The range of different consumption and demand models can be divided into three classes: correlation – regression models; normative consumer budget models; and structural models.

1 Correlation – regression models

The models of the first class in our classification are based, at least partially, on the ideas of Sir Richard Stone (Stone, 1954). The version of the linear expenditure system which is used can formally be described by the equations:

$$R_{jt} = P_{jt}C_{jt} = \alpha_j P_{jt} + \beta_j(R_t - P'_{jt}\alpha_j) \tag{1}$$

$$i'\beta = 1 \tag{2}$$

$$\left.\begin{array}{l} \alpha_j = \alpha_j^* + \dfrac{1}{t}\,\alpha_j^{**} \\[2mm] \beta_j = \beta_j^* + \dfrac{1}{t}\,\beta_j^{**} \end{array}\right\} \tag{3)[1]}$$

$$C_{lt}^j = f_i(R_{jt}, P_{C_u}^j, u_{it}) \tag{4}$$

where R stands for the total consumer income (expenditure), R_{jt} is the money demand for the group of commodities or services j, C_{it}^j is the demand for the commodity i within the group j, P_{jt}, P_{Cit}^j are the prices for the group j and the commodity i in the group j respectively, and α_j and β_j are parameters to be estimated. The quantity $\alpha_j P_{jt}$ is the so-called 'committed expenditure', i.e. the expenditure needed to keep up with the traditional level of life; $(R_t - P'_{jt}\alpha_j)$ is supernumerary income (expenditure), while $\beta_j(R_t - P'_{jt}\alpha_j)$ is the fraction of supernumerary income (expenditure) going to group j. There are thus two sets of parameters at the upper level. The parameters of the first kind describe the subsistence level at a certain time (α^*) and its rate of change (α^{**}), while those of the second kind describe the structure of utilization of additional income (β^*) at the same time and its rate of change (β^{**}). The upper and lower levels of the model (1)–(4) are connected both through these estimates, which are obtained at the upper level and serve as inputs for regression equations, and secondly through elasticity coefficients. The latter can be formalised as follows.

The coefficient of elasticity of the demand for the group of commodities j for the total expenditure R_t is equal to

$$\epsilon_{R_t}^j = \frac{\partial R_{jt}}{\partial R_t} \frac{R_t}{R_{jt}} \tag{5}$$

As to the coefficients of elasticity of the demand for any commodity i with respect to expenditure on the group of commodities j (obtained from the upper level of the model), they may be defined by the equation

$$\epsilon_{R_\mu}^i = \frac{\partial C_{it}^j}{\partial R_{jt}} \frac{R_{jt}}{C_{it}} \tag{6}$$

As a result, the product of the equations (5) and (6) represents the elasticity of the demand for commodity i with respect to total expenditure, i.e.

$$\epsilon_R^i = \frac{\partial C_{jt}^i}{\partial R_t} \frac{R_t}{C_{jt}} \tag{7}$$

The implementation of the model (1)–(4) requires reliable and qualitatively homogeneous statistical data in addition to adequate computer software. The necessary software is currently available and can not only be used for demand analysis but also for a number of other economic, demographic and social problems. The main programs are as follows: a pro-

---

1 The representation of the trend for these parameters as linear functions of time (Drucker and Soloviev, 1975) $\beta_j = \beta_j^* + t\beta_1^{**}$, $\alpha_j = \alpha_j^* + t\beta_j^{**}$ is commonly used. However this representation is unfortunate for forecasting since it is too inflexible. We prefer (3) for representing the dynamic behaviour of the parameters.

gram that solves the simultaneous equations at the upper level, a program for non-linear functions, and a program for linear functions and functions reducible to linear ones. The practical implementation of the two-stage model (1)–(4) uses official statistical data for the period from 1950 to 1977. It uses information about the population size, the price index, the volume and the structure of sales, and the dynamics of monetary savings. However the available statistical information does not meet the needs of the model, so that laborious and time-consuming processing is inevitable. First of all the accounting statistics for the volume of sales have to be evaluated at comparable prices. Then the indices of *per capita* consumption and the relative price indices are estimated. The figures for services and savings are taken directly from the accounts. Finally the expenditures for the upper level of the model (1)–(4) were aggregated into the following groups: animal production, crop production, other alimentary products, drinks included, light industry products, durable goods, other non-foods, payable services and the growth of monetary savings. After this processing, the statistical data are ready for simulation and analysis at both levels of aggregation.

We now consider the potential applications of the above model both in general and for each separate level. The upper level model, that is, the set of simultaneous linear equations in expenditures, can be used for analysis as well as for forecasting. In the latter case we need to know the trends of (1) the parameters α and β; (2) the prices of the groups of commodities P_i, $i = 1, 2, \ldots$ under consideration; (3) the volume of the extended consumption fund (the aggregate income) *per capita* R_θ. They serve as input parameters. We consider each of these factors in turn.

(i) The population size for the forecast period is exogenous.

(ii) The trend of the parameters α and β is estimated by (3).

(iii) The price index for the total forecast period was assumed to be constant and equal to that in the last year of the reference period.

(iv) The evaluation of population income is a complex process.

One should take into consideration a large number of socio-economic factors concerning the production, distribution and consumption of commodities. This process is feasible provided there is a balance between population income on the one hand and the supply of the economic system on the other hand. Theoretically this problem can be solved with the help of input-output analysis. However, so far, this has not been done, because input–output models consider solely material production, which is not sufficient for studies of consumption. To achieve this further stage, a considerable change in the schema of the input–output model would be necessary both at the accounting and the planning stages. Under such conditions an iterative technique may be recommended based on a combination of demographic, normative and input–output models. The procedure is as follows. Total income of the population is estimated using demographic, normative and input–output models independently. Here every aspect of the extended consumption fund (commodities and services) and personal consumption fund forming is taken into account. The input–output model matches personal consumption with available economic resources. The comparison of these valuations reveals and helps to eliminate various errors. We then obtain independent evaluations by the three types of models once more and again make the proper corrections. This procedure goes on until a balance is obtained, see Drucker and Soloviev (1975a; 1975b).

The simultaneous linear expenditure system can be used not only for demand forecasting but also for the evaluation of future price indices. In the latter case we need to know the parameters and the volume of purchases *per capita*. Let us rewrite formula (2) for the group of commodities *j* in the following way:

$$P_j C_j - P_j \alpha_j + \beta_j \sum_{i=1}^{n} P_i \alpha_i = \beta_j R \qquad (8)$$

(we omit the index *t* for simplicity). After some transformation we get the following equation in the unknown price indices P_j,

$$\sum_{j=1}^{n} [(C_j - \alpha_j)\delta_{ij} + \beta_i \alpha_j]P_j = \beta_i R \qquad (9)$$

where

$$\delta_{ij} = \begin{cases} 1, & \text{if } i = j \\ 0, & \text{if } i \neq j \end{cases} \qquad (10)$$

Hence P_j is given by

$$P_j = \frac{\beta_j R/(C_j - \alpha_j)}{1 + \sum_{j=1}^{n} \dfrac{\alpha_j \beta_j}{C_j - \alpha_j}} \qquad (11)$$

The upper stage of this two-stage system is in wide use for forecasting the prices needed for the evaluation of both the level of consumption and its allocation (Kirichenko, 1976).

After evaluating the volumes of consumer expenditures for the major aggregates of commodities and calculating the elasticities for these aggregates during the accounting period, we get rather a good idea of market satiation, of trends in demand, structural changes, and so on. However this gives us only a superficial picture of the state of affairs because of the highly aggregative nature of the data and it is necessary to analyze the fine structure of these aggregates. Thanks to the hierarchical nature of the linear expenditure system, we are able to achieve any level of disaggregation. But, for this, one has to assume that the consumption of less aggregative groups of commodities is also linear in prices and the total expenditure. But the assumptions which are valid for large groups are not necessarily valid for smaller ones and especially for a single commodity, because there may be large differences between commodities within the same aggregate group. To study these properties we need to deal with each commodity separately, using for this purpose a wide class of linear and non-linear functions. Since we have to deal with a large number of important items in the consumption fund and each item has its own specific features and regularities, our purpose is to reveal these regularities and to discover appropriate approximations for them. This is a hard job, especially since the researcher is supposed to know the specific features of the dynamics of every aggregate and its components in each accounting period.

Up till now we have been discussing mainly one-factor and two-factor models. In addition to these models mathematical economics makes wide use of multi-factor models. These models are usually of the multiple regression type. The dependent variable for these models stands for the demand for a certain commodity, and the independent variables stand for factors that influence it. According to our calculations, for most of the commodities this dependence can be approximated by linear and power functions (Bredov and Levin, 1969, 1972)

$$y = a_0 + a_1 x_1 + a_2 x_2 + a_3 x_3 + \ldots + a_n x_n \tag{12}$$

$$y = e^{a_0} x_1^{a_1} x_2^{a_2} x_3^{a_3} \ldots x_n^{a_n} \tag{13}$$

where y is the demand (or consumption) of a certain commodity

$x_1, x_2, \ldots, x_n$ are regression factors and

$a_0, a_1, a_2, \ldots, a_n$ are the parameters of the model.

Sometimes the best approximation is obtained by regression equations, expressed by power functions and so-called mixed regression equations, which combine both linear and non-linear relations.

The problem of selecting factors for these models is crucial. Both demand and consumption depend on a number of different factors: social, economic, demographic, natural, climatic and others. In particular the volume and the structure of demand and consumption depend on production, social structure, the ratio of urban to rural population, the monetary income of people and its distribution among different socio-economic groups, the level and the structure of state retail prices, the volume of subsistence agriculture production, the age–sex structure of the population, the size of the population, the number, the size and the structure of families, fashions, the preferences of consumers and so on. It is obvious that this whole variety of factors cannot be explicitly taken into account in mathematical economic models of demand. These models can consider only a limited number of factors determined by the size of the statistical sample to be used in correlation and regression analysis. In order that such analysis be reliable, the number of observations should be 5–6 times the number of factors considered in the regression model. But the number of observations is usually small. Thus, as a rule, the maximum duration of time series does not exceed 15–17 years, while in the demand and consumption simulation on the basis of the sample statistics of family budgets the number of economic groups with different income levels is limited to 12–15. All this results in a need to keep down the number of factors included in the model.

Hence, only the most essential factors in the determination of demand and consumption are explicitly taken into account in the model. Prime amongst these is the monetary income of the population and the retail prices that influence demand and consumption of nearly all commodities. In addition, demand and consumption depend upon a number of specific factors. Thus the demand for furniture depends on the level of housing construction, the demand for washing and sewing machines depends on the availability of laundries and dressmaking services, the demand for foodstuffs produced by state enterprises depends on the consumption of foodstuffs produced in private households, the demand for TV sets depends on the range of quality reception of the TV signal, and so on. All these specific factors influencing demand together with general factors (such as monetary income and retail prices) are allowed for in demand and consumption models. Together, these procedures result in an integrated system of demand and consumption models for separate commodities, differing in the specific factors taken into account and encompassing all the commodities that are covered by the statistics. All in all the number of these commodities is about 100, and we have developed the same number of commodity models.

No doubt many such models will use the same set of factors. Thus, for instance, the demand models for all agricultural foodstuffs (i.e. meat, milk products, potatoes, vegetables, fruit) may be described by the equation

$$y = a_0 + a_1 x_1 + a_2 x_2 + a_3 x_3$$

where y stands for the demand for the commodity under consideration, x_1 the monetary income of the population, x_2 the retail price of the commodity, x_3 the volume of commodity subsistence provided by the private household, and a_0, a_1, a_2, a_3 the parameters of the model.

As to the group of consumer durables (i.e. TV sets, refrigerators, radio sets, washing machines, vacuum cleaners and the like) we have to take into consideration such additional factors as the level of provision of these goods as well as scientific and technological advance in the corresponding industries which can be evaluated by specific indexes characterizing the ratio of the new makes to the total volume of production. As a result the demand for these commodities will be as follows

$$y = a_0 + a_1 x_1 + a_2 x_2 + a_3 x_3 + a_4 x_4$$

where y stands for this commodity demand, x_1 the monetary income of the population, x_2 the level of the retail prices for this commodity, x_3 the level of supply of this commodity, x_4 the ratio of the new products to the total volume of production, and a_0, a_1, a_2, a_3, a_4 the parameters of the model.

It is necessary to underline the fact that these models are not only of analytical significance, though they may be used for the precise quantitative evaluation of consumption trends in relation to their determining factors. The main purpose is to provide the means for making demand and consumption forecasts for various time horizons and this is what most of them are used for in the USSR.

2 Normative consumer budget models

Along with pure statistical models, the normative–statistical models have become more and more popular for forecasting demand and consumption. The main distinguishing feature of the models in this class is the fact that they consider the so-called 'rational' levels of consumption for different commodities to be one of the factors determining changes in consumption patterns and in effective demand.

The conceptual feasibility of defining rational consumption levels is tied up with the validity of the hypothesis of the existence of demand satiation points relevant to each of the consumer goods. This hypothesis seems to be more plausible than the non-satiation axiom that constitutes the basis for utility analysis. The latter axiom states that if for two commodity bundles $\{x_g\}$ $g \in G$ and $\{x'_g\}$ $g \in G$ we have $x_g \geq x'_g$ for all $g \in G$, and there exists at least one commodity for which $x_g > x'_g$, then the utility function for the first bundle is strictly more than that for the second one

$$u(x_g, g \in G) < u(x'_g, g \in G) \tag{14}$$

It turns out, however, that for all known commodities (whether actually produced or under consideration) there are consumption levels such that, after they are exceeded, further amounts of the commodity do not increase satisfaction so that further consumption growth does not imply an increase in utility. Given the limits on the length of this paper we are in no position to consider the practical aspects of the determination of rational consumption levels. The problem is not easy to deal with and it merits special investigation. We would only claim that due to the research in the USSR we possess an approximate procedure for the calculation of consumption levels for the most important foodstuffs, textiles, footwear and various durables, which were lately accepted by the planning institutions as the guide for forecasting welfare in the long-term (Sarkisyan and Kuznezova, 1967; Maier, 1977). The data on rational consumption levels also provide us with an opportunity to make a closer link between utility analysis and the practical problems of economic and social planning.

Our economists have suggested several approaches to the utilisation of the rational consumption levels while forecasting demand and individual consumption. Let us consider one of them from Lahman and Sokolovskaya (1978).

The whole set of commodities is divided into 2 groups: the group of current consumer goods G_T, that includes all foodstuffs, non-durable and semi-durable goods; and the group of durable goods G_D that includes the major part of cultural and household goods and some products of light industry. For each of these groups the demand and consumption forecast is made in two stages. First of all, for the current consumer goods G_T we make a forecast of the total *per capita* expenditure for the group $- W_T$. This forecast is based on the following idea about the dynamics of expenditure. If the real expenditure for the commodities belonging to G_T is considerably less than the cost of the bundle of these commodities formed in accordance with the rational consumption levels, then the relation between W_T and the income volume W is close to linear. As soon as the consumption approaches the rational norms the growth of $W_T(W)$ slows down. And when the expenditure for the group G_T reaches the rational level $\overline{W}_T (\overline{W}_T = \Sigma_{g \in G_T} \bar{x}_g \Pi)$ (where $\bar{x}_g$ stands for the rational consumption level for the commodity $g_1 \Pi$ and Π is the price of this commodity) the further growth of W_T depends only on changes in retail prices Π, that take place as a result of the improvements in quality and variety of the commodities and some other factors.

This dependence can be described by the relation

$$[W_T - (AW + B)](W_T - \overline{W}_T) = a \quad a > 0, \ W_T < \overline{W}_T \tag{15}$$

The first equation represents a curve that consists of two separate parts, while the inequalities point out the part essential for our forecast. The parameters A, B and a are chosen in such a way that the $W_T(W)$ function, described implicitly by (15), provides the best approximation to the reference period $W_T(W)$ function. Keeping in mind the inequality $W_T < \overline{W}_T$ we solve the equation and obtain the forecast formula

$$W_T(W) = \frac{AW + B + \overline{W}_T}{2} - \left[\frac{(AW + B + \overline{W}_T)^2}{4} + a \right]^{1/2} \tag{16}$$

Taking into account the W_T values for the forecast period, we can estimate the consumption levels x_g and the *per capita* expenditure $x_g\Pi_g$ at specific times. Consumer behaviour at each moment t is assumed to be determined by each consumer attempting to maximize his satisfaction of wants for the commodities of group G_T within the constraints of his given expenditure value $W_T(t)$. That is, at each t we have to solve

$$\max u'(x_g g \in G_T) = u_{\max} - \sum \left(\frac{a_g}{2}(\bar{x}_g - x)^2\right)$$

$$\text{with } \sum_{g \in G} x_g\Pi_g = W_T(t), x_g \geq 0 \quad (17)$$

(where the parameter a_g stands for the utility index for the relevant commodity). The solution of this problem can be obtained with the help of the Lagrange multiplier approach.

As for durables, the main factor that is to be optimized by the consumer is the *per capita* supply of each commodity. Hence, the model described above has to be essentially modified. The total volume of purchased durables $x_g(t)$ at the moment t consists of two parts. One part is needed to replace physical depreciation and is equal to $M_g(t)\, G_g(t)$, where $M_g(t)$ stands for the depreciation rate. The other part is used to increase the individual (or household) ownership and is equal to $(Y_g(t) - Y_g(t-1))$. We have

$$X_g(t) = Y_g(t) - Y_g(t-1) + M_g.Y_g(t) \quad (18)$$

To forecast the *per capita* (per household) purchases of each durable we transform (18) into

$$x_g(t) = Y_g(t) - Y_g(t-1).L(t-1)/L(t) + Y_g(t).M_g(t) \quad (19)$$

where $L(t)$ stands for the size of the population or the number of households.

Similarly to the nondurable case we introduce an asymptotic function $W_D(t)$ that reflects the cost dynamics of the purchased commodities from the G_D group with $y_g(t) = \bar{y}_g$ (where $\bar{y}_g$ is the rational supply level for the durable consumer goods). Finally we may construct a $W_D(t)$ function corresponding to the function $W_D(t)$ for the reference period at the very beginning of the forecast period and which asymptotically approaches W_D at the end of it.

To predict the *per capita* supply for individual commodities $y_g(t)$, the utility functions U can also be used. But for this it should be defined on the set of $\{y_g(t)\}g \in G_D$. The utility of vector y_g is assumed to reach its maximum when $y_g = \bar{y}$. Equating $\partial u/\partial y_g$ to $a_g(\bar{y}_g - \min(y_g\bar{y}_g))$ we have to find $y_g(t)$ and $x_g(t)$ such that the utility function U reaches its maximum provided

$$\sum x_g(t)\Pi_g(t) = W_D(t)$$

As to the practical implementation of these models we should acknowledge that the adequacy of the forecast estimates obtained using them depends to a large extent upon the validity of the rational consumption levels and the degrees of satisfaction of the latent demand for the commodities as well as on the reliability and completeness of the information concerning other factors accounted for by the model (i.e. the dynamics of income, prices, life expectancy for durables and so on). Even so, as practice shows, this approach is much more realistic and practical than dealing with unknown and possibly even constructively undefinable utility functions.

3 Structural models

Another important direction for consumption studies that has come into being quite recently, deals with the investigation of the consumption typology and the design of structural models (Karapetyan and Rimashevskaya, 1977; Aivazyan and Rimashevskaya, 1978). Many investigators have acknowledged the importance and urgency of establishing a consumption 'typology', that is, of detecting comparatively steady and characteristic consumption types created under certain conditions of the consumer's life. Until recently they were treated, as a rule, with the help of statistical clustering techniques and correlation – regression analysis. But one can take another point of view and study consumption using multivariate statistical techniques, in particular pattern recognition techniques, principal component techniques and others.

Multivariate statistical theory regards multivariate objects as a set of points or vectors in the space of their characteristics. In the consumption area the set of elementary consumer units–households stands for the set of objects to be studied. Each family is characterized on the one hand by a given set of determinants (i.e. factors that determine the household life style) and on the other hand by the set of behavioural parameters reflecting the real expenditures of a household for various commodities. In studying the consumption typology one can in theory lean upon the fact that the actual consumption structure is the result of free choice by consumers and thus satisfies their wants in the best possible way within the budget constraint.

Differences in welfare among the population and corresponding differences in consumption result from the socialist principle of distribution of the major part of the produced commodities according to the amount of labour, given that labour is itself distributed unevenly. Households differ also in their demographic composition. In addition, individual features of educational status and working skills, cultural standards, professional training and so on influence the consumption structure of different social groups and strata.

We may distinguish at least three ways that the consumer's life style influences the consumption pattern:

(i) The regional level, which takes into account the economic, natural and climatic particularities of the region;

(ii) The household level, which considers household conditions such as the family income, the quality and the size of the residence, accumulated ownership, the age of the family, its size, composition and so on;

(iii) The personal level, which takes into account the age, education and occupation of the consumer. Here we must take into account also such vague and implicit features of the individual as his moral, ethical and psychological norms and aspirations.

To each level of welfare, that is, every combination of objective conditions of family activity, there corresponds its own set of wants and preferences that determine the specific nature of consumer behaviour and the actual consumption structure. Hence, families that differ in the conditions of their activity differ in their consumer behaviour as well. And this gives grounds for the belief that such a detection of several steady consumption types is possible. The problem of establishing consumption types can be reduced formally to the research of clusters of points or vectors in the multi-dimensional space of attributes associated with the families under investigation. Each cluster of points corresponds to a certain class and the corresponding families are close in their consumer behaviour. To formalize, let $\{y_i\}$ $i = 1, 2, ..., n$ be a set of points in the multi-dimensional space of behavioural attributes. We look for some partition of the set S_y into an unknown number N of disjoint classes $S_y^{(1)}$, $S_y^{(2)}$, $S_y^{(3)}$, ..., $S_y^{(N)}$.

The study and analysis of the differentiations of consumer behaviour consist of the following stages:

(i) The initial formulation of economic problems, where we determine research objectives and prove the conceptual feasibility of a multivariate analytical approach;

(ii) The gathering of all the necessary information and preliminary data processing, including its comprehension and its reading into the computer;

(iii) The selection of a taxonomy algorithm and the determination of the main types of consumer behaviour through the partitioning of the set of household-points in the space of the chosen consumption attributes;

(iv) The meaningful analysis of the consumer behaviour within the consumption classes so obtained;

(v) The selection of consumption classification factors and the design of the consumer 'images'.

The choice of attributes that gives the best description of the objects under classification is the most important point of the second stage. It is quite natural to take those attributes for which the differentiation of consumer expenditures is the greatest. As a result of such a choice the dimension of the attribute space is reduced by neglecting irrelevant information. The reduced number of attributes together with their high information content makes it easier to study the phenomenon and makes the interpretation of the results of our taxonomy more straightforward and more meaningful. As to the way we diminish the dimension of the attribute space we have two alternatives. The first consists of the selection of a limited number of attributes from the initial set of given objective features, while the second is the aggregation of characteristics and expenditures. In both cases one may employ both formal and informal techniques for attribute selection and aggregation.

In reference to the socio-demographic and economic characteristics of the family it is advisable to consider the level of material welfare (that is the monetary *per capita* income of the family), the size of the family, the fertility of the family (that is the presence and number of children), the social affiliation of the family, the profession of the head of the family, the size and quality of the dwelling, and the number of durables owned. However, the number of these factors can be extended when available information permits.

The factors that determine the classification of the family according to consumption type can be considered as type-forming. They play the main role in the formation of the consumption structure, while all other factors determine only random fluctuations within the same type of consumer behaviour. No doubt the values of the separate type-forming factors vary within every consumption type, that is, they are characterized by some distribution law. Thus it is quite natural to consider as type-forming those factors, whose distribution laws for different consumer behaviour classes differ most of all. In accordance with this principle we have selected the specific attributes contributing to the formation of consumption behaviour classes and as a result constructed a socio-demographic 'image' for each class.

If the size of the sample is not very large, and each household can be recognized as a separate entity, the choice of type-forming attributes for each class of consumer behaviour can be performed without resorting to a formal treatment. Instead we obtain the average socio-demographic estimates for families in each class and then try to correlate the predominant structural indices of socio-demographic attributes with the distinguishing features of the consumer behaviour of the given household class. Along with structural indices the analysis also takes into account data on each characteristic distribution within classes as well as intra- and inter-class variability and the correlation between socio-demographic attributes and the indices of consumer behaviour. However, for large sample sizes, formal techniques for consumer image identification are needed; in particular, one may use factor analysis and other taxonomic techniques. After one of these methods has provided us with the division of the total set of attributes into groups, we may regard every such a group as an aggregate. This approach carries through the idea of reducing the number of socio-demographic attributes with minimal loss of information about the sample as a whole.

In studying consumption processes we have to deal with data of a multivariate nature due to the fact that both the number of registered attributes in each family and the number of objects to be considered are very large. The selection of the most informative attributes among these characteristics is performed by interpreting the variation of these characteristics and their relation to the main consumption-forming factors. At this stage we may take into consideration the *a priori* conceptions of the investigator about the informative significance of the factors for the differentiation of consumption. The aggregation of behavioural characteristics may be based on various principles. Thus, for the aggregation of the expenditures on foodstuffs one may lean upon the principle of allocation of limited raw material, while for that on non-foods one may lean upon the principle of specific wants to be satisfied. This approach has resulted in the reduction of the number of attributes by nearly a factor of 3 – from 100 to 37.

At the second stage of aggregation all the characteristics of consumer behaviour can be reduced to 4 expenditure groups in accordance with the following classification of expenditures: (1) foodstuffs; (2) non-foods; (3) services; (4) public catering. Together with the choice of informative attributes and their aggregation one may also use formal techniques. However, their use meets with difficulties in the economic interpretation of the results. These techniques are only to be advised if the feasibility of consumption types classification can be established and the classification can be interpreted. This latter fact may be regarded as a kind of a check for the results obtained by some formal technique of partitioning the attribute space. If two different formal approaches lead to the same partitioning of the attribute space, one may regard this as the confirmation of the validity of the technique, which in turn reduces consumption classification time and provides a unified computer program for the solution of the problem.

The classification structure so obtained represents a rather stable system of consumption models for some household types. The consumption behaviour of each of these types can be considered constant for the medium-range period (i.e. 7–10 years). Under such conditions, changes of some factors in the household activity can be viewed as a transition of this household to another type group, while the changes of the consumption structure in general can be viewed as an effect of modifications of weight of different types of consumer behaviour within the totality of households. Here we have a forecast based on structural consumption models, while in the present structural model (Karapetyan and Rimashevskaya, 1977) we take into account only one factor, namely, income; in the structural models based on the consumer taxonomy we account for a series of factors that allow us to adjust the forecast calculations and make them more stable over time. This is an obvious advantage of these models.

The decomposition into consumer groups which are homogeneous in the given set of characteristics also opens the way for the wide use of correlation – regression techniques for analysis and forecasting. The parameters of models based on homogeneous household classification are more reliable and meaningful than those built from a more heterogeneous set. Thus we bypass one of the most important and unsolved problems of the proper representation of consumption. Combining the classification methods and the correlation techniques we may expect to achieve a good agreement between the results and reality, for current estimates as well as for forecasts. The identification of stable types of consumers, with each having its own system of values and preferences governing the choice of commodities, opens entirely new vistas for the simulation of normative consumer budgets.

Thus, the studies of consumption and demand in the USSR follow various directions, each aimed at the improvement of planning practice in this country.

References

Aivazyan, S. A. and N. M. Rimashevskaya (1972), *Consumption Typology:* Moscow, Nauka.

Bazarov, V. A. (1927), 'Use of budget data for urban demand mix elaboration within a perspective general plan', *Planned Economy*, p. 5.

Bredov, V. M. and A. I. Levin (1969), 'Economic and mathematical models of demand', *Economica* (Moscow).

(1972), 'Forecasting methods', *Economica* (Moscow).

Drucker, S. G. and J. P. Soloviev (1975a), 'Modelling of consumer demand', *Economica i Matematicheski Metodi*, Vol. II.

(1975b), 'A two-level model for analysis and forecasting of population demand', *Economica i Matematischeski Metodi,* Vol. II.

Karapetyan, A. H. and N. M. Rimashevskaya (1977), *Family Income and Consumption Differential Balance:* Moscow, Nauka.

Kirichenko, N. (1976), 'Rational consumer budgeting in the system of long-term forecasts', in *Problems of Long-Term National Economic Forecasting,* Central Economic Mathematical Institute, Moscow.

Lahman, I. L. and T. A. Sokolovskaya, (1978), 'A normative model for forecasting personal consumption', *Economica i Matematicheski Metodi,* Vol. 8.

Maier, V. F. (1977), *The Living Standard of the Population of the USSR,* Moscow, Misl.

Sarkisyan, G. S. and N. P. Kuznezova (1967), 'Family demand and income', *Economica* (Moscow).

Stone, R. (1954), 'Linear expenditure systems and demand analysis: an application to the pattern of British demand', *Economic Journal,* Vol. 64, pp. 511–27.

Strumilin, S. G. (1965), *Selected Works,* Vol. 5, Moscow, Nauka.

The theory of index numbers

Introduction to part two

The theory and measurement of economic index numbers presents side by side some of the most difficult and abstruse theory with the most immediately practical issues of everyday measurement. The construction of index numbers is an essential part of all social accounting; without compression and aggregation the mass of quantities and prices thrown up by the economic system would be incomprehensible. Yet from the outset such aggregation has been known to be meaningful only in the context of welfare measurement. But to what extent are welfare-based index numbers practical? In his book on index numbers [56] written for the OEEC (now OECD), Sir Richard Stone addressed the question of whether practical international standards for index number construction could be established in line with his earlier standardized system of national accounts. Sir Richard gives the following reasons why the welfare approach is useful:

First, they give content to such concepts as real consumption which might otherwise be vague and obscure; second, they bring out the fundamental difficulties in establishing empirical correlates to concepts such as real consumption and so help to show what can and what cannot usefully be attempted in the present state of knowledge; finally they show the circumstances in which particular empirical correlates, such as a measure of real consumption which can actually be constructed, are likely to provide a good or a bad approximation to the concepts of the theory. ([56], pp. 18–19)

Much of the material in this section is an elaboration of these three points.

Although index number theory is at least as old as consumer theory itself, it has been a somewhat neglected area at least until the last few years. However, the world-wide increase in inflation rates over the last decade accompanied by rapid changes in relative prices has caused a recent upsurge of interest in both theory and measurement. When relative prices show large changes, it makes a great difference exactly how price index numbers are constructed. At the same time, the fact that different consumers consume different bundles of goods means that the index number which measures one family's welfare may be quite misleading if applied to another. Poor families have different price indices from rich families, families with children differ from those without, old families

130

from young families, and so on. These differences were well understood in Cambridge in the 1950s (see in particular Prais, 1959) and have certainly been empirically important in recent times both in Britain and the United States (see, for example, Deaton and Muellbauer, 1980, chapter 7, for some evidence and further references).

In this section, however, it is the theory which is highlighted. In the first chapter, that by Sydney Afriat, the question at issue is whether it is conceptually possible to construct a price index from a given set of observations on prices and quantities. If price indices are to be based on welfare, welfare itself must be well-defined and we can do this only from data which are consistent with rational behaviour. For example, if we have two periods with price vectors p^0, p^1 and quantities q^0 and q^1, then if $p^0 . q^0 > p^0 . q^1$ we know that, in situation 0, q^1 could have been chosen but was not. Hence if we also find that $p^1 . q^1 > p^1 . q^0$, behaviour is not consistent with rationality, no utility function exists and a price index cannot be constructed. Afriat goes further than this and insists that the existence of a preference ordering by itself is not sufficient for the existence of the price index. If this latter is to be unique and unambiguous, it cannot vary from individual to individual and this will occur only if demand patterns in terms of budget shares are the same for everyone. As Afriat has shown elsewhere (e.g. Afriat, 1977), two observations will allow the construction of a utility function consistent with such behaviour if and only if $p^1 \cdot q^1/p^0 \cdot q^1 \leq p^1 \cdot q^0/p^0 \cdot q^0$, that is if the Paasche price index is no greater than the Laspeyres price index, a condition which also rules out the possibility of the earlier contradiction. The question of how this analysis extends to many observations is the subject of the present paper. In it, Afriat defines generalized Paasche and Laspeyres indices which allow an extension of the theorem; he also presents an algorithm for calculating the relevant quantities so that his results can be applied straightforwardly to any finite set of data.

The second chapter in the section is an extremely comprehensive and clear survey of the whole area of economic index numbers by Erwin Diewert. Basing his analysis on modern duality theory, he provides an integrated treatment of index numbers encompassing not only consumer behaviour but also the theory of the firm. The cost or expenditure function is used to derive the Konüs or 'true' cost-of-living index number and the conventional bounds theorems proved. The dual quantity index numbers due originally to Malmquist (1953) are also fully discussed as is their relationship to the Konüs price indices. The duality framework renders the results easily proved and provides a straightforward way of understanding how the various concepts relate to one another. In the final sections of the paper, Diewert shows how particular well-known index number formulae, for example Fisher's 'ideal' index, can be derived from specific preference structures. Perhaps the most interesting of these theorems shows that the Törnqvist logarithmic price index number, in which the logarithmic price relatives are weighted by the average of the two periods' budget shares, can be justified exactly in terms of a specific but flexible formation of preferences. Such theorems take us a long way towards an integration of theory and practice.

References for introduction to part two

Afriat, S. N. (1977), *The price index,* Cambridge University Press, New York.

Deaton, A. S. and J. Muellbauer (1980), *Economics and consumer behavior,* Cambridge University Press, New York.

Malmquist, S. (1953), 'Index numbers and indifference surfaces', *Tradajos de Estadistica,* **4,** pp. 209–41.

Prais, S. J. (1959), 'Whose cost of living?', *Review of Economic Studies,* **26,** pp. 126–34.

6 On the constructability of consistent price indices between several periods simultaneously[1]

S. N. AFRIAT

Introduction

A price index refers to a pair of consumption periods, and price-index formulae usually involve demand data from the reference periods alone.' When there are many periods, a price index can be determined from any one period to any other, in each case using the data from just those two periods. But then consistency questions arise for the set of price indices so obtained. Especially, they must have the consistency that would follow from their being ratios of 'price levels'. The well-known tests of Irving Fisher have their origin in such questions. When these tests are regarded as giving identities to be satisfied by a standard formula and are taken in combination, it is impossible to satisfy them. Such impossibility remains even with partial combinations. Eichhorn and Voeller (1976) have given a full account of the inconsistencies between Fisher's tests. Reference is made there for their results and for the history of the matter.

Fisher recognizes the consistency question also in his idea of the 'rectification of pair comparisons'. In this the price indices are all calculated, as usual, separately and regardless of any consistency they should have together, and then they are all adjusted in some manner so that they can form a consistent set. For instance, by 'crossing' a formula with its 'antithesis' you got one that satisfied the 'reversal' test. Here he takes one of the tests separately as if any one could mean anything on its own, and contrives a formula to satisfy it. This is how he arrived at his 'ideal' index. It is 'ideal' because it satisfies the 'reversal' test but not so when those other tests are brought in. The search for a really ideal index seemed a hopeless task.

In any case these tests are just negative criteria for index-number-making, showing how a formula can be rejected and telling nothing of how one should be arrived at. Something is to be measured and it is not yet

1 Support of this work by the National Research Council of Canada is acknowledged with thanks.

133

considered what, but whatever it is it must fit a certain mould. Here is not measurement but a ritual with form. In the background thought, what is to be measured is the price level, though prices are many so no one quite knows what that means, and a price index is a ratio of price levels. Therefore the set m^2 price indices $P_{rs}(r, s = 1, ..., m)$ between m periods $1, ..., m$ must at least have the consistency required by their being ratios $P_{rs} = P_s/P_r$ of m 'price levels' $P_r(r = 1, ..., m)$. Therefore $P_{rr} = 1$, $P_{rs} = P_{sr}^{-1}$, $P_{rs}P_{st} = P_{rt}$ and so forth. There are other parts to Fisher's tests and here we have the part that touches just the ratio aspect.

In a seemingly more coherent approach, utility makes the base for what is being measured. There would be no problem there at all if only the utility function or order to be used could be known. But it is not known and therefore it is dealt with hypothetically. Its existence is entertained and inferences are made from that position. With utility in the picture the natural object of measurement is the 'cost of living', and at first we know nothing of the price-level or of a price-index. Giving intelligibility to the price index in the utility framework involves imposing a special restriction on utility.

Let M_0 be any income in a period 0 when the prices are given by a vector p_0. Hypothetically, the bundle of goods x_0 consumed with this income has the highest utility among all those which might have been consumed instead. Then it is asked what income M_1 in a period 1 when the prices are p_1 provides the standard of living, or utility, attained with the income M_0 in period 0. With p_0, p_1 fixed and the utility order given, M_1 is determined as a function $M_1 = F_{10}(M_0)$ of M_0, where the function F_{10} depends on the prices p_0, p_1 and the utility order. Without making any forbidding extra assumptions it can be allowed that this is a continuous increasing function, and that is all. However, turning to practice with price-indices, we find that to offer a relationship between M_0 and M_1 is the typical use given to a price index. The relationship in this case has the form $M_1 = P_{10}M_0$, P_{10} being the price index. In other words, using a price-index corresponds to the idea that there is a homogeneous linear relation between M_0, M_1 or that the relation is a line through the origin, the price-index being the slope.

To give the function F_{10}, just this form has implications about the utility from which it is derived. That utility must have a conical structure that is a counterpart of linear homogeneity of that function: if any commodity bundle x has at least the utility of another y then the same holds when x and y are replaced by their multiples xt and yt by any positive number t. To talk about a price-index and at the same time about utility, this assumption about the utility must be made outright.

If a conical utility is given, relative to it a price-index P_{10} can be computed for any prices p_0, p_1. Then, as explained further in section 11, it has the form $P_{10} = P_1/P_0$ where $P_0 = \theta(p_0)$, $P_1 = \theta(p_1)$ are the values of a concave conical function θ depending on prices alone. Price indices so computed for many periods automatically satisfy various tests of Fisher. The issue about those tests therefore becomes empty in this context, and pair-comparisons so obtained need no 'rectification'. But a remaining issue comes from the circumstance that a utility usually is not given. Should one be proposed arbitrarily as a basis for constructing price indices, there can be no objection to it merely on the basis of the tests, at least with those that concern the ratio-aspect of price indices.

With each price-index formula P_{10} of the very many he surveyed, Fisher associated a quantity-index formula X_{10} in such a way that the product is the ratio of consumption expenditures $M_0 = p_0x_0$, $M_1 = p_1x_1$ in the two periods. For instance with the Laspeyres price index $P_{10} = p_1x_0/p_0x_0$, the corresponding quantity-index is $X_{10} = p_1x_1/p_1x_0$, and then

$$P_{10}X_{10} = (p_1x_0/p_0x_0)(p_1x_1/p_1x_0) = p_1x_1/p_0x_0 = M_1/M_0$$

As a possible sense to this scheme, it is as if, beside the price-index being a ratio $P_{10} = P_1/P_0$ of price-levels, also the quantity-index is a ratio $X_{10} = X_1/X_0$ of quantity levels, and price-level multiplied with quantity level is the same as price-vector multiplied with quantity-vector, that is

$$P_0X_0 = p_0x_0 = M_0, \quad P_1X_1 = p_1x_1 = M_1$$

to give

$$P_{10}X_{10} = (P_1/P_0)(X_1/X_0) = (P_1X_1)/(P_0X_0) = M_1/M_0$$

Here there is the simple result that all prices are effectively summarized by a single number and all quantities by a single quantity number, and instead of doing accounts by dealing with each price and quantity separately, and also with their product that gives the cost of the quantity at the price, the entire account can be carried on just as well in terms of these two summary price and quantity numbers, or levels, whose product is, miraculously, the cost of that quantity level at that price level. Though there are many goods and so-many prices and quantities, still it is just as if there was effectively just one good with a price and obtainable in any quantity at a cost which is simply, as with a simple goods, the product of price times quantity. Any mystery about the meaning of a price index vanishes, because it becomes simply a price. Were this scheme valid we could ask for so much utility, enquire the price and pay the right amount by the usual multiplication. When applied to income M_0 in period 0 when the price level is P_0, the level of utility it purchases is $X_0 = M_0/P_0$.

Then the income that purchases the same level of utility in period 1 when the price level is P_1 is given by $M_1 = P_1 X_0$. Hence, by division, $M_1/M_0 = P_1/P_0 = P_{10}$, giving the relation $M_1 = P_{10}M_0$ as usual.

Whether or not this scheme has serious plausibilities, it is implicit whenever a price index based on utility is in view. However, though such a scheme has here been imputed as belonging to Fisher's system, or conjured up as though that seems to belong to it or at least gives it an intelligibility, it cannot be considered to have clear presence there. For Fisher's system does not have a basis in utility and this scheme does. While this circumstance is not evidence of a union it still might not seem to force a separation. However, a symptom of a decided separation is that, even when many periods are involved, Fisher still followed standard custom in regarding an index formula as one involving the demand data just from its pair of reference periods, and really his system is about such formulae. Then he worried about the incoherence of the set of price indices for many periods so obtained. The utility formulation cares nothing about the form of the formula. When many periods are involved and all the price indices between them are to be calculated, the calculation of one and all should involve the data for all periods simultaneously. In the utility approach immediate thought is not of the demand data and of formulae in these at all, but rather it is of the utility order which gives the basis of the calculations, and necessarily gives coherent results. Instead, Fisher forces incoherence by rigidly following the standard idea of what constitutes an index formula. The main issue with the utility approach is about the utility function or order. When that utility is settled all that remains to be dealt with is a well-defined objective of calculation based on that utility. The role of the demand data is just to put constraints on the permitted utility order, and consequently price indices based on utility become based on that data. Having such constraints, the first question then is about the existence of a utility order that satisfies them. If none exists then no price indices exist and there the matter ends. Though that is so in the present treatment, by making the constraints more tolerant it is possible to go further (see Afriat, 1972b and 1973).

In the standard model of the consumer, choice is governed by utility, to the effect that any bundle of goods consumed has greater utility than any other attainable with the same income at the prevailing prices. With this model, the obvious constraint on a utility for it to be permitted by given data is, firstly, that it validate the model for the consumer on the evidences provided by that data. Then further, since price-indices are to be dealt with, the conical property of utility should be required.

With this method of constraint and the other definitions that have been outlined, everything is available for developing the questions that are in view. But first there will be a change in formulation that has advantages.

Instead of requiring that a chosen bundle of goods be represented as being the unique best among all those attainable for no greater cost at the prevailing prices, or as being definitely better than any others in utility, it will be required that it be just one among the possibly many best, or one at as least as good as any other. This alters nothing if certain prior assumptions are made about the utility order, for instance that it is representable by an increasing strictly quasiconcave utility function. With the latter assumption a utility maximum under a budget constraint must in any case be a unique maximum, and so adding that the maximum is unique just makes a redundance. But we do not want to introduce additional assumptions about utility. A utility is wanted that fits the data in a certain way, and if all that is now wanted in such a fit is that some commodity bundles be represented as having at least the utility of certain others then we can always count on a utility function that is constant everywhere to do that service. In making what could at first seem a slight change in the original formulation of the constraint on permitted utilities, the result is no constraint at all: whatever the data there always exists a permitted utility, for instance the one mentioned which will give zero as the cost of attaining any given standard of living. That change is drastic and no such change is sought. All that is in view is a change that alters nothing important in the results, the effect being something like replacing an open interval by a closed one, while it is better to work with and in any case is conceptually fitting. One possibility is to add a monotonicity condition as an assumption about utility expressing that 'more is better'. But, as said, we do not want any such prior assumptions. Instead consider again the original strict condition, that the chosen bundle be the unique best attainable at no greater cost. It implies the considered weaker condition in which the uniqueness has been dropped. But also it implies a second condition: the cost of the bundle is the minimum cost for obtaining a bundle that is as good as it. These two conditions are generally independent, even though relations between them can be produced from prior assumptions about utility, of which we have none, and their combination is implied by the stricter and analytically more cumbersome original condition.

They are just what is wanted. They have equal warrant as economic principles. In the context of cost – benefit analysis they are familiar as constituting the two main criteria about a project, that it be *cost-effective* or gives best value for the cost, and *cost-efficient* or the same value is unattainable at lower cost.

Now the wanted constraint on an admissible utility can be stated by the requirement that every bundle of goods given in the demand data be represented by it as cost-effective and cost-efficient. Such a utility can be said to be *compatible* with the demand data. Then the data is *consistent* if there exists a compatible utility. It is *homogeneously consistent* if there exists a compatible utility that moreover has the property of being conical, or homogeneous, required whenever dealing with price-indices. A *compatible price-index,* or a 'true' one, is one derived on the basis of a homogeneous utility that is compatible with the given data.

The first problem therefore is to find a test for the homogeneous consistency of the data. In the case where there are just two periods, the test found reduces to a relation that is quite familiar, in a context where it is not at all connected with this test but is offered as a 'theorem', though certainly it is not that. The relation is simply that the Paasche index from one period to the other does not exceed that of Laspeyres. The relation is symmetrical between the data in the two periods, and so there is no need to put it in this unsymmetrical form where one period is distinguished as the base. But this is the form in which it is familiar and known as the 'Index-Number Theorem'. That the 'Theorem', or relation, *is necessary and sufficient for homogeneous consistency* of the demands in the two periods is a theorem in the ordinary sense. It is going to be generalized for any number of periods.

Related to the Index-Number Theorem is the proposition that the Laspeyres and Paasche indices are upper and lower 'limits' for the 'true index'. From the foregoing consistency considerations it is recognized that even the existence of a price index, at least in the sense entertained here, can be contradicted by the data, so certainly some additional qualification is needed in the 'limits' proposition. Also, what makes an index 'true' has obscurities in early literature. An interpretation emerging in later discussions is that a true index is simply one derived on the basis of utility. This could be accepted to mean one that, in present terms, is compatible with the given demand data.

With demand data given for any number of periods and satisfying the homogeneous consistency test, a price index compatible with those data can be constructed from any period to any other. It has many possible values corresponding to the generally many compatible homogeneous utilities. These values *describe a closed interval* whose endpoints are given by certain formulae in the given demand data.

A special case of this result applies to the situation usually assumed in index-number discussions. In this, the only data involved in a price-index construction between two periods are the data from the two reference periods themselves. For this case *the formulae for the endpoints of the interval of values for the price index reduce to the Paasche and Laspeyres formulae.* Here therefore is a generalization of those well-known formulae for when demand data from any number of periods can be permitted to enter the calculation of a price-index between any two. *The values* of these generalized Paasche and Laspeyres formulae *are well defined just in the case of homogeneous consistency* of the data, under which condition they have the price-index significance just stated. Then a counterpart of the 'Index-Number Theorem' condition in the context of many periods is that *the generalized Paasche formula does not exceed the generalized Laspeyres formula*. There seems to be one such condition for each ordered pair of periods, making a collection of conditions. However, all are redundant because they are *automatically satisfied* whenever the formulae have well-defined values, as they do just in the case of homogeneous consistency of the data.

For price-indices P_{rs} between many periods to be *consistent* they should have the form $P_{rs} = P_s/P_r$ for some P_r. Let $\hat{P}_{rs}$, $\check{P}_{rs}$ be the generalized Laspeyres and Paasche formulae. These, when they have well-defined values, are connected by the relation $\hat{P}_{rs}\check{P}_{sr} = 1$ and have the properties $\hat{P}_{rs}\hat{P}_{st} \leq \hat{P}_{rt}$, $\check{P}_{rs}\check{P}_{st} \leq \check{P}_{rt}$. Then it is possible to solve the system of simultaneous inequalities $\hat{P}_{rs} \geq P_s/P_r$ for the P_r. The system $\check{P}_{rs} \leq P_s/P_r$ is identical with this, so solutions automatically satisfy

$$\check{P}_{rs} \leq P_s/P_r \leq \hat{P}_{rs}$$

Now it is possible to describe all the price-indices P_{rs} between periods that are compatible with the data and form a consistent set: they are exactly those *having the form $P_{rs} = P_s/P_r$ where P_r is any solution of the above system of inequalities*. The condition for their existence is just the homogeneous consistency of the data. For any solution P_r there exists a homogeneous utility compatible with the data on the basis of which $P_{rs} = P_s/P_r$ is the price-index from period r to period s. This will be shown by actual construction of such a utility.

Now to be remarked is the *extension property* of any given price-indices for a subset of the periods that are compatible with the data and together are consistent: *it is always possible to determine further price indices involving all the other periods so that the collection price-indices so obtained between all periods are both compatible with the data and together are consistent*. There is an ambiguity here about a set of price indices being compatible with the data: they could be that with each taken separately, or in another stricter sense where they are taken simultaneously together. But in the conjunction with consistency the ambiguity loses effect. *For price-indices P_{rs} that are all independently compatible with the data*, the compatibility of each one with the data being established by means of a possibly different utility, *if they are all consistent there also they are jointly compatible* in that also there exists a single utility, homogeneous and compatible with the data, that establishes their compatibility with the data simultaneously.

This completes a description of the main concepts and results dealt with in this paper. Further remarks concern computation of the $m \times m -$ matrix of generalized Laspeyres indices $\hat{P}_{rs}$, and hence also the generalized Paasche indices $\check{P}_{rs} = \hat{P}_{sr}^{-1}$, from the matrix of ordinary Laspeyres indices $L_{rs} = p_s x_r / p_r x_r$. An algorithm proposed goes as follows. The matrix L with elements L_{rs} is raised to powers in a sense that is a variation of the usual, in which $a + b$ means min$[a, b]$. With the modification of matrix addition and multiplication that results associativity and distributivity laws are preserved, and matrix 'powers' can be defined in the usual way by repeated 'multiplication'. The condition for the powers $L, L^2, L^3, \ldots$ to converge is simply the homogeneous consistency of the data. Then for some $k \le m$, $L^{k-1} = L^k$, and in that case also $L^k = L^{k+1} = \ldots$ so the calculation of powers can be broken-off as soon as one is found that is identical with its predecessor. Finding such a $k \le m$ by this procedure is a test for homogeneous consistency; finding a diagonal element less than unity denies this condition and terminates the procedure. With such a k let $\hat{P} = L^k$. The elements $\hat{P}_{rs}$ of $\hat{P}$ are the generalized Laspeyres indices. A programme for this algorithm is available for the TI-59 programmable calculator applicable to $m \le 6$, and another in Standard BASIC for a microcomputer.

1 Demand

With n commodities, Ω^n is the *commodity space* and Ω_n is the *price* or *budget space*. These are described by non-negative column and row vectors with n elements, Ω being the non-negative numbers. Then $x \in \Omega^n$, $p \in \Omega_n$ have a product $px \in \Omega$, giving the value of the commodity bundle x at the prices p. Any $(x, p) \in \Omega^n \times \Omega_n$ with $px > 0$ defines a *demand*, of quantities x at prices p, with expenditure given by $M = px$. Associated with it is the *budget vector* given by $u = M^{-1}p$ and such that $ux = 1$. Then (x, u) is the *normal demand* associated with $(x, p)(px > 0)$.

Some m periods of consumption are considered, and it is supposed that demands $(x_t, p_t)(t = 1, \ldots, m)$ are given for these. With expenditures $M_t = p_t x_t$ and budgets $u_t = M_t^{-1} p_t$, so that $u_t x_t = 1$, the associated normal demands are the (x_t, u_t). Then $L_{rs} = u_r x_s = p_r x_s / p_r x_r$ is the Laspeyres quantity index from r to s, or with r, s as base and current periods. It is such that $L_{rr} = 1$. Then the coefficients $D_{rs} = L_{rs} - 1$ are such that $D_{rr} = 0$. To be used also are the Laspeyres *chain-coefficients* $L_{rij \ldots ks} = L_{ri} L_{ij} \ldots L_{ks}$.

Any collection $D \subseteq \Omega^n \times \Omega_n$ of demands is a *demand relation*. Here we have a finite demand relation D with elements (x_t, p_t). For any demand (x, p), the collection of demands of the form (xt, p), where $t > 0$ is its *homogeneous extension*, and the homogeneous extension of a demand relation is the union of the homogeneous extensions of its elements. A *homogeneous demand relation* has the property

$xDp,\ t > 0 \rightarrow xtDp$

making it identical with its homogeneous extension.

For a normal demand relation E, or one such that $xEu \rightarrow ux = 1$, homogeneity is expressed by the condition

$$xEu,\ t > 0 \rightarrow xtEt^{-1}u$$

If E is the normal demand relation associated with D, or the *normalization* of D, then this is the condition for D to be homogeneous.

2 Utility

A *utility relation* is any binary relation $R \subseteq \Omega^n \times \Omega^n$ that is reflexive, xRx, and transitive, $xRyRz \rightarrow xRz$, by which properties it is an order. Then the symmetric part $E = R \cap R'$, for which

$$xEy \leftrightarrow xRy \wedge xR'y \leftrightarrow xRy \wedge yRx$$

is a symmetric order, or an equivalence, and the antisymmetric part $P = R \cap \bar{R}'$, for which

$$xPy \leftrightarrow xRy \wedge x\bar{R}'y \leftrightarrow xRy \wedge y\bar{R}x \leftrightarrow xRy \wedge {\sim}yRx$$

is irreflexive and transitive, or a strict order.

A *homogeneous, or conical,* utility relation is one that is a cone in $\Omega^n \times \Omega^n$, that is $xRy,\ t > 0 \rightarrow xtRyt$. Any $\phi: \Omega^n \rightarrow \Omega$ is a utility function, and it is homogeneous or conical if its graph is a cone, the condition for this being $\phi(xt) = \phi(x)t(t > 0)$. A utility function ϕ represents a utility relation R if $xRy \leftrightarrow \phi(x) \geq \phi(y)$. If ϕ is conical so is R.

3 Demand and utility

A demand (x, p) and a utility R are *compatible* if

$$\text{(i)}\ py \leq px \rightarrow xRy \quad \text{(ii)}\ yRx \rightarrow py \geq px \tag{3.1}$$

They are *homogeneously compatible* if (xt, p) and R are compatible for all $t > 0$, in other words if the homogeneous extension of (x, p) is compatible with R. If R is homogeneous, compatibility is equivalent to homogeneous compatibility. Demand and utility relations D and R are compatible if the elements of D are all compatible with R, and homogeneously compatible if the homogeneous extension of D is compatible with R.

A demand relation D is *consistent* if it is compatible with some utility relation, and *homogeneously consistent* if moreover that utility relation can be chosen to be homogeneous. Homogeneous consistency of any demand relation is equivalent to consistency of its homogeneous extension. That the former implies the latter is seen immediately, and the converse will be shown later.

It should be noted that (3.1 (ii)) in contrapositive is $py < px \rightarrow y\bar{R}x$, and, with the definition of P in section 2, this with (3.1 (i)) gives

$$py < px \rightarrow xPy \tag{3.2}$$

so this is a consequence of (3.1).

4 Revealed preference

A relation $W \subset \Omega^n \times \Omega_n$ is defined by $xWu \equiv ux \leq 1$. Then xWu, that is $ux \leq 1$, means the commodity bundle x is *within* the budget u, and

$$Wu = [x : xWu] = [x : ux \leq 1]$$

is the *budget set* for u, whose elements are the commodity bundles within u.

The *revealed preference relation* of a demand (x, p) is $[(x, y) : py \leq px]$. For a normal demand $(x, u)(ux = 1)$ it is $(x, Wu) = [(x, y) : y \in Wu] = [(x, y) : uy \leq 1]$. The revealed homogeneous preference relation is the conical closure of the revealed preference relation, so it is $[(xt, y) : py \leq pxt, t > 0]$ for a demand and $\cup_{t>0}(xt, Wt^{-1}u)$ for the normal demand. The condition (3.1), which is a part of the requirement for compatibility between a demand and utility (x, p) and R, asserts simply that the utility relation contains the revealed preference relation. If the utility relation is homogeneous, this is equivalent to its containing the revealed homogeneous preference relation.

Let R_t be the revealed preference relation of the demand (x_t, p_t), and $\dot{R}_t$ the revealed homogeneous preference relation. Then, as remarked, compatibility of that demand with a utility R requires that

$$R_t \subseteq R \tag{4.1}$$

and if R is homogeneous this is equivalent to

$$\dot{R}_t \subseteq R \tag{4.2}$$

Now let R_D, the revealed preference relation of the given demand relation D, be defined as the transitive closure of the union of the revealed preference relations R_t of its elements, $R_D = \vec{\cup}_t R_t$. The compatibility of R with D requires (4.1) for all t, and because R is transitive this is equivalent to $R_D \subset R$. Also let $\dot{R}_D = \vec{\cup}_t \dot{R}_t$, the transitive closure of the union of the revealed homogeneous preference relation $\dot{R}_t$ of the elements of D, define the *revealed homogeneous preference relation* of D. Then, by similar argument, with (4.2), compatibility of D with a homogeneous R implies

$\dot{R}_D \subseteq R$. While R_D is transitive from its construction, and reflexive at the points x_t, because R_t is reflexive at x_t, $\dot{R}_D$ is both transitive and conical, and reflexive on the cone through the x_t.

5 Revealed contradictions

A demand relation D with elements (x_r, p_r) is *compatible* with a utility relation R if

$$\text{(i)} \ p_t x \leq p_t x_t \rightarrow x_t R x \quad \text{(ii)} \ x R x_t \rightarrow p_t x \geq p_t x_t \tag{5.1}$$

and D is *consistent* if some compatible order R exists. It has been seen that (5.1) is equivalent to

$$R_D \subseteq R \tag{5.2}$$

Therefore, if D is compatible with R, $x R_D x_t \rightarrow x R x_t$ for any t and x, and also $p_t x < p_t x_t \rightarrow x \bar{R} x_t$. Therefore, on the hypothesis that D is compatible with some R, the condition

$$x R_D x_t, \ p_t x < p_t x_t \tag{5.3}$$

implies $x R x_t$, $x \bar{R} x_t$ making a contradiction, so the hypothesis is impossible and D is inconsistent.

The condition (5.3) for any t and x is a *revealed contradiction*, denying the consistency of D. Thus:

The existence of a revealed contradiction is sufficient
for D to be inconsistent. (5.4)

Now it will be seen to be also necessary.

The condition for there to be no revealed contradictions is the denial of (5.3), for all t and x; equivalently

$$x R_D x_t \rightarrow p_t x \geq p_t x_t \tag{5.5}$$

But this is just the condition (5.1 (ii)) with $R = R_D$. Because (5.1 (i)) is equivalent to (5.2), and because in any case $R_D \subseteq R_D$ so (5.2) is satisfied with $R = R_D$, it is seen that (5.4) is necessary and sufficient for (5.1 (i) and (ii)) to be satisfied with $R = R_D$, in other words for D to be compatible with R_D. Thus:

The absence of revealed contradictions is necessary and
sufficient for D to be compatible with R_D. (5.6)

As a corollary:

The absence of revealed contradictions implies the consistency of D.

$$(5.7)$$

For consistency means the existence of some compatible order, and by (5.5) under this hypothesis R_D is one such order. Now with (5.5):

> *The absence of revealed contradictions is necessary and*
> *sufficient for the consistency of D and implies*
> *compatibility with R_D.*   (5.8)

By exactly similar argument, $x\dot{R}_D x_t\theta$ and $p_r x < p_r x_r \theta$, for any r, x and $\theta > 0$, make a *homogeneously revealed contradiction* denying the homogeneous consistency of D, or the existence of a compatible homogeneous utility. Then $x\dot{R}_D x_t\theta \rightarrow p_r x \geq p_r x_r \theta$ for all r, x and $\theta > 0$ asserts the absence of homogeneously revealed contradictions. Then there is the following:

Theorem. For a demand relation to be compatible with some homogeneous utility relation, and so homogeneously consistent, it is necessary and sufficient that its revealed homogenous preference relation be one such relation, and for this the absence of homogeneously revealed contradictions is necessary and sufficient.

This theorem holds unconditionally, regardless of whether or not D is finite. However, when D is finite the homogeneous consistency condition has a finite test, developed in the next two sections.

Because the revealed preference relation of the homogeneous extension of a demand relation is identical with its revealed homogeneous preference relation, it appears now, as remarked in section 3, that *homogeneous consistency of a demand relation is equivalent to consistency of its homogeneous extension.* For, as just seen, the first stated condition on D is equivalent to compatibility with $\dot{R}_D$ and the second with $R_{\dot{D}}$, so this conclusion follows from $\dot{R}_D = R_{\dot{D}}$.

6 Consistency

Though R_D, $\dot{R}_D$ and the L_{rs} which give the base for the following work are derived from D, they are also derivable from the normal demand relation E derived from D. Therefore there would be no loss in generality if only normal demand relations were considered.

As a preliminary, the definition of the revealed homogeneous preference relation $\dot{R}_D$ will be put in a more explicit form. This requires identification of the transitive closure of any relation R with its chain-extension $\vec{R}$. An R-chain is any sequence of elements x, y, ..., z in which each has the relation $\vec{R}$ to its successor, that is $xRyR ... Rz$. Then the chain-extension R is the relation that holds between extremities of R-chains, so $x\vec{R}z \equiv (\bigvee y, ...)xRyR ... Rz$. The relation $\vec{R}$ so defined can be identified with the transitive closure of R, that is as the smallest transitive relation containing R, it being such that it is transitive, contains R and is contained in every transitive relation that contains R. Therefore $x\dot{R}_D y$ means x, y are extremities of a chain in the relation $\cup_t \dot{R}_t$. This means there exist $r, i, ..., k$ and $z_i, ..., z_k$ such that $xR_r z_i R_i ... z_k R_k y$. But, considering the form of the elements of the R_t, now we must have $x_r = x_r \theta_r$, $z_i = x_i \theta_i, ..., z_k = x_k \theta_k$ for some $\theta_r, \theta_i, ..., \theta_k > 0$, and $u_k y \leq \theta_k$. Accordingly, the condition $x\dot{R}_D x_s \theta_s \rightarrow u_s x \geq \theta_s$ *for all x, s and $\theta_s > 0$*, for the absence of homogeneously revealed contradictions, can be restated as the condition

$$x_r \theta_r \dot{R}_r x_i \theta_i \dot{R}_i ... x_k \theta_k \dot{R}_k x_s \theta_s \rightarrow U_s x_r \theta_r \geq \theta_s \qquad (6.1)$$

for all $r, i, ..., k, s$ and $\theta_r, \theta_i, ..., \theta_k, \theta_s > 0$. From the form of the elements of the $\dot{R}_t$, that is

$$u_r x_i \theta_i \leq \theta_r, ..., u_k x_s \theta_s \leq \theta_k \rightarrow u_s x_r \theta_r \geq \theta_s$$

or, in terms of the Laspeyres coefficients,

$$L_{ri} \leq \theta_r/\theta_i, ..., L_{ks} \leq \theta_k/\theta_s \rightarrow L_{sr} \geq \theta_s/\theta_r \qquad (6.2)$$

Another way of stating this condition is that

$$(L_{ri}, ..., L_{ks}, L_{sr}) \leq (\theta_r/\theta_i, ..., \theta_k/\theta_s, \theta_s/\theta_r) \qquad (6.3)$$

is impossible for all $r, i, ..., k, s$ and $\theta_r, \theta_i, ..., \theta_k, \theta_s > 0$. This condition will be denoted $\dot{K}$.

While theory based on homogeneity is here the main object, in the background is the further theory without that restriction. Some account of that is given here, but it is mainly given elsewhere as already indicated. The dots used in the notation are to distinguish features in this homogeneous theory from their counterparts without homogeneity. The homogeneous theory is required in dealing with price indices, but still it has its source in the more general theory. It is useful in this section and later to bring counterparts of the two theories together for recognition of the connections and the differences.

Condition (6.1) has been identified with the condition for the absence of homogeneously revealed contradictions that in the last section was shown necessary and sufficient for the consistency of the given demands, that is, for the existence of a homogeneous utility compatible with them all simultaneously. The weaker condition that is the counterpart without homogeneity, put in a form that assists comparison, is the condition K given by

$$(L_{ri}, ..., L_{ks}, L_{sr}) \leq (1, ..., 1, 1) \qquad (6.4)$$

is impossible for all $r, i, ..., k, s$. By taking the θs all unity in (6.3), (6.4) is obtained, so (6.3) implies (6.4) as should be expected.

If compatibility between demand and utility is replaced by *strict compatibility*, by replacing cost-efficacy or cost-efficiency by their strict counterparts, which conditions in fact are equivalent to each other, and *strict consistency* of any demands means the existence of a strictly compatible utility, then the test for this condition which is a counterpart of (6.4) is the condition K^* given by

$$(L_{ri}, ..., L_{ks}, L_{sr}) \leq (1, ..., 1, 1) \tag{6.5}$$

is impossible for all r, i, ..., k, s unless $x_r = x_i = ... = x_k = x_s$, in which case the equality holds. This is just a way of stating the condition of Houthakker (1950), known as the Strong Axiom of Revealed Preference, for when that condition is applied to a finite set of demands instead of to the infinite set associated with a demand function. Here the *finiteness is not essential* and is just a matter of notation, though in later results it does have an essential part. Corresponding to the results obtained for the less strict consistency, and for homogeneous consistency, as in the Theorem of section 5, *Houthakker's condition is necessary and sufficient for the existence of strictly compatible utility, and for the revealed preference relation to be one such utility.*

While (6.5) is the 'strict' counterpart of (6.4), the corresponding counterpart for (6.3) is the condition K given by

$$(L_{ri}, ..., L_{ks}, L_{sr}) \leq (\theta_r/\theta_i, ..., \theta_k/\theta_s, \theta_s/\theta_r) \tag{6.6}$$

is impossible for all r, i, ..., k, s and θ_r, θ_i, ..., θ_k, $\theta_s > 0$ unless $x_r\theta_r = x_i\theta_i = ... = x_s\theta_s$ in which case the equality holds.

Just as a dot signifies a condition associated with homogeneity, a star signifies belonging to the 'strict' theory. The various conditions that have been stated have the relations

$$
\begin{array}{ccc}
\dot{K} & \rightarrow & K \\
\uparrow & & \uparrow \\
\dot{K}^* & \rightarrow & K^*
\end{array}
$$

The main result of this section, which is about $\dot{K}$ in (6.3) being a consistency condition, will be part of a theorem in the next section where it is developed into another form.

It can be noted that (6.3) is equivalent to the same condition with r, i, ..., k, s restricted to be all distinct. For the second condition is part of the first. Also, the inequalities stated in the first, involving a cycle of elements, can be partitioned into groups of inequalities involving simple cycles, each without repeated elements, showing that also the first follows from the second.

A finite consistency test is wanted, one that can be decided in a known finite number of steps. The last conclusion goes a step towards finding such a test, though it does not give one. That will be left to the next section. However, (6.4) and (6.5) taken with the indices all distinct already represent finite tests. But still this is not the case for Houthakker's condition (6.5), or for (6.4), when these are regarded as applying to a demand function, for which the number of cycles of distinct demands is unlimited.

7 Finite test

Theorem. For any finite demand relation D the following conditions are equivalent

($\dot{H}$) *D is homogeneously consistent, that is, there exists a compatible homogeneous utility relation;*

($\dot{R}$) *D is compatible with its own revealed homogeneous utility relation $\dot{R}_D$;*

($\dot{K}$) $(L_{rs}, L_{st}, ..., L_{qr}) \leq (\theta_r/\theta_s, \theta_s/\theta_t, ..., \theta_q/\theta_r)$ *is impossible for all distinct r, s, ..., q and $\theta_r, \theta_s, ..., \theta_q > 0$;*

($\dot{L}$) $L_{rst...qr} \geq 1$ *for all distinct r, s, ..., q.*

Arguments for the equivalences between $\dot{H}$, $\dot{R}$ and $\dot{K}$ have already been given in the last two sections. It is enough now to show $\dot{K}$ and $\dot{L}$ are equivalent. By multiplying the inequalities stated for any case where $\dot{K}$ is denied, it follows that

$$L_{rst...qr} < (\theta_r/\theta_s)(\theta_s/\theta_t) ... (\theta_q/\theta_r) = 1$$

contrary to $\dot{L}$. Thus $\dot{L} \rightarrow \dot{K}$. Now, contrary to $\dot{L}$, suppose $L_{rst...qr} < 1$, and let

$$\theta_r = L_{rst...qr}, \quad \theta_s = L_{st...qr}, \quad ..., \quad \theta_q = L_{qr}$$

Then

$$L_{rs} = \theta_r/\theta_s, \quad L_{st} = \theta_s/\theta_t, \quad ...$$

and finally, $\theta_r < 1$ and $\theta_q = L_{qr}$, so that $L_{qr} < \theta_q/\theta_r$, showing a denial of K. Thus $\dot{K} \rightarrow \dot{L}$, and the two conditions are now equivalent.

Because the number of simple cycles that can be formed from m elements is finite and given by

$$\sum_{r=1}^{m} (r - 1)!\binom{m}{r} = \sum_{r=1}^{m} (r - 1)!m!/r!(m - r)!$$

$$= \sum_{r=1}^{m} (m - r + 1) ... m/r$$

$\dot{L}$ is a finite test.

The counterpart of $\dot{K}$ for the general non-homogeneous theory has already been stated, and that for $\dot{L}$ is

(L) *There exist positive λs such that for all distinct r, s, t, ..., q*

$$(\lambda_r L_{rs} + \lambda_s L_{st} + ... + \lambda_q L_{qr})/(\lambda_r + \lambda_s + ... + \lambda_q) \geq 1$$

It can be noted that while $\dot{L}$ shows a finite test and $\dot{K}$ does not, L does not and K does.

There are several routes for proving the equivalence of K and L, all of some length. From that equivalence it is known that $\dot{L} \to L$. But this can be seen also directly. From the theorem that the geometric mean does not exceed the arithmetic,

$$(L_{rs} + L_{st} + ... + L_{qr})/k \geq L_{rst...qr}^{1/k}$$

k being the number of elements in the cycle. Therefore $\dot{L}$ implies

$$(L_{rs} + L_{st} + ... + L_{qr})/k \geq 1$$

But this validates L with all the λs equal to unity.

The counterpart of L for the 'strict' theory, equivalent to Houthakker's revealed preference axiom, is

(L^*) *There exist positive λs such that, for all distinct $r, s, t, ..., q$*

$$(\lambda_r L_{rs} + \lambda_s L_{st} + ... + \lambda_q L_{qr})/(\lambda_r + \lambda_s + ... + \lambda_q) \geq 1$$

the equality holding just when $x_r = x_s = x_t = ... = x_q$.

8 A system of inequalities

The test $L_{rs...qr} \geq 1$ *for all distinct r, s, ..., q*, that was found for the homogeneous consistency of a demand relation is also the test for solubility of the system of inequalities

$$L_{rs} \geq \phi_s/\phi_r \text{ for all } r, s \tag{8.1}$$

for numbers $\phi_r(r = 1, ..., m)$. Such numbers obtained by solving the inequalities will be identified as utility-levels for the demand periods, because for any demand period there exists a homogeneous utility compatible with the demands that identify them all as such, in that the numbers $X_{rs} = \phi_s/\phi_r$ are identified as quantity-indices, compatible with the data, and price indices correspond to these. By taking logarithms the system (7.1) comes into the form

$$a_{rs} \geq x_s - x_r \tag{8.2}$$

where $x_r = \log \phi_r$ and $a_{rs} = \log L_{rs}$. An account of the system in this form has been given in Afriat (1960), and in the last section here it is developed to suit needs of the present application.

The same system, in the additive form, arises also in the version of this theory unrestricted by homogeneity. It is required to find a positive solution of the system of homogeneous linear inequalities

$$\lambda_r(L_{rs} - 1) \geq \phi_s - \phi_r \tag{8.3}$$

That the ϕs be positive is inessential because they enter through their differences, and so a constant can always be added to make them so, but the restriction is essential. The λs occurring in solutions of (7.3) are identical with the λs that are solutions of (6.4), so they can be determined separately. With any λs so determined, and $a_{rs} = \lambda_r(L_{rs} - 1)$, (7.3) is in the form (7.2) for determining the ϕs. The ϕs and λs in any solution become utilities and marginal utilities at the demanded xs with a compatible utility that is constructed by means of the solution. In the case of a homogeneous utility, $\lambda_r = \phi_r$, and with this substitution (7.3) reduces to (7.1).

An entirely different connection for the system (7.2) is with minimum paths in networks. With the coefficient a_{rs} as direct path-distances, a solution of (7.2) corresponds to the concept of a *subpotential* for the network, as described by Fiedler and Ptak (1967). Whereas there it is an auxiliary that came in later, here it is a principal objective and a starting point. Then there is the linear programming formula $A_{ij} = \min[x_j - x_i : a_{rs} \geq x_r - x_s]$ expressing the minimum path-distance A_{ij} as the minimum subpotential difference, as learnt from Edmunds (1973). It is familiar under the assumption $a_{rs} \geq 0$, and in the integer programming context. Close to hand in the 1960 account is this formula without the non-negativity restriction on the coefficients and a quite different method of proof.

9 Utility construction

Now to be considered is how, for any number $\phi_t > 0$ such that

$$u_s x_t \geq \phi_t/\phi_s \tag{9.1}$$

it is possible to construct a linearly homogeneous, or conical, utility that is compatible with the given demands D_t and such that

$$\phi(x_t) = \phi_t \tag{9.2}$$

The utility constructed will moreover be semi-increasing, $x < y \rightarrow \phi(x) < \phi(y)$, and, being both conical and superadditive, $\phi(x + y) \geq \phi(x) + \phi(y)$; also it is concave.

The existence of numbers ϕ_t satisfying (9.1) is necessary and sufficient that there should exist any compatible homogeneous utility R at all, without further qualification. But here it is seen that if there exists one then also there exists one with these additional classical properties. A conclusion is that these classical properties are unobservable in the observational framework of choice under linear budgets, or are without empirical test or meaning and are just a property of the framework.

The consistency condition generally becomes more restrictive as additional restrictions are put on utility. Thus homogeneous consistency is more restrictive than the more general consistency that is free of the homogeneity. Then *classical consistency,* where utility is required to be representable by a utility function with the classical properties, might seem to be more restricted than general consistency, and also the same might be supposed for when homogeneity is added to both these conditions. But the contrary is a theorem: *the imposition of the classical properties makes no difference whatsoever.*

Let

$$\phi(x) = \min_t \phi_t u_t x \tag{9.3}$$

so, for all x,

$$\phi(x) \le \phi_t u_t x \text{ for all } t, \quad \phi(x) = \phi_t u_t x \text{ for some } t \tag{9.4}$$

Then, with $x = x_t$, so $u_t x = 1$, we have $\phi(x_t) < \phi_t$. But from (9.1), $\phi_s u_s x_t \ge \phi_t$ for all s. Hence, with (9.3), $\phi(x_t) = \min_s \phi_s u_s x_t \ge \phi_t$. Thus (9.2) is shown.

Now further, from (9.4) with $\phi_t > 0$,

$$u_t x < 1 \to \phi_t u_t x < \phi_t \to \phi(x) < \phi_t$$

Hence, with (9.2), $u_t x < 1 \to \phi(x) < \phi(x_t)$, and similarly, or from here by continuity, $u_t x \le 1 \to \phi(x) \le \phi(x_t)$, showing that the utility $\phi(x)$ and the normal demand (x_t, u_t) are compatible.

10 Utility cost

Because

$$u_t = M_t^{-1} p_t \tag{10.1}$$

where

$$M_t = p_t x_t \tag{10.2}$$

and because $X_t = \phi_t(x_t)$, another statement of (9.1), in view of (9.2), is that

$$p_s x_t / p_s x_s \ge X_t / X_s \tag{10.3}$$

Then introducing

$$P_t = M_t / X_t \tag{10.4}$$

so that, as a parallel to (10.2) $M_t = P_t X_t$, (10.3) and (10.4) give

$$p_s x_t / p_s x_s \ge (p_t x_t / P_t)/(p_s x_s / P_s) = (p_t x_t / p_s x_s)(P_s / P_t)$$

and consequently

$$p_s x_t / p_t x_t \ge P_s / P_t \tag{10.5}$$

Or again, introducing

$$U_t = M_t^{-1}P_t \tag{10.6}$$

in analogy with (10.1), so that $U_t X_t = 1$, this being, in analogy with the normalized budget identity $u_t x_t = 1$, an equivalent of (10.3), and also of (10.5), is that $u_s x_t \geq U_s/U_t$. Let $\theta(p)$ be the cost function associated with the classical homogeneous utility function $\phi(x)$, so that

$$\theta(p) = \min[px : \phi(x) \geq 1] \tag{10.7}$$

this again being classical homogeneous, that is semi-increasing, concave and conical. Then by taking x in the form xt^{-1}, where $t > 0$,

$$\theta(p) = \min[pxt^{-1} : \phi(xt^{-1}) \geq 1] = \min[pxt^{-1} : \phi(x) \geq t]$$

because ϕ is conical. Then by taking $t = \phi(x)$, $\theta(p) = \min_x px(\phi(x))^{-1}$ is obtained as an alternative formula for θ. From this formula the functions θ and ϕ are such that

$$\theta(p)\phi(x) \leq px \tag{10.8}$$

for all p, x with equality just in the case of compatibility between the demand (x, p) and the utility ϕ. For the equality signifies cost efficiency, and because ϕ is continuous this implies also cost effectiveness, and hence also the compatibility. Because ϕ is concave it is recovered from θ by the same formula by which θ is derived from it, with an exchange of roles between θ and ϕ; that is

$$\phi(x) = \min[px : \theta(p) \geq 1] = \min_p (\theta(p))^{-1}px \tag{10.9}$$

In the case of a normal demand (x, u), that is one for which $ux = 1$, (10.8) becomes

$$\theta(u)\phi(x) \leq 1 \tag{10.10}$$

with equality just in the case of a demand that is compatible with ϕ.

In section 9 it was shown that the function $\phi(x)$ constructed there is compatible with the given normal demands (x_t, u_t). Therefore $\theta(u_t)\phi(x_t) = 1$ for all t, while, by (10.10), $\theta(u_s)\phi(x_t) \leq 1$ for all s, t. Also it was shown that

$$\phi(x_t) = \phi_t \tag{10.11}$$

Hence, introducing

$$\theta_t = \phi_t^{-1} \tag{10.12}$$

it is shown that $\theta(u_t) = \theta_t$. It is possible to verify that also directly by inspection of the cost function. Thus, with $\phi(x) = \min_t \phi_t u_t x$, so that $\phi(x) \geq 1$ is equivalent to $\phi_t u_t x \geq 1$ for all t, which, with (10.12), is equivalent to $u_t x \geq \theta_t$ for all t, the cost function in (10.7) is also

$$\theta(u) = \min[ux : u_t x \geq \theta_t] \tag{10.13}$$

so that $\theta(u_t) \geq \theta_t$. Therefore, by (10.11) and (10.12), $\theta(u_t)\phi(x_t) \geq 1$. Then $u_t x_t = 1$ with (10.10) shows that $\theta(u_t)\phi(x_t) = 1$ and hence, again with (10.11) and (10.12), that $\theta(u_t) = \theta_t$.

By the linear programming duality theorem (Dantzig 1963) applied to (10.13), another formula for the cost function is

$$\theta(u) = \max \left[\sum s_t \theta_t : \sum s_t u_t \leq u \right] \tag{10.14}$$

Then, as known from the theory of linear programming, for any x, $\theta(u) \leq ux$ for all u if and only if x solves (10.13). Similarly, with the θ_t now variable while u is fixed, for any s_t, $\theta(u) \geq \Sigma s_t \theta_t$ for all θ_t if and only if the s_t solve (10.14).

If the θ_t are a strict solution of (9.1), that is $u_s x_t > \phi_t/\phi_s (s \neq t)$, then $x = x_t \theta_t$ is the unique solution of (10.13) when $u = u_t$. In just that case $\theta(u)$ is differentiable at the point $u = u_t$. In that case θ is locally linear, and has a unique support gradient, and the differential gradient which now exists coincides with it. Thus in this case $\theta(u) \leq ux$ for all u, and $\theta(u_t) = u_t x$ if and only if $x = x_t \theta_t$, so $\theta(u)$ has gradient $x_t \theta_t$ at $u = u_t$.

It can be added that this entire argument could have gone just as well with an interchange of roles between u and x. By solving $u_s x_t \geq \theta_s/\theta_t$ for the θ_t, a cost function θ could be constructed first, with the form originally given to ϕ, and then ϕ could have been derived. Also, ϕ need not have been given the polyhedral form (9.5). It could have been given the polytope form (10.13) or (10.14). Then θ would have had the polyhedral form (9.5).

11 Price and quantity

The method established for the determination of index numbers can be stated in a way that treats price and quantity both simultaneously and in a symmetrical fashion. With the given demands (x_t, p_t), numbers (X_t, P_t) should satisfy

$$p_s x_t \geq P_s X_t \text{ for all } s, t \tag{11.1}$$

Then, in particular,

$$p_t x_t = P_t X_t \tag{11.2}$$

Then division of (11.1) by (11.2) gives

$$p_s x_t / p_t x_t \geq P_s / P_t \tag{11.3}$$

as a condition for the 'price levels', and also

$$p_s x_t / p_s x_s \geq X_t / X_s \tag{11.4}$$

for 'quantity levels'. Reversely, starting with a solution P_t of (11.3), let X_t be determined from (11.2). Then X_t is a solution of (11.4) and the P_t and X_t together make a solution of (11.1). Just as well, the procedure could start with a solution X_t of (11.4) and go on similarly.

It has been established that the existence of solutions to these inequalities is necessary and sufficient for homogeneous consistency of the demand data. The investigation now concerns the identification of the numbers $P_{rs} = P_s / P_r$ obtained from solutions with *all possible* price indices that are compatible with the data, that is, derivable on the basis of compatible homogeneous utilities. Then it will be possible to go further with a description of all possible price indices in terms of closed intervals specified by formulae for their end-points, or limits.

For any utility order R, the derived utility – cost function $\rho(p, x) = \min[py : yRx]$ is defined for all p, x if the sets Rx are closed. If R is a complete order and the sets Rx, xR are closed then, for any p, $\rho(p, x)$ is a utility function representing R (see Afriat, 1979). It follows that, for any p and q, there exists an increasing function $w(t)$, independent of x and carrying p, q as parameters, such that $\rho(p, x) = w(\rho(q, x))$ for all x.

If R is conical then so is $\rho(p, x)$ as a function of x, for any p. In that case so is $w(t)$ as a function of t. But a conical function of one variable must be homogeneous linear, so $w(t)$ has the form wt where w is a function of p, q independent of x. That is, $\rho(p, x)/\rho(q, x) = w$ is independent of x. Then w must have the form $w = \theta(p)/\theta(q)$ where $\theta(p)$ is a function of p alone, so it follows that $\rho(p, x)/(\theta(p)$ must be a function of x alone, and so $\rho(p, x) = \theta(p)\phi(x)$, where θ, ϕ are functions p, x alone. Now ϕ must be a utility that represents R, and be conical because ρ is conical in x. Then the condition for ϕ to be quasi-concave is that the sets Rx be convex. But because ϕ is conical this is also the condition that ϕ be concave (Berge, 1963). Moreover, because in any case $\rho(p, x)$ is concave conical in p, so also is $\theta(p)$.

The reflexivity of R gives in any case $\rho(p, x) \leq px$, so now $\theta(p)\phi(x) \leq px$ for all x. Hence, for all p, $\theta(p) \leq \min_x px(\phi(x))^{-1}$, while $\rho(p, x) = px$ for some x gives $\theta(p)\phi(x) = px$ for some x, so that now $\theta(p) = \min px(\phi(x))^{-1}$. Similarly $\phi(x) \leq \min_p(\theta(p))^{-1} px$. Then let $\bar{\phi}(x) = \min_p(\theta(p))^{-1}px$, so $\phi(x) \leq \bar{\phi}(x)$ for all x and $\bar{\phi}$ is concave conical. Then, for any x, $\phi(x) = \bar{\phi}(x)$ is equivalent to $\theta(p)\phi(x) = px$ for some p. The condition for this to be so for any x is that $\phi(x)$ be quasi-concave, having a quasi-support p at x, for which

$$py < px \rightarrow \phi(y) < \phi(x), \quad py \leq px \rightarrow \phi(y) \leq \phi(x)$$

in other words the demand (x, p) is compatible with x for some p. This condition, which means that, with choice governed by ϕ, x could be demanded at some prices, can define compatibility between ϕ and x. The condition that ϕ be compatible with all x is just that it be quasi-concave, and that now is equivalent to $\phi(x) = \bar{\phi}(x)$ for all x. In any case, any x compatible with ϕ is also compatible with $\bar{\phi}$. Hence, if utility R is constrained by compatibility with given demands, if ϕ is acceptable then so is $\bar{\phi}$, and moreover ϕ and $\bar{\phi}$ have the same conjugate price function θ. This suggests that, instead of constructing a utility ϕ compatible with the data having a concave form that is a generally unwarranted restriction on utility and, for all we know now, might make some added restriction on price-index values, it is both possible and advantageous to construct the price function θ first instead, and so be free of such a suspicion. It has already been remarked that this might have been done instead, following an identical procedure as that for the ϕ, so in fact that issue is already disposed of. From any compatible homogeneous utility a price function θ is derived, giving the $P_r = \theta(p_r)$ as a system of 'price-levels' compatible with the data, and determining the $P_{rs} = P_s/P_r$ as compatible prices. But the possible such P_r are already identified with the possible solutions of (11.3). Also, for any solution P_r and the θ that must exist, the X_r determined from (11.2) have the identification $X_r = \phi(x_r)$ where $\phi(x) = \min_p(\theta(p))^{-1}px$. This ϕ is concave conical. But also any other ϕ^*, not necessary concave but having the same conjugate θ, would do, so there is no inherent restriction to concave utilities here. For such a ϕ^*, generally $\phi^*(x) \leq \phi(x)$, while $\phi^*(x_r) = \phi(x_r)$ for all r, and all that is required of ϕ^* is that $\theta(x) = \min_p px(\phi^*(x))^{-1}$, and there are many ϕ^* for which this is so, that given being just one.

The argument in this section permits by-passing complications of the argument involving 'critical cost functions' that was used formerly, such as in the exposition of Afriat (1977b) for the special case of just two demand-periods. An interesting point is that the care taken in both arguments to avoid imposing on a compatible utility the requirement that also it be concave makes no difference at all to the range of possible values for a price-index.

12 Extension and exhaustion properties

For any coefficients $a_{rs}(r, s = 1, \ldots, k)$, consider the system $S(a)$ of simultaneous linear inequalities

$$a_{rs} \geq x_s - x_r \tag{12.1}$$

to be solved for numbers x_r. This is an alternative form for the system (7.1), and the form that applies directly to the system (7.3). Introduce *chain-coefficients*

$$a_{rij...ks} = a_{ri} + a_{ij} + ... + a_{ks} \tag{12.2}$$

so that

$$a_{r...s...t} = a_{r...s} + a_{s...t} \tag{12.3}$$

If the system $S(a)$ has a solution x then

$$a_{ri} \geq x_i - x_r, \; x_{ij} \geq x_j - x_i, \; ..., \; a_{ks} \geq x_s - x_k$$

so by addition,

$$a_{r...s} \geq x_s - x_r \tag{12.4}$$

In particular $a_{r...r} \geq x_r - x_r = 0$, so that $a_{r...r} \geq 0$, that is,

$$a_{ri} + a_{ij} + ... + a_{kr} \geq 0 \tag{12.5}$$

for every cyclic sequence of elements r, i, j, ..., k, r. This can be called the *cyclical non-negativity* condition C on the system $S(a)$, and it has been seen *necessary for the existence of a solution.* Because

$$a_{r...s...s...r} = a_{r...s...r} + a_{s...s}$$

the coefficient on a cycle with a repeated element s can be expressed as a sum of terms that are coefficients on cycles where the repetition multiplicity is reduced, and this decomposition can be performed on those terms and so forth until an expression is obtained with only simple cycles, without repeated elements. From this it follows that the condition C is equivalent to the same condition on cycles that are restricted to be simple, or have elements all distinct.

Under the condition C,

$$a_{r...s...s...t} = a_{r...s...t} + a_{s...s} \geq a_{r...s...t}$$

so the cancellation of a loop in a chain does not increase the coefficient along it. It follows that the *derived coefficient*

$$A_{rs} = \min_{ij...} a_{rij...s} \tag{12.6}$$

exists for any r, s and moreover

$$A_{rs} = a_{rij...s} \tag{12.7}$$

for some simple chain rij ... s from r to s. Thus C is sufficient for the existence of the derived coefficients. Also it is necessary. For if $a_{s...s} < 0$ then for any r, t by taking the chain that goes from r to t, following the loop $s ... s$ any number K of times and then going from s to t, we have

$$A_{rt} \leq a_{rs} + Ka_{s...s} + a_{st} \to -\infty(K \to \infty) \tag{12.8}$$

so A_{rt} cannot exist. Therefore also *C is sufficient for the existence of the derived coefficients.* Evidently then either the derived coefficients all exist or none do. Given that they exist, from (12.3) it follows that $A_{rs} + A_{st} \geq A_{rt}$, *so they satisfy the triangle inequality.*

The system $S(a)$ and the derived system $S(A)$, of inequalities

$$A_{rs} \geq x_s - x_r \tag{12.9}$$

have the same solutions. For from (12.4), any solution of (12.1) is a solution of (12.9). Also from $A_{rs} \leq a_{rs}$, that follows from the definition (12.6) of the A_{rs}, it is seen that any solution of (12.9) is a solution of (12.1).

The triangle inequality is necessary and sufficient for a system to be identical with its derived system, that is for $A_{rs} = a_{rs}$ for all r, s. It is necessary because any derived system has that property. Also it is sufficient. For the triangle inequality on $S(a)$ is equivalent to $a_{rij...ks} \geq a_{rs}$, but (12.9) implies both that the derived coefficients A_{rs} exist and that $A_{rs} \geq a_{rs}$, which because of (12.8) is equivalent to (12.9).

Now the *extension property* for the solutions of a system that satisfies the triangle inequality will be proved. Let $S(A)$ be any such system, so if this is the derived system of some other system then this hypothesis must be valid.

A subsystem of $S(A)$ is obtained when the indices are restricted to any subset of $1, ..., n$. Without loss in generality consider the subsystem $S_{m-1}(A)$ on the subset of $1, ..., m - 1$. Let $x_r (r < m)$ be any solution for this subsystem, so that

$$A_{rs} \geq x_s - x_r \quad \text{for} \quad r, s < m \tag{12.10}$$

Now consider any larger system obtained by adjoining a further element to the set of indices. Without loss in generality, let m be that element and $S_m(A)$ the system obtained. It will be shown that there exists x_m so that the $x_r (r \leq m)$ that extend the solution $x_r (r < m)$ of $S_{m-1}(A)$ are a solution of $S_m(A)$, that is

$$A_{rs} \geq x_s - x_r \quad \text{for} \quad r, s \leq m \tag{12.11}$$

With the $x_r (r < m)$ satisfying (12.10), x_m has to satisfy

$$A_{rm} \geq x_m - x_r \quad \text{for} \quad r < m, \quad A_{ms} \geq x_s - x_m \quad \text{for} \quad s < m \tag{12.12}$$

Equivalently, $x_s - A_{ms} \leq x_m \leq x_r + A_{rm}$ for $r, s < m$. But a necessary and sufficient condition for the existence of such x_m is that $x_s - A_{ms} \leq x_r + A_{rm}$ for $r, s < m$, equivalently $A_{rm} + A_{ms} \geq x_s - x_r$ for $r, s < m$. By the triangle inequality, (12.11) implies this, so the existence of such x_m is now proved. Thus *any solution of $S_{m-1}(A)$ can be extended to a solution of $S_m(A)$.* Then by an inductive argument it follows that, for any $m \leq n$, *any solution* $x_r (r \leq m)$ *of* $S_m(A)$ *can be extended to a solution of* $S_n(A) = S(A)$, by adjunction of further elements $x_r (r > m)$. It can be concluded that *any system with the triangle inequality has a solution*, because the triangle inequality requires in particular that $A_{11} + A_{11} \geq A_{11}$, or equivalently $A_{11} \geq 0$. This assures that $S_1(A)$ has a solution x_1 and then any such solution x_1 can be extended to a solution $x_r (r \leq n)$ of $S(A)$.

From the foregoing, each of the conditions in the following sequence implies its successor: (i) The existence of a solution. (ii) The cyclical non-negativity test. (iii) The existence of the derived system. (iv) The existence of a solution for the derived system. (v) The existence of a solution.

It was shown first that (i) → (ii) → (iii). Then because any derived system satisfies the triangle inequality and any system with that property has a solution, (iii) ↔ (iv) is shown. Now the identity between the solutions of a system and its derived system shows (iv) ↔ (i) and establishes equivalence between all the conditions, in particular between (i) and (ii).

The derived system $S(A)$ can be stated in the form

$$-A_{sr} \leq x_s - x_r \leq A_{rs} \quad (r \leq s)$$

requiring the differences $x_s - x_r (r \leq s)$ to belong to the intervals $(-A_{sr}, A_{rs})$. The extension property of solutions assures also the *interval exhaustion property*, that *every point in these intervals is taken by some solution*. Whenever the derived system exists these intervals automatically are all non-empty.

An order U of the indices determined from the coefficients A_{rs} is given by the transitive closure $U = \vec{A}$ of the relation A given by $rAs \equiv A_{rs} \leq 0$. Also, any solution x determines an order $V(x)$ of the indices, where $rV(x)s \equiv x_s \leq x_r$. Whatever the solution, *this is always a refinement of the order* U, that is $V(x) \subset U$ for every solution x. Moreover, *for any order V that is a refinement of U, there always exists a solution x such that* $V(x) = V$. This *order exhaustion property* can be seen from the interval exhaustion property and also by means of the proof of the extension property of solutions by taking the extensions in the required order.

These results can all be translated to apply to a system in the form $a_{rs} \geq x_s / x_r$, now with *multiplicative chain coefficients*, $a_{rij...ks} = a_{ri}a_{ij}...a_{ks}$ and derived coefficients A_{rs} defined from these as before and satisfying the *multiplicative triangle inequality* $A_{rs}A_{st} \geq A_{rt}$. The cyclical non-negativity test becomes $a_{rs}a_{st} ... a_{qr} \geq 1$. For any solution x, the ratios x_s / x_r are required to lie in the intervals $I_{rs} = (1/A_{sr}, A_{rs})$. From their form these intervals remind of the Paasche – Laspeyres (*PL*) interval $(1/L_{sr}, L_{rs})$. Also, the multiplicative chain coefficients correspond to the familiar procedure of multiplying chains of price indices, except that there are many chains with given extremities and here one is taken on which the coefficient is minimum. While the non-emptiness of the *PL*-intervals, whether or not the one index exceeds the other, is a well known issue, there is no such issue at all with the intervals I_{rs} *because whenever they are defined they are non-empty,* this following from the multiplicative triangle inequality that gives

$$A_{rs}A_{sr} \geq A_{rr} \geq 1$$

13 The power algorithm

For a system with coefficients a_{rs}, and any $k \leq m \leq n$, let

$$a_{rs}^{[k]} = \min_{i_2 i_k} (a_{ri_2} + a_{i_2 i_3} + \ldots + a_{i_k s}), \quad a_{rs}^{(m)} = \min_{k \leq m} a_{rs}^{[k]} \qquad (13.1)$$

According to (12.6), if the derived coefficients exist any one has the form

$$A_{rs} = a_{ri} + a_{ij} + \ldots + a_{ks} \qquad (13.2)$$

for some $i, j, \ldots, k$ making $r, i, j, \ldots, s$ all distinct except possibly for the coincidence of r and s. Because there are just n possible values $1, \ldots, n$ for the indices, it follows from (13.1) and (13.2) that $A_{rs} \geq a_{rs}^{(n)}$. But from the definition of the A_{rs} in (12.6) and from (13.1) again, also $A_{rs} \leq a_{rs}^{(n)}$, so now $A_{rs} = a_{rs}^{(n)}$, that is $A = a^{(n)}$. Now writing $+$ as $.$ and $\min$ as $+$, (13.1) becomes

$$a_{rs}^{[k]} = \sum_{i, \ldots i_{m-1}} a_{ri_1} \cdot a_{i_1 i_2} \cdot \ldots \cdot a_{i_{k-1}s}$$

$$= (a \cdot a \cdot \ldots a)_{rs} (k \text{ factors})$$

$$= (a^k)_{rs}$$

that is $a^{[k]} = a^k$, where the 'power' a^k so defined is unambiguous because of associativity of 'multiplication' and 'addition' and the distributivity of 'multiplication' over 'addition' and is determined recurrently from

$$a^1 = a \quad \text{and} \quad a^k = a \cdot a^{k-1} \qquad (13.3)$$

Then (13.2) becomes $a^{(m)} = \Sigma_1^m a^k$, and is determined from

$$a^{(1)} = a \quad \text{and} \quad a^{(m)} = aa^{(m-1)} + a \qquad (13.4)$$

This algorithm with powers in the context of minimum paths in networks is from Bainbridge (1978). Observed now is a simplification that is applicable to the special case of importance here where $a_{rr} = 0$, or where $a_{rr} = 1$ in the multiplicative formulation. If $a_{rr} = 0$, in which case chains of any length include all those of lesser length, we have

$$a \geq a^2 \geq \ldots \geq a^k \geq \ldots \geq a^m$$

where the matrix relation $\geq$ means that relation simultaneously for all elements. Therefore in this case $a^{(m)} = a^m$. This with $A = a^{(n)}$, together with (13.3), shows that the matrix A of derived coefficients can be calculated by raising the matrix a of the original coefficients to successive powers, the nth power being A. Should $a^m = a^{m-1}$ for any $m \leq n$ then also $a^m = a^{m+1} = \ldots = a^n = \ldots$ so that $A = a^m$. But in any case the formula $A = a^n$ is valid. Then evidently $A = A^2 = \ldots$, so *the derived matrix is idempotent.* This property is characteristic of any matrix having the triangle inequality.

By taking exponentials, these procedures can be translated to apply to the system in the multiplicative form (7.1), $L_{rs} \geq \phi_s/\phi_r$ with $L_{rr} = 1$. Matrix powers have been defined in a sense where $+$ means min and . means $+$. Taking exponentials turns $+$ into . and leaves min as min, so we are back with . meaning. . This makes $\hat{L} = L^n$ a formula for the derived coefficient matrix, where powers now are defined in the ordinary sense except that $+$ now means min. As before, n here can be replaced by any $m \leq n$ for which $L^m = L^{m+1}$, in particular by the first such m found.

References

Afriat, S. N. 1956. 'Theory of Economic Index Numbers'. Mimeographed. Department of Applied Economics, Cambridge.

1960. 'The system of inequalities $a_{rs} > X_s - X_r$'. *Research Memorandum No. 18*, Econometric Research Program, Princeton University, Princeton, NJ. *Proc. Cambridge Phil. Soc.*, **59** (1963), 125–33.

1964. 'The construction of utility functions from expenditure data'. *Cowles Foundation Discussion Paper No.* 144, Yale University. Paper presented at the First World Congress of the Econometric Society, Rome, September 1965. *International Economic Review*, **8** (1967), 67–77.

1967a. 'The Cost of Living Index'. In *Studies in Mathematical Economics: In Honor of Oskar Morgenstern*. Edited by M. Shubik. Princeton, NJ: Princeton University Press.

1970a. 'The Concept of a Price Index and Its Extension'. Paper presented at the Second World Congress of the Econometric Society, Cambridge, August 1970.

1970b. 'The Cost and Utility of Consumption'. Mimeographed. Department of Economics, University of North Carolina at Chapel Hill, North Carolina.

1970c. 'Direct and Indirect Utility'. Mimeographed. Department of Economics, University of North Carolina at Chapel Hill, North Carolina.

1972a. 'Revealed Preference Revealed'. Waterloo Economic Series No. 60, University of Waterloo, Ontario.

1972b. 'The Theory of International Comparisons of Real Income and Prices'. In *International Comparisons of Prices and Output*, Proceedings of the Conference at York University, Toronto, 1970. Edited by D. J. Daly, 13–84. Studies in Income and Wealth, vol. 37. New York: National Bureau of Economic Research.

1973. 'On a System of Inequalities in Demand Analysis: an Extension of the Classical Method'. *International Economic Review*, **14**, 460–72.

1974. 'Sum-symmetric matrices'. *Linear Algebra and its Applications*, **8**, 129–40.

1976. *Combinatorial Theory of Demand*. London: Input – Output Publishing Co.

1977a. 'Minimum paths and subpotentials in a valuated network'. Research Paper 7704, Department of Economics, University of Ottawa.

1977b. *The Price Index*. Cambridge and New York: Cambridge University Press.

1978a. '*Index Numbers in Theory and Practice* by R. G. D. Allen'. *Canadian Journal of Economics*, **11**, 367–9.

1978b. '*Theory of the Price Index* by Wolfgang Eichhorn and Joachim Voeller'. *Journal of Economic Literature*, **16**, 129–30.

1979. *Demand Functions and the Slutsky Matrix*. Princeton, NJ: Princeton University Press.

1980. 'Matrix Powers: Classical and Variations'. Paper presented at the Matrix Theory Conference, Auburn University, Auburn, Alabama, 19–22 March 1980.

Allen, R. G. D. 1975. *Index Numbers in Theory and Practice*. London: Macmillan.

Bainbridge, S. 1978. 'Power algorithm for minimum paths', private communication. Department of Mathematics, University of Ottawa, Ontario.

Berge, C. 1963. *Topological Spaces*. New York: Macmillan.

Berge, C. and Ghouila-Houri, A. 1965. *Programming, Games and Transportation Networks*. London: Methuen & Co. New York: John Wiley and Sons.

Dantzig, G. 1963. 'Linear Programming and Its Extensions'. Princeton, NJ: Princeton University Press.

Edmunds, J. 1973. 'Linear programming formula for minimum paths', private communication. Department of Combinatorics and Optimization, Faculty of Mathematics, University of Waterloo, Ontario.

Eichhorn, W. and Voeller, J. 1976. *Theory of the Price Index: Fisher's Test Approach and Generalizations*. Berlin, Heidelburg and New York: Springer-Verlag.

Fiedler, M. and Ptak, V. 1967. 'Diagonally dominant matrices'. *Czech. Math J.*, **17**, 420–33.

Fisher, I. 1927. *The Making of Index Numbers*. Third edition. Boston and New York: Houghton Mifflin Company.

Geary, R. C. 1958. 'A note on the comparison of exchange rates and purchasing power between countries'. *J. Roy Stat. Soc.* A, **121**, 97–9.

Hicks, J. R. 1956. *A Revision of Demand Theory*. Oxford: Clarendon Press.

Houthakker, H. S. 1950. 'Revealed Preference and the Utility Function', *Economica*, New Series, **17**, 159–74.

Samuelson, P. A. 1947. *The Foundations of Economic Analysis*. Cambridge, Mass.: Harvard University Press.

Samuelson, P. A. and Swamy, S. 1974. 'Invariant Economic Index Numbers and Canonical Duality: Survey and Synthesis'. *American Economic Review*, **64**, 566–93.

Shephard, R. W. 1953. *Cost and Production Functions*. Princeton, NJ: Princeton University Press.

Theil, H. 1960. 'Best linear index numbers of prices and quantities'. *Econometrica*, **28**, 464–80.

1975–1976. *Theory and Measurement of Consumer Demand*. Two volumes. Amsterdam: North-Holland Publishing Company.

1979. *The System-wide Approach to Microeconomics*. The University of Chicago Press.

Yen, J. Y. 1975. *Shortest Path Network Problems*. Meisenheim am Glan: Verlag Anton Hain.

7 The economic theory of index numbers: a survey[1]

W. E. DIEWERT

1 Introduction

The literature on index numbers is so vast that we can cover only a small fraction of it in this chapter. Frisch (1936) distinguishes three approaches to index number theory: (i) 'statistical' approaches, (ii) the test approach, and (iii) the functional approach, which Wold (1953, p. 135) calls the preference field approach and Samuelson and Swamy (1974, p. 573) call the economic theory of index numbers. We shall mainly cover the essentials of the third approach. In the following two sections, we define the different index number concepts that have been suggested in the literature and develop various numerical bounds. Then in section 4, we briefly survey some of the other approaches to index number theory. In section 5, we relate various functional forms for utility or production functions to various index number formulae. In section 6, we develop the link between 'flexible' functional forms and 'superlative' index number formulae. The final section offers a few historical notes and some comments on some related topics such as the measurement of consumer surplus and the Divisia index.

2 Price indexes and the Konüs cost of living index

We assume that a consumer is maximizing a utility function $F(x)$ subject to the expenditure constraint $p^T x \equiv \Sigma_{i=1}^{N} p_i x_i \leq y$ where $x \equiv (x_1, \ldots, x_N)^T \geq 0_N$ is a non-negative vector of commodity rentals, $p \equiv (p_1, \ldots, p_N)^T \gg 0_N$ is a positive vector of commodity prices[2] and $y > 0$ is expenditure on the N commodities. We could also assume that a producer is maximizing a production function $F(x)$ subject to the expenditure constraint $p^T x \leq y$ where $x \geq 0_N$ is now an input vector, $p \gg 0_N$ is an input price vector and $y > 0$ is expenditure on the inputs. In order to cover both the consumer and producer theory applications, we shall call the utility or production function F an *aggregator function* in what follows.

   The consumer's (or producer's) aggregator maximization problem can be decomposed into two stages: in the first stage, the consumer (or pro-

163

ducer) attempts to minimize the cost of achieving a given utility (or output) level, and, in the second stage, he chooses the maximal utility (or output) level that is just consistent with his budget constraint.

The solution to the first stage problem defines the consumer's (or producer's cost function C:

$$C(u, p) \equiv \min_x\{p^T x: F(x) \geq u, x \geq 0_N\} \tag{1}$$

The cost function C turns out to play a pivotal role in the economic approach to index number theory.

Throughout much of this chapter, we shall assume that the aggregator function F satisfies the following *Conditions I:* F is a real valued function of N variables defined over the non-negative orthant $\Omega \equiv \{x: x \geq 0_N\}$ which has the following three properties: (i) continuity, (ii) increasingness[3] and (iii) quasi-concavity.[4]

Let U be the range of F. From I(i) and (ii), it can be seen that $U \equiv \{u: \underline{u} \leq u \leq \bar{u}\}$ where $\underline{u} \equiv F(0_N) < \bar{u}$. Note that the least upper bound $\bar{u}$ could be a finite number or $+\infty$. In the context of production theory, typically $\underline{u} = 0$ and $\bar{u} = +\infty$, but, for consumer theory applications, there is no reason to restrict the range of the utility function F in this manner.

Define the set of positive prices $p \equiv \{p: p \gg 0_N\}$. It can be shown that (see Diewert, 1978c) if F satisfies Conditions I, then the cost function C defined by (1) satisfies the following *Conditions II:*

(i) $C(u, p)$ is a real valued function of $N + 1$ variables defined over $U \times P$ and is jointly *continuous* in (u, p) over this domain.

(ii) $C(\underline{u}, p) = 0$ for every $p \in P$.

(iii) $C(u, p)$ is *increasing in u* for every $p \in P$; i.e., if $p \in P$, $u', u'' \in U$, with $u' < u''$, then $C(u', p) < C(u'', p)$.

(iv) $C(\bar{u}, p) = +\infty$ for every $p \in P$; i.e., if $p \in P$, $u^n \in U$, $\lim_n u^n = \bar{u}$, then $\lim_n C(u^n, p) = +\infty$.

(v) $C(u, p)$ is (positively) *linearly homogenous in p* for every $u \in U$: i.e. $u \in U$, $\lambda > 0$, $p \in P$ implies $C(u, \lambda p) = \lambda C(u, p)$.

(vi) $C(u, p)$ is *concave in p* for every $u \in U$; i.e., if $p' \gg 0_N$, $p'' \gg 0_N$, $0 \leq \lambda \leq 1$, $u \in U$, then $C(u, \lambda p' + (1 - \lambda) p'') \geq \lambda C(u, p') + (1 - \lambda)C(u, p'')$.

(vii) $C(u, p)$ is increasing in p for $u > \underline{u}$ and $u \in U$.

(viii) C is such that the function $F^*(x) \equiv \max_u\{u: p^T x \geq C(u, p)$ for every $p \in P$, $u \in U\}$ is continuous for $x \geq 0_N$.

For some of the theorems to be presented in this chapter, we can weaken the regularity conditions on the aggregator function F to just *continuity from above.*[5] Under this weakened hypothesis on F, the cost function C defined by (1) will still satisfy many of the properties in Conditions II above.[6]

Finally, some of the theorems below make use of the following (stronger) regularity conditions on the aggregator function: we say that F is a *neoclassical aggregator function* if it is defined over the positive orthant $\{x: x \gg 0_N\}$ and is (i) *positive,* i.e. $F(x) > 0$ for $x \gg 0_N$, (ii) (positively) *linearly homogeneous,* and (iii) *concave* over $\{x: x \gg 0_N\}$. Under these conditions (let us call them *Conditions III*) F can be extended to the non-negative orthant Ω, and the extended F will be non-negative, linearly homogeneous, concave, increasing and continuous over Ω (see Diewert, 1978c). Moreover, if F is neoclassical, then F's cost function C factors into

$$C(u, p) \equiv u \, C(1, p) \equiv u \, c(p) \tag{2}$$

for $u \geq 0$ and $p \gg 0_N$ where $c(p) \equiv C(1, p)$ is F's *unit cost function.* It can be shown that c satisfies the same regularity conditions as F; i.e. c is also a neoclassical function. Also, if we are given a neoclassical unit cost function c, then the underlying aggregator function F can be defined for $x \gg 0_N$ by

$$
\begin{aligned}
F(x) &\equiv \max_u \{u: C(u, p) \leq p^T x \text{ for every } p > 0_N\} \\
&= \max_u \{u: u \, c(p) \leq p^T x \text{ for every } p \geq 0_N, \, p^T x = 1\} \\
&= \min_p \{1/c(p): p \geq 0_N, \, p^T x = 1\} \tag{3}
\end{aligned}
$$

$$= 1/\max_p \{c(p): p^T x = 1, \, p \geq 0_N\} \tag{4}$$

Now that we have disposed of the mathematical preliminaries, we can define the Konüs (1924) *cost of living index*[7] P_K: for $p^0 \gg 0_N$, $p^1 \gg 0_N$ and $x > 0_N$

$$P_K(p^0, p^1, x) \equiv C[F(x), p^1]/C[F(x), p^0] \tag{5}$$

Thus P_K depends on three sets of variables: (i) p^0, a vector of period 0 or base period prices, (ii) p^1, a vector of period 1 or current period prices,[8] and (iii) x, a reference vector of quantities.[9] In the consumer context, P_K can be interpreted as follows. Pick a reference indifference surface indexed by the quantity vector $x > 0_N$. Then $P_K(p^0, p^1, x)$ is the minimum cost of achieving the standard of living indexed by x when the consumer faces period 1 prices p^1 relative to the minimum cost of achieving the same standard of living when the consumer faces period 0 prices p^0. Thus P_K can be interpreted as a level of prices in period 1 relative to a level of prices in period 0. If the number of goods is only one (i.e. $N = 1$), then it is easy to see that $P_K(p_1^0, p_1^1, x_1) = p_1^1/p_1^0$ for all $x_1 > 0$.

Note that the mathematical properties of P_K with respect to p^0, p^1 and x are determined by the mathematical properties of F and C given by Conditions I and II above. In particular, for $\lambda > 0$, $p^0 \gg 0_N$ $p^1 \gg 0_N$ and $x \gg 0_N$, we have $P_K(p^0, \lambda p^0, x) = \lambda$ and $P_K(p^0, p^1, x) = 1/P_K(p^1, p^0, x)$. Thus if period 1 prices are proportional to period 0 prices, then P_K is equal to the common factor of proportionality for any reference quantity vector x. However, if prices are not proportional, then in general P_K depends on the reference vector x, except when preferences are homothetic as is shown in the following result.

Theorem 1[10] ((Malmquist (1953, p. 215), Pollak (1971, p. 31), Samuelson and Swamy (1974, pp. 569–70)): Let the aggregator function F satisfy Conditions I. Then $P_K(p^0, p^1, x)$ is independent of x if and only if F is homothetic.

Proof: If F is homothetic, then, by definition, there exists a continuous, monotonically increasing function of one variable G, with $G(\bar{u}) = 0$ such that $G[F(x)] \equiv f(x)$ is a neoclassical aggregator function (i.e. f satisfies Conditions III above). Under these conditions, F's cost function decomposes as follows: for $u > 0$, $p \gg 0_N$,

$$
\begin{aligned}
C(u, p) &\equiv \min_x\{p^T x: F(x) \geq u\} \\
&= \min_x\{p^T x: G[F(x)] \geq G(u)\} \\
&= G(u)c(p)
\end{aligned}
\tag{6}
$$

where c is the unit cost function which corresponds to the neoclassical aggregator function f. Thus for $p^0 \gg 0_N$, $p^1 \gg 0_N$ and $x > 0_N$, we have

$$
\begin{aligned}
P_K(p^0, p^1, x) &\equiv C[F(x), p^1]/C[F(x), p^0] \\
&= G[F(x)]c(p^1)/G[F(x)]c(p^0) \\
&= c(p^1)/c(p^0)
\end{aligned}
\tag{7}
$$

which is independent of x.

Conversely, if P_K is independent of x, then we must have the factorization (7); i.e. we must have for every $x \gg 0_N$, $p \gg 0_N$

$$
C(F(x), p) = G[F(x)]c(p)
\tag{8}
$$

for some functions G and c, whose regularity properties must be such that C satisfies Conditions II. It can be verified that the regularity conditions on C and the decomposition (8) imply that the functions c and $G[F]$ both satisfy Conditions III,[11] so that, in particular, $G[F(x)]$ is (positively) linearly homogeneous in x. Thus F is homothetic.   Q.E.D.

Thus in the case of a homothetic aggregator function, the Konüs cost of living index $P_K(p^0, p^1, x)$ is independent of the reference quantity vector x and is equal to a ratio of unit cost functions, $c(p^1)/c(p^0)$.

If we knew the consumer's preferences (or the producer's production function), then we could construct the cost function $C(u, p)$ and the Konüs price index P_K. However, usually we do not know F or C and thus it is useful to develop *non-parametric bounds* on P_K; i.e. bounds that do not depend on the functional form for the aggregator function F (or its cost function dual C).

Theorem 2 (Lerner, 1935–36; Joseph, 1935–36, p. 149; Samuelson, 1947, p. 159; Pollak, 1971, p. 12): If the aggregator function F is continuous from above, then, for every $p^0 \equiv (p_1^0, \ldots, p_N^0)^T \gg 0_N$, $p^1 \equiv (p_1^1, \ldots, p_N^1)^T \gg 0_N$ and $\bar{x} > 0_N$ where $F(\bar{x}) > F(0_N)$,

$$\min_i\{p_i^1/p_i^0: i = 1, \ldots, N\} \leq P_K(p^0, p^1, \bar{x})$$
$$\leq \max_i\{p_i^1/p_i^0: i = 1, \ldots, N\} \quad (9)$$

i.e. P_K lies between the smallest and the largest price ratio.

Proof: Let $p^0 \gg 0_N$, $p^1 \gg 0_N$, $\bar{x} > 0_N$ where $F(\bar{x}) > F(0_N)$ and let $x^0 \geq 0_N$ and $x^1 \geq 0_N$ solve the following cost minimization problems:

$$C[F(\bar{x}), p^0] \equiv \min_x\{p^{0T}x: F(x) \geq F(\bar{x})\} = p^{0T}x^0 > 0 \quad (10)$$

$$C[F(\bar{x}), p^1] \equiv \min_x\{p^{1T}x: F(x) \geq F(\bar{x})\} = p^{1T}x^1 > 0 \quad (11)$$

$$\begin{aligned}
\therefore \quad C[F(\bar{x}), p^1] &\equiv \min_x\{p^{1T}x: F(x) \geq F(\bar{x})\} \\
&\geq \min_x\{p^{1T}x: p^{0T}x \geq p^{0T}x^0, x \geq 0_N\} \\
&\quad \text{since } \{x: F(x) \geq F(\bar{x})\} \\
&\quad \subset \{x: p^{0T}x \geq p^{0T}x^0, x \geq 0_N\} \\
&= \min_i\{p_i^1(p^{0T}x^0/p_i^0): i = 1, \ldots, N\} \quad (12)
\end{aligned}$$

since the solution to the linear programming problem $\min_x\{p^{1T}x: p^{0T}x \geq p^{0T}x^0, x \geq 0_N\}$ can be taken to be a corner solution. Similarly,

$$C[F(\bar{x}), p^0] \geq \min_i\{p_i^0(p^{1T}x^1/p_i^1): = 1, \ldots, N\}$$

or

$$1/C[F(\bar{x}), p^0] \leq \max_i\{p_i^1/p_i^0 \, p^{1T}x^1: i = 1, \ldots, N\} \quad (13)$$

Since $P_K(p^0, p^1, \bar{x}) \equiv C[F(\bar{x}), p^1]/C[F(\bar{x}), p^0]$, (10) and (12) imply the lower limit in (9) while (11) and (13) imply the upper limit. Q.E.D.

The geometric idea behind the above algebraic proof is that the sets $\{x: p^{0T}x \geq p^{0T}x^0, x \geq 0_N\}$ and $\{x: p^{1T}x^1 \geq p^{1T}x^1, x \geq 0_N\}$ form outer approximations to the true utility (or production) possibility set $\{x: F(x) \geq F(\bar{x})\}$. Moreover, it can be seen that the bounds on P_K given by (9) are the best possible,[12] i.e. if $F(x) \equiv p^{0T}x$, then P_K will attain the lower bound while, if $F(x) \equiv p^{1T}x$, then P_K will attain the upper bound in (9).

It is natural to assume that we can observe the consumer's (or producer's) quantity choices $x^0 > 0_N$ and $x^1 > 0_N$, made during periods 0 and 1 in addition to the prices which prevailed during those periods, $p^0 \gg 0_N$ and $p^1 \gg 0_N$. In the remainder of this section, we shall also assume that the consumer (or producer) is engaging in cost minimizing behaviour during the two periods. Thus we assume:

$$p^{0T}x^0 = C[F(x^0), p^0]; \; p^{1T}x^1 = C[F(x^1), p^1]; \; p^0, p^1 \gg 0_N; \; x^0, x^1 > 0_N \quad (14)$$

Given the above assumptions, we now have two natural choices for the quantity vector x which occurs in the definition of the Konüs cost of living index $P_K(p^0, p^1, x)$: x^0 or x^1. The *Laspeyres–Konüs cost of living index* is defined as $P_K(p^0, p^1, x^0)$ and the *Paasche–Konüs cost of living index* is defined as $P_K(p^0, p^1, x^1)$.[13] It turns out that the Laspeyres–Konüs index $P_K(p^0, p^1, x^0)$ is related to the *Laspeyres price index* $P_L(p^0, p^1, x^0, x^1) \equiv p^{1T}x^0/p^{0T}x^0$ while the Paasche–Konüs index $P_K(p^0, p^1, x^1)$ is related to the *Paasche price index* $P_P(p^0, p^1, x^0, x^1) \equiv p^{1T}x^1/p^{0T}x^1$.

Theorem 3 (Konüs, 1924, pp. 17–19): Suppose F is continuous from above and (14) holds. Then

$$P_K(p^0, p^1, x^0) \le p^{1T}x^0/p^{0T}x^0 \equiv P_L \quad \text{and} \tag{15}$$

$$P_K(p^0, p^1, x^1) \ge p^{1T}x^1/p^{0T}x^1 \equiv P_P, \tag{16}$$

Proof:

$$
\begin{aligned}
P_K(p^0, p^1, x^0) &\equiv C[F(x^0), p^1]/C[F(x^0), p^0] \\
&= C[F(x^0), p^1]/p^{0T}x^0 \text{ using (14)} \\
&\equiv \min_x\{p^{1T}x: F(x) \ge F(x^0)\}/p^{0T}x^0 \\
&\le p^{1T}x^0/p^{0T}x^0
\end{aligned}
$$

since x^0 is feasible for the cost minimization problem (but is not necessarily optimal), which proves (15). Similarly,

$$
\begin{aligned}
P_K(p^0, p^1, x^1) &= p^{1T}x^1/C[F(x^1), p^0] \\
&= p^{1T}x^1/\min_x\{p^{0T}x: F(x) \ge F(x^1)\} \\
&\ge p^{1T}x^1/p^{0T}x^1 \quad\quad\quad\quad \text{Q.E.D.}
\end{aligned}
$$

Corollary 3.1 (Pollak, 1971, p. 17):

$$\min_i\{p_i/p_i^0: i = 1, ..., N\} \le P_K(p^0, p^1, x^0) \le p^{1T}x^0/p^{0T}x^0 \equiv P_L \tag{17}$$

Corollary 3.2 (Pollak, 1971, p. 18):

$$P_P \equiv p^{1T}x^1/p^{0T}x^1 \le P_K(p^0, p^1, x^1) \le \max_i\{p_i^1/p_i^0: i = 1, ..., N\} \tag{18}$$

Corollary 3.3 (Frisch, 1936, p. 25): If in addition, F is homothetic, then for $x \gg 0_N$,

$$P_P \equiv p^{1T}x^1/p^{0T}x^1 \le P_K(p^0, p^1, x) \le p^{1T}x^0/p^{0T}x^0 \equiv P_L \tag{19}$$

The first two corollaries follow from Theorems 2 and 3, while the third corollary follows from Theorems 1 and 2. Note that

$$
\begin{aligned}
P_L &\equiv p^{1T}x^0/p^{0T}x^0 = \sum_{i=1}^{N} (p_i^1/p_i^0)(p_i^0 x_i^0/p^{0T}x^0) \\
&\equiv \sum_{i=1}^{N} (p_i^1/p_i^0)s_i^0 \le \max_i\{p_i^1/p_i^0: i = 1, 2, ..., N\}
\end{aligned}
$$

since a share weighted average of the price ratios p_i^1/p_i^0 will always be equal to or less than the maximum price ratio. Thus the bounds given by (17) will generally be sharper than the Joseph–Pollak bounds given by (9). Similarly,

$$P_P \equiv p^{1T}x^1/p^{0T}x^1 \equiv \sum_{i=1}^{N} (p_i^1/p_i^0)(p_i^0 x_i^1/p^{0T}x^1)$$

$$\geq \min_i\{p_i^1/p_i^0: i = 1, 2, ..., N\},$$

so that the bounds (18) are generally sharper than the bounds (9).

The geometric idea behind the proof of Theorem 3 is that the sets $\{x: x = x^0\}$ and $\{x: x = x^1\}$ form inner approximations to the true utility (or production) possibility sets $\{x: F(x) \geq F(x^0)\}$ and $\{x: F(x) \geq F(x^1)\}$ respectively. Moreover, it can be seen that the bounds on P_K given by (15) and (16) are attainable if F is a Leontief aggregator function (so that the corresponding cost function is linear in prices).[14]

Theorem 4 (Konüs, 1924, pp. 20–1): Let F satisfy Conditions I and suppose (14) holds. Then there exists a λ^* such that $0 \leq \lambda^* \leq 1$ and $P_K(p^0, p^1, \lambda^*x^1 + (1 - \lambda^*)x^0)$ lies between P_L and P_P; i.e. *either*

$$P_L \equiv p^{1T}x^0/p^{0T}x^0 \leq P_K(p^0, p^1, \lambda^*x^1 + (1 - \lambda^*)x^0)$$
$$\leq p^{1T}x^1/p^{0T}x^1 \equiv P_P \quad (20)$$

or

$$P_P \leq P_K(p^0, p^1, \lambda^*x^1 + (1 - \lambda^*)x^0) \leq P_L \quad (21)$$

Proof: Define $h(\lambda) \equiv P_K(p^0, p^1, \lambda x^1 + (1 - \lambda)x^0) \equiv C[F(\lambda x^1 + (1 + \lambda)x^0), p^1]/C[F(\lambda x^1 + (1 - \lambda)x^0), p^0]$. Since both F and C are continuous with respect to their arguments, h is continuous over the closed interval [0,1]. Note that $h(0) = P_K(p^0, p^1, x^0)$ and $h(1) = P_K(p^0, p^1, x^1)$. There are $4! = 24$ possible inequalities between the 4 numbers P_L, P_P, $h(0)$ and $h(1)$. However, from Theorem 3, we have the restrictions $h(0) \leq P_L$ and $P_P \leq h(1)$. These restrictions imply that there are only 6 possible inequalities between the 4 numbers: (1) $h(0) \leq P_L \leq P_P \leq h(1)$, (2) $h(0) \leq P_P \leq P_L \leq h(1)$, (3) $h(0) \leq P_P \leq h(1) \leq P_L$, (4) $P_P \leq h(0) \leq P_L \leq h(1)$, (5) $P_P \leq h(1) \leq h(0) \leq P_L$ and (6) $P_P \leq h(0) \leq h(1) \leq P_L$. Since $h(\lambda)$ is continuous over [0, 1] and thus assumes all intermediate values between $h(0)$ and $h(1)$, it can be seen that we can choose λ between 0 and 1 so that $P_L \leq h(\lambda^*) \leq P_P$ for case (1) or so that $P_P \leq h(\lambda^*) \leq P_L$ for cases (2) to (6), which establishes (20) or (21). Q.E.D.

It should be noted that λ^* can be chosen so that (20) or (21) is satisfied and in addition $F(\lambda^*x^1 + (1 - \lambda^*)x^0)$ lies between $F(x^0)$ and $F(x^1)$. Thus the Paasche and Laspeyres indexes provide bounds for the Konüs cost of living index for some reference indifference surface which lies between the period 0 and period 1 indifference surfaces.

The above theorems provide bounds for the Konüs price index $P_K(p^0,$ $p^1, x)$ under various hypotheses. We cannot improve upon these bounds unless we are willing to make specific assumptions about the functional form for the aggregator function F, a strategy we will pursue in sections 5 and 6.

3 The Konüs, Allen and Malmquist quantity indexes

In the case of only one commodity, a quantity index could be defined as x_1^1/x_1^0, the ratio of the quantity in period 1 to the quantity in period 0. This ratio is also equal to the ratio of expenditures in the two periods, $p_1^1 x_1^1/p_1^0 x_1^0$, divided by the price index p_1^1/p_1^0. This suggests that a reasonable notion of a quantity index in the general N commodity case could be the expenditure ratio deflated by the Konüs cost of living index. Thus we define the *Konüs–Pollak* (1971, p. 64) *implicit quantity index* for $p^0 \gg$ 0_N, $p^1 \gg 0_N$, $x^0 > 0_N$, $x^1 > 0_N$ and $x > 0_N$ as

$$\tilde{Q}_K(p^0, p^1, x^0, x^1, x) \equiv p^{1T}x^1/p^{0T}x^0 \, P_K(p^0, p^1, x) \tag{22}$$

$$= \frac{C[F(x^1), p^1]}{C[F(x^0), p^0]} \Big/ \frac{C[F(x), p^1]}{C[F(x), p^0]} \tag{23}$$

where (23) follows if the consumer or producer is engaging in cost minimizing behaviour during the two periods; i.e. (23) follows if (14) is true. Note that $\tilde{Q}_K$ depends on the period 0 prices and quantities, p^0 and x^0, the period 1 prices and quantities, p^1 and x^1, and the reference indifference surface indexed by the quantity vector x.

The following result shows that $\tilde{Q}_K$ gives the correct answer (at least ordinally) if the reference quantity vector x is chosen appropriately.

Theorem 5: Suppose F satisfies Conditions 1 and (14) holds. (i) If $F(x^1) > F(x^0)$, then for every $x \geq 0_N$ such that $F(x^1) \geq F(x) \geq F(x^0)$, $\tilde{Q}_K(p^0, p^1, x^0, x^1, x) > 1$. (ii) If $F(x^1) = F(x^0)$, then, for every $x \geq 0_N$ such that $F(x) = F(x^1) = F(x^0)$, $\tilde{Q}_K(p^0, p^1, x^0, x^1, x) = 1$. (iii) If $F(x^1) < F(x^0)$, then for every $x \geq 0_N$ such that $F(x^1) \leq F(x) \leq F(x^0)$, $\tilde{Q}_K(p^0, p^1, x^0, x^1, x) < 1$.

Proof of (i):

$$\tilde{Q}_K(p^0, p^1, x^0, x^1, x) = \frac{C[F(x^1), p^1]}{C[F(x), p^1]} \frac{C[F(x), p^0]}{C[F(x^0), p^0]} \quad \text{using (23)}$$
$$> 1$$

since $F(x^1) \geq F(x)$ implies $C[F(x^1), p^1] \geq C[F(x), p^1]$ and $F(x) \geq F(x^0)$ implies $C[F(x), p^0] \geq C[F(x^0), p^0]$ with at least one of the inequalities holding strictly, using property (iii) on the cost function C.

Parts (ii) and (iii) follow in an analogous manner.　　　　　　Q.E.D.

It can be verified that if $F(x^1) > F(x^0) > F(x)$, then, if F is not homothetic, it is not necessarily the case that $\tilde{Q}_K(p^0, p^1, x^0, x^1, x) > 1$. However, if we choose x to be x^0 or x^1, then the resulting $\tilde{Q}_K$ will have the desirable properties outlined in Theorem 5. Thus define the *Laspeyres–Konüs implicit quantity index* as

$$
\begin{aligned}
\tilde{Q}_K(p^0, p^1, x^0, x^1, x^0) &\equiv p^{1T}x^1/p^{0T}x^0 \, P_K(p^0, p^1, x^0) \\
&= C[F(x^1), p^1]/C[F(x^0), p^0] \cdot \\
&\quad (C[F(x^0), p^1]/C[F(x^0), p^0]) \\
&\quad \text{using (5) and (14)} \\
&= C[F(x^1), p^1]/C[F(x^0), p^1]
\end{aligned}
\tag{24}
$$

and the *Paasche–Konüs implicit quantity index* as

$$
\begin{aligned}
\tilde{Q}_K(p^0, p^1, x^0, x^1, x^1) &\equiv p^{1T}x^1/p^{0T}x^0 \, P_K(p^0, p^1, x^1) \\
&= C[F(x^1), p^0]/C[F(x^0), p^0]
\end{aligned}
\tag{25}
$$

where (25) follows using definition (5) for P_K and the assumptions (14) of cost minimizing behaviour.

It turns out that the quantity indexes defined by (24) and (25) are special cases of another class of quantity indexes. For $x^0 > 0_N$, $x^1 > 0_N$ and $p \gg 0_N$, define the *Allen (1949, p. 199) quantity index* as

$$
Q_A(x^0, x^1, p) \equiv C[F(x^1), p]/C[F(x^0), p],
\tag{26}
$$

Note that $\tilde{Q}_K(p^0, p^1, x^0, x^1, x) = Q_A(x^0, x, p^0)Q_A(x, x^1, p^1)$ and that the *Laspeyres–Allen quantity index* $Q_A(x^0, x^1, p^0)$ equals the Paasche–Konüs implicit quantity index $\tilde{Q}_K(p^0, p^1, x^0, x^1, x^1)$ while the *Paasche–Allen quantity index* $Q_A(x^0, x^1, p^1)$ equals $\tilde{Q}_K(p^0, p^1, x^0, x^1, x^0)$, assuming that (14) holds.

Theorem 6: Suppose F satisfies Conditions I. (i) If $F(x^1) > F(x^0) > \bar{u}$, then $Q_A(x^0, x^1, p) > 1$ for every $p \gg 0_N$. (ii) If $F(x^1) = F(x^0) > \bar{u}$, then $Q_A(x^0, x^1, p) = 1$ for every $p \gg 0_N$. (iii) If $\bar{u} < F(x^1) < F(x^0)$, then $Q_A(x^0, x^1, p) < 1$ for every $p \gg 0_N$.

The proof of the above lemma follows directly from definition (26) and property (iii) for the cost function $C(u, p)$: increasingness in u.[15]

It turns out that Allen quantity indexes do not satisfy bounds analogous to those given by Theorem 2 for the Konüs price indexes. However, there is a counterpart to Theorem 3.

Theorem 7 (Samuelson, 1947, p. 162; Allen, 1949, p. 199): If the aggregator function F is continuous from above and (14) holds, then

$$
Q_A(x^0, x^1, p^0) \leq p^{0T}x^1/p^{0T}x^0 \equiv Q_L(p^0, p^1, x^0, x^1) \quad \text{and}
\tag{27}
$$

$$
Q_A(x^0, x^1, p^1) \geq p^{1T}x^1/p^{1T}x^0 \equiv Q_P(p^0, p^1, x^0, x^1)
\tag{28}
$$

i.e. the Laspeyres–Allen quantity index is bounded from above by the

Laspeyres quantity index Q_L and the Paasche–Allen quantity index is bounded below by the Paasche quantity index Q_P.

Proof:

$$Q_A[x^0, x^1, p^0] = C[F(x^1), p^0]/p^{0T}x^0 \quad \text{using (26) and (14)}$$
$$\equiv \min_x\{p^{0T}x: F(x) \geq F(x^1)\}/p^{0T}x^0$$
$$\leq p^{0T}x^1/p^{0T}x^0$$

since x^1 is feasible for the minimization problem. Similarly,

$$Q_A(x^0, x^1, p^1) = p^{1T}x^1/\min_x\{p^{1T}x: F(x) \geq F(x^0)\}$$
$$\geq p^{1T}x^1/p^{1T}x^0$$

since x^0 is feasible for the minimization problem and $p^{1T}x^0 > 0$.   Q.E.D.

Theorem 8: If F is homothetic (so that there exists a continuous, monotonically increasing function of one variable such that $G[F(x)]$ is neoclassical) and (14) holds, then for every $x \gg 0_N$ and $p \gg 0_N$

$$\tilde{Q}_K(p^0, p^1, x^0, x^1, x) = Q_A(x^0, x^1, p)$$
$$= G[F(x^1)]/G[F(x^0)] \tag{29}$$

Proof:

$$\tilde{Q}_K(p^0, p, x^0, x^1, x) = \frac{C[F(x^1), p^1]}{C[F(x^0), p^0]} \Big/ \frac{C[F(x), p^1]}{C[F(x), p^0]} \quad \text{using (23)}$$
$$= \frac{G[F(x^1)]c(p^1)}{G[F(x^0)]c(p^0)} \Big/ \frac{G[F(x)]c(p^1)}{G[F(x)]c(p^0)}$$
$$\qquad \text{by homotheticity of } F$$
$$= G[F(x^1)]/G[F(x^0)]$$
$$= G[F(x^1)]c(p)/G[F(x^0)]c(p)$$
$$= C[F(x^1), p]/C[F(x^0), p]$$
$$\qquad \text{by homotheticity again}$$
$$\equiv Q_A(x^0, x^1, p) \tag{Q.E.D.}$$

Corollary 8.1 (Samuelson and Swamy, 1974, p. 570): If $Q_A(x^0, x^1, p)$ is independent of p and F satisfies Conditions I, then F must be homothetic.

Proof: If $Q_A(x^0, x^1, p)$ is independent of p, then $C[F(x^1), p]/C[F(x^1), p]$ is independent of p for all $x^0 \gg 0_N$ and $x^1 \gg 0_N$. Thus we must have $C[F(x), p] = G[F(x)]c(p)$ for some functions G and c which implies that F is homothetic.   Q.E.D.

Corollary 8.2: If F is neoclassical (so that $G(u) \equiv u$) and (14) holds, then for every $x \gg 0_N$, and every $p \gg 0_N$:

$$\tilde{Q}_K(p^0, p^1, x^0, x^1, x) = Q_A(x^0, x^1, p) = F(x^1)/F(x^0) \tag{30}$$

Corollary 8.3: If F is homothetic and (14) holds, then for every $x \gg 0_N$ and $p \gg 0_N$:

$$Q_P \equiv p^{1T}x^1/p^{1T}x^0 \le \tilde{Q}_K(p^0, p^1, x^0, x^1, x) = Q_A(x^0, x^1, p)$$
$$\le p^{0T}x^1/p^{0T}x^0 \equiv Q_L \qquad (31)$$

Proof: From (28),

$$Q_P \le Q_A(x^0, x^1, p^1) = \tilde{Q}_K(p^0, p^1, x^0, x^1, x) = Q_A(x^0, x^1, p)$$
$$= Q_A(x^0, x^1, p^0) \quad \text{using (29)} \le Q_L \text{ using (27)}$$

Q.E.D.

Thus if the aggregator function is homothetic, then the Allen and Implicit Konüs quantity indexes coincide for all reference vectors p and x, and their common value is bounded from below by the Paasche quantity index Q_P and above by the Laspeyres quantity index Q_L. Note that Q_P and Q_L can be computed from observable data.

In the general case when F is not necessarily homothetic, the following results give bounds for $\tilde{Q}_K$ and Q_A.

Theorem 9: Let F satisfy Conditions I and suppose (14) holds. Then there exists a λ^* such that $0 \le \lambda^* \le 1$ and $Q_K(x^0, x^1, p^0, p^1, \lambda^*x^1 + (1 - \lambda^*)x^0)$ lies between Q_P and Q_L.

Proof: From Theorem 4, either (20) or (21) holds for $P_K(p^0, p^1, \lambda^*x^1 + (1 - \lambda^*)x^0)$ for some λ^* between 0 and 1. If (20) holds, then, using definition (22):

$$Q_L = (p^{1T}x^1/p^{0T}x^0)/P_P \le \tilde{Q}_K(x^0, x^1, p^0, p^1, \lambda^*x^1 + (1 - \lambda^*)x^0)$$
$$\le (p^{1T}x^1/p^{0T}x^0)/P_L = Q_P$$

Similarly, if (21) holds then $Q_P \le Q_K(x^0, x^1, p^0, p^1, \lambda^*x^1 + (1 - \lambda^*)x^0)$ $\le Q_L$. Q.E.D.

Theorem 10: Let F be continuous from above and suppose (14) holds. Then there exists a λ^* such that $0 \le \lambda^* \le 1$ and $Q_A(x^0, x^1, \lambda^*p^1 + (1 - \lambda^*)p^0)$ lies between Q_L and Q_P.

Proof: Define $h(\lambda) \equiv Q_A(x^0, x^1, \lambda p^1 + (1 - \lambda)p^0) \equiv C[F(x^1), \lambda p^1 + (1 - \lambda)p^0]/C[F(x^0), \lambda p^1 + (1 - \lambda)p^0]$. Since F is continuous from above, $C(u, p)$ is continuous in p and thus $h(\lambda)$ is continuous for $0 \le \lambda \le 1$. Note that $h(0) = Q_A(x^0, x^1, p)$ and $h(1) = Q_A(x^0, x^1, p^1)$. From Theorem 7, $h(0) \le Q_L$ and $Q_P \le h(1)$. Now repeat the proof of Theorem 9 with Q_L and Q_P replacing P_L and P_P. Q.E.D.

Thus the Paasche and Laspeyres quantity indexes (which are observable) bound both the implicit Konüs quantity index $\tilde{Q}_K$ and the Allen quantity index Q_A, provided that we choose appropriate reference vectors between x^0 and x^1 or p^0 and p^1 respectively. However, it is also necessary to assume cost minimizing behaviour on the part of the consumer or producer during the two periods in order to derive the above bounds.

Recall that the Konüs price index P_K had the desirable property that $P_K(p^0, \lambda p^0, x) = \lambda P_K(p^0, p^0, x)$ for all $\lambda > 0$, $p^0 \gg 0_N$, and $x \gg 0_N$; i.e.

if the current period prices were proportional to the base period prices, then the price index equalled this common factor of proportionality λ. It would be desirable if an analogous homogeneity property held for the quantity indexes. Unfortunately, it is *not* always the case that $\hat{Q}_K(x^0, \lambda x^0, p^0, p^1, x) = \lambda$ or that $Q_A(x^0, \lambda x^0, p) = \lambda$. However, the following quantity index does have this desirable homogeneity property.

For $\bar{x} \gg 0_N$, $x^0 \gg 0_N$, $x^1 \gg 0_N$, define the *Malmquist* (1953, p. 232) *quantity index* as

$$Q_M(x^0, x^1, \bar{x}) \equiv D[F(\bar{x}), x^1]/D[F(\bar{x}), x^0] \tag{32}$$

where $D[u, \bar{x}] \equiv \max_k\{k: F(\bar{x}/k) \geq u, k > 0\}$ is the *deflation function*[16] which corresponds to the aggregator function F. Thus $D[F(\bar{x}), x^1]$ is the biggest number which will just deflate the period 1 quantity vector x^1 onto the boundary of the utility (or production) possibility set $[x: F(x) \geq F(\bar{x}), x \geq 0_N]$ indexed by the quantity vector $\bar{x}$ while $D[F(\bar{x}), x^0]$ is the biggest number which will just deflate the period 0 quantity vector x onto the utility possibility set indexed by $\bar{x}$, and Q_M is the ratio of these two deflation factors.

Note that the assumption of cost minimizing behaviour is *not* required in order to define the Malmquist quantity index Q_M.

Theorem 11 (Malmquist, 1953, p. 231; Pollak, 1971, p. 62): If F satisfies Conditions I, then (i) $\lambda > 0$, $x^0 \gg 0_N$, $\bar{x} \gg 0_N$ implies $Q_M(x^0, \lambda x^0, \bar{x}) = \lambda$ and (ii) $x^0 \gg 0_N$, $x^1 \gg 0_N$, $x^2 \gg 0_N$, $\bar{x} \gg 0_N$ implies $Q_M(x^0, x^1, \bar{x}) \times Q_M(x^1, x^2, \bar{x}) = Q_M(x^0, x^2, \bar{x})$.

Proof: (i) If F is merely continuous from above and increasing, then $D[F(\bar{x}), x]$ is well defined for all $\bar{x} \gg 0_N$ and $x \gg 0_N$. Moreover, if $\lambda > 0$, D has the following homogeneity property (recall property (v) of Conditions IV on D): $D[F(\bar{x}), \lambda x] = \lambda D[F(\bar{x}), x]$. Thus $Q_M(x^0, \lambda x^0, \bar{x}) \equiv D[F(\bar{x}), \lambda x^0]/D[F(\bar{x}), x^0] = \lambda D[F(\bar{x}), x^0]/D[F(\bar{x}), x^0] = \lambda$. (ii) follows directly from definition (32).   Q.E.D.

Property (ii) in the above theorem is a desirable transitivity property of Q_M. $\hat{Q}_K$, Q_A and P_A and P_K all possess the analogous transitivity property (or circularity property as it is sometimes called in the index number literature).

Theorem 12: If F satisfies Conditions I, $x^0 \gg 0_N$, $x^1 \gg 0_N$, $\bar{x} \gg 0_N$ and $F(\bar{x})$ is between $F(x^0)$ and $F(x^1)$, then the Malmquist quantity index $Q_M(x^0, x^1, \bar{x})$ will correctly indicate whether the aggregate has remained constant, increased or decreased from period 0 to period 1.

Proof: (i) Suppose $F(x^0) = F(\bar{x}) = F(x^1)$. Then $Q_M(x^0, x^1, \bar{x}) = D[F(\bar{x}), x^1]/D[F(\bar{x}), x^0] = 1/1 = 1$. (ii) Suppose $F(x^0) \leq F(\bar{x}) \leq F(x^1)$ with $F(x^0) < F(x^1)$. Then $Q_M(x^0, x^1, \bar{x}) = k^1/k^0$ where $F(x^1/k^1) = F(\bar{x}) \leq F(x^1)$ which implies $k^1 \geq 1$ and $F(x^0/k^0) = F(\bar{x}) \geq F(x^0)$ which implies $0 < k^0 \leq 1$. Since at least one of the inequalities $F(\bar{x}) \leq F(x^1)$ and $F(\bar{x}) \geq F(x^0)$ is strict, at least one of the inequalities $k^1 \geq 1$ and $k^0 \leq 1$ must also be strict. Thus $Q_M(x^0, x^1, \bar{x}) = k^1/k^0 > 1$. The remaining case is similar. Q.E.D.

If F is non-homothetic, then the restriction that the reference indifference surface indexed by $F(\bar{x})$ lie between the indifference surfaces indexed by $F(x^0)$ and $F(x^1)$ is necessary in order to prove Theorem 12; e.g., if $F(x^0) < F(x^1) < F(\bar{x})$, then it *need not* be the case that $Q_M(x^0, x^1, \bar{x}) > 1$.

The following result shows that the Malmquist quantity index satisfies the analogue to the Joseph–Pollak bounds for the Konüs price index.

Theorem 13: If F satisfies Conditions I and $x^0 \gg 0_N$, $x^1 \gg 0_N$, $\bar{x} \gg 0_N$, then

$$\min_i\{x_i^1/x_i^0: i = 1, ..., N\} \leq Q_M(x^0, x^1, \bar{x})$$
$$\leq \max_i\{x_i^1/x_i^0: i = 1, ..., N\} \quad (33)$$

Proof: If F satisfies Conditions I, then the deflation function D satisfies Conditions IV. Thus $D(u, x)$ satisfies the same mathematical regularity properties with respect to x as $C(u, p)$ satisfies with respect to p. Since $C[F(\bar{x}), p^1]/C[F(\bar{x}), p^0] \equiv P_K(p^0, p^1, \bar{x})$ satisfies the inequalities in (9), $D[F(\bar{x}), x^1]/D[F(\bar{x}), x^0] \equiv Q_M(x^0, x^1, \bar{x})$ will satisfy the analogous inequalities (33).[17] Q.E.D.

In general, the Malmquist quantity index will depend on the reference indifference surface indexed by $\bar{x}$. As usual, two natural choices for $\bar{x}$ are x^0 or x^1, the observed quantity choices during period 0 or 1. Thus the *Laspeyres–Malmquist quantity index* is defined as $Q_M(x^0, x^1, x^0) \equiv D[F(x^0), x^1]/D[F(x^0), x^0] = D[F(x^0), x^1]$ since $D[F(x^0), x^0] = 1$ if F is continuous from above and increasing, and the *Paasche–Malmquist quantity index* is defined as $Q_M(x^0, x^1, x^1) \equiv D[F(x^1), x^1]/D[F(x^1), x^0] = 1/D[F(x^1), x^0]$ since $D[F(x^1), x^1] = 1$ if F is continuous from above and increasing.

Theorem 14 (Malmquist, 1953, p. 231): Suppose F satisfies Conditions I and (14) holds. Then

$$Q_M(x^0, x^1, x^0) \leq p^{0T}x^1/p^{0T}x^0 \equiv Q_L \quad \text{and} \quad (34)$$

$$Q_M(x^0, x^1, x^1) \geq p^{1T}x^1/p^{1T}x^0 \equiv Q_P \quad (35)$$

Proof:

$$Q_M(x^0, x^1, x^0) \equiv D[F(x^0), x^1]$$
$$\equiv \max_k\{k: F(x^1/k) \geq F(x^0), k > 0\}$$
$$= k^1 \text{ where } F(x^1/k^1) = F(x^0)$$

Now

$$p^{0T}x^0 = C[F(x^0), p^0]$$
$$\equiv \min_x\{p^{0T}x: F(x) \geq F(x^0)\}$$
$$\leq p^{0T}x^1/k^1$$

since x^1/k^1 is feasible for the cost minimization problem. Thus $k^1 =$

$Q_M(x^0, x^1, x^0) \leq p^{0T}x^1/p^{0T}x^0 \equiv Q_L$ which proves (34). The proof of (35) is similar.   Q.E.D.

Theorem 15: Suppose F satisfies Conditions I and (14) holds. Then there exists a λ^* such that $0 \leq \lambda^* \leq 1$ and $Q_M(x^0, x^1, \lambda^*x^1 + (1 - \lambda^*)x^0)$ lies between Q_L and Q_P.

Proof: Define $h(\lambda) \equiv Q_M(x^0, x^1, \lambda x^1 + (1 - \lambda)x^0) \equiv D[F(\lambda x^1 + (1 - \lambda)x^0), x^1]/D[F(\lambda x^1 + (1 - \lambda)x^0), x^0]$. Since $F(\lambda x^1 + (1 - \lambda)x^0)$ is continuous with respect to λ and $D(u, x)$ is continuous with respect to u (recall property (i) of Conditions IV on D, $h(\lambda)$ is continuous for λ between 0 and 1. Moreover, $h(0) = Q_M(x^0, x^1, x^0)$ and $h(1) = Q_M(x^0, x^1, x^1)$. From Theorem 14, $h(0) \leq Q_L$ and $Q_P \leq h(1)$. Now repeat the proof of Theorem 10.   Q.E.D.

It should be noted that λ^* can be chosen so that $0 \leq \lambda^* \leq 1$ and $Q_M(x^0, x^1, \lambda^*x^1 + (1 - \lambda^*)x^0)$ lies between Q_L and Q_P, and in addition, $F(\lambda^*x^1 + (1 - \lambda^*)x^0)$ lies between $F(x^0)$ and $F(x^1)$. Thus the Paasche and Laspeyres quantity indexes provide bounds for the Malmquist quantity index for some reference indifference surface which lies between the period 0 and period 1 indifference surfaces.

The following theorem relates the Paasche and Laspeyres Malmquist quantity indexes to the Paasche and Laspeyres implicit Konüs and Allen quantity indexes.

Theorem 16 (Malmquist, 1953, p. 233): Suppose F satisfies Conditions I and (14) holds. Then

$$Q_M(x^0, x^1, x^0) \leq \tilde{Q}_K(p^0, p^1, x^0, x^1, x^0) = Q_A(x^0, x^1, p^1) \quad \text{and} \tag{36}$$

$$Q_M(x^0, x^1, x^1) \geq \tilde{Q}_K(p^0, p^1, x^0, x^1, x^1) = Q_A(x^0, x^1, p^0) \tag{37}$$

Proof:

$$Q_M(x^0, x^1, x^0) = D[F(x^0), x^1]$$
$$= k^1 \quad \text{say where } F(x^1/k^1) = F(x^0)$$
$$Q_A(x^0, x^1, p^1) = p^{1T}x^1/C[F(x^0), p^1] \quad \text{using (26) and (14)}$$
$$= \tilde{Q}_K(p^0, p^1, x^0, x^1, x^0) \quad \text{using (23)}$$
$$= p^{1T}x^1/\min_x\{p^{1T}x: F(x) \geq F(x^0)\}$$
$$\leq p^{1T}x^1/p^{1T}(x^1/k^1) \quad \text{since } x^1/k^1 \text{ is}$$
$$\text{feasible but not necessarily optimal}$$
$$= k^1$$

which establishes (36). (37) follows in a similar manner.   Q.E.D.

It is obvious that an *implicit Malmquist price index* $\tilde{P}_M$ can be defined as the expenditure ratio for the two periods deflated by Q_M: i.e. define

$$\tilde{P}_M(p^0, p^1, x^0, x^1, \bar{x}) \equiv p^{1T}x^1/p^{0T}x^0 \, Q_M(x^0, x^1, \bar{x}) \tag{38}$$

However, the resulting price index does not have the desirable homogeneity property $\tilde{P}_M(p^0, \lambda p^0, x^0, x^1, \bar{x}) = \lambda$. Thus $\tilde{P}_M$ has properties analogous to the implicit Konüs quantity index $\bar{Q}_K$, except that the role of prices and quantities is reversed.

Now that we have studied price and quantity indexes separately, it is time to observe that it is essential to study them together. For empirical work, it is highly desirable that the product of the price index P and the quantity index Q equal the actual expenditure ratio for the two periods under consideration, $p^{1T}x^1/p^{0T}x^0$. If P and Q satisfy this property, then we say that P and Q satisfy the *weak factor reversal test*[18] or the *product test*.[19] We have seen that the Konüs price index P_K is a desirable price index and that the Malmquist quantity index Q_M is a desirable quantity index since they each have a desirable homogeneity property. The following result shows that there exists at least one reference indifference surface such that P_K and Q_M satisfy the product test.

Theorem 17 (Malmquist, 1953, p. 234): Suppose the aggregator function F satisfies Conditions I and (14) holds. Then there exists a λ^* such that $0 \leq \lambda^* \leq 1$ and

$$P_K(p^0, p^1, \lambda^*x^1 + (1 - \lambda^*)x^0) \, Q_M(x^0, x^1, \lambda^*x^1$$
$$+ (1 - \lambda^*)x^0) = p^{1T}x^1/p^{0T}x^0 \quad (39)$$

Proof: For $0 \leq \lambda \leq 1$, define the continuous function $h(\lambda) \equiv P_K(p^0, p^1, \lambda x^1 + (1 - \lambda)x^0) \, Q_M(x^0, x^1, \lambda x^1 + (1 - \lambda)x^0)$. Thus

$$h(0) \equiv P_K(p^0, p^1, x^0) \, Q_M(x^0, x^1, x^0)$$
$$\equiv (C[F(x^0), p^1]/C[F(x^0), p^0])(D[F(x^0), x^1]/D[F(x^0), x^0])$$

by (5) and (32)

$$\leq \frac{C[F(x^0), p^1]}{C[F(x^0), p^0]} \frac{C[F(x^1), p^1]}{C[F(x^0), p^1]} \quad \text{using (36) and (26)}$$

$$= p^{1T}x^1/p^{0T}x^0 \quad \text{using (14)}$$
$$= (C[F(x^1), p^1]/C[F(x^1), p^0])(C[F(x^1), p^0]/C[F(x^0), p^0])$$

$$\leq \frac{C[F(x^1), p^1]}{C[F(x^1), p^0]} \frac{D[F(x^1), x^1]}{D[F(x^1), x^0]} \quad \text{using (37), (26) and (32)}$$

$$= P_K(p^0, p^1, x^1) \, Q_M(x^0, x^1, x^1) \quad \text{using (5) and (32)}$$
$$\equiv h(1)$$

Since $h(\lambda)$ is continuous over $[0, 1]$ and since $h(0) \leq p^{1T}x^1/p^{0T}x^0 \leq h(1)$, there exists $0 \leq \lambda^* \leq 1$ such that $h(\lambda^*) = p^{1T}x^1/p^{0T}x^0$ and thus (39) is satisfied. Moreover, since $h(\lambda) \equiv (C[F(\lambda x^1 + (1 - \lambda)x^0), p^1]/C[F(\lambda x^1 + (1 - \lambda)x^0), p^0])(D[F(\lambda x^1 + (1 - \lambda)x^0), x^1]/D[F(\lambda x^1 + (1 - \lambda)x^0), x^0])$, we can choose λ^* so that $F(\lambda^*x^1 + (1 - \lambda^*)x^0)$ lies between $F(x^0)$ and $F(x^1)$. Q.E.D.

Thus the reference indifference surface indexed by $\lambda^*x^1 + (1 - \lambda^*)x^0$ which occurs in the above theorem lies between the surfaces indexed by x^0 and x^1, the quantity vectors observed during periods 0 and 1.

The final result in this section shows that all three quantity indexes that we have considered coincide (and are independent of reference price or quantity vectors) if the aggregator function is homothetic.

Theorem 18 (Pollak, 1971, p. 65): If F is homothetic (so that there exists a continuous, monotonically increasing function of one variable such that $G[F(x)]$ is neoclassical) and (14) holds, then for every $x \gg 0_N$ and $p \gg 0_N$

$$Q_M(x^0, x^1, x) = \tilde{Q}_K(p^0, p^1, x^0, x^1, x) = Q_A[x^0, x^1, p]$$
$$= G[F(x^1)]/G[F(x^0)] \tag{40}$$

Proof:

$$\begin{aligned}
Q_M(x^0, x^1, x) &\equiv D[F(x), x^1]/D[F(x), x^0] \\
&\equiv \max_{k>0}\{k: F(x^1/k) \geq F(x)\}/\max_{k>0}\{k: F(x^0/k) \\
&\quad \geq F(x)\} \\
&= \frac{\max_k\{k: G[F(x^1/k)] \geq G[F(x)], k > 0\}}{\max_k[k: G[F(x^0/k)] \geq G[F(x)], k > 0]} \\
&= k^1/k^0 \quad \text{say}
\end{aligned}$$

where $G[F(x^1/k^1)] = G[F(x)]$ and $G[F(x^0/k^0)] = G[F(x)]$. Since $G[F(x)]$ is linearly homogeneous in x, the last two equations imply $k^1 = G[F(x^1)]/G[F(x)]$ and $k^0 = G[F(x^0)]/G[F(x)]$ which in turn implies $k^1/k^0 = Q_M(x^0, x^1, x) = G[F(x^1)]/G[F(x^0)]$. The other two equalities in (40) now follow from (29) and (30). Q.E.D.

Corollary 18.1: $Q_P \leq Q_M(x^0, x^1, x) = \tilde{Q}_K(p^0, p^1, x^0, x^1, x) = Q_A(x^0, x^1, p) \leq Q_L$.

Proof: Follows from (40) and (31). Q.E.D.

Corollary 18.2: If $Q_M(x^0, x^1, x)$ is independent of $x \gg 0_N$ for all $x^0 \gg 0_N$ and $x^1 \gg 0_N$ and F satisfies Conditions I, then F must be homothetic.

Proof: If $Q_M(x^0, x^1, x)$ is independent of x, then $D[F(x), x^1]/D[F(x), x^0]$ is independent of x for all $x^0 \gg 0_N$ and $x^1 \gg 0_N$. Thus we must have $D[F(x), x^0] = f(x^0)/G[F(x)]$ for some functions f and G. Since F satisfies Conditions I, D must satisfy Conditions IV and it is evident that f can be taken to be neoclassical and G can be taken to be a monotonically increasing, continuous function of one variable with $G(u) > 0$ if $u > \bar{u} \equiv F(0_N)$. Since $D[F(x), x] = 1 = f(x)/G[F(x)]$ for every $x \gg 0_N$, we have $G[F(x)] = f(x)$, a positive, increasing, concave, linearly homogeneous and continuous function for $x \gg 0_N$. Thus F is homothetic. Q.E.D.

Finally, we note that if F is neoclassical and (14) holds, then: (i) all quantity indexes coincide and equal the value of the aggregator function evaluated at the period 1 quantities x^1 divided by the value of F evaluated at the period 0 quantities x^0: i.e. we have

$$Q_M(x^0, x^1, x) = \bar{Q}_K(p^0, p^1, x^0, x^1, x) = Q_A(x^0, x^1, p)$$
$$= F(x^1)/F(x^0) \quad (41)$$

for all $x \gg 0_N$ and $p \gg 0_N$; (ii) all price indexes coincide and equal the ratio of unit costs for the two periods: i.e. we have

$$P_K(p^0, p^1, x) = \bar{P}_M(p^0, p^1, x^0, x^1, x) = c(p^1)/c(p^0) \quad (42)$$

for all $x \gg 0_N$; and (iii) the expenditure ratio for the two periods is equal to the product of the price index times the quantity index:

$$p^{1T}x^1/p^{0T}x^0 = [c(p^1)/c(p^0)][F(x^1)/F(x^0)] \quad (43)$$

4 Other approaches to index number theory

During the period 1875–1925, perhaps the main approach to index number theory was what Frisch (1936) called the 'atomistic' or 'statistical' approach. This approach assumes that all prices are affected proportionately (except for random errors) by the expansion of the money supply. Therefore, it does not matter which price index is used to measure the common factor of proportionality, as long as the index number contains a sufficient number of statistically independent price ratios. Proponents of this approach were Jevons and Edgeworth but the approach was rather successfully attacked by Bowley (1928) and Keynes. For references to this literature, see Frisch (1936, pp. 2–5).

A 'neostatistical' approach has been initiated by Theil (1960). For the case of two observations, Theil's best linear *price and quantity indexes* P_0, P_1, Q_0, Q_1 are the solution to the following constrained least squares problem:

$$\min_{P_0, P_1, Q_0, Q_1, e_1, e_2, e_3, e_4} \left\{ \sum_{i=1}^{4} e_i^2 \text{ subject to} \right.$$

$$\begin{matrix} \text{(i) } p^{0T}x^0 = P_0Q_0 + e_1, & \text{(ii) } p^{0T}x^1 = P_0Q_1 + e_2 \\ \text{(iii) } p^{1T}x^0 = P_1Q_0 + e_3, & \text{(iv) } p^{1T}x^1 = P_1Q_1 + e_4 \end{matrix} \right\} \quad (44)$$

and one other normalization such as $P_0 = 1$ is required. As usual, p^0 and p^1 are price vectors for the two periods while x^0 and x^1 are the corresponding quantity vectors. P_0 and P_1 are scalars which are interpreted as the price level in periods 0 and 1 respectively while Q_0 and Q_1 are the quantity levels for the two periods. Finally, the e_i are regarded as errors. Kloek and de Wit (1961) suggested a number of modifications to Theil's approach: they suggested (44) for the case of two observations, but with the following 3 sets of additional normalizations: (1) $P_0 = 1$, $e_1 = 0$, (2) $P_0 = 1$, $e_1 + e_4 = 0$, and (3) $P_0 = 1$, $e_1 = 0$, $e_4 = 0$. Stuvel (1957) and Banerjee (1975) have suggested similar 'neostatistical' index number formulae: Stuvel's index numbers P_1/P_0 and Q_1/Q_0 can be generated by solving (44) subject to the additional normalizations $P_0 = 1$, $e_1 = 0$, $e_4 = 0$ and $e_2 = e_3$.

The other major approach to index number theory is the test or axiomatic approach, initiated by Irving Fisher (1911; 1922). The test approach assumes that the price and quantity indexes are functions of the price and quantity vectors pertaining to two periods, say $P(p^0, p^1, x^0, x^1)$ and $Q(p^0, p^1, x^0, x^1)$. Tests are a priori 'reasonable' properties that the functions P and Q should possess. However, several researchers (e.g. Frisch, 1930; Wald, 1937; Samuelson, 1974; Eichhorn, 1976; 1978; Eichhorn and Voeller, 1976) have shown that not all a priori reasonable properties for P and Q can be consistent with each other: i.e. there are various impossibility theorems. Moreover, if one works with a restricted set of tests which are consistent, the resulting family of index number formulae is often not uniquely determined.

However, it turns out that the economic and test approaches to index number theory can be partially reconciled. In the following two sections, we shall assume explicit functional forms for the underlying aggregator function plus the assumption of cost minimizing behaviour on the part of the consumer or producer. We shall show that certain functional forms for the aggregator function can be associated with certain functional forms for index number formulae. Many of the resulting index number formulae (e.g. Fisher's (1922) ideal formula) have been suggested as desirable in the literature on the test approach to index number theory.

5 Exact index number formulae

Suppose we are given price and quantity data for two periods, p^0, p^1, x^0 and x^1. A *price index* P is defined to be a function of prices and quantities, $P(p^0, p^1, x^0, x^1)$, while a *quantity index* Q is defined to be another function of the observable prices and quantities for the two periods, $Q(p^0, p^1, x^0, x^1)$. Given either a price index or a quantity index, the other function can be defined implicitly by the following equation (Fisher's (1922) weak factor reversal test):

$$P(p^0, p^1, x^0, x^1) \, Q(p^0, p^1, x^0, x^1) = p^{1T}x^1/p^{0T}x^0 \tag{45}$$

i.e. the product of the price index times the quantity index should equal the expenditure ratio between the two periods.

Assume that the producer or consumer is maximizing a neoclassical[20] aggregator function f subject to a budget constraint during the two periods. Under these conditions, it can be shown that the consumer (or producer) is also minimizing cost subject to a utility (or output) constraint and that the cost function C which corresponds to f can be written as

$$C(f(x), p) = f(x)c(p) \tag{46}$$

for $x \geq 0_N$ and $p \gg 0_N$ where $c(p) \equiv \min_x\{p^T x: f(x) \geq 1, x \geq 0_N\}$ is f's unit cost function.[21]

A quantity index $Q(p^0, p^1, x^0, x^1)$ is defined to be *exact* for a neoclassical aggregator function f if, for every $p^0 \gg 0_N$, $p^1 \gg 0_N$,[22] $x^r \gg 0_N$ a solution to the aggregator maximization problem $\max_x\{f(x): p^{rT} x \leq p^{rT} x^r, x \geq 0_N\} = f(x^r) > 0$ for $r = 0, 1$, we have

$$Q(p^0, p^1, x^0, x^1) = f(x^1)/f(x^0) \tag{47}$$

Thus in (47), the price and quantity vectors (p^0, p^1, x^0, x^1) are *not* regarded as completely independent variables – on the contrary, we assume that (p^0, x^0) and (p^1, x^1) satisfy the following restrictions in order for the price and quantity vectors to be consistent with 'utility' maximizing behaviour during the two periods:

$$p^r \gg 0_N, x^r \gg 0_N, f(x^r) = \max_x\{f(x): p^{rT} x \leq p^{rT} x^r, x \geq 0_N\} > 0;$$
$$r = 0, 1 \quad (48)$$

If f is neoclassical, then, using (46), it can be verified that (48) implies (49) and vice versa:

$$p^r \gg 0_N, \ x^r \gg 0_N, \ p^{rT} x^r = f(x^r)c(p^r) = C(f(x^r), p^r) > 0; \quad r = 0, 1 \tag{49}$$

Now we are ready to define the notion of an exact price index.

A *price index* $P(p^0, p^1, x^0, x^1)$ is defined to be *exact* for a neoclassical aggregator function f which has the dual unit cost function c, if for every (p^0, x^0) and (p^1, x^1) which satisfies (48) or (49), we have

$$P(p^0, p^1, x^0, x^1) = c(p^1)/c(p^0) \tag{50}$$

Note that if Q is exact for a neoclassical aggregator function f, then Q can be interpreted as a Malmquist, Allen or implicit Konüs quantity index (recall (41)), and the corresponding price index P defined implicitly by Q via (45) can be interpreted as a Konüs or implicit Malmquist price index (recall (42)).

Some examples of exact index number formulae are presented in the following theorems. Before proceeding with these theorems, it is convenient to develop some implications of (48) and (49). If f is neoclassical, (48) is satisfied, and f is differentiable at x^0 and x^1, then

$$p^r/p^{rT} x^r = \nabla f(x^r)/x^{rT} \nabla f(x^r) = \nabla f(x^r)/f(x^r); \quad r = 0, 1 \tag{51}$$

The first equality in (51) follows from the Hotelling (1935, p. 71), Wold (1944, pp. 69–71; 1953, p. 145) identity[23] while the second equality follows from Euler's Theorem on linearly homogeneous functions, $f(x^r) =$

$x^{rT}\nabla f(x^r)$. Also if f is neoclassical, (49) holds and f's unit cost function c is differentiable at p^0 and p^1, then

$$x^r/p^{rT}x^r = \nabla_p C[f(x^r), p^r]/C[f(x^r), p^r] = \nabla c(p^r)/c(p^r); \quad r = 0, 1 \quad (52)$$

The first equality in (52) follows from Shephard's (1953, p. 11) Lemma while the second equality follows from (49).

Theorem 19 (Konüs and Byushgens, 1926, p. 162; Pollak, 1971, p. 21; Samuelson and Swamy, 1974, p. 574): The Paasche and Laspeyres price indexes, $P_P(p^0, p^1, x^0, x^1) \equiv p^{1T}x^1/p^{0T}x^1$ and $P_L(p^0, p^1, x^0, x^1) \equiv p^{1T}x^0/p^{0T}x^0$, and the Paasche and Laspeyres quantity indexes, $Q_P(p^0, p^1, x^0, x^1) \equiv p^{1T}x^1/p^{1T}x^0$ and $Q_L(p^0, p^1, x^0, x^1) \equiv p^{0T}x^1/p^{0T}x^0$, are exact for a Leontief (1941) aggregator function, $f(x) \equiv \min_i\{x_i/b_i: i = 1, ..., N\}$, where $x \equiv (x_1, ..., x_N)^T \geq 0_N$ and $b \equiv (b_1, ..., b_N)^T \gg 0_N$ is a vector of positive constants.

Proof: If f is the Leontief or fixed coefficients aggregator function defined above, then its unit cost function is $c(p) \equiv p^T b$ for $p \gg 0_N$. Now assume (49). Then

$$\begin{aligned}
P_L &\equiv p^{1T}x^0/p^{0T}x^0 \\
&= p^{1T}(\nabla c(p^0)/c(p^0)) \quad \text{using (52)} \\
&= p^{1T}b/c(p^0) \quad \text{since } \nabla c(p^0) = b \\
&\equiv c(p^1)/c(p^0)
\end{aligned}$$

Similarly,

$$\begin{aligned}
P_P &\equiv p^{1T}x^1/p^{0T}x^1 = 1/[p^{0T}x^1/p^{1T}x^1] \\
&= 1/[p^{0T}(\nabla c(p^1)/c(p^1)] \quad \text{using (52)} \\
&= c(p^1)/p^{0T}b \quad \text{since } \nabla c(p^1) = b \\
&\equiv c(p^1)/c(p^0)
\end{aligned}$$

Thus P_L and P_P are exact price indexes for f, and thus the corresponding quantity indexes, Q_P and Q_L, defined implicitly by the weak factor reversal test (45), are exact quantity indexes for f. Q.E.D.

Theorem 20 (Pollak, 1971, pp. 24–6; Samuelson and Swamy, 1974, p. 574): The Paasche and Laspeyres price and quantity indexes are also exact for a linear aggregator function, $f(x) \equiv a^T x$ where $a^T \equiv (a_1, ..., a_N) \gg 0_N$ is a vector of fixed constants.

Proof: Assume (48).[24] Then

$$\begin{aligned}
Q_L &\equiv p^{0T}x^1/p^{0T}x^0 \\
&= x^{1T}(\nabla f(x^0)/f(x^0)) \quad \text{using (51)} \\
&= x^{1T}a/f(x^0) \quad \text{since } \nabla f(x) = a \\
&\equiv f(x^1)/f(x^0)
\end{aligned}$$

Similarly, $Q_P = f(x^1)/f(x^0)$ and so Q_L and Q_P are exact for the linear aggregator function f defined above. Thus the corresponding price indexes, P_P and P_L, defined implicitly by the weak factor reversal test (45) are exact price indexes for f and its corresponding unit cost function, $c(p) \equiv \min_x\{p^T x: a^T x \geq 1, x \geq 0_N\} = \min_i\{p_i/a_i: i = 1, \ldots, N\}$. Q.E.D.

The above theorems show that more than one index number formula can be exact for the same aggregator function, and one index number formula can be exact for quite different aggregator functions.

Theorem 21 (Konüs and Byushgens, 1926, pp. 163–6; Afriat, 1972b, p. 46; Pollak, 1971, p. 37; Samuelson and Swamy, 1974, p. 574): The family of geometric price indexes defined by $P_G(p^0, p^1, x^0, x^1) \equiv \Pi_{i=1}^N (p_i^1/p_i^0)^{s_i}$ (where for $i = 1, 2, \ldots, N$, $s_i \equiv m_i(s_i^0, s_i)$, $s_i^0 \equiv p_i^0 x_i^0/p^{0T} x^0$, $s_i^1 \equiv p_i^1 x_i^1/p^{1T} x^1$ and m_i is any function which has the property $m_i(s, s) \equiv s$) is exact for a Cobb–Douglas (1928) aggregator function f defined by

$$f(x) \equiv \alpha_0 \prod_{i=1}^N x_i^{\alpha_i} \quad \text{where } \alpha_0 > 0, \ \alpha_1 > 0, \ \ldots, \ \alpha_N > 0, \ \sum_{i=1}^N \alpha_i = 1 \tag{53}$$

The family of geometric quantity indexes,

$$Q_G(p^0, p^1, x^0, x^1) \equiv \prod_{i=1}^N (x_i^1/x_i^0)^{s_i}, \ s_i \equiv m_i(s_i^0, s_i^1)$$

is also exact for the aggregator function defined by (53).

Proof: If f is Cobb–Douglas and (48) holds, then for $r = 0, 1$, differentiating (53) yields

$$x_i^r \frac{\partial f(x^r)}{\partial x_i} \Big/ f(x^r) = \alpha_i = x_i^r p_i^r/p^{rT} x^r$$

using (51) $\equiv s_i^r$. Thus $s_i^0 = s_i^1 = \alpha_i = s_i \equiv m_i(s_i^0, s_i^1)$ and

$$P_G(p^0, p^1, x^0, x^1) \equiv \prod_{i=1}^N (p_i^1/p_i^0)^{s_i} = \prod_{i=1}^N (p_i^1/p_i^0)^{\alpha_i}$$

$$= k \prod_{i=1}^N (p_i^0)^{\alpha_i} \Big/ k \prod_{i=1}^N (p_i^0)^{\alpha_i} = c(p^1)/c(p^0)$$

since it can be verified by Lagrangian techniques that the Cobb–Douglas function defined by (53) has the unit cost function

$$c(p) \equiv k \prod_{i=1}^N p_i^{\alpha_i} \quad \text{where } k \equiv 1/\alpha_0 \prod_{i=1}^N \alpha_i^{\alpha_i}.$$

Thus P_G is exact for f. Similarly,

$$Q_G(p^0, p^1, x^0, x^1) \equiv \prod_{i=1}^N (x_i^1/x_i^0)^{s_i} = \prod_{i=1}^N (x_i^1/x_i^0)^{\alpha_i}$$

$$= \alpha_0 \prod_{i=1}^N (x_i^1)^{\alpha_i} \Big/ \alpha_0 \prod_{i=1}^N (x_i^0)^{\alpha_i} = f(x^1)/f(x^0)$$

and so Q_G is also exact for f defined by (53). Q.E.D.

Theorem 22 (Buscheguennce (Byushgens), 1925; Konüs and Byushgens, 1926, p. 1971; Frisch, 1936, p. 30; Wald, 1939, p. 331; Afriat, 1972b, p. 45; 1977; Pollak, 1971, p. 49; and Diewert, 1976a, p. 132):[25] Irving Fisher's (1922) ideal quantity index $Q_F(p^0, p^1, x^0, x^1) \equiv [p^{1T}x^1/p^{1T}x^0]^{1/2} \times [p^{0T}x^1/p^{0T}x^0]^{1/2} = [Q_P Q_L]^{1/2}$ and the corresponding price index $P_F(p^0, p^1, x^0, x^1) \equiv [p^{1T}x^1/p^{0T}x^1]^{1/2}[p^{1T}x^0/p^{0T}x^0]^{1/2} = [P_P P_L]^{1/2} = p^{1T}x^1/p^{0T}x^0 Q_F(p^0, p^1, x^0, x^1)$ are exact for the homogeneous quadratic function f defined by

$$f(x) \equiv (x^T A x)^{1/2}, \quad x \in S \tag{54}$$

where A is a symmetric $N \times N$ matrix of constants and S is any open, convex subset of the non-negative orthant Ω such that f is positive, linearly homogeneous and concave over this subset.[26]

Proof: We suppose that the following modified version of (48) holds:[27]

$$p^r \gg 0_N, x^r \gg 0_N, f(x^r) = \max_x\{f(x): p^{rT}x \leq p^{rT}x^r, x \in S\};$$
$$r = 0, 1 \tag{55}$$

Since only the budget constraints $p^{rT}x \leq p^{rT}x^r$ will be binding in the concave programming problems defined in (55), the Hotelling–Wold relations (51) will also hold, since the f defined by (54) is differentiable. Thus

$$p^r/p^{rT}x^r = \nabla f(x^r)/f(x^r) \quad \text{for } r = 0, 1 \text{ by (51)}$$

$$= \frac{1}{2}(x^{rT}Ax^r)^{-1/2}2Ax^r/(x^{rT}Ax^r)^{1/2} \quad \text{differentiating (54)}$$

$$= Ax^r/x^{rT}Ax^r \tag{56}$$

$$\begin{aligned}\therefore \quad Q_F(p^0, p^1, x^0, x^1) &\equiv [x^{1T}(p^0/p^{0T}x^0)/x^{0T}(p^1/p^{1T}x^1)]^{1/2}\\ &= [x^{1T}(Ax^0/x^{0T}Ax^0)/x^{0T}(Ax^1/x^{1T}Ax^1)]^{1/2} \quad \text{using (56)}\\ &= [x^{1T}Ax^1]^{1/2}/[x^{0T}Ax^0]^{1/2} \quad \text{since } x^{1T}Ax^0 = x^{0T}Ax\\ &\equiv f(x^1)/f(x^0) \quad \text{using (54)}\end{aligned}$$

Thus Q_F and the corresponding implicit price index

$$\begin{aligned}P_F(p^0, p^1, x^0, x^1) &= p^{1T}x^1/p^{0T}x^0 \, Q_F(p^0, p^1, x^0, x^1)\\ &= f(x^1)c(p^1)/f(x^0)c(p^0)[f(x^1)/f(x^0)]\\ &\quad \text{using (49)}\\ &= c(p^1)/c(p^0)\end{aligned}$$

are exact for the aggregator function f defined by (54) where c is the unit cost function which is dual to f.   Q.E.D.

The set S which occurs in (54) will be non-empty if we take A to be a symmetric matrix with one positive eigenvalue (and the corresponding eigenvector is positive) while the other eigenvalues of A are zero or negative. For example, take $A = aa^T$ where $a \gg 0_N$ is a vector of positive constants. In this case, S can be taken to be the positive orthant and $f(x) \equiv (x^T aa^T x)^{1/2} = a^T x$, a linear aggregator function. Thus the Fisher price and quantity indexes are also exact for a linear aggregator function.

The above example shows that the matrix A in (54) does not have to be invertable. However if A^{-1} does exist, then, using Lagrangian techniques, it can be shown[28] that $c(p) \equiv (p^T A^{-1} p)^{1/2}$ for $p \in S^*$ where S^* is the set of positive prices where $c(p)$ is positive, linearly homogeneous and concave.

6 Superlative index number formulae

The last example of an exact index number formula is very important for the following reason: unlike the linear aggregator function $a^T x$ or the geometric aggregator function defined by (53), the homogeneous quadratic aggregator function $f(x) \equiv (x^T A x)^{1/2}$ can provide a second order differential approximation to an arbitrary, linearly homogeneous, twice continuously differentiable aggregator function, i.e. $(x^T A x)^{1/2}$ is a *flexible functional form*.[29] Thus if the true aggregator function can be approximated closely by a homogeneous quadratic, and the producer or consumer is engaging in competitive maximizing behaviour during the two periods, then the Fisher price and quantity indexes will closely approximate the true ratios of unit and output (or utility). Note that it is not necessary to econometrically estimate the (generally unknown) coefficients which occur in the A matrix, *only the observable price and quantity vectors are required*.

Diewert (1976a, p. 117) defined a quantity index Q to be *superlative*[30] if it is exact for an aggregator function f which is capable of providing a second order differential approximation to an arbitrary twice continuously differentiable linearly homogeneous aggregator function. Thus Theorem 22 implies that Fisher's ideal index number formula Q_F is superlative.

Theorem 23 (Konüs and Byushgens, 1926, pp. 167–72; Pollak, 1971, pp. 49–52; Diewert, 1976a, pp. 133–4): Irving Fisher's ideal price and quantity indexes, P_F and Q_F, are exact for the aggregator function which is dual to the unit cost function c defined by

$$c(p) \equiv (p^T B p)^{1/2} \tag{57}$$

where B is a symmetric matrix of constants and S^* is any convex subset of Ω such that c is positive, linearly homogeneous and concave over S^*.[31]

Proof: Assume that (49) is satisfied where p^0, $p^1 \in S^*$, c is defined by (57) and f is the aggregator function dual to this c. Then, since c is differentiable, (52) also holds. Thus we have

$$\begin{aligned}
P_F(p^0, p^1, x^0, x^1) &\equiv (p^{1T} x^1 / p^{0T} x^1)^{1/2} (p^{1T} x^0 / p^{0T} x^0)^{1/2} \\
&= (p^{0T} \nabla c(p^1) / c(p^1))^{-1/2} (p^{1T} \nabla c(p^0) / c(p^0))^{1/2} \\
&\quad \text{using (52)} \\
&= (p^{0T} B p^1 / p^{1T} B p^1)^{-1/2} (p^{1T} B p^0 / p^{0T} B p^0)^{1/2} \\
&\quad \text{differentiating (57)} \\
&= (p^{1T} B p^1)^{1/2} / (p^{0T} B p^0)^{1/2} \quad \text{since } p^{0T} B p^1 = p^{1T} B p^0 \\
&\equiv c(p^1) / c(p^0) \quad \text{using (57)}
\end{aligned}$$

Thus P_F and the corresponding implicit quantity index

$$\begin{aligned}
Q_F(p^0, p^1, x^0, x^1) &= p^{1T}x^1/p^{0T}x^0 \, P_F(p^0, p^1, x^0, x^1) \\
&= f(x^1)c(p^1)/f(x^0)c(p^0)[c(p^1)/c(p^0)] \\
&\quad \text{using (49)} \\
&= f(x^1)/f(x^0)
\end{aligned}$$

are exact for the unit cost function defined by (57).   Q.E.D.

The set S^* which occurs in (57) will be non-empty if we take B to be a symmetric matrix with one positive eigenvalue (and the corresponding eigenvector is a vector with positive components) while the other eigenvalues of B are zero or negative. For example, take $B \equiv bb^T$ where $b \gg 0_N$ is a vector of positive constants. In this case, S^* can be taken to be the positive orthant and $c(p) \equiv (p^Tbb^Tp)^{1/2} = p^Tb$, a Leontief unit cost function. Thus the Fisher price and quantity indexes are also exact for a Leontief aggregator function.[32] This example shows that the f and c defined by Theorem 23 do not have to coincide with the f and c defined in Theorem 22. However, Q_F and P_F are exact for both classes of functions. Of course, if B^{-1} or A^{-1} exist, then the f and c defined in Theorem 22 coincide with the f and c defined in Theorem 23 (for a subset of prices and quantities at least).

A price index P is defined to be *superlative* if it is exact for a unit cost function c which can provide a second order differential approximation to an arbitrary twice continuously differentiable unit cost function. Since the c defined by (57) can provide such an approximation, Theorem 23 implies that P_F is a superlative price index.

If P is a superlative price index and $\tilde{Q}$ is the corresponding quantity index defined implicitly by the weak factor reversal test (45), then we define the pair of index number formulae $(P, \tilde{Q})$ to be *superlative*. Similarly, if Q is a superlative quantity index and $\tilde{P}$ is the corresponding implicit price index defined by (45), then the pair of index number formulae $(\tilde{P}, Q)$ is also defined to be *superlative*.

Before defining some additional pairs of superlative indexes, it is necessary to note the following result. If

$$f^*(z_1, \ldots, z_N) \equiv \alpha_0 + \sum_{i=1}^N \alpha_i z_i + \frac{1}{2} \sum_{i=1}^N \sum_{j=1}^N \alpha_{ij} z_i z_j$$

is a quadratic function defined over an open convex set S, then for every $z^0, z^1 \in S$, the following identity is true:

$$f^*(z^1) - f^*(z^0) = \frac{1}{2} [\nabla f^*(z^1) + \nabla f^*(z^0)]^T (z^1 - z^0) \tag{58}$$

where $\nabla f^*(z^r)$ is the gradient vector of f^* evaluated at z^r, $r = 0, 1$. The above identity follows simply by differentiating f^* and substituting the partial derivatives into (58).[33]

Now define the Törnqvist (1936) price and quantity indexes, P_0 and Q_0:

$$P_0(p^0, p^1, x^0, x^1) \equiv \prod_{i=1}^{N} (p_i^1/p_i^0)^{1/2(s_i^0+s_i^1)} \tag{59}$$

$$Q_0(p^0, p^1, x^0, x^1) \equiv \prod_{i=1}^{N} (x_i^1/x_i^0)^{1/2(s_i^0+s_i^1)} \tag{60}$$

where $p^0 \gg 0_N$, $p^1 \gg 0_N$, $x^0 \gg 0_N$, $x^1 \gg 0_N$, $s_i^0 \equiv p_i^0 x_i^0/p^{0T}x^0$ and $s_i^1 \equiv p_i^1 x_i^1/p^{1T}x^1$ for $i = 1, 2, ..., N$.

Theorem 24 (Diewert, 1976a, p. 119): Q_0 is exact for the homogeneous translog aggregator function f defined as[34]

$$\ln f(x) \equiv \alpha_0 + \sum_{i=1}^{N} \alpha_i \ln x_i + \frac{1}{2} \sum_{i=1}^{N} \sum_{j=1}^{N} \alpha_{ij} \ln x_i \ln x_j, \quad x \in S \tag{61}$$

where $\Sigma_{i=1}^{N} \alpha_i = 1$, $\alpha_{ij} = \alpha_{ji}$ for all i, j, $\Sigma_{j=1}^{N} \alpha_{ij} = 0$ for $i = 1, ..., N$ and S is an open convex subset of Ω such that f is positive and concave over S (the above restrictions on the αs ensure that f is linearly homogeneous).

Proof: Assume that the producer or consumer is engaging in maximizing behaviour during periods 0 and 1 so that (55) holds. Now define $z_i \equiv \ln x_i^r$ for $r = 0, 1$ and $i = 1, 2, ..., N$. If we define $f^*(z) \equiv \alpha_0 + \Sigma_{i=1}^{N} \alpha_i z_i + \frac{1}{2} \Sigma_{i=1}^{N} \Sigma_{j=1}^{N} \alpha_{ij} z_i z_j$ where the αs are as defined in (61), then, since f^* is quadratic in z, we can apply the identity (58). Since $\partial f^*(z^r)/\partial z_j \equiv \partial \ln f(x^r)/\partial \ln x_j = [x_j^r/f(x^r)][\partial f(x^r)/\partial x_j]$ for $r = 0, 1$ and $j = 1, ..., N$, (58) translates into the following identity involving the partial derivatives of the f defined by (61):

$$\ln f(x^1) - \ln f(x^0) = \frac{1}{2} \sum_{i=1}^{N} \left[\frac{x_i^1}{f(x^1)} \frac{\partial f(x^1)}{\partial x_i} + \frac{x_i^0}{f(x^0)} \frac{\partial f(x^0)}{\partial x_i} \right] (\ln x_i^1 - \ln x_i^0)$$

or

$$\ln f(x^1)/f(x^0) = \frac{1}{2} \sum_{i=1}^{N} \left[\frac{x_i^1 p_i^1}{p^{1T}x^1} + \frac{x_i^0 p_i^0}{p^{0T}x^0} \right] \ln [x_i^1/x_i^0] \quad \text{using (51)}$$

$$\therefore \quad f(x^1)/f(x^0) = \prod_{i=1}^{N} (x_i^1/x_i^0)^{1/2[s_i + s_i^0]} \equiv Q_0(p^0, p^1, x^0, x^1)$$

Q.E.D.

Define the implicit Törnqvist price index, $\bar{P}_0(p^0, p^1, x^0, x^1) \equiv p^{1T}x^1/p^{0T}x^0 \times Q_0(p^0, p^1, x^0, x^1)$. Since Q_0 is exact for the homogeneous translog f defined by (61), and since the homogeneous translog f is a flexible functional form (it can provide a second order differential approximation to an arbitrary twice continuously differentiable linearly homogeneous aggregator function), $(\tilde{P}_0, Q_0)$ is a superlative pair of index number formulae.

Theorem 25 (Diewert, 1976a, p. 121):[35] P_0 defined by (59) is exact for the translog unit cost function c defined as

$$\ln c(p) \equiv \alpha_0^* + \sum_{i=1}^{N} \alpha_i^* \ln p_i + \frac{1}{2} \sum_{i=1}^{N} \sum_{j=1}^{N} \alpha_{ij}^* \ln p_i \ln p_j, \quad p \in S^* \tag{62}$$

where $\Sigma_{i=1}^{N} \alpha_i^* = 1$, $\alpha_{ij}^* = \alpha_{ji}^*$ for all i, j, $\Sigma_{j=1}^{N} \alpha_{ij}^* = 0$ for $i = 1, ..., N$ and S^* is an open, convex subset of Ω such that c is positive and concave over S^*.

Proof: Assume that the producer or consumer is engaging in cost minimizing behaviour during periods 0 and 1 and thus we assume that (49) and its consequence (52) hold, with p^0, $p^1 \in S^*$. Since $\ln c(p)$ is quadratic in the variables $z_i \equiv \ln p_i$, we can again apply the identity (58) which translates into the following identity involving the partial derivatives of the c defined by (62):

$$\ln c(p^1) - \ln c(p^0) = \frac{1}{2} \sum_{i=1}^{N} \left[\frac{p_i^1}{c(p^1)} \frac{\partial c(p^1)}{\partial p_i} + \frac{p_i}{c(p^0)} \frac{\partial c(p^0)}{\partial p_i} \right]$$

$$\times (\ln p_i^1 - \ln p_i^0)$$

or

$$\ln c(p^1)/c(p^0) = \frac{1}{2} \sum_{i=1}^{N} \left[\frac{p_i^1 x_i^1}{p^{1T} x^1} + \frac{p_i^0 x_i^0}{p^{0T} x^0} \right] \ln (p_i^1/p_i^0)$$

using (52)

$$\therefore \quad c(p^1)/c(p^0) = P_0(p^0, p^1, x^0, x^1) \quad \text{using definition (59)}$$

Q.E.D.

Now define the implicit Törnqvist quantity index, $\tilde{Q}_0(p^0, p^1, x^0, x^1) \equiv p^{1T} x^1 / p^{0T} x^0 P_0(p^0, p^1, x^0, x^1)$. Since P_0 is exact for the flexible functional form defined by (62), $(\tilde{Q}_0, P_0)$ is also a superlative pair of index number formulae. It should be noted that the translog unit cost function is in general *not* dual to the homogeneous translog aggregator function defined by (61) (except when all $\alpha_{ij} = 0 = \alpha_{ij}^*$ and $\alpha_i = \alpha_i^*$, in which case (61) and (62) reduce to the Cobb–Douglas functional form).

Thus far, we have found 3 pairs of superlative index number formulae: (P_F, Q_F), $(P_0, \tilde{Q}_0)$ and $(\tilde{P}_0, Q_0)$. It turns out that there are many more such formulae. For $r \neq 0$, define the *quadratic mean of order r aggregator function*[36] f_r as

$$f_r(x) \equiv \left(\sum_{i=1}^{N} \sum_{j=1}^{N} a_{ij} x_i^{r/2} x_j^{r/2} \right)^{1/r}, \quad x \in S \tag{63}$$

where S is an open subset of Ω where f_r is neoclassical, and define the *quadratic mean order r unit cost function*[37] c_r as

$$c_r(p) \equiv \left(\sum_{i=1}^{N} \sum_{j=1}^{N} b_{ij} p_i^{r/2} p_j^{r/2} \right)^{1/r}, \quad p \in S^* \tag{64}$$

where S^* is an open subset of Ω where c_r is neoclassical. For $r \neq 0$, define the following price and quantity indexes:

$$P_r(p^0, p^1, x^0, x^1) \equiv \left\{ \sum_{i=1}^{N} s_i^0 (p_i^1/p_i^0)^{r/2} \right\}^{1/r} \left\{ \sum_{j=1}^{N} s_j^1 (p_j^1/p_j^0)^{-r/2} \right\}^{-1/r}$$

$$Q_r(p^0, p^1, x^0, x^1) \equiv \left\{ \sum_{i=1}^{N} s_i^0 (x_i^1/x_i^0)^{r/2} \right\}^{1/r} \left\{ \sum_{j=1}^{N} s_j^1 (x_j^1/x_j^0)^{-r/2} \right\}^{-1/r} \tag{65}$$

where $p^0, p^1, x^0, x^1 \gg 0_N$, $s_i^0 \equiv p_i^0 x_i^0 / p^{0T} x^0$ and $s_i^1 \equiv p_i^1 x_i^1 / p^{1T} x^1$ for $i = 1, 2, ..., N$.

It can be shown[38] (in a manner analogous to the proof of Theorem 22), that for each $r \neq 0$, Q_r defined by (65) is exact for f_r defined by (63). Similarly, it can be shown[39] (in a manner analogous to the proof of Theorem 23), that P_r defined by (65) is exact for c_r defined by (64). Since it is easy to show (cf. Diewert, 1976a, p. 130) that f_r and c_r are flexible functional forms for each $r \neq 0$, if can be seen that $(P_r, \tilde{Q}_r)$ and $(\tilde{P}_r, Q_r)$ are pairs of superlative index number formulae for each $r \neq 0$, where $\tilde{Q}_r \equiv p^{1T} x^1 / p^{0T} x^0 P_r$ and $\tilde{P}_r \equiv p^{1T} x^1 / p^{0T} x^0 Q_r$. Note that $P_2 = P_F$ (Fisher's ideal price index) and $Q_2 = Q_F$ (Fisher's ideal quantity index), so that $(P_2, \tilde{Q}_2) = (\tilde{P}_2, Q_2) = (P_F, Q_F)$. Moreover, it can be shown that the homogeneous translog aggregator function defined by (61) is a limiting case of f_r defined by (63) as r tends to zero (similarly, the translog unit cost function defined by (62) is a limiting case of c_r as r tends to zero)[40] and that Q_0 defined by (60) is a limiting case of Q_r as r tends to 0 while P_0 defined by (59) is a limiting case of P_r as r tends to 0.[41]

Given such a multiplicity of superlative indexes, the question arises: which index number formula should be used in empirical applications? The answer appears to be that it doesn't matter, provided that the variation in prices and quantities is not too great going from period 0 to period 1. This is because it has been shown[42] that the functions P_r and P_s differentially approximate each other to the second order for all r and s, provided that the derivatives are evaluated at any point where $p^0 = p^1$ and $x^0 = x^1$: i.e. we have $P_r(p^0, p^1, x^0, x^1) = \tilde{P}_s(p^0, p^1, x^0, x^1)$, $\nabla P_r(p^0, p^1, x^0, x^1) = \nabla \tilde{P}_s(p^0, p^1, x^0, x^1)$ and $\nabla^2 P_r(p^0, p^1, x^0, x^1) = \nabla^2 \tilde{P}_s(p^0, p^1, x^0, x^1)$ for all r and s, provided that $p^0 = p^1 \gg 0_N$. ∇P_r stands for the $4N$ dimensional vector of first order partials of P_r, $\nabla^2 P_r$ stands for the $4N$ matrix of second order partials of P_r, etc. The quantity indexes Q_r and $\tilde{Q}_s$ similarly differentially approximate each other to the second order for all r and s, provided that prices and quantities are the same for the two periods. These results are established by straightforward but tedious calculations – moreover, the assumption of optimizing behaviour on the parts of the consumer or producer is not required in order to derive these results.

Diewert (1978b) also shows that the Paasche and Laspeyres price indexes, P_P and P_L, differentially approximate each other and the superlative indexes, P_r and $\tilde{P}_s$, to the *first* order for all r and s, provided that prices and quantities are the same for the two periods. Thus if the variation in prices and quantities is relatively small between the two periods, the indexes P_L, P_P, P_r and $\tilde{P}_s$ will all yield approximately the same answer.

Diewert (1978b) argues that the above results provide a reasonably strong justification for using the *chain principle* when calculating official indexes such as the consumer price index or the GNP deflator, rather than using a fixed base, since in using the chain principle the base is changed every year, and thus the changes between p^0 and p^1 and x^0 and x^1 will be minimized, leading to smaller discrepancies between P_L and P_P, and even smaller discrepancies between the superlative indexes P_r and $\tilde{P}_s$.[43]

However, in some situations (e.g. in cross country comparisons or when decennial census data are being used), there can be considerable variation in the price and quantity data going from period (or observation) 0 to period (or observation) 1, in which case the indexes P_r and $\tilde{P}_s$ can differ considerably. In this situation, it is sometimes useful to compare the variation in the N quantity ratios (x_i^1/x_i^0) to the variation in the N price ratios (p_i^1/p_i^0). If there is less variation in the quantity ratios than in the price ratios, then the quantity indexes Q_r defined by (66) are share weighted averages of the quantity ratios and will tend to be more stable than the implicit indexes $\tilde{Q}_r$. On the other hand, if there is less variation in the price ratios than in the quantity ratios (the more typical case), then the price indexes P_r defined by (65) are share weighted averages of the price ratios (p_i^1/p_i^0) and will tend to be in closer agreement with each other than the implicit price indexes $\tilde{P}_r$. Thus, in the first situation, we would recommend the use of $(\tilde{P}_r, Q_r)$ for some r,[44] while in the second situation we would recommend the use of $(P_r, \tilde{Q}_r)$ for some r.[45] Notice that the Fisher index, $(P_F, Q_F) = (P_2, \tilde{Q}_2) = (\tilde{P}_2, Q_2)$ can be used in either situation. A further advantage for the Fisher formulae (P_F, Q_F) is that Q_F is consistent with revealed preference theory: i.e., even if the true aggregator function f is non-homothetic, under the assumption of maximizing behaviour, Q_F will correctly indicate the direction of change in the aggregate when revealed preference theory tells us that the aggregate is decreasing, increasing or remaining constant (cf. Diewert, 1976a, p. 137). Recall also that Q_F is consistent both with a linear aggregator function (perfect substitutability) and a Leontief aggregator function (no substitutability). No other superlative index number formula Q_r or $\tilde{Q}_r$, $r \neq 2$, has the above rather nice properties.

We conclude this section by showing that some of the above superlative index number formulae are also exact for non-homothetic aggregator functions.

Theorem 26 (Diewert, 1976a, p. 122): Let the functional form for the cost function $C(u, p)$ be a general translog defined by

$$\ln C(u, p) \equiv \alpha_0 + \sum_{i=1}^{N} \alpha_i \ln p_i + \frac{1}{2} \sum_{i=1}^{N} \sum_{j=1}^{N} \gamma_{ij} \ln p_i \ln p_j$$

$$+ \delta_0 \ln u + \sum_{i=1}^{N} \delta_i \ln p_i \ln u + \frac{1}{2} \varepsilon_0 (\ln u)^2 \quad (66)$$

where the parameters satisfy the following restrictions:

$$\sum_{i=1}^{N} \alpha_i = 1; \quad \gamma_{ij} = \gamma_{ji} \text{ for all } i, j; \quad \sum_{j=1}^{N} \gamma_{ij} = 0$$

$$\text{for } i = 1, 2, ..., N, \quad \text{and} \quad \sum_{i=1}^{N} \delta_i = 0 \quad (67)$$

Let (u^0, p^0) and (u^1, p^1) belong to a (u, p) region where $C(u, p)$ satisfies Conditions II where $u^0 > 0$, $u^1 > 0$, $p^0 \gg 0_N$, $p^1 \gg 0_N$ and the corresponding quantity vectors are $x^0 \equiv \nabla_p C(u^0, p^0) > 0_N$ and $x^1 \equiv \nabla_p C(u^1, p^1) > 0_N$ respectively. Then

$$P_0(p^0, p^1, x^0, x^1) = C(u^*, p^1)/C(u^*, p^0) \quad (68)$$

where P_0 is the Törnqvist price index defined by (59) and the reference utility level $u^* \equiv (u^0 u^1)^{1/2}$.

Proof: For a fixed u^*, $\ln C(u^*, p)$ is quadratic in the variables $z_i \equiv \ln p_i$ and thus we may apply the identity (53) to obtain

$$\ln C(u^*, p^1) - \ln C(u^*, p^0)$$

$$= \frac{1}{2} \sum_{i=1}^{N} [p_i^1 \ln C(u^*, p^1)/\partial p_i$$

$$+ p_i^0 \ln C(u^*, p^0)/\partial p_i][\ln p_i^1 - \ln p_i^0]$$

$$= \frac{1}{2} \sum_{i=1}^{N} [p_i^1 \partial \ln C(u^1, p^1)/\partial p_i$$

$$+ p_i^0 \partial \ln C(u^0, p^0)/\partial p_i][\ln p_i^1 - \ln p_i^0]$$

where the equality follows upon evaluating the derivatives of C and noting that
$$2 \ln u^* = \ln u^1 + \ln u^0$$
$$= \ln P_0(p^0, p^1, x^0, x^1)$$

using the definitions of x^0, x^1 and P_0 and equations (52).   Q.E.D.

Note that the right hand side of (68) is the true Konüs price index which corresponds to the general translog cost function defined by (66), evaluated at the reference utility level u^*, the square root of the product of the period 0 and 1 utility levels, u^0 and u^1. We note that the translog cost function can provide a second order differential approximation to an arbitrary twice continuously differentiable cost function.

Theorem 27 (Diewert, 1976a, pp. 123–4): Let the aggregator function F be such that F's distance function D is the translog distance function defined by $\ln D(u, x) \equiv \ln C(u, x)$ where C is defined by (66) and (67). Let (u^0, x^0) and (u^1, x^1) belong to a (u, x) region where $D(u, x)$ satisfies Conditions IV where $u^0 > 0$, $u^1 > 0$, $x^0 \gg 0_N$, $x^1 \gg 0_N$, $D(u^0, x^0) = 1$, $D(u^1, x^1) = 1$ and the corresponding vectors of normalized prices are $p^0/p^{0T}x^0 \equiv \nabla_x D(u^0, x^0) > 0_N$ and $p^1/p^{1T}x^1 \equiv \nabla_x D(u^1, x^1) > 0_N$ respectively.[46] Then

$$Q_0(p^0, p^1, x^0, x^1) = D(u^*, x^1)/D(u^*, x^0) \qquad (69)$$

where Q_0 is the Törnqvist quantity index defined by (60) and the reference utility level $u^* \equiv (u^0 u^1)^{1/2}$.

Proof: For a fixed u^*, $\ln D(u^*, x)$ is quadratic in the variables $z_i \equiv \ln x_i$ and thus we may apply the identity (58) to obtain

$$\ln D(u^*, x^1) - \ln D(u^*, x^0)$$

$$= \frac{1}{2} \sum_{i=1}^{N} [x_i^1 \, \partial \ln D(u^*, x^1)/\partial x_i$$
$$+ x_i^0 \, \partial \ln D(u^*, x^0)/\partial x_i][\ln x_i^1 - \ln x_i^0]$$

$$= \frac{1}{2} \sum_{i=1}^{N} [x_i^1 \ln D(u^1, x^1)/\partial x_i$$
$$+ x_i^0 \, \partial \ln D(u^0, x^0)/\partial x_i] \ln (x_i^1/x_i^0)$$

where the equality follows upon evaluating
the derivatives of D and noting that
$2 \ln u^* = \ln u^1 + \ln u^0$

$$= \frac{1}{2} \sum_{i=1}^{N} [x_i^1 \, p_i^1/p^{1T}x^1 D(u^1, x^1)$$
$$+ x_i^0 p_i^0/p^{0T}x^0 D(u^0, x^0)] \ln (x_i^1/x_i^0)$$
using $p^r/p^{rT}x^r = \nabla_x D(u^r, x^r)$, $r = 0, 1$[47]
$$= \ln Q_0(p^0, p^1, x^0, x^1)$$

using $D(u^1, x^1) = 1$, $D(u^0, x^0) = 1$ and the definition of Q_0.   Q.E.D.

Note that the right hand side of (69) is the Malmquist quantity index which corresponds to the translog distance function, evaluated at the reference utility level $u^* \equiv (u u^1)^{1/2}$. Theorem 27 provides a fairly strong justification for the use of Q_0 in empirical applications, since the translog distance function can differentially approximate an arbitrary twice continuously differentiable distance function to the second order.[48] However, the Fisher ideal index Q_2 can be given a similar strong justification in the context of non-homothetic aggregator functions.[49]

7 Historical notes and additional related topics

Our survey of the economic theory of index numbers is based on the work of Konüs (1924), Frisch (1936), Allen (1949), Malmquist (1953), Pollak (1971), Afriat (1972; 1977) and Samuelson and Swamy (1974). The results noted in sections 2 and 3 are either taken directly from or are straightforward modifications of results obtained by the above authors, except that in many cases we have weakened the original author's regularity conditions.[50]

The reader will have noted that many of the proofs in sections 2 and 3 use arguments that are used in revealed preference theory. For further material on the interconnections between revealed preference theory and index number theory, see Leontief (1936), Samuelson (1947, pp. 146–63), Allen (1949), Diewert (1976b), Vartia (1976b, p. 144) and Afriat (1977).

There is an extensive literature on the measurement of real output or real value added that is analogous to our discussion on the measurement of utility or real input: see Samuelson (1950), Bergson (1961), Moorsteen (1961), Fisher and Shell (1972, pp. 49–113) (the last 3 references make use of a quantity index analogous to the Malmquist index), Samuelson and Swamy (1974, pp. 588–92), Sato (1976b), Archibald (1977) and Diewert (1980).

Background material on the duality between cost, production or utility, and distance or deflation functions can be found in Shephard (1953; 1970), McFadden (1978), Hanoch (1978), Blackorby, Primont and Russell (1978), Diewert (1974a; 1978c), Deaton (1979) and Weymark (1978).

Turning now to sections 5 and 6, for theorems which prove converses to Theorems 19 to 25 under various regularity conditions, see Byushgens (1925), Konüs and Byushgens (1926), Pollak (1971), Diewert (1976a) and Lau (1979).

Sato (1976a) shows that a certain index number formula (which was defined independently by Vartia (1974)) is exact for the CES aggregator function defined by (63) with $a_{ij} \equiv 0$ for $i \neq j$ for all r, while Lau (1979) develops a partial converse theorem.

In Theorem 22, preferences were assumed to be represented by the transformed quadratic function, $(x^T A x)^{1/2}$. The assumption that preferences can be represented, at least locally, by a general quadratic function of the form $a_0 + a^T x + \frac{1}{2} x^T A x$ has a long history in economics, perhaps starting with Bennet (1920). Other authors who have approximated preferences quadratically, in addition to those mentioned in Theorem 22, include Bowley (1928), Hotelling (1938), Hicks (1946, pp. 331–3), Kloek (1967), Theil (1967, pp. 200–12; 1968), and Harberger (1971).

Kloek and Theil utilize quadratic approximations in the logarithms of prices and quantities and they obtain results which are related to Theorems 25 and 26 above. Kloek (1967) shows that the Törnqvist price index $P_0(p^0, p^1, x^0, x^1)$ approximates the true Konüs price index $P_K(p^0, p^1, u^m)$ to the second order where u^m, an intermediate utility level, is defined implicitly by the equation $C(u^m, p^0)/C(u^0, p^0) = C(u^1, p^1)/C(u^m, p^1)$ and C is the true cost function. On the quantity side, Kloek (1967) shows that the implicit Törnqvist quantity index $\tilde{Q}_0(p^0, p^1, x^0, x^1)$ approximates the true Allen quantity index $Q_A(x^0, x^1, p^m) \equiv C[F(x^1), p^m]/C[F(x^0), p^m]$ to the second order where $p^m \equiv (p_1^m, p_2^m, ..., p_N^m)^T$, an intermediate price vector, is defined by $p_i^m \equiv (p_i^0 p_i^1)^{1/2}$, $i = 1, ..., N$ and F is the aggregator function dual to the true cost function C. On the other hand, Theil (1968) shows that $P_0(p^0, p^1, x^0, x^1)$ approximates the true Konüs price index $P_K(p^0, p^1, \bar{u})$ to the second order where $\bar{u}$, an intermediate utility level, is defined as $\bar{u} \equiv G(p^m/y^m)$ where G is the indirect utility function dual to the true cost function C,[51] p^m is Kloek's intermediate price vector defined above and $y^m \equiv (p^{0T}x^0 p^{1T}x^1)^{1/2}$ is an intermediate expenditure. Finally, on the quantity side, Theil (1967; 1968) proves Kloek's result (i.e. that $\tilde{Q}_0(p^0, p^1, x^0, x^1)$ approximates $Q_A(x^0, x^1, p^m)$ to the second order) and in addition, shows that the direct Törnqvist quantity index $Q_0(p^0, p^1, x^0, x^1)$ also approximates $Q_A(x^0, x^1, p^m)$ to the second order.

It should be noted that index number theory and consumer surplus analysis are closely related. Thus the Paasche–Allen quantity index $Q_A(x^0, x^1, p^1) \equiv C[F(x^1), p^1]/C[F(x^0), p^1]$, is closely related to Hicks' (1941–42, p. 128; 1946, pp. 40–1) *compensating variation in income*,[52] $C[F(x^1), p^1] - C[F(x^0), p^1]$, and the Laspeyres–Allen quantity index, $Q_A(x^0, x^1, p^0) \equiv C[F(x^1), p^0]/C[F(x^0), p^0]$, is closely related to Hicks' (1941–42, p. 128; 1946, p. 331) *equivalent variation in income*, $C[F(x^1), p^0] - C[F(x^0), p^0]$. Thus the various bounds we developed for index numbers in the previous section have counterparts in consumer surplus analysis. Hicks (1941–42) and Samuelson (1947, pp. 189–202) emphasized the interconnection between index number theory and consumer surplus measures. For additional results and references to the literature on consumer surplus, see Hotelling (1938), Samuelson (1942), Harberger (1971), Silberberg (1972), Hause (1975), Chipman and Moore (1976) and Diewert (1976b). The attractiveness of the Malmquist quantity index $Q_M(x^0, x^1, x)$ does not seem to have been noted in the applied welfare economics literature, although the closely related concept inherent in Debreu's (1951) coefficient of resource utilization has been recognized. Perhaps in the future there will be more applications of the Kloek–Theil approximation results, or of Theorem 27 above which shows that the Törnqvist quantity index Q_0 is numerically equal to a certain Malmquist index.

Another type of price and quantity index which we must mention is the Divisia (1925; 1926, p. 40) index, (which is perhaps due to Bennet (1920, p. 461)). The Bennet–Divisia justification for these indexes proceeds as follows. Regard $(x_1, ..., x_N)^T \equiv x$ and $(p_1, ..., p_N)^T \equiv p$ as functions of time, $x(t)$ and $p(t)$ for $i = 1, ..., N$. Now differentiate expenditure with respect to time and we obtain:[53]

$$\partial \left[\sum_{i=1}^{N} p_i(t)x_i(t) \right] \Big/ \partial t = \sum_{i=1}^{N} p_i(t)\partial x_i(t)/\partial t + \sum_{i=1}^{N} x_i(t)\partial p_i(t)/\partial t \qquad (70)$$

Now divide both sides of the above equation through by $\Sigma_{i=1}^{N} p_i(t)x_i(t) \equiv p(t)^T x(t)$ and we obtain the identity:

$$\partial \ln [p(t)^T x(t)]/\partial t = \sum_{i=1}^{N} s_i(t)\partial \ln x_i(t)/\partial t$$
$$+ \sum_{i=1}^{N} s_i(t)\partial \ln p_i(t)/\partial t \qquad (71)$$

where $s_i(t) \equiv p_i(t)x_i(t)/p(t)^T x(t)$ for $i = 1, 2, ..., N$. The term on the left hand side of (70) is the rate of change of expenditures, which is decomposed into a share weighted rate of change of quantities plus a share weighted rate of change of prices. Denote $\dot{x}_i(t) \equiv \partial x_i(t)/\partial t$ and $\dot{p}_i(t) \equiv \partial p_i(t)/\partial t$ and integrate both sides of (70) to obtain

$$\ln p(1)^T x(1)/p(0)^T x(0) = \int_0^1 \left[\sum_{i=1}^{N} s_i(t)\dot{x}_i(t)/x_i(t) \right] dt$$
$$+ \int_0^1 \left[\sum_{i=1}^{N} s_i(t)\dot{p}_i(t)/p_i(t) \right] dt \qquad (72)$$

The first term on the right hand side of the above equation is defined to be the natural logarithm of the *Divisia quantity index*, $\ln [X(1)/X(0)]$, while the second term is the logarithm of the *Divisia price index*, $\ln [P(1)/P(0)]$.

The above derivation of the Divisia indexes, $X(1)/X(0)$ and $P(1)/P(0)$, is devoid of any economic interpretaton. However, Ville (1951), Malmquist (1953, p. 227), Wold (1953, pp. 134–47), Solow (1957), Gorman (1959, p. 479; 1970), Jorgenson and Griliches (1967, p. 253) and Hulten (1973) show that if the consumer or producer is continuously maximizing a well behaved linearly homogeneous aggregator function subject to a budget constraint between $t = 0$ and $t = 1$, then $P(1)/P(0) = P_K(p(0), p(1), \bar{x})$ (i.e. the Divisia price index equals the true Konüs price index for any reference quantity vector $\bar{x} \gg 0_N$) and we can deduce that $X(1)/X(0) = Q_M(x(0), x(1), \bar{x}) = Q_A(x(0), x(1), \bar{p}) = \tilde{Q}_K(p(0), p(1), x(0), x(1), \bar{x})$ (i.e. the Divisia quantity index equals the Malmquist, Allen, and implicit Konüs quantity indexes for all reference vectors $\bar{x} \gg 0_N$ and $\bar{p} \gg 0_N$). On the other hand, Ville (1951, p. 127), Malmquist (1953, pp. 226–7), Gorman (1970, p. 7), Silberberg (1972, p. 944) and Hulten (1973, pp. 1021–2) show that if the aggregator function is not homothetic, then the line integrals defined on the right hand side of (72) are not independent of the path of integration and thus the Divisia indexes are also path dependent.

We have not stressed the Divisia approach to index numbers in this survey since economic data typically are not collected on a continuous time basis. Since there are many ways of approximating the line integrals in (72) using discrete data points, the Divisia approach to index number theory does not significantly narrow down the range of discrete type index number formulae, $P(p^0, p^1, x^0, x^1)$ and $Q(p^0, p^1, x^0, x^1)$, that are consistent with the Divisia approach.

The line integral approach also occurs in consumer surplus analysis: see Samuelson (1942; 1947, pp. 189–202), Silberberg (1972), Rader (1976) and Chipman and Moore (1976).

Divisia indexes and exact index number formulae also play a key role in another area of economics which has a vast literature, namely the *measurement of total factor productivity*. A few references to this literature are Solow (1957), Domar (1961), Richter (1966), Jorgenson and Griliches (1967; 1972), Gorman (1970), Ohta (1974), Star (1974), Usher (1974), Christensen, Cummings and Jorgenson (1980), Diewert (1976a, pp. 124–9; 1980, pp. 487–98) and Allen (1978). To see the relationship of this literature to superlative index number formulae, consider the following example: Let $u^r \equiv f(x^r) > 0$, $r = 0, 1$ be 'intermediate' output produced by a competitive (in input markets) cost minimizing firm where $x^r \gg 0_N$ is a vector of inputs utilized during period r, and f is the homogeneous translog production function defined by (61). Letting $w^0 \gg 0_N$ and $w^1 \gg 0_N$ be the vectors of input prices the producer faces during periods 0 and 1, Theorem 24 tells us that

$$f(x^1)/f(x^0) = Q_0(w^0, w^1, x^0, x^1) \tag{73}$$

where Q_0 is the Törnqvist quantity index defined by (60). Using (49), we also have

$$c(w^r)f(x^r) = w^{rT}x^r, \quad r = 0, 1 \tag{74}$$

where $c(w)$ is the unit cost function which is dual to $f(x)$. Suppose now that 'final' output is $y^r \equiv a^r f(x^r)$, $r = 0, 1$ where $a^r > 0$ is defined to be a technology index for period r. The ratio a^1/a^0 can be defined to be a measure of Hicks neutral technical progress.[54] Using (73),

$$a^1/a^0 \equiv [y^1/y^0]/[f(x^1)/f(x^0)] = y^1/y^0 Q_0(w^0, w^1, x^0, x^1) \tag{75}$$

Thus a^1/a^0 can be calculated using observable data.[55] The unit cost function for y in period r is $c(w)/a^r$. Now suppose the producer behaves monopolistically on his output market and sells his period r output y^r at a price p^r equal to unit cost times a markup factor $m^r > 0$, i.e.

$$p^r \equiv m^r c(w^r)/a^r, \quad r = 0, 1 \tag{76}$$

Using (76),

$$m^1/m^0 = [p^1/p^0][a^1/a^0]/[c(w^1)/c(w^0)] = [p^1 y^0/p^0 y^0]/[w^{1T}x^1/w^{0T}x^0] \tag{77}$$

using (74) and (75). Thus the rate of markup change m^1/m^0 can be calculated by (77), the value of output ratio deflated by the value of inputs ratio, using observable data.[56] However, if pure profits are zero in each period, then $p^r y^r = w^{rT} x^r = [m^r c(w^r)/a^r][a^r f(x^r)]$ (using (76)) $= m^r w^{rT} x^r$ (using (74)) so that $m^r = 1$ for $r = 0, 1$.

Another area of research which somewhat surprisingly is closely related to index number theory is the measurement of inequality: see Blackorby and Donaldson (1978; 1980; 1981).

Typically, a price or quantity index is not constructed in a single step. For example, in constructing a cost of living index, first food, clothing, transportation and other sub-indexes are constructed and then they are combined to form a single cost of living index. Vartia (1974, pp. 39–42; 1976a, p. 124; 1976b, pp. 84–9) defines an index number formula $P(p^0, p^1, x^0, x^1)$ to be *consistent in aggregation* if the numerical value of the index constructed in two (or more) stages necessarily coincides with the value of the index calculated in a single stage. Vartia (1976b; p. 90) stresses the importance of the consistency in aggregation property for national income accounting and notes that the Paasche and Laspeyres indexes have this property (as do the geometric indexes P_G and Q_G defined in Theorem 21 above). Vartia (1976b, pp. 121–40) exhibits many other index number formulae that are consistent in aggregation. Unfortunately, the two families of superlative indexes, $(P_r, \tilde{Q}_r)$ and $(\tilde{P}_s, Q_s)$, are *not* consistent in aggregation for any r or s. However, Diewert (1978b) using some of Vartia's results shows that the superlative indexes are *approximately* consistent in aggregation (to the second order in a certain sense). Additional results are contained in Blackorby and Primont (1980). Related to the consistency in aggregation property for an index number formula are the following issues which have been considered by Pollak (1975), Primont (1977), Blackorby and Russell (1978) and Blackorby, Primont and Russell (1978, chapter 9): (i) under what conditions do well defined Konüs cost of living sub-indexes exist for a subset of the commodity space and (ii) under what conditions can the sub-indexes be combined into the true overall Konüs cost of living index P_K? Finally, a related result is due to Gorman (1970, p. 3) who shows that the line integral Divisia indexes defined above 'aggregate conformably' or are consistent in aggregation, to use Vartia's term.

If we are given more than two price and quantity observations, then some ideas due to Afriat (1967) can be utilized in order to construct *non-parametric index numbers*. Let there be I given price–quantity vectors (p^i, x^i) where $p^i \gg 0_N$, $x^i > 0_N$, $i = 1, 2, ..., I$. Use the given data in order to define Afriat's ijth cross coefficient, $D_{ij} \equiv (p^{iT}x^j/p^{iT}x^i) - 1$ for $1 \le i, j \le I$. Now consider the following linear programming problem in the $2I + 2I^2$ variables λ_i, ϕ_i, s_{ij}^+, s_{ij}^-, $i, j = 1, ..., I$:

$$\text{minimize} \sum_{i=1}^{I} \sum_{j=1}^{I} s_{ij}^- \quad \text{subject to} \tag{78}$$

(i) $\lambda_i D_{ij} = \phi_j - \phi_i + s_{ij}^+ - s_{ij}^-$; $i, j = 1, 2, ..., I$,

(ii) $\lambda_i \ge 1$; $i = 1, 2, ..., I$,   and

(iii) $\phi_i \ge 0$, $s_{ij}^+ \ge 0$, $s_{ij}^- \ge 0$; $i, j = 1, 2, ..., I$

Diewert (1973)[57] shows that if x^i is a solution to

$$\max_x \{F(x): p^{iT}x \le p^{iT}x^i, x \ge 0_N\} \tag{79}$$

for $i = 1, 2, ..., I$ where F is a continuous from above aggregator function which is subject to local non-satiation (so that the budget constraint $p^{iT}x \le p^{iT}x^i$ will always hold as an equality for an x which maximizes $F(x)$ subject to the budget constraint), then the objective function in the programming problem (78) will attain its lower bound of zero. On the other hand, Afriat (1967) shows that if the objective function in (78) attains its lower bound of 0 so that $\lambda_i^* D_{ij} \ge \phi_j^* - \phi_i^*$ for all i and j where λ_i^*, ϕ_i^* denote solution variables to (78), then the given quantity vector x^i is a solution to the utility maximization problem (79) for $i = 1, 2, ..., I$. Moreover, Afriat (1967, pp. 73–4) shows that a utility function F^* which is consistent with the given data in the sense that $F^*(x^i) = \max_x \{F^*(x): p^{iT}x \le p^{iT}x^i; x \ge 0_N\}$ for $i = 1, 2, ..., I$ can be defined as $F^*(x) \equiv \min_i \{F_i^*(x): i = 1, ..., I\}$ where

$$F_i^*(x) \equiv \phi_i^* + \lambda_i^*[(p^{iT}x/p^{iT}x^i) - 1]; \quad i = 1, 2, ..., I \tag{80}$$

where the number ϕ_i^* and λ_i^* are taken from the solution to (78). Afriat notes that this F^* is continuous, increasing and concave over the non-negative orthant and that $F^*(x^i) = \phi_i^*$ for $i = 1, ..., I$. Thus if the observed data are consistent with a decision maker maximizing a continuous from above, locally non-satiated aggregator function $F(x)$ subject to I budget constraints, then the solution to the linear programming problem (78) can be used in order to construct an approximation F^* to the true F, and this F^* will satisfy much stronger regularity conditions. Diewert (1973, p. 424) notes that we can test whether the given data are consistent with the additional hypothesis that the true aggregator function is homothetic or linearly homogeneous by adding the following restrictions to (78): (iv) $\lambda_i = \phi_i$, $1 = 1, ..., I$. Geometrically, these additional restrictions force all of the hyperplanes defined by (61) through the origin: i.e. $F_i^*(0_N) = 0$ for all i. Once the linear program (78) is solved, either with or without the additional normalizations (iv), we can calculate $F^*(x^i) = \phi_i^*$ for all i and thus the quantity indexes $F^*(x^{i+1})/F^*(x^i)$ can readily be calculated. Diewert and Parkan (1978) calculated these non-parametric quantity indexes using some Canadian time series data[58] and compared them with the superlative indexes Q_2, Q_0 and $\bar{Q}_0$. The differences between all of these indexes turned out to be small.[59] The above method for constructing parametric indexes is of course closely related to revealed preference theory.

Finally, we mention that there is an analogous 'revealed production theory' which allows one to construct non-parametric index numbers and non-parametric approximations to production functions and production possibility sets by solving various linear programming problems:[60] see Farrell (1957), Afriat (1972a), Hanoch and Rothschild (1972) and Diewert and Parkan (1979).

Notes

1 University of British Columbia, Vancouver, Canada. The financial support of the Canada Council is gratefully acknowledged as are the helpful comments of R. C. Allen, C. Blackorby, and A. Deaton, who are not responsible for the remaining shortcomings of this chapter. It is a pleasure to dedicate this chapter to Professor Stone, since the author first learned of the existence of the index number problem as a graduate student at Berkeley by reading some of Professor Stone's work.

2 Notation: $x \geq 0_N$ means each component of the column vector x is non-negative, $x \gg 0_N$ means each component is positive, $x > 0_N$ means $x \geq 0_N$ but $x \neq 0_N$ where 0_N is an N dimensional vector of zeros, and x^T denotes the transpose of x.

3 If $x'' \gg x' \geq 0_N$, then $F(x'') > F(x')$.

4 For every $u \in$ Range F, the upper level set $L(u) \equiv \{x: F(x) \geq u\}$ is a convex set. A set S is convex iff $x' \in S$, $x'' \in S$, $0 \leq \lambda \leq 1$ implies $\lambda x' + (1 - \lambda)x'' \in S$: i.e. the line segment joining any two points belonging to S also belongs to S.

5 F is continuous from above over $x \geq 0_N$ iff for every $u \in$ Range F, $L(u) \equiv \{x: F(x) \geq u\}$ is a closed set.

6 Specifically, Diewert (1978c) shows that C will satisfy the following Conditions II'': (i) $C(u, p)$ is a real valued function of $N + 1$ variables defined over $U \times P$ and is continuous in p for fixed u and continuous from below in u for fixed p (the set U is now the convex hull of the range of F), (ii) $C(u, p) \geq 0$ for every $u \in U$ and $p \in P$, (iii) $C(u, p)$ is non-decreasing in u for fixed p, (iv) $C(u, p)$ is non-decreasing in p for fixed u, and properties (v) and (vi) are the same as (v) and (vi) of Conditions II.

7 Or *cost of production index* in the producer context.

8 In the theory of international comparisons, p^0 and p^1 can be interpreted as

price vectors that a given consumer (whose utility level is indexed by the quantity vector x) faces in countries 0 and 1.

9 The index P_K can also be written as $P_K(p^0, p^1, u) \equiv C(u, p^1)/C(u, p^0)$ where u is the reference output or utility level. Written in this form, the symmetry of the Konüs price index P_K with the Malmquist quantity index to be introduced later becomes apparent. However, our present notation for P_K is more convenient when we set the reference consumption vector x equal to the observed consumption vector x^r in period r.

10 It seems clear that earlier researchers such as Frisch (1936, p. 25) also knew this result, but they had some difficulty in stating it precisely, since the concept of homotheticity was not invented until 1953 (by Shephard (1953) and Malmquist (1953)).

11 Linear homogeneity of $G[F]$ follows from the following identity which can be derived in a manner analogous to (4): $G[F(x)] = 1/\max_p \{c(p): p \geq 0_N, p^T x = 1\}$ for every $x \gg 0_N$.

12 This point is made by Pollak (1971, p. 28).

13 The terminology is due to Wold (1953, p. 136).

14 Pollak (1971, p. 20) makes this well known point. F is a Leontief aggregator function if $F(x_1, x_2, ..., x_N) \equiv \min_i\{x_i/a_i: i = 1, 2, ..., N\}$ where $a^T \equiv (a_1, a_2, ..., a_N) > 0_N$. In this case $C(u, p) = u\, p^T a$.

15 We also utilize property (ii) for C: $C(\bar{u}, p) = 0$ for every $p \gg 0_N$.

16 If F satisfies *Conditions I*, then it can be shown (e.g., see Diewert, 1978c), that the deflation function D satisfies *Conditions IV*: (i) $D(u, x)$ is a real valued function of $N + 1$ variables defined over Int $\Omega = \{u: \underline{u} < u < \bar{u}\} \times \{x: x \gg 0_N\}$ and is *continuous* over this domain, (ii) $D(\bar{u}, x) = +\infty$ for every $x \in$ Int Ω; i.e., $u^n \in$ Int U, $\lim u^n = \bar{u}$, $x \in$ Int Ω implies $\lim_n D(u^n, x) = +\infty$, (iii) $D(u, x)$ is *decreasing in* u for every $x \in$ Int Ω, i.e. if $x \in$ Int Ω, u', $u'' \in$ Int U with $u' < u''$, then $D(u', x) > D(u'', x)$, (iv) $D(\underline{u}, x) = 0$ for every $x \in$ Int Ω; i.e. $u^n \in$ Int U, $\lim u^n = \underline{u}$, $x \in$ Int Ω implies $\lim_n D(u^n, x) = 0$, (v) $D(u, x)$ is (positively) *linearly homogeneous in* x for every $u \in$ Int U; i.e., $u \in$ Int U, $\lambda > 0$, $x \in$ Int Ω implies $D(u, \lambda x) = \lambda D(u, x)$, (vi) $D(u, x)$ is *concave in* x for every $u \in$ Int U, (vii) $D(u, x)$ is increasing in x for every $u \in$ Int U; i.e., $u \in$ Int U, x', $x'' \in$ Int Ω implies $D(u, x' + x'') > D(u, x')$, and (viii) D is such that the function $\tilde{F}(x) \equiv \{u: u \in$ Int U, $D(u, x) = 1\}$ defined for $x \gg 0_N$ has a continuous extension to $x \geq 0_N$.

17 More explicitly, $C[F(\bar{x}), p]$ is the support function for the set $L[F(\bar{x})] \equiv \{x: p^T x \geq C[F(\bar{x}), p]$ for every $p \gg 0_N\}$ and the sets $\{x: p^{0T} x \geq p^{0T}x^0, x \geq 0_N\}$ and $\{x: p^{1T}x \geq p^{1T}x^1, x \geq 0_N\}$ form outer approximations to this set where $x^0 \in \partial_p C[F(\bar{x}), p^0]$ and $x^1 \in \partial_p C[F(\bar{x}), p^1]$. $\partial_p C(u, p^0)$ denotes the set of supergradients to the concave function of p, $C(u, p)$, evaluated at the point p^0. Analogously, $D[F(\bar{x}), x]$ is the support function for the set $L^*[F(\bar{x})] \equiv \{p: p^T x \geq D[F(\bar{x}), x]$ for every $x \gg 0_N\}$ and the sets $\{p: p^T x^0 \geq p^{0T}x^0, p \geq 0_N\}$ and $\{p: p^T x^1 \geq p^{1T}x^1, p \geq 0_N\}$ form outer approximations to this set where $p^0 \in \partial_x D[F(\bar{x}), x^0]$ and $p^1 \in \partial_x D[F(\bar{x}), x^1]$.

18 The concept is associated with Irving Fisher (1922).

19 This terminology is due to Frisch (1930).

20 f is positive, linearly homogeneous and concave over the positive orthant and is extended to the non-negative orthant Ω by continuity.

21 Recall (6) with $G(u) \equiv u$. The function c is also neoclassical.

22 Sometimes p^0 and p^1 are restricted to a subset of the positive orthant.

23 Alternatively, the first equality in (51) is implied by the Kuhn–Tucker condi-

tions for the concave programming problem in (48) upon eliminating the Lagrange multiplier for the binding constraint $p^{rT}x \leq p^{rT}x^r$. The non-negativity constraints $x \geq 0_N$ are not binding because we assume the solution $x^r \gg 0_N$.

24 Note that the definition of exactness requires $x^r \gg 0_N$ and x^r is a solution to the appropriate aggregator maximization problem. Thus it can be seen that p^0 must be proportional to a.

25 Samuelson (1947, p. 155) states that S. Alexander also derived this result in an unpublished Harvard paper.

26 f can be extended to the non-negative orthant as follows. Because $(x^TAx)^{1/2}$ is linearly homogeneous, S can be taken to be a convex cone. Extend f to $\bar{S}$, the closure of S, by continuity. Now define the free disposal level sets of f by $L(u) \equiv \{x: x \geq x', f(x') \geq u, x' \in \bar{S}\}$ for $u \geq 0$. The extended f is defined as $f(x) \equiv \max_u\{u: x \in L(u), u \geq 0\}$ for $x \geq 0_N$.

27 The non-negativity constraints $x \geq 0_N$ have been replaced by $x \in S$. Because we assume that S is an open set and we assume that $x^r \in S$, the constraints $x \in S$ are not binding in (55).

28 See Pollak (1971, pp. 47–9) and Afriat (1972b, p. 45).

29 f is a flexible functional form if it can provide a second order (differential) approximation to an arbitrary twice continuously differentiable function f^* at a point x^*. f differentially approximates f^* at x^* iff (i) $f(x^*) = f^*(x^*)$, (ii) $\nabla f(x^*) = \nabla f^*(x^*)$ and (iii) $\nabla^2 f(x^*) = \nabla^2 f^*(x^*)$, where both f and f^* are assumed to be twice continuously differentiable at x^* (and thus the two Hessian matrices in (iii) will be symmetric). Thus a general flexible functional form f must have at least $1 + N + N(N + 1)/2$ free parameters. If f and f^* are both linearly homogeneous, then $f^*(x^*) = x^{*T}\nabla f^*(x^*)$ and $\nabla^2 f^*(x^*)x^* = 0_N$, and thus a flexible linearly homogeneous functional form f need have only $N + N(N - 1)/2 = N(N + 1)/2$ free parameters. The term 'differential approximation' is in Lau (1974, p. 184). Diewert (1974b, p. 125) or (1976a, p. 130) shows that $(x^TAx)^{1/2}$ is a flexible linearly homogeneous functional form.

30 The term is due to Fisher (1922, p. 247) who defined a quantity index Q to be superlative if it was numerically close to his ideal index, Q_F.

31 The aggregator function f which is dual to c defined by (57) can be constructed using the local duality techniques explained in Blackorby and Diewert (1979).

32 This fact was first noted by Pollak (1971, p. 52).

33 On the other hand if f^* satisfies (58) for all $z^0, z^1 \in S$, then Diewert (1976a, p. 138) (assuming that f^* is thrice differentiable) and Lau (1979) (assuming that f^* is once differentiable) show that f^* must be a quadratic function.

34 This functional form is due to Christensen, Jorgenson and Lau (1971) and Sargan (1971).

35 Theil (1965, pp. 71–2) virtually proved this theorem; however, he did not impose linear homogeneity on $c(p)$ defined by (62), which is required in order for (52) to be valid.

36 An ordinary mean of order r (see Hardy, Littlewood and Polya, 1934) is defined as $F_r(x) \equiv (\sum_{i=1}^N a_i x_i^r)^{1/r}$ for $x \gg 0_N$ where $a_i \geq 0$ and $\sum_{i=1}^N a_i = 1$. Note that $kF_r(x)$ where $k > 0$ is the constant elasticity of substitution functional form (see Arrow, Chenery, Minhas and Solow, 1961) so that f_r defined by (63) contains this functional form as a special case.

37 See Denny (1974) who introduced c_r to the economics literature.

38 See Diewert (1976a, p. 132).

39 See Diewert (1976a, pp. 133–4).

40 See Diewert (1980, p. 451).

41 See Khaled (1978; pp. 95–6).

42 See Diewert (1978b) who utilizes the work of Vartia (1976a; 1976b). Vartia (1978) provides an alternative proof.

43 The chain principle can also be justified from the viewpoint of Divisia indexes; see Wold (1953, pp. 134–9) and Jorgenson and Griliches (1967).

44 If $(x_i^1/x_i^0) = k > 0$ for all i, then $(\tilde{P}_r, Q_r) = (p^{1T}x^1/p^{0T}x^0k, k)$ for all r, and the use of $(\tilde{P}_r, Q_r)$ can be theoretically justified using Leontief's (1936, pp. 54–7) Aggregation Theorem.

45 If $(p_i^1/p_i^0) = k > 0$ for all i, then $(P_r, \tilde{Q}_r) = (k, p^{1T}x^1/p^{0T}x^0k)$ for all r, and the use of $(P_r, \tilde{Q}_r)$ can be theoretically justified using Hicks' (1946, pp. 312–13) Composite Commodity Theorem. See also Wold (1953, pp. 102–10), Gorman (1953, pp. 76–7) and Diewert (1978a, p. 23).

46 These assumptions imply that x^r is a solution to the aggregator maximization problem $\max_x\{F(x): p^{rT}x = p^{rT}x^r, x \geq 0_N\} = F(x^r) \equiv u^r$ for $r = 0, 1$ where F is locally dual (cf. Blackorby and Diewert, 1979) to the translog distance function D defined above.

47 This identity is due to Shephard (1953, pp. 10–13) and Hanoch (1978, p. 116).

48 Let D be a distance function which satisfies certain local regularity properties and let F be the corresponding local aggregator function, and C be the corresponding local cost function. Blackorby and Diewert (1979) show that if D differentially approximates D^* to the second order, then F differentially approximates F^*, and C differentially approximates C^* to the second order where F^*, and C^* are dual to D^*.

49 See Diewert (1976b, p. 149).

50 Our regularity conditions can be further weakened: for all of the results in sections 2 and 3 which do not involve the Malmquist quantity index, we need only assume that F be continuous and be subject to local non-satiation (it turns out that the corresponding C will still satisfy Conditions II). Also Theorems 11, 12, 14 and 16 can be proven provided that F be only continuous from above and increasing.

51 $G(p^m/y^m) \equiv \max_u\{u: C(u, p^m/y^m) \leq 1\} \equiv \max_x\{F(x): (p^m/y^m)^T x \leq 1, x \geq 0_N\}$ where C is the cost function and F is the aggregator function.

52 Hicks' verbal definition of the compensating variation can be interpreted to mean $C[F(x^0), p^1] - C[F(x^0), p^0]$, and this interpretation is related to the Laspeyres–Konüs cost of living index.

53 'The fundamental idea is that over a short period the rate of increase of expenditure of a family can be divided into two parts x and l, where x measures the increase due to change of prices and l measures the increase due to increase of consumption; x is the total of the various quantities consumed, each multiplied by the appropriate rate of increase of price, and l is the total of the prices of commodities, each multiplied by the rate of increase in its consumption' (Bennet, 1920, p. 455). l is the first term on the right hand side of (70) while x is the second term.

54 See Blackorby, Lovell and Thursby (1976) for a discussion of the various types of neutral technological change.

55 This part of the analysis is due to Diewert (1976a, pp. 124–9).

56 This argument is essentially due to Allen (1978). Allen also generalized his results to many outputs and to non-neutral measures of technical change.

57 Afriat (1967) has essentially this result. However, there is a slight error in his proof and he does not phrase the problem as a linear programming problem. (78) corrects some severe typographical errors in Diewert's (1973, p. 421) equation (3.2).

58 However, slightly different but equivalent normalizations were used. In particular, when the general non-homothetic problem (78 (i), (ii) and (iii)) was solved, (78 (iii)) was replaced by $\lambda_i \geq 0$ for $i = 1, ..., I$, $\phi_1 \equiv 1$ and $\phi_I \equiv Q_2(p^1, p^I, x^1, x^I)$ in order to make the nonhomothetic nonparametric quantity indexes, ϕ_{i+1}^*/ϕ_i^*, comparable to $Q_2(p^i, p^{i+1}, x^i, x^{i+1})$ for $i = 1, 2, ..., I - 1$.

59 Diewert and Parkan (1978) also investigated empirically the consistency in aggregation issue. Price indexes were constructed residually using (45).

60 In the context of production theory, the (output) aggregate $F(x)$ is observable, in contrast to the utility theory context where $F(x)$ is unobservable.

References

Afriat, S. N. (1967), 'The Construction of Utility Functions from Expenditure Data', *International Economic Review* **8**, 67–77.

——— (1972a), 'Efficiency Estimation of Production Function', *International Economic Review* **13**, 568–98.

——— (1972b), 'The Theory of International Comparisons of Real Income and Prices', pp. 13–69 in *International Comparisons of Prices and Output*, D. J. Daly (ed.), New York: National Bureau of Economic Research.

——— (1977), *The Price Index*, London: Cambridge University Press.

Allen, R. C. (1978), 'Accounting for Price Changes', Discussion Paper 78–14, Department of Economics, University of British Columbia, Vancouver, Canada.

Allen, R. G. D. (1949), 'The Economic Theory of Index Numbers', *Economica NS* **16**, 197–203.

Archibald, R. B. (1977), 'On the Theory of Industrial Price Measurement: Output Price Indexes', *Annals of Economic and Social Measurement* **6**, 57–72.

Arrow, K. J., Chenery, H. B., Minhas, B. S. and Solow, R. M. (1961), 'Capital–Labor Substitution and Economic Efficency', *Review of Economics and Statistics* **63**, 225–50.

Banerjee, K. S. (1975), *Cost of Living Index Numbers: Practice, Precision and Theory*, New York: Marcel Dekker, Inc.

Bennet, T. L. (1920), 'The Theory of Measurement of Changes in Cost of Living', *Journal of the Royal Statistical Society* **83**, 455–62.

Bergson, A. (1961), *National Income of the Soviet Union since 1928*, Cambridge, Mass.: Harvard University Press.

Blackorby, C. and Diewert, W. E. (1979), 'Expenditure Functions, Local Duality, and Second Order Approximations', *Econometrica* **47**, 579–601.

Blackorby, C. and Donaldson, D. (1978), 'Measures of Relative Equality and Their Meaning in Terms of Social Welfare', *Journal of Economic Theory* **18**, 59–80.

——— (1980), 'A Theoretical Treatment of Indices of Absolute Inequality', *International Economic Review* **21**, 107–36.

——— (1981), 'Ethical Indices for the Measurement of Poverty', *Econometrica* **22**.

Blackorby, C., Lovell, C. A. K. and Thursby, M. (1976), 'Extended Hicks Neutral Technical Change', *Economic Journal* **86**, 845–52.

Blackorby, C. and Primont, D. (1980), 'Index Numbers and Consistency in Aggregation', *Journal of Economic Theory* **22**, 87–98.

Blackorby, C., Primont, D. and Russell, R. R. (1978), *Duality, Separability and Functional Structure: Theory and Economic Applications*, New York: American Elsevier.

Blackorby, C. and Russell, R. R. (1978), 'Indices and Subindices of the Cost of Living and the Standard of Living', *International Economic Review* **19**, 229–40.

Bowley, A. L. (1928), 'Notes on Index Numbers', *Economic Journal* **38**, 216–37.

Buscheguennce, S. S. (1925), 'Sur une classe des hypersurfaces: A propos de "l'index ideal" de M. Irving Fischer', *Recueil Mathematique* (Moscow) **32**, 625–31 [Russian title: Byushgens, S. S., 1925, 'Ob odnom klasse giperpoverkhnostey: po povodu "idealnovo indeksa" Irving Fischer' a pokupatelnoi sili deneg', *Mathematischeskii Sbornik* **32**, 625–31].

Chipman, J. S. and Moore, J. C. (1976), 'The Scope of Consumer's Surplus Arguments', in *Evolution, Welfare and Time in Economics*, A. M. Tang, F. M. Westfield, and J. S. Worley (eds.), Lexington, Mass.: D. C. Heath and Co.

Christensen, L. R., Cummings, D. and Jorgenson, D. W. (1980), 'Economic Growth, 1947–1973: An International Comparison', pp. 595–691 in *New Developments in Productivity Measurement and Analysis*, J. W. Kendrick and B. N. Yaccard (eds.), Chicago: University of Chicago Press.

Christensen, L. R., Jorgenson, D. W. and Lau, L. J. (1971), 'Conjugate Duality and the Transcendental Logarithmic Production Function', *Econometrica* **39**, 255–6.

Cobb, C. and Douglas, P. H. (1928), 'A Theory of Production', *American Economic Review* **18**, 139–65.

Darrough, M. N. and Southey, C. (1977), 'Duality in Consumer Theory Made Simple: The Revealing of Roy's Identity', *The Canadian Journal of Economics* **10**, 307–17.

Deaton, A. (1979), 'The Distance Function in Consumer Behavior with Applications to Index Numbers and Optimal Taxation', *Review of Economic Studies*, **46**, pp. 391–405.

Debreu, G. (1951), 'The Coefficient of Resource Utilization', *Econometrica* **19**, 273–92.

Denny, M. (1974), 'The Relationship Between Functional Forms for the Production System', *Canadian Journal of Economics* **7**, 21–31.

Diewert, W. E. (1973), 'Afriat and Revealed Preference Theory', *Review of Economic Studies* **40**, 419–26.

(1974a), 'Applications of Duality Theory', in *Frontiers of Quantitative Economics* Vol. II, ed. M. D. Intriligator and D. A. Kendrick, Amsterdam: North-Holland Publishing Company.

(1974b), 'Functional Forms for Revenue and Factor Requirements Functions', *International Economic Review* **15**, 119–30.

(1976a), 'Exact and Superlative Index Numbers', *Journal of Econometrics* **4**, 115–45.

(1976b), 'Harberger's Welfare Indicator and Revealed Preference Theory', *The American Economic Review* **66**, 143–52.

(1980), 'Aggregation Problems in the Measurement of Capital', pp. 453–528 in *The Measurement of Capital*, D. Usher (ed.), Chicago: University of Chicago Press.

(1978a), 'Hicks' Aggregation Theorem and the Existence of a Real Value-Added Function', pp. 17–51 in M. Fuss and D. McFadden (eds.), *Production Economics: A Dual Approach to Theory and Applications* Vol. 2, Amsterdam: North-Holland Publishing Company.

(1978b), 'Superlative Index Numbers and Consistency in Aggregation', *Econometrica* **46**, 883–900.

(1978c), 'Duality Approaches to Microeconomic Theory', IMSSS Technical Report No. 281, Stanford University, Stanford, California.

Diewert, W. E. and Parkan, C. (1978), 'Tests for the Consistency of Consumer Data and Nonparametric Index Numbers', Discussion Paper 78–27, Department of Economics, University of British Columbia, Vancouver, Canada.

(1979), 'Linear Programming Tests of Regularity Conditions for Production Functions', Discussion Paper 79–01, Department of Economics, University of British Columbia, Vancouver, Canada.

Divisia, F. (1925), 'L'indice monétaire et la théorie de la monnaie', *Revue d'Economie Politique* **39**, 842–61, 980–1008, and 1121–51.

(1926), *L'indice monétaire et la théorie de la monnaie*, Paris: Societe anonyme du Recueil Sirey.

Domar, E. D. (1961), 'On the Measurement of Technological Change', *The Economic Journal* **71**, 709–29.

Eichhorn, W. (1976), 'Fisher's Tests Revisited', *Econometrica* **44**, 247–56.

(1978), 'What is an Economic Index? An Attempt of an Answer', pp. 3–42 in W. Eichhorn, R. Henn, O. Optiz and R. W. Shephard (eds.), *Theory and Economic Applications of Economic Indices*, Würzburg: Physica-Verlag.

Eichhorn, W. and Voeller, J. (1976), *Theory of the Price Index: Fisher's Test Approach and Generalizations*, Lecture Notes in Economics and Mathematical Systems, Berlin: Springer-Verlag.

Farrell, M. J. (1957), 'The Measurement of Productive Efficiency', *Journal of the Royal Statistical Society* (Series A) 120, 253–81.

Fisher, I. (1911), *The Purchasing Power of Money*, London: Macmillan.

(1922), *The Making of Index Numbers*, Boston Mass.: Houghton Mifflin.

Fisher, F. M., and Shell, K. (1972), *The Economic Theory of Price Indices*, New York: Academic Press.

Frisch, R. (1930), 'Necessary and Sufficient Conditions Regarding the Form of an Index Number Which Shall Meet Certain of Fisher's Tests', *American Statistical Association Journal* **25**, 397–406.

(1936), 'Annual Survey of General Economic Theory: The Problem of Index Numbers', *Econometrica* **4**, 1–39.

Gorman, W. M. (1953), 'Community Preference Fields', *Econometrica* **21**, 63–80.

(1959), 'Separable Utility and Aggregation', *Econometrica* **27**, 469–81.

(1970), 'Notes on Divisia Indices', Department of Economics, University of North Carolina, Chapel Hill, October.

Hanoch, G. (1978), ''Symmetric Duality and Polar Production Functions', pp. 111–31 in M. Fuss and D. McFadden (eds.), *Production Economics: A Dual Approach to Theory and Applications* Vol. 1, Amsterdam: North-Holland.

Hanoch, G. and Rothschild, M. (1972), 'Testing the Assumptions of Production Theory: A Nonparametric Approach', *Journal of Political Economy* **80**, 256–75.

Harberger, A. C. (1971), 'Three Basic Postulates for Applied Welfare Economics: An Interpretive Essay', *Journal of Economic Literature* **9**, 785–97.

Hardy, G. H., Littlewood, J. E. and Polya, G. (1934), *Inequalities*, Cambridge: Cambridge University Press.

Hause, J. C. (1975), 'The Theory of Welfare Cost Measurement', *Journal of Political Economy* **83**, 1145–82.

Hicks, J. R. (1941–42), 'Consumers' Surplus and Index-Numbers', *Review of Economic Studies* **9**, 126–37.

(1946), *Value and Capital*, Oxford: Clarendon Press.

Hotelling, H. (1935), 'Demand Functions with Limited Budgets', *Econometrica* **3**, 66–78.

(1938), 'The General Welfare in Relation to Problems of Taxation and of Railway and Utility Rates', *Econometrica* **6**, 242–69.

Hulten, C. R. (1973), 'Divisia Index Numbers', *Econometrica* **41**, 1017–26.

Jorgenson, D. W. and Griliches, Z. (1967), 'The Explanation of Productivity Change', *Review of Economic Studies* **34**, 249–83.

(1972), 'Issues in Growth Accounting: A Reply to Edward F. Denison', *Survey of Current Business* **52**, No. 5, Part II, 65–94.

Joseph, M. F. W. (1935–36), 'Mr. Lerner's Supplementary Limits for Price Index Numbers', *Review of Economic Studies* **3**, 155–7.

Khaled, M. S. (1978), *Productivity Analysis and Functional Specification: A Parametric Approach*, PhD thesis, University of British Columbia, Vancouver, Canada.

Kloek, T. (1967), 'On Quadratic Approximations of Cost of Living and Real Income Index Numbers', Report 6710, Econometric Institute, Netherlands School of Economics, Rotterdam.

Kloek, T. and de Wit, G. M. (1961), 'Best Linear Unbiased Index Numbers', *Econometrica* **29**, 602–16.

Konüs, A. A. (1924), 'The Problem of the True Index of the Cost of Living', translated in *Econometrica* **7**, 1939, 10–29.

Konüs, A. A. and S. S. Byushgens (1926), 'K probleme pokupatelnoi cili deneg', *Voprosi Konyunkturi,* **II**, 151–72. [English title: Conus, A. A. and S. S. Buscheguennce, On the Problem of the Purchasing Power of Money', *The Problems of Economic Conditions* (supplement to the Economic Bulletin of the Conjuncture Institute) **2**, 151–72.]

Lau, L. J. (1974), 'Applications of Duality Theory: Comments', pp. 176–99 in M. D. Intriligator and D. A. Kendrick (eds.), *Frontiers of Quantitative Economics*, vol. II, Amsterdam: North-Holland.

(1979), 'On Exact Index Numbers', *Review of Economics and Statistics* **61**, 73–82.

Leontief, W. W. (1936), 'Composite Commodities and the Problem of Index Numbers', *Econometrica* **4**, 39–59.

(1941), *The Structure of the American Economy 1919–1929*, Cambridge, Mass.: Harvard University Press.

Lerner, A. P. (1935–36), 'A Note on the Theory of Price Index Numbers', *Review of Economic Studies* **3**, 50–6.

McFadden, D. (1978), 'Cost, Revenue and Profit Functions', pp. 3–109 in M. Fuss and D. McFadden (eds.), *Production Economics: A Dual Approach to Theory and Applications* Vol. 1, Amsterdam: North-Holland.

Malmquist, S. (1953), 'Index Numbers and Indifference Surfaces', *Trabajos de Estatistica* **4**, 209–42.

Moorsteen, R. H. (1961), 'On Measuring Productive Potential and Relative Efficiency', *Quarterly Journal of Economics* **75**, 451–67.

Ohta, M. (1974), 'A Note on Duality between Production and Cost Functions: Rate of Returns to Scale and Rate of Technical Progress', *Economic Studies Quarterly* **25**, 63–5.

Pollak, R. A. (1969), 'Conditional Demand Functions and Consumption Theory', *Quarterly Journal of Economics* **83**, 60–78.

(1971), 'The Theory of the Cost of Living Index', Research Discussion Paper No. 11, Office of Prices and Living Conditions, US Bureau of Labor, Statistics, Washington, DC.

(1975), 'Subindexes of the Cost of Living', *International Economic Review* **16**, 135–50.

Primont, D. (1977), 'Necessary and Sufficient Conditions for the Consistent Aggregation of Cost-of-Living Subindexes', Discussion Paper 77–08, Department of Economics, University of British Columbia, Vancouver, Canada.

Rader, T. (1976), 'Equivalence of Consumer Surplus, the Divisia Index of Output and Eisenberg's Addilog Social Utility Function', *Journal of Economic Theory* **13**, 58–66.

Richter, M. K. (1966), 'Invariance Axioms and Economic Indexes', *Econometrica* **34**, 739–55.

Samuelson, P. A. (1942), 'Constancy of the Marginal Utility of Income', in O. Lange *et al.* (eds.), *Studies in Mathematical Economics and Econometrics, in Memory of Henry Schultz,* Chicago: University of Chicago Press.

(1947), *Foundations of Economic Analysis,* Cambridge, Mass.: Harvard University Press.

(1950), 'Evaluation of Real National Income', *Oxford Economic Papers* **2**, 1–29.

(1974), 'Remembrances of Frisch', *European Economic Review* **5**, 7–23.

Samuelson, P. A. and Swamy, S. (1974), 'Invariant Economic Index Numbers and Canonical Duality: Survey and Synthesis', *American Economic Review* **64**, 566–93.

Sargan, J. D. (1971), 'Production Functions', Part V of P. R. G. Layard, J. D. Sargan, M. E. Ager, and D. J. Jones, *Qualified Manpower and Economic Performance,* Harmondsworth: Penguin.

Sato, K. (1976a), 'The Ideal Log-Change Index Number', *Review of Economics and Statistics* **58**, 223–8.

(1976b), 'The Meaning and Measurement of the Real Value Added Index', *The Review of Economics and Statistics* **58**, 434–42.

Shephard, R. W. (1953), *Cost and Production Functions,* Princeton: Princeton University Press.

(1970), *Theory of Cost and Production Functions,* Princeton: Princeton University Press.

Silberberg, E. (1972), 'Duality and the Many Consumer's Surpluses', *American Economic Review* **62**, 942–52.

Solow, R. M. (1957), 'Technical Change and the Aggregate Production Function', *Review of Economics and Statistics* **39**, 312–20.

Star, S. (1974), 'Accounting for the Growth of Output', *American Economic Review* **64**, 123–35.

Stuvel, G. (1957), 'A New Index Number Formula', *Econometrica* **25**, 123–31.

Theil, H. (1960), 'Best Linear Index Numbers of Prices and Quantities', *Econometrica* **28**, 464–80.

(1965), 'The Information Approach to Demand Analysis', *Econometrica* **33**, 67–87.

(1967), *Economics and Information Theory,* Amsterdam: North-Holland.

(1968), 'On the Geometry and the Numerical Approximation of Cost of Living and Real Income Indices', *De Economist* **116**, 677–89.

Törnqvist, L. (1936), 'The Bank of Finland's Consumption Price Index', *Bank of Finland Monthly Bulletin* **10**, 1–8.

Usher, D. (1974), 'The Suitability of the Divisia Index for the Measurement of Economic Aggregates', *Review of Income and Wealth* **20**, 273–88.

Vartia, Y. O. (1974), *Relative Changes and Economic Indices,* Licensiate Thesis in Statistics, University of Helsinki, June.

(1976a), 'Ideal Log-Change Index Numbers', *Scandanavian Journal of Statistics* **3**, 121–6.

(1976b), *Relative Changes and Index Numbers*, Helsinki: The Research Institute of the Finnish Economy.

(1978), 'Fisher's Five Tined Fork and Other Quantum Theories of Index Numbers', pp. 271–95 in W. Eichhorn, R. Henn, O. Opitz and R. W. Shephard (eds.) *Theory and Economic Applications of Economic Indices*, Würzburg: Physica-Verlag.

Ville, J. (1951) ['Sur les conditions d'existence d'une ophélimité totale et d'un indice due niveau des prix', *Annales de l'Université de Lyon* **9** (1946), 32–9], English translation: 'The Existence Conditions of a Total Utility Function', *Review of Economic Studies* **19** (1951–52), 123–8.

Wald, A. (1937), 'Zur Theorie des Preisindexziffern', *Zeitschrift für Nationalökonomie* **8**, 179–219.

(1939), 'A New Formula for the Index of the Cost of Living', *Econometrica* **7**, 319–31.

Weymark, J. A. (1978), 'Durality Results in Demand Theory', Discussion Paper 78–38, Department of Economics, University of British Columbia, Vancouver, Canada.

Wold, H. (1943, 1944), 'A Synthesis of Pure Demand Analysis', *Skandinavisk Aktuarietidskrift* **26**, 85–144 and 220–75; **27**, 69–120.

(1953), *Demand Analysis*, New York: John Wiley and Sons.

The consumption function and durable goods

Introduction to part three

One of the most difficult areas in consumer theory is that which concerns itself with intertemporal choice. Theory which ignores uncertainty lacks credibility while theory taking it into account is complex and hard to implement. On the empirical side, the analysis of the consumption function and of durable goods presents all the classic time-series problems of dynamics, seasonality and serial correlation. Even after 40 years of continual econometric activity, and in spite of their contemporary treatment as standard classroom examples of applied econometric analysis, both durable goods and consumption functions are still subject to lively controversy.

Much the most influential work on what is still called the 'modern' theory of the consumption function is that of Modigliani and Brumberg (1955a, b) on the life-cycle model, although the ideas go back to Fisher and Ramsey. The life-cycle model has the inestimable advantage of viewing the theory of the consumption function as a part of consumption theory in general. This work, together with that of Friedman (1957), provided the basic model of the consumption function which has dominated theoretical and empirical discussion ever since. In its applied form at least, the basic regression is one of consumption on its own lagged value and on income although a number of other variables (lagged income, wealth, liquid assets, the distribution of income) make periodic appearances. Such equations are at the heart of most macroeconometric models and have been widely estimated in both the United States and Britain; indeed Sir Richard Stone's own work in the area is very much in this tradition, see [84], [99], [117] and [140].

Purchases of durable goods, although recognized in principle as part of the general intertemporal choice problem, tend to be handled rather differently, at least in practice. On the one hand, the distinction between use and purchase has always been clear and the best work on the consumption function allows for the use or depreciation of durables as a part of household consumption. On the other hand, the price associated with that use, or user cost, has rarely been used in empirical work on the demand for household durable goods themselves. Instead, the focus has been much more on the dynamics of the relationship between durable purchases and income which is induced by the fact that the former is a stock while the latter is a flow. The main vehicle for this analysis has been the stock-adjustment model pioneered in consumer demand studies by Sir

210

Richard Stone [55], [58], [60], [64], [67] and, at about the same time, by Chow (1957). Like the permanent income consumption function, the stock-adjustment model has become a standard tool of applied econometrics and, indeed, as the 'state' adjustment model of Houthakker and Taylor (1966; 1970), is now undergoing something of a revival. However, like the standard consumption function model, durable goods models of this type, particularly for cars, have not performed consistently well, especially in recent years. Hence the theory and empirics of both durables and non-durables has been undergoing increasing scrutiny.

In the first chapter in this section, by John Muellbauer, the intertemporal theory is taken seriously and an integrated model of both durable and non-durable consumption is developed and estimated. The user cost concept is presented and its empirical counterpart is calculated for British post-war data. A considerable amount of ingenuity is displayed in the construction of expected magnitudes which correspond as closely as possible to the future price and income variables which appear in the theory. The major testable implication of the model is that once stocks are correctly measured, the dynamic relationship between non-durable consumption and income must be the same as that between durable stocks and income. Hence the only difference between the dynamics of durable and non-durable *purchases* must be explicable in terms of the relationship between durable flows and stocks. This conclusion is emphatically rejected by the evidence. Muellbauer suggests that this is because of 'imperfections' in the durable goods market, such as the asymmetry between buying and selling prices for cars predicted by models such as that of Akerlof (1970). Clearly, such phenomena will have to be explicitly modelled if successful progress is to be made in integrating theory and empirical work on durable goods.

The second paper, by David Hendry and Thomas von Ungern-Sternberg, is an important contribution to the very active current debate on the nature of the consumption function. Two issues are central here. In the first place, the empirical failure of the conventional consumption function in recent years has provoked a search for previously omitted variables. Since the difficulties occurred during a period of price inflation higher than anything in post-war history, the obvious candidates have been variables associated with the rate of inflation, particularly the real value of liquid assets, increased uncertainty, or the rate of inflation itself. As recent work has shown (see particularly the paper by Davidson, Hendry, Srba and Yeo (1978) (upon which the current work builds) and also Deaton (1977), Howard (1978) and Juster and Wachtel (1972a,b)), such variables can take us a considerable way in reconciling evidence with theory. In the current paper, the authors show that the hypothesis that, in the long run, real consumption and real income are proportional, together with a 'correction' of real income for at least some of the loss in real liquid assets consequent on price inflation, provides an extremely parsimonious and efficient explanation of the British consumption data. The second issue relates to the dynamics of the relation between income and consumption. Here, much of the recent interest has come from theoretical work on the implications of 'rational expectations' for the structure of consumption functions based on the actions of consumers who plan ahead according to the life-cycle model. In this context, see particularly the recent paper by Hall (1978). At the same time, the fact that quarterly data series are now relatively long permits the application of much more sophisticated time-series techniques than were available in the 1950s or 1960s. The current paper is remarkable for the care with which the dynamics are estimated and it is especially valuable in providing a description of the data in terms of stylized dynamic facts which cannot be ignored by future work in this field.

References for introduction to part three

Akerlof, G. (1970), 'The market for lemons', *Quarterly Journal of Economics*, **84**, pp. 488–500.

Chow, G. (1957), *Demand for automobiles in the US: a study in consumer durables*, Amsterdam: North-Holland.

Davidson, J. E. H., D. F. Hendry, F. Srba and S. Yeo (1978), 'Econometric modelling of the aggregate time-series relationship between consumers' expenditure and income in the United Kingdom', *Economic Journal*, **88**, pp. 661–92.

Deaton, A. S. (1977), 'Involuntary savings through unanticipated inflation', *American Economic Review*, **67**, pp. 899–910.

Friedman, M. (1957), *A theory of the consumption function*, Princeton University Press.

Hall, R. E. (1978), 'Stochastic implications of the life cycle – permanent income hypothesis: theory and evidence', *Journal of Political Economy*, **86**, pp. 971–87.

Houthakker, H. S. and L. D. Taylor (1966; 1970), *Consumer demand in the United States 1929–70, Analysis and projections*, Harvard University Press, 1st and 2nd editions.

Howard, D. H. (1978), 'Personal saving behavior and the rate of inflation', *Review of Economics and Statistics*, **60**, pp. 547–54.

Juster, F. T. and P. Wachtel (1972a), 'Inflation and the consumer', *Brookings Papers*, Vol. 1, pp. 71–114.

(1972b), 'A note on inflation and the saving rate', *Brookings Papers*, Vol. 3, pp. 765–78.

Modigliani, F. and R. Brumberg (1955a), 'Utility analysis and the consumption function: an interpretation of cross-section data', in Kurihara, K. K. (ed.), *Post-Keynesian Economics*, George Allen and Unwin, London.

(1955b), 'Utility analysis and aggregate consumption functions: an attempt at integration', mimeo.

8 Testing neoclassical models of the demand for consumer durables[1]

JOHN MUELLBAUER

Introduction

Modelling the demand for consumer durables is not one of the easiest topics in applied economics. Much of the most creative work in the field was done in Cambridge in the 1950s in the group around Stone. Thus the classic paper by Farrell (1954) was the first systematic application of discrete choice theory to the problem and made a notable contribution also in analysing the interaction of the markets for new and used cars. Under the direct influence of Stone, Cramer (1957), in another classic, first put forward a neoclassical model integrating the demand for durable and non-durable goods with the life cycle theory of Ramsey (1928), Fisher (1930), Tintner (1938) and Modigliani and Brumberg (1955). The essence of the model lies in the assumptions that the budget constraint is linear and known with confidence and that, in efficiency-corrected units, new and used durables are perfect substitutes. Stone and Rowe (1957) simultaneously with Chow (1957) first applied the stock adjustment model to the demand for durables. The latter remains the most popular tool of analysis for aggregate time-series data though more recently Smith (1974; 1975) and Westin (1975) have put forward the 'discretionary replacement' model as a simple alternative. Though the neoclassical model of investment has been widely applied since Haavelmo (1960) and Jorgenson (1963), application to consumer durables have been less frequent. Diewert (1974) is one and contains a useful discussion of the theory. Hess (1977), which is another, finds parameter estimates which are interpreted as favouring the neoclassical model. Although the stock adjustment model is typically rationalized by costs of adjustment, in applications to consumer durables it is typically not derived from an optimizing problem. The same is true of the discretionary replacement model. The systematic connection between theory and empirical implementation in the neoclassical model as well as the empirical success which has been claimed for it therefore make it worthwhile to carry out a systematic test. The present test complements the wider-ranging discussion of durables in Deaton and Muellbauer (1980).

213

Section 1 reviews the theory and suggests an extended form of the linear expenditure system, see Stone (1954), as the vehicle for implementation. The application is in section 2. This discusses the form taken by price and income expectations which makes this extended LES more general and realistic than those proposed by Lluch (1973) and Lluch, Powell and Williams (1977). There is also a brief review of the national accounts treatment of income, saving, assets and durables, to put the empirical application which follows into context. The fact that a long time series on assets and durables exists in Britain again reflects the beneficial influence of the work done by the Stone group in Cambridge. The theory implies some cross-equation restrictions between the non-durables and durables equations and testing these is the object. The model fails this test and in section 3 two possible explanations are suggested. One feature of the neoclassical model is that the rental price of durables is fairly volatile and this is one reason why the model suggests that purchases should also be volatile. Both of the alternative hypotheses suggest limitations on the speed of adjustment: uncertainty and transactions costs which stem from the asymmetry of information between buyers and owners of used durables. It is suggested therefore that either or both the perfect markets (linear budget constraint) assumption and the assumption that the constraint is perceived with confidence are erroneous even as approximations to reality.

1 The neoclassical model and the extended linear expenditure system

The presentation of the neoclassical model follows the same logic as that in the classic paper by Cramer (1957). By working here in discrete rather than continous time, the intertemporal optimization problem is more accessible, being the maximization of utility with respect to a finite number of decision variables and subject to a standard linear budget constraint.

It is assumed that the stock of the durable good yields a consumption service flow proportional to its magnitude. Hence the stock is itself the measure of the service flow and it is thus stocks at various dates which must appear in the intertemporal utility function. Let d_s denote purchases of the durable at time s, v_s denote the corresponding price, and D_s the stock in existence at the end of period s. Further assume that deterioration is proportional to stocks with a constant of proportionality, δ, which is independent of use and remains constant over time. This assumes that, in efficiency-corrected units, older and younger durables are perfect substitutes. Hence, stocks are linked to purchases by

$$D_s = d_s + (1 - \delta)D_{s-1} \tag{1.1}$$

For simplicity of presentation the small amount of deterioration on current purchases within the period is ignored here but, as in Stone and Rowe (1958) allowed for in the empirical work below.

The utility function relevant for intertemporal planning can now be written

$$u_t = v(q_t, q_{t+1}, \ldots, q_\tau, D_t, D_{t+1}, \ldots, D_\tau, A_\tau/P_\tau) \tag{1.2}$$

where q_s is the amount of non-durable purchases at time s, τ is the date of the planning horizon and A_τ/P_τ is the real value of financial assets at the end of period τ which, together with D_τ, represents the consumer's provision for periods beyond τ. Both q_s and D_s could easily be made vectors with an obvious generalization of the demand functions below. But since in the empirical application which follows they are treated as aggregates, the same is done here. The omission of leisure from the utility function is rationalized by the assumption of separability of leisure from non-durable and durable consumption. The wage incomes, y_s all s, are treated as exogenous variables in the budget constraint. On the assumption that all markets are perfect so that consumers face parametric prices and can lend or borrow at the same interest rate, the period to period budget constraint takes the form

$$
\begin{aligned}
A_s &= (1 + r_s)A_{s-1} + y_s - p_s q_s - v_s d_s \\
&= (1 + r_s)A_{s-1} + y_s - p_s q_s - v_s\{D_s - (1 - \delta)D_{s-1}\}
\end{aligned} \tag{1.3}
$$

from (1.1). Equation (1.3) can be used to write $A_{\tau-1}$ as a function of A_τ, $A_{\tau-2}$ as a function of $A_{\tau-1}$, and so on recursively until we have an intertemporal budget constraint linking A_{t-1} to A_τ. This takes the form

$$
\sum_{s=t}^{\tau} \hat{p}_s q_s + \sum_{s=t}^{\tau} \{\hat{v}_s - (1 - \delta)\hat{v}_{s+1}\}D_s + \hat{A}_\tau
$$
$$
= v_t(1 - \delta)D_{t-1} + \hat{y}_t + \hat{y}_{t+1} + \ldots + \hat{y}_\tau + (1 + r_t)A_{t-1} \tag{1.4}
$$

where $\hat{v}_s$ and $\hat{p}_s$ are discounted prices obtained by dividing v_s and p_s by the discounting factor $\Pi_{i=t+1}^{s} (1 + r_i)$. The values $\hat{y}_{t+1}, \ldots, \hat{y}_\tau$ and $\hat{A}_\tau$ are $y_{t+1}, \ldots$ y_τ and A_τ discounted by the appropriate value of the same factor. Note that since the discount factor is unity when $s = t$, there is no distinction between y_t and $\hat{y}_t$ or v_t and $\hat{v}_t$. Clearly, the left-hand side of (1.4) is the present discounted value of present and future consumption of durable and non-durable goods plus the discounted value of bequests. The right-hand side is discounted present value of purchasing power including the value of starting stocks of the durable. Denote it by W_t. The intertemporal budget constraint thus takes the 'standard form':

$$
\sum_{t}^{\tau} \hat{p}_s q_s + \sum_{t}^{\tau} v_s^* D_s + \hat{A}_\tau = W_t \tag{1.5}
$$

where the (discounted) implicit price of durable services $\hat{v}_s^*$ is defined by

$$\hat{v}_s^* \equiv \hat{v}_s - (1 - \delta)\hat{v}_{s+1} \qquad (1.6)$$

this is often referred to as the rental equivalent price or user cost. Since,

$$\hat{v}_s^* = \hat{v}_s \left\{ 1 - (1 - \delta) \frac{\hat{v}_{s+1}}{\hat{v}_s} \right\}$$

$$= \hat{v}_s \left(r_{s+1} + \delta - (1 - \delta) \frac{\Delta v_{s+1}}{v_s} \right) \Big/ (1 + r_{s+1}) \qquad (1.7)$$

it can readily be seen that an increase in the expected rate of capital gains, $\Delta v_{s+1}/v_s$ can very substantially reduce the (discounted) price of durable services $\hat{v}_s^*$.

The maximization of (1.2) with leisure exogenous, subject to (1.5), is now a standard problem, with solutions, in period t,

$$q_t = g_t(W_t, \hat{p}_t, \dots \hat{p}_\tau, \hat{v}_t^*, \dots \hat{v}_\tau^*)$$

$$D_t = f_t(W_t, \hat{p}_t, \dots \hat{p}_\tau, \hat{v}_t^*, \dots \hat{v}_\tau^*) \qquad (1.8)$$

Purchases of the durable good are given by

$$d_t = f_t(W_t, \hat{p}, \hat{v}^*) - (1 - \delta)D_{t-1} \qquad (1.9)$$

where p and $\hat{v}^*$ are vectors of length $\tau - t$ of discounted prices and user cost.

Thus the neoclassical approach, by defining appropriate flows and prices, transforms the demand for durable stocks into a form precisely analogous to the demand for non-durable goods. Indeed, the distinction between durables and non-durables vanishes entirely when δ is unity so that, by (1.7), user cost reduces to price, and stocks to consumption.

One implication of the model deserves some discussion. The rental price can, in principle, fall to zero or below, which should lead consumers to demand infinite quantities to profit from the expected capital gains. Even allowing for uncertainty on the part of consumers and for quantity constraints on the supply side, price fluctuations could well imply powerful advancement and postponement effects in purchases. Even a cursory look at some of the price changes, which, at least in Britain, have taken place in durables markets in the last twenty-five years, suggests that, unless expectations or price increases are quite insensitive to actual changes, service prices have at times reached quite low levels. Yet these periods do not, by and large, coincide with large booms in sales.

Before we turn to the proposed test, we must discuss the exogeneity of prices. According to the model, new and used durables are perfect substitutes so that in a simple supply and demand model of durables, total market supply is $(1 - \delta)D_{t-1}$ + new supply. Suppose that new supply is

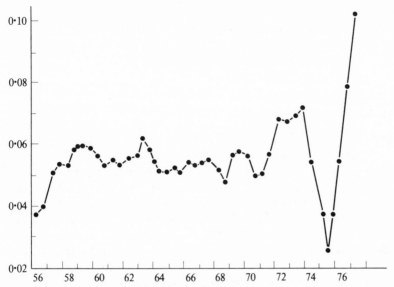

Figure 1. User cost series for British consumer durable stock for 1955–76, as computed in section 2 below

$F(v_t,$ prices of production inputs). Then assuming that v_t clears the market, in market equilibrium, $(1 - \delta)D_{t-1} + F(v_t,$ prices of production inputs) $= f_t(W_t, \hat{p}_t, ..., \hat{p}_\tau, \hat{v}_t^*, ..., \hat{v}_\tau^*)$ where $\hat{v}_t^* = v_t - (1 - \delta)\hat{v}_{t+1}$ and $f_t(\ )$ is the aggregate demand equation for the stock. This can be solved to give v_t and $D_t = f_t(\ )$ as functions of $(1 - \delta)D_{t-1}, W_t, \hat{p}_t, ..., \hat{p}_\tau, \hat{v}_{t+1}, \hat{v}_{t+1}^*,$ ..., $\hat{v}_\tau^*$ and prices of production inputs. If one believed this model, these reduced form equations are the ones to estimate. However, the model lacks plausibility except perhaps in the long run. Prices of new durables such as cars tend to be fixed in the short run with inventory changes, production changes and import changes taking up demand fluctuations. And even when they do change it seems to be more in response to cost conditions than to demand conditions, except perhaps perversely as increasing excess manufacturing capacity raises unit cost. For example, in Britain, prices of cars rose sharply relative to other goods in the recession of 1974–77. In a quarterly model, therefore, it seems reasonable to regard prices of durables as exogenous.

The vehicle for testing is the linear expenditure system (see Stone (1954)) extended intertemporally and for durables. This model comes from maximizing the following utility function subject to the constraint (1.5):

$$\log u_t = \sum_{s=t}^{\tau} \alpha_s \log(q_s - a_s) + \sum_{s=t}^{\tau} \gamma_s \log(D_s - b_s) + \lambda \log A_\tau \qquad (1.10)$$

where $\Sigma \, \alpha_s + \Sigma \, \gamma_s + \lambda = 1$

The period t demand functions are

$$q_t = a_t + \frac{\alpha_t}{p_t} \left(W_t - \sum_t^\tau a_s \hat{p}_s - \sum_t^\tau b_s \hat{v}_s^* \right) \tag{1.11}$$

$$D_t = b_t + \frac{\gamma_t}{v_t^*} \left(W_t - \sum_t^\tau a_s \hat{p}_s - \sum_t^\tau b_s \hat{v}_s^* \right) \tag{1.12}$$

where W_t is defined from (1.4) and (1.5). Note that, unlike previous work with the extended linear expenditure system, a_s and b_s are not eliminated for all s greater than t – which would remove all price expectations – nor is W_t replaced by the plainly unsatisfactory proxy of measured income or even conventionally defined permanent income. $\Sigma_{t+1}^\tau a_s \hat{p}_s$, $\Sigma_{t+1}^\tau b_s \hat{v}_s^*$ and the expected labour income component of W_t are represented by expectational proxies while assets are treated explicitly.

These proxies are one way in which lags come into the model. Another way is from lagged social interactions somewhat along the lines of Duesenberry (1949). Suppose the committed purchases a_t and b_t of each household are linear functions of the observed purchases in the previous period of non-durables and durables by the reference group with which the household identifies and of which it is a member. If different households have the same parameters then, as Gaertner (1974) points out, in the aggregate the a_ts and b_ts are linear functions of aggregate purchases in the previous period. This motivation for lags avoids the charge of myopia which would be justified if similar lags were derived in an intertemporal context from the individualistic theory of habit formation – see, for example, Pollak (1970; 1978) and Phlips (1974).

As far as the aggregation properties of (1.11) and (1.12) are concerned, the as and bs can differ over households[2] but for exact linear aggregation the αs and βs must be the same across households. While this may not be too bothersome for households of the same demographic structure, it is implausible for households whose heads differ widely in age. To obtain exact aggregation then it must be assumed that the distribution of W_t over age is constant over time though slightly weaker conditions permit stochastic aggregation – see Theil (1954).

This concludes the discussion of the basic theory of the model. The more empirical questions of how to deal with seasonality, expectations, and the construction and use of the asset and stock data on durables are discussed in the next section.

The essence of the proposed test is as follows. The extended linear expenditure system (1.11) and (1.12) is applied to quarterly British data on non-durable purchases and stocks of durables. One implication of (1.11) and (1.12) lies in the restrictions across equations on various parameters and these are tested. Independently of any specific functional form restrictions, (1.8) implies that all the elements which make up long-run purchasing power are wrapped up in the variable W_t. These include existing financial and real assets, current income and discounted expected labour income. Because the same W_t appears in both equations, the parameters which reflect the proxying of income expectations ought to be the same in both equations and this gives a more robust test in which the other cross-equation parameter restrictions of (1.11) and (1.12) are ignored.

2 Empirical implementation of the extended linear expenditure system

Seasonality

In practice, it is necessary to take seasonal differences in expenditure into account. This is done by permitting α_t and γ_t to differ between quarters. This allows seasonal effects to expand with expenditure rather than to remain either absolutely fixed or to expand with lagged q and D, which would be the result of the more obvious procedure of allowing seasonal variation in the committed quantities a and b. Attaching seasonal effects to lagged values of q and D would raise the problem of whether to interpret large positive coefficients on lagged variables of q and D as reflecting genuine lags or merely widening seasonal effects.

Expectations

Two alternative formulations of the expectational proxies were tried and they will be illustrated by taking the case of labour income. The first assumes that income expectations are generated in money terms. We want to proxy

$$\sum_t^\tau \hat{y}_s = y_t \left(1 + \sum_{t+1}^\tau \hat{y}_s/y_t \right) \tag{2.1}$$

Now suppose $\hat{y}_{s+1}/\hat{y}_s = 1 + \rho_t$, $s = t + 1, ..., \tau$. Then

$$\sum_t^\tau y_s/y_t = 1 + (1 + \rho_t) + (1 + \rho_t)^2 + ... + (1 + \rho_t)^{\tau-1}$$

$$= [(1 + \rho_t)^\tau - 1]/\rho_t \tag{2.2}$$

By the first three terms of the Binomial expansion this is a linear function of ρ_t. Now we suppose that expectations on ρ_t are given as the weighted average of some steady state view ρ_0 and recent experience. The latter is represented by $(\frac{1}{4})DFD(y_t)$ where $DFD(y_t)$ is the 'discounted fourth difference of income' which is $[y_t/(1 + r_t)(1 + r_{t-1})(1 + r_{t-2})(1 + r_{t-3}) - y_{t-4}]/y_{t-4}$. Note that the first term in [ ] is exactly the discounted income which would have been relevant one year ago had incomes been correctly anticipated. Working with annual changes removes seasonal irregularities and, as Davidson, Hendry *et al.* (1978) argue, is likely to reflect the way in which consumers themselves make forecasts. Thus

$$\sum_t \hat{y}_t = {}_{yt}(\text{linear function of } DFD(y_t)) \tag{2.3}$$

The terms $\Sigma_t^7 a_s \hat{p}_s$ and $\Sigma_t^7 b_s \hat{v}_s^*$ are similarly represented by $a_t p_t \times$ (linear function of $DFD(p_t)$) and $b_t v_t^* \times$ (linear function of $DFD(v_t^*)$), where a_t and b_t are themselves respectively linear functions of expenditure on non-durables and the stock of durables one year ago. This represents the lagged spread of behaviour patterns discussed at the end of section 1.

To meet the potential charge that the conclusions rest on the specific expectational hypothesis rather than on the neoclassical model in itself, a second expectational hypothesis was investigated. This assumes a similar structure to that above for the generation of expectations on non-durable prices but takes a much more flexible view for incomes and durable prices. The term in (1.11) and (1.12) which involves expectations is $\Sigma_t^7 \hat{y}_s - \Sigma_t^7 a_s \hat{p}_s - \Sigma_t^7 b_s \hat{v}_s^*$ which we can write as

$$\sum (a_s/a_t)\hat{p}_s \left(\frac{\sum \hat{y}_s}{\sum (a_s/a_t)\hat{p}_s} - a_t - \frac{b_t \sum (b_s/b_t)\hat{v}_s^*}{\sum (a_s/a_t)\hat{p}_s} \right) \tag{2.4}$$

It seems reasonable to think that consumers regard the terms a_s/a_t and b_s/b_t as fairly constant and, with a similar discounting structure in $\hat{y}_s$, $\hat{p}_s$ and $\hat{v}_s^*$, it makes sense to proxy the terms

$$\frac{\sum \hat{y}_s}{\sum (a_s/a_t)\hat{p}_s} \quad \text{and} \quad \frac{\sum (b_s/b_t)\hat{v}_s^*}{\sum (a_s/a_t)\hat{p}_s}$$

by fairly general distributed lags in real income y_t/p_t and the relative price of durables v_t^*/p_t. That expectations might be generated in real terms in this way does make sense: even with inflation running at 25% per annum one would not expect that consumers' expectations of real long-term labour (and transfer) income would alter by much because of inflation itself. The same thing goes for the relative price of durables, where short-term increases in capital gains because of general inflation are unlikely to lead to permanent reductions in durable rental prices, because the interest rate will eventually adjust to inflation. Further, while the expectational hypothesis in (2.3) may be reasonable for non-durable prices it suffers from an objection when applied to income. The transitory component in income changes is likely to be much more considerable than in price changes. The disadvantage of (2.3) is that current income y_t is always taken as the base for projections even when it is particularly high or low because of transitory components. In fact, it turned out that the second expectational hypothesis gave better empirical results than the first though the results of the tests were similar in the two cases.

The role of financial assets

In the exposition of the neoclassical model it was assumed that the financial asset is not subject to revaluation in its money value. In reality, households own a wide range of financial assets, from money and other liquid assets to claims on life insurance companies and pension funds, and government and company securities. For a number of reasons it may not be relevant to measure assets A by the sum total of the market value of household net worth. In the first place, even for a single household, fluctuations in the value of marketable securities may have limited relevance within the total portfolio. By the argument of Stiglitz (1970), a risk averse widow living in an inflation free environment could arrange the maturity pattern of her portfolio to guarantee a constant income every period. Asset price changes would not alter her ability to do this, though of course inflation in consumer goods would make this an undesirable objective and would make the total purchasing power in terms of consumer good prices of financial assets once more a good proxy for long-term purchasing power. A second point is that, especially in the wealthiest households, part of assets will be held for bequest, and then for tax or other reasons a specific composition of assets may be desired so that again the simple money value of the aggregate is not a sufficient measure. Note, however, that the aggregate value of bequests is included in the utility function. Finally the personal sector includes not only family trusts, but also unincorporated enterprises such as small builders, retail shops, farmers and stockbrokers as well as non-profit institutions such as private schools, trade unions, friendly societies and universities. Hence, personal savings and asset holdings contain a substantial element not relevant to the consumption decisions of households, as usually defined. In the empirical work below, some allowance (although necessarily crude) will be made for these factors. The lower relevance of many non-liquid assets is modelled by letting $A = LA + \beta NLA$, for liquid and non-liquid assets LA and NLA where β is expected to be substantially less than unity. In the British national accounts the accumulation of housing and land is treated as part of the accumulation of personal sector assets. Thus total A_t including housing and land is constructed from the formula

$$A_t = A_{t-1} + S_t + \Delta P_t^A A_{t-1} \tag{2.5}$$

where S_t is personal saving and $\Delta P_t^A A_{t-1}$, which represents asset revaluation, uses a specially constructed price index P_t^A based on price indices of land, housing, company securities and government securities. In addition, liquid assets are distinguished using asset data from *Financial Statistics* linked to earlier data from Roe (1969). Non-liquid assets NLA_t is determined as a residual given A_t and LA_t.

Income, non-durable expenditures and durable stocks

In the British as in most national accounts, housing among durable goods is given special treatment. Income and expenditure both include an imputation for housing, while rents, rates (property taxes), repairs and maintenance and improvements make up housing expenditure. Personal disposable income is measured net of interest payments such as mortgage interest but repayments of principal are part of personal savings and not part of housing expenditure. No imputation is made for the services of other durables. Housing expenditure is treated as part of non-durable expenditure only and it is assumed that housing rental prices are correctly reflected in the non-durables price index. However, the value of the housing stock is included in non-liquid assets.

An alternative procedure which has been followed by Simmons (1978) is to treat housing (and one might do the same for land) as a separate durable category. Then saving is redefined as the accumulation of financial assets only and becomes much smaller. However, one can argue that, for most people, paying off their mortgage debt is a type of saving which is very similar to that of accumulating a financial asset with future price prospects as rosy as those of housing, and this argues for the more conventional and less ambitious grouping followed in this paper.[3]

A last point to note about the national accounts is that the surplus of life-insurance companies and pension funds is treated as part of personal disposable income. In the equations we estimate, no special allowance other than permitting non-liquid assets to have a different weight from liquid ones, is made for the behaviour of what are essentially firms in the personal sector. No special allowances are made for the contractual part of savings or of total assets, as reflected, for example, in pension rights.

The data are quarterly from 1955.1 to 1976.3 with 1970 the base year for the price series. The stock data on durables are constructed from constant price purchase data in *Economic Trends* and the *Monthly Digest of Statistics* on cars and motorcycles, household durables and furnishings and floorcoverings aggregated into one category. Stock is defined as

$$D_t = \left(1 - \frac{\delta}{2}\right) d_t + (1 - \delta)D_{t-1} \tag{2.6}$$

which makes allowance for deterioration of new purchases. The deterioration rate δ is assumed to be 1/18 per quarter, following earlier work, while the benchmark estimate comes from Roe (1969). (2.6) implies that v_t^* is $v_t[1 - (\hat{v}_{t+1}/v_t)(1 - \delta)]/(1 - \delta/2)$. $\hat{v}_{t+1}/v_t$ is proxied by $1 + (\frac{1}{4})DFD(v_t)$, which assumes that capital gains will continue at the rate experienced over the previous year.

The empirical specification

The non-durable expenditure equation (1.11) is estimated in the following form:

$$
\begin{aligned}
q_t = {}&(\alpha_7 + \alpha_8 q_{t-4}) + (1/p_t)(\alpha_1 DU_{1t} + \alpha_2 DU_{2t} + \alpha_3 DU_{3t} + \alpha_4 DU_{4t} \\
&+ \alpha_5 CLP_t)\{LA_{t-1} + \alpha_6 NLA_{t-1} + v_t(1 - \delta)D_{t-1} \\
&+ (\alpha_{11}p_t + \alpha_{12}p_t DFD(p_t))[y_t/p_t + \alpha_{13}\Delta_4(y_t/p_t) \\
&+ \alpha_{14}\Delta_4(y/p)_{t-1} + \alpha_{15}\Delta_4(y/p)_{t-4} + \alpha_{16}\Delta_4(y/p)_{t-8} \\
&- (\alpha_7 + \alpha_8 q_{t-4}) - (\alpha_9 + \alpha_{10}D_{t-4})(v_t^*/p_t) + \alpha_{17}\Delta_4(v_t^*/p_t) \\
&+ \alpha_{18}\Delta_4(v^*/p)_{t-1})]\} + \alpha_{19}HP_t \\
&+ \alpha_{20}DU_{5t} + \alpha_{21}DU_{6t} + \varepsilon_{1t}
\end{aligned}
\tag{2.7}
$$

The relationship between (1.11) and (2.7) is as follows: a_t in (1.11) is given by $\alpha_7 + \alpha_6 q_{t-4}$ and α_t by the linear combination of the seasonal dummies DU_1 to DU_4 and the dummy CLP, which reflects the possible changes in seasonality after the month in which new car licences are issued was changed in 1962. Then in the curly bracket we have liquid and non-liquid assets and the value of the durable stock. Then comes the proxy for the expression (2.4). $\Sigma_t^7 (a_s/a_t)\hat{p}_s$ is represented by $\alpha_{11}p_t + \alpha_{12}p_t DFD(p_t)$ and the square bracket represents the rest of (2.4). Strictly speaking, y_t should exclude asset income but since disposable labour and transfer income are not separately available in the accounts, personal disposable income is used instead. Finally, HP_t is a measure of hire purchase restrictions as used in Townend (1976), DU_{5t} is a dummy reflecting the widely anticipated changes in the 1968 budget and DU_{6t} is a dummy reflecting the 1972.1 miners' strike and the transitory income reductions and other special features of that quarter. Strictly speaking, HP_t should have no role if the assumption of no borrowing restrictions which underlies the neoclassical model is valid.

The analogous empirical form of the durables equation (1.12) is

$$
\begin{aligned}
D_t = {}&(\beta_9 + \beta_{10}D_{t-4}) + (1/v_t^*)(\beta_1 DU_{1t} + \beta_2 DU_{2t} + \beta_3 DU_{3t} \\
&+ \beta_4 DU_{4t} + \beta_5 CLP_t)\{LA_{t-1} + \beta_6 NLA_{t-1} + v_t(1 - \delta)D_{t-1} \\
&+ (\beta_{11}p_t + \beta_{12}p_t DFD(p_t))[y_t/p_t + \beta_{13}\Delta_4(y_t/p_t) \\
&+ \beta_{14}\Delta_4(y/p)_{t-1} + \beta_{15}\Delta_4(y/p)_{t-4} + \beta_{16}\Delta_4(y/p)_{t-8} \\
&- (\beta_7 + \beta_8 q_{t-4}) - (\beta_9 + \beta_{10}D_{t-4})(v_t^*/p_t) + \beta_{17}\Delta_4(v_t^*/p_t) \\
&+ \beta_{18}\Delta_4(v^*/p)_{t-1}]\} + \beta_{19}HP_t + \beta_{20}DU_{5t} \\
&+ \beta_{21}DU_{6t} + \varepsilon_{2t}
\end{aligned}
\tag{2.8}
$$

If the extended LES form of the neoclassical model is valid then all αs should be identical to the corresponding βs from α_6 to α_{18}. These 13 restrictions are clearly rather powerful. If one regards (2.7) and (2.8) merely as linear approximations to the basic neoclassical demand functions (1.8) then we can test the much weaker hypothesis that merely the terms in W_t should be the same in each of the two equations: i.e. that α_6 and α_{11} to α_{16} should be identical to the corresponding βs. There are seven restrictions here.

The results are given in table 1. The first two columns give estimates of (2.7) and (2.8) without any cross-equation restrictions; the second two columns impose the W_t restrictions only; the last two columns impose the full LES restrictions. In estimation it is assumed that the error terms ε_{1t} and ε_{2t} are serially independent but have a cross-equation correlation ρ. The equations are non-linear in the parameters and together with ρ they are estimated by non-linear maximum likelihood using Angus Deaton's NLFIML.

Let us begin with the unrestricted non-durables equation. The average value of α_t is about 0.015 which, together with $\gamma_t \approx 0.0025$ for durables, implies, ignoring bequests, a time horizon of around 14 years. With bequests this falls a little further. Though on the low side, this is not impossible. The coefficient α_t on NLA at around 0.05 is also very low and the two phenomena are undoubtedly related: restricting α_6 to unity lowers α_1, ..., α_4 and hence raises the length of the planning period. However, the fit becomes significantly worse. With $\alpha_{11} \simeq 12$ and $\alpha_{13} \simeq 0.2$ the impact effect of real disposable income on non-durable expenditures is about 0.21. Note that $DFD(p_t)$ is approximately the annual rate of inflation minus the annual interest rate so that when the former exceeds the latter by one percentage point this lowers the impact effect of real disposable income by 2%. The interest rate used is a lending rate: the Building Society Deposit rate adjusted for income tax relief. If the interest rate reflects anticipated inflation the negative coefficient α_{12} can be regarded as supporting Deaton's (1977) 'rational money illusion' theory of inflation effects: note that the wiping out of the real value of financial assets by increases in consumer good prices is already incorporated since W_t is deflated by p_t in (1.11) and (2.7).

Though the impact effect of real income is only 0.21, after 1 quarter this goes up to 0.32 plus the effect (around 0.01) of the increase in financial and durable assets made in the previous period. The latter long-term effect builds up over time. It is augmented by the $0.8q_{t-4}$ term after one year but diminished by the negative coefficients on $(y/p)_{t-4}$, $(y/p)_{t-5}$. It appears then that it takes considerable time for all the effects of an increase in real income to be reflected in non-durable consumption.

In the 'committed ownership of durables', β_9 could not in practice be

Table 1. *Unrestricted and restricted estimates of the extended LES*

i	No restrictions Non-durables α_i	No restrictions Durables β_i	W_t restrictions only Non-durables α_i	W_t restrictions only Durables β_i	Full ELES restrictions Non-durables α_i	Full ELES restrictions Durables β_i
1	0.0131 (0.0058)	0.00248(0.00063)	0.0196 (0.0040)	0.00158(0.00049)	0.0194 (0.0059)	−0.00006 (0.00006)
2	0.0148 (0.0064)	0.00252(0.00066)	0.0219 (0.0043)	0.00119(0.00033)	0.0217 (0.0064)	−0.00005 (0.00007)
3	0.0151 (0.0064)	0.00249(0.00064)	0.0222 (0.0044)	0.00120(0.00033)	0.0221 (0.0065)	−0.00006 (0.00006)
4	0.0165 (0.0069)	0.00247(0.00066)	0.0241 (0.0046)	0.00092(0.00024)	0.0240 (0.0069)	−0.00006 (0.00007)
5	0.00015(0.0001)	−0.00001(0.00004)	0.00019(0.0001)	−0.00009(0.00008)	0.00020(0.0001)	0.000003(0.00004)
6	0.049 (0.028)	0.092 (0.030)	0.050(0.014)		0.039(0.019)	
7	546 (120)	1000*	529 (70)	1000*	590(113)	
8	0.799 (0.053)	0.533 (0.15)	0.784 (0.029)	3.04 (0.81)	0.767(0.050)	
9	1000*	540 (59)	1000*	883 (76)		759(82)
10	−0.154 (0.033)	0.897 (0.026)	−0.142 (0.037)	1.036 (0.015)		1.020(0.012)
11	11.1 (6.0)	−7.80 (1.6)	3.41 (2.0)		7.25 (3.2)	
12	−24.2 (18)	−9.62 (9.5)	−6.74 (3.7)		−19.1 (12)	
13	0.165 (0.27)	−0.934 (0.13)	0.937(0.87)		0.185(0.31)	
14	0.606 (0.21)	−0.556 (0.25)	1.43 (0.71)		0.557(0.23)	
15	−0.657 (0.18)	−0.826 (0.19)	−1.20 (0.57)		−0.764(0.23)	
16	−0.0753 (0.15)	−0.236 (0.17)	−0.499(0.30)		−0.127(0.16)	
17	10.1 (8.8)	2.58 (0.80)	30.9 (28)	5.44 (4.0)	−0.385(0.51)	
18	−18.6 (11)	−0.453 (0.47)	−33.2 (26)	−5.81 (4.2)	0.223(0.58)	
19	−1.17 (0.63)	−14.1 (1.6)	−1.06 (0.67)	−12.4 (2.3)	−1.38 (0.63)	−18.0 (2.6)
20	36.5 (29)	176 (72)	66.3 (30)	−39 (107)	38.1 (31)	52 (144)
21	114 (34)	116 (89)	109 (35)	67 (138)	102 (37)	110 (181)
R^2	0.9990	0.9992	0.9988	0.9979	0.9988	0.9961
R_1^2	0.9959	−0.2423	0.9951	−2.167	0.9953	−5.018
R_4^2	0.9275	0.8859	0.9142	0.709	0.9179	0.447
DW_1	2.24	0.86	1.96	0.58	2.08	0.21
DW_2	2.03	1.56	2.07	1.28	2.10	0.57
DW_3	1.96	1.88	1.90	1.74	1.90	0.95
DW_4	2.28	2.00	2.33	1.85	2.24	1.23
σ	29.8	78.6	32.4	125.5	31.7	173.0
ρ	−0.125		−0.137		−0.106	
2 log likelihood	−1673		−1755		−1808	

identified separately from β_{10} and was set at 1000. Because of the negative value of β_{10} the term as a whole is close to zero at the mean value of D_{t-4} and negative for the latter part of the estimation period, thus implying that non-durables are gross substitutes for durables.

A tightening of hire purchase restrictions seems to reduce non-durable expenditure marginally and the dummies DU_{5t} and DU_{6t} have the anticipated effects.

The diagnostic statistics look quite favourable. R_1^2 and R_4^2 are defined as $1 - SSE_1/SST_1$ and $1 - SSE_4/SST_4$ respectively where for example SSE_1 is the sum of squares of residuals and SST_1 is the sum of squared deviations around the mean of first differences of the dependent variable. DW_1 is the conventional Durbin–Watson statistic while DW_2, DW_3, DW_4 are analogous measures for 2 quarter etc. differences. Thus there seems to be no obvious sign of serial correlation in the residuals. $\hat{\sigma}$ is the maximum likelihood estimate (MLE) of the standard error of the equation. The degree of freedom correction appropriate for an equation linear in the parameters would raise $\hat{\sigma}$ from 29.7 to about 34.3 which still seems quite acceptable.[4] $\hat{\rho}$ measures the correlation in the residuals of the two equations which here is negative.

Perhaps the most striking contrast in the unrestricted durables equation is in the income coefficients. When $DFD(p_t)$ is zero the income terms appear as

$$\frac{0.0025}{v_t^*} p_t(-8.8(y/p)_t + 8.2\Delta_4(y/p)_t + 4.9\Delta_4(y/p)_{t-1}$$
$$+ 7.3\Delta_4(y/p)_{t-4} + 2.1\Delta_4(y/p)_{t-8})$$

This seems to suggest that income changes rather than levels have the dominant effect, but must be considered in the context of β_{10}, the coefficient on D_{t-4}, being about 0.9. Another notable feature of the equation is the very significant negative effect of hire purchase restrictions. This would seem to be direct evidence that the linear budget constraint hypothesis on which the neoclassical model is based is not valid.

The diagnostic statistics are much less satisfactory than those of the non-durables equation. The implication of negative R_1^2 is that the fit of the equation when durable purchases is the dependent variable is very poor, since $d_t \simeq \Delta D_t$. A standard error more than 2½ times as great as for non-durables when durable purchases are on the average only 10% of non-durable expenditures supports this. The high R^2 for levels is therefore quite meaningless. The Durbin–Watson statistics are strong evidence for positive first order serial correlation. But rather than taking a Cochrane–Orcutt transformation, this should be interpreted as evidence of a more fundamental mis-specification.

Then the cross-equation restrictions on the parameters in W_t are imposed. Note that the impact effect of real income on non-durable expenditure is 0.19, which is almost the same as before, but that the fit of the durables equation becomes quite terrible. Thus the information in the non-durables equation dominates these estimates and clearly imposes a quite unacceptable structure on the durables equation. The fall in the 2 log-likelihood is close to 120 for 7 restrictions which can therefore be strongly rejected.

When the further 6 restrictions that α_7 to α_{10} and α_{17} and α_{18} are the same in the two equations are imposed, which correspond to the extended LES specification, the 2 log-likelihood falls by a further 53 so that the full LES specification can be strongly rejected in the framework of the unrestricted forms of (2.7) and (2.8). Very similar results but worse fits throughout were obtained when expectations proxies of the first type considered above were used.

In one respect even the unrestricted forms of (2.7) and (2.8) are not very general: they permit only a wealth role for prices of other assets, especially those of houses. Had houses been distinguished as a second type of durable in a three group system of equations, house prices could have been given a separate systematic role. Though imputed rental income from housing should then be excluded from income, the wealth term otherwise stays the same. As an approximation to this specification, the house price index and, for good measure, the *Financial Times* ordinary share index were included as extra linear terms in each equation and the tests described above repeated. Briefly, the same rejections take place: when the restrictions on the coefficients in W_t are imposed, the drop in the 2 log-likelihood is 52 for 7 restrictions which is still very significant. But it is worth noting that the fit of the durables equation is improved, though the Durbin–Watson statistics are little altered: higher house prices raise purchases of durables.

Some other checks can be carried out which are even less dependent on the specific expectational hypothesis. For example, note that from (1.11) and (1.12), $p_t(q_t - a_t)/\alpha_t = v_t^*(D_t - b_t)/\gamma_t = W_t - \Sigma \, a_s \hat{p}_s - \Sigma \, b_s \hat{v}_s^*$. This implies

$$D_t = b_t + (\gamma_t/\alpha_t)(p_t/v_t^*)(q_t - a_t) \tag{2.9}$$

Using the empirical forms (2.7) and (2.8) the equation (2.9) becomes

$$
\begin{aligned}
D_t = {} & \beta_9 + \beta_{10}D_{t-4} \\
& + \left(\frac{\beta_1^* DU_{1t} + \beta_2^* DU_{2t} + \beta_3^* DU_{3t} + \beta_4^* DU_{4t} + \beta_5^* \, CLP_t}{DU_{1t} + \alpha_2^* DU_{2t} + \alpha_3^* DU_{3t} + \alpha_4^* DU_{4t} + \alpha_5^* CLP_t} \right) \frac{p_t}{v_t^*} \\
& \{q_t - \alpha_7 - \alpha_8 q_{t-4} - \alpha_{19}HP_t - \alpha_{20}DU_{5t} - \alpha_{21}DU_{6t} - \varepsilon_{1t}\} \\
& \qquad\qquad\qquad + \beta_{19}HP_t + \beta_{20}DU_{5t} + \beta_{21}DU_{6t} + \varepsilon_{2t} \tag{2.10}
\end{aligned}
$$

Note that $\beta_i^* = \beta_i/\alpha_1$ and $\alpha_i^* = \alpha_i/\alpha_1$ for $i > 1$, since an identifying restriction $\alpha_1 = 1$ imposed. Since $- \varepsilon_{1t}$ is negatively correlated with q_t one would expect some downward bias on the β^* coefficients but not a large one since the variance of ε_{1t} is rather small and since there is probably some offsetting bias because of the negative correlation between ε_{1t} and ε_{2t} revealed in table 1. The results are in table 2 and are broadly in line with those of table 1.[5] The fit is rather less poor than when the full ELES restrictions are imposed in table 1 as one might expect with an endogenous regressor. However, it remains very bad, with obvious autocorrelation in the residuals. A somewhat more general test of this kind without cross-equation restrictions on the terms $\Sigma\ a_s\hat{p}_s$ and $\Sigma\ b_s v_s^*$, so that W_t is substituted out but price expectations are not, gives similar results. So one can reject the idea that any inadequacies in the expectational proxies or in the asset data were responsible for the negative results of table 1.

Table 2. *Estimates of (2.10)*

i	Non-durables αs	Durables βs	Diagnostics	
1	0.0572(0.0132)	1*	R^2	0.9976
2	0.0491(0.38)	0.891(7.0)	R_1^2	−2.719
3	0.0473(0.23)	0.832(4.3)	R_4^2	0.658
4	0.0740(0.56)	1.214(9.9)	DW_1	1.08
5	0.0021(0.15)	0.512(5.3)	DW_2	1.14
7	1112 (213)	—	DW_3	1.93
8	0.868 (0.033)	—	DW_4	1.67
9	—	1003 (132)	$\hat{\sigma}$	136
10	—	0.970(0.015)		
19	−2.35 (2.8)	−13.1 (3.8)		
20	263 (210)	253 (270)		
21	143*	272 (142)		

3 Alternative hypotheses

I shall consider two reasons for the failure of the simple neo-classical model. Both involve liquidity considerations, but of rather different kinds, which can be regarded as representative of the two main ways the Keynesian concept of liquidity has been treated in the post-war literature.

(i) Uncertainty about future asset prices and income

There is a substantial literature on portfolio models of asset demand since Tobin (1958) and Markovitz (1959) and a largely separate literature on the effects of income uncertainty on savings (see Sandmo (1974) and Deaton and Muellbauer (1980, ch. 14). One consideration that comes out of an attempt to integrate the two approaches by setting up an appropriate dynamic programming problem with uncertainty suggests that one might expect different income dynamics for durables than for non-durables. Suppose that for next period, income and the prices of bonds and of durables are uncertain but the price of non-durables is not. This introduces an asymmetry which makes the form of the solution for durables demand rather different from that of non-durables and is a possible rationalization of the above results. Even if there were uncertainty about both prices one would expect, because of the capital gains element in the demand for durables, that uncertainty about prices of durables would be more important. However, setting up and estimating formal models of this type is a substantial research project in its own right, though it seems to me to be a feasible one.

(ii) Transactions costs

The neoclassical model predicts pronounced volatility of durable purchases. Uncertainty about the price of durables next period is one reason why one might expect only limited volatility. Another reason comes out of informational assymetries and other, more mundane transactions costs. A major reason for volatility lies in the assumption that, next period, durables purchased this period can be liquidated at the price prevailing next period taking into account the efficiency loss through deterioration at the rate δ. But as Akerlof (1970) points out, the potential buyer has less information on a used durable than the owner and is likely to fear that the owner wishes to sell because it is a 'lemon'. Even if it is not, there may be no cheap way the owner can give this information to the buyer. The effect is like having to pay a fixed transaction cost in order to sell. This must reduce speculative activity in durables purchases.

One way of representing this in the budget constraint is to add to the expenditure $v_s(D_s - (1 - \delta)D_{s-1})$ the following non-convex transaction cost

$$\begin{cases} k_1 v_s D_s + k_2 v_s (1 - \delta)D_{s-1} & \text{if} \quad D_s - (1 - \delta)D_{s-1} \neq 0 \\ 0 & \text{if} \quad D_s - (1 - \delta)D_{s-1} = 0 \end{cases} \tag{3.1}$$

The idea is the following: let v_s be some average index of new and used durable prices. If no investment is made then $D_s - (1 - \delta)D_{s-1}$ is zero and no transactions are carried out. Otherwise the used durable, e.g. a car, is traded in at a return of $v_s(1 - k_2)(1 - \delta)D_{s-1}$ where k_2, which might for example be 20%, represents the transaction cost margin of selling. The new durable is bought for $v_s(1 + k_1)D_s$ where k_1 is the transaction cost margin of buying. In empirical applications $k_1 = k_2$ seems a reasonable approximation and it also seems reasonable that k_1 and k_2 should be proportional to the difference between the price of the new durable and the price of a representative used version of that durable. This would give the value of trade-ins a plausible role in the demand for new durables. The current period budget constraint where x is total expenditure is

$$x_t = \begin{cases} p_t q_t + v_t(1 + k_1)D_t - v_t(1 - k_2)(1 - \delta)D_{t-1} \\ \qquad\qquad\qquad\qquad \text{if} \quad D_t - (1 - \delta)D_{t-1} \neq 0 \\ p_t q_t \qquad\qquad\qquad \text{if} \quad D_t - (1 - \delta)D_{t-1} = 0 \end{cases}$$
(3.2)

This is illustrated in figure 2 where a consumer with the indifference curve shown would choose not to invest in that period. As the durable deteriorates, the point A moves north-west and in due course the decision to invest is taken.

The intertemporal budget constraint then takes the form

$$W_t = \sum \hat{p}_s q_s + \sum \xi_s[\hat{v}_s(1 + k_1)D_s - \hat{v}_s(1 - k_2)(1 - \delta)D_{s-1}] \quad (3.3)$$

where

$$\xi_s = 1 \quad \text{if} \quad D_s - (1 - \delta)D_{s-1} \neq 0$$
$$\quad = 0 \quad \text{if} \quad D_s - (1 - \delta)D_{s-1} = 0,$$

To maximize utility subject to this constraint yields a rather complicated programming problem since there is a mixture of integer (the ξ_ss) and continuous decision variables. Nevertheless, it can be seen that the marginal condition $\partial u/\partial q_t = \lambda p_t$ still governs the decision to purchase nondurables. An unanticipated reduction in income has an effect through the Lagrange multiplier λ on q_t but a more complicated effect on D_t: not only

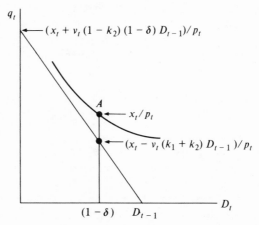

Figure 2. Non-convex transaction costs

is there a reduction for those who had planned to invest but there is a shift in the extensive margin in the population of those making some investment: some will postpone. How the latter effect operates depends on the joint distributions of income, income expectations and durable stocks and is quite different from the way these variables enter the non-durable demand functions. This rationalizes the quite different income dynamics found empirically in the two equations.

The demand functions conditional on the ξs which come out of (3.3) are manageable at least for certain classes of utility functions. Note that the model sketched here is most applicable to data disaggregated into specific kinds of different durables so that the budget constraint (3.3) is really defined for a vector of stocks of different durables. For such data aggregated across households, the mean value of ξ_t is simply the proportion of households with non-zero purchases of that durable good. The inequalities which determine ξ_t are very complicated and involve distributional data. Thus the model is most suitable to be applied to data, especially panel data, on the purchases by individual households of particular durable goods.

When different durable goods are aggregated into one the zero–one aspect of purchases is likely to be lost so that even on quarterly data a single household always has positive durable purchases. Aggregation over different kinds of durables tends to smooth and make convex the non-convex adjustment costs for each kind in (3.3). It may therefore be that, as an approximation, the assumption of convex (e.g. quadratic) adjustment costs at the level of aggregated durables data is a reasonable one. If so, the route leads back to the stock adjustment model but suggests two modifications to the conventional analysis. The first is that the measure of durable prices v_t should be an average of new and used prices and that adjustment costs increase with the margin between the two. The second is that expectations should be treated more systematically than is usually the case in estimates of stock adjustment models.

Summary and conclusions

Section 1 reviews the neoclassical theory of demand for durables. The definition of 'neoclassical' here is a narrow one: optimizing consumers face given prices and endowments at which they can buy or sell, have point expectations about future prices and endowments and do not incur costs of adjustment. If, as seems plausible, costs of adjustment as usually understood are merely a proxy for non-linearities in the budget constraint, their absence is simply an implication of the assumption of given prices. Notice that point expectations excludes portfolio considerations, which is consistent with the simplifying assumption usually made in life cycle consumption or savings theories that financial assets can be aggregated into a single asset with a given rate of interest and not subject to revaluation. Assuming, in addition, that durables of different vintages can be aggregated in efficiency corrected units gives a linear intertemporal budget constraint in which the prices are the discounted prices of non-durables and the discounted user cost or rental equivalent prices of durables. The wealth term consists of the present value of current and expected income, and initial endowments of durables and the financial asset. The linear expenditure system extended intertemporally and for durables gives the demand functions for purchases of non-durables and the stock of durables a linear structure which allows the aggregate behaviourial equations to have the same form as the ones for individual households. The committed consumption levels in the ELES are assumed through the influence of lagged social interactions to depend on past consumption levels.

Section 2 begins with the treatment of expectations: it is assumed that expectations of non-durable prices, real incomes and relative prices are each formed on the basis of past observations of the dependent variable. By giving income and income expectations a quite distinct role from assets, by introducing future committed consumption levels, which makes price expectations important, and by permitting the committed consumption levels to depend upon past consumption, the form of the ELES which emerges is much more general than that of Lluch (1973) and Lluch, Powell and Williams (1977). There is also a brief review of the national accounts treatment of income, savings, assets and durables to put the empirical application which follows in context. This is to quarterly data going back to 1955: the existence of the asset and durables data going back this far owes much to the work of the Stone group in Cambridge. The theory implies some cross-equation restrictions between the non-durables and durables equations and testing these is the main point of this exercise. These restrictions are conclusively rejected. One might argue that this is understandable for a particular form of utility function which may be a poor approximation to preferences. However, in much more general forms of the test, in which the ELES restrictions are ignored and only the hypothesis that the wealth term has the same asset and income expectations parameters in both the non-durables and the durables equations is tested, the result is the same: rejection. This implies that non-durable purchases and durable ownership are not consistent with the same neoclassical budget constraint. Other aspects of the results worth mentioning are that the non-durables equation is quite reasonable, fits well and has residuals which look like white noise. However, non-liquid assets have a much lower coefficient relative to liquid assets than simple theory would suggest. The durables equation is rather poor with positively auto-correlated residuals even in the most general specification and very significant coefficients on the terms for credit restrictions – which is another reason for arguing that behaviour is inconsistent with the inter-temporal neo-classical budget constraint.

Section 3 suggests two possible explanations. One feature of the neo-classical model is that the rental price of durables is fairly volatile and this is one reason why the model suggests that purchases should also be volatile. Both of the alternative hypotheses suggest limitations on the speed of adjustment; uncertainty and transactions costs which stem from the a-symmetry of information between buyers and owners of used durables. It is suggested therefore that either or both the perfect markets (linear budget constraint) assumption and the assumption that the constraint is perceived with confidence are erroneous even as approximations. By considering a model where the budget constraint is non-linear because of transactions costs, it is possible to give a theoretical justification to the empirical result that assets, income and income expectations enter the non-durables and durables equations in quite different ways.

Notes

1 Support for this research under SSRC grant HR4577/1 is gratefully acknowledged. I am indebted to Angus Deaton and Gerald Kennally for stimulating discussions and comments and to Gerald Kennally for effective programming. John Dorrington and Alan Roe were helpful in providing missing pieces of data. Responsibility for errors remains with the author.
2 If households have the same price expectations.
3 However, see the discussion of portfolio models in section 3.
4 In the base year, 1970, quarterly non-durable consumption ≈ 7500.
5 Not surprisingly only β_1^* of the seasonal parameters is well determined. For similar reasons separate estimates of α_{21} and β_{21} could not be obtained and α_{21} was therefore restricted.

References

Akerlof, G. (1970), 'The market for lemons', *Quarterly Journal of Economics*, **84**, pp. 488–500.
Chow, G. (1957), *Demand for Automobiles in the US: a study in consumer durables*, Amsterdam: North Holland.
Cramer, J. S. (1957), 'A dynamic approach to the theory of consumer demand', *Review of Economic Studies*, **24**, pp. 73–86.
Davidson, J. E. H., Hendry, D. F. *et al.* (1978), 'Econometric modelling of the aggregate time-series relationship between consumers' expenditure and income in the United Kingdom', *Economic Journal*, **88**, pp. 661–92.
Deaton, A. S. (1977), 'Involuntary saving through unanticipated inflation', *American Economic Review*, **67**, pp. 899–910.
Deaton, A. S. and Muellbauer, J. (1980), *Economics and Consumer Behavior*, New York and Cambridge: Cambridge University Press.
Diewert, W. E. (1974), 'Intertemporal consumer theory and the demand for durables', *Econometrica*, **42**, pp. 497–516.

Duesenberry, J. S. (1949), *Income, Saving, and the Theory of Consumer Behaviour*, Cambridge, Mass.: Harvard University Press.

Farrell, M. J. (1954), 'The demand for motor cars in the United States', *Journal of the Royal Statistical Society*, Series A, **117**, pp. 171–201.

Fisher, I. (1930), *The Theory of Interest*, New Haven, Connecticut: Yale University Press, 1930.

Gaertner, W. (1974), 'A dynamic model of interdependent consumer behaviour', *Zeitschrift für Nationalökonomie*, **34**, pp. 327–44.

Haavelmo, T. (1960), *A Study in the Theory of Investment*, Chicago: University of Chicago Press.

Hess, A. C. (1977), 'A comparison of automobile demand equations', *Econometrica*, **45**, pp. 683–702.

Jorgenson, D. W. (1963), 'Capital theory and investment behaviour', *American Economic Review*, **53**, Papers and Proceedings, pp. 247–59.

Lluch, C., (1973), 'The extended linear expenditure system', *European Economic Review*, **4**, pp. 21–32.

Lluch, C., Powell, A. A., and Williams, R. A. (1977), *Patterns in Household Demand and Saving*, Oxford University Press.

Markowitz, H. M. (1959), *Portfolio Selection*, John Wiley.

Modigliani, F. and Brumberg, R. (1955), 'Utility analysis and the consumption function: an interpretation of cross-section data', in Kurihara, K. K. (ed.), *Post Keynesian Economics*, George Allen & Unwin, London.

Phlips, L. (1974), *Applied Consumption Analysis*, North-Holland, Amsterdam and Oxford.

Pollak, R. A. (1970), 'Habit formation and dynamic demand functions', *Journal of Political Economy*, **78**, pp. 60–78.

—— (1978), 'Endogenous tastes in demand and welfare analysis', *American Economic review*, **68**, (papers and proceedings), pp. 374–9.

Ramsey, F. P. (1928), 'A mathematical theory of saving', *Economic Journal*, **38**, pp. 543–59.

Roe, A. (1969), 'A quarterly series of personal sector assets and liabilities', Cambridge Growth Project Paper no. 8, mimeo.

Sandmo, A. (1974), 'Two-period models of consumption decisions under uncertainty: a survey', pp. 24–35 in Dreze, J. H. (ed.) *Allocation under Uncertainty: Equilibrium and Optimality*, Macmillan.

Simmons, P. J. (1978), *Models for the analysis of consumer demand in the post-war UK*, unpublished PhD thesis, Southampton University.

Smith, R. P. (1974), 'A note on car replacement', *Review of Economic Studies*, **41**, pp. 567–70.

—— (1975), *Consumer Demand for Cars in the U.S.A.*, Cambridge University Press.

Stiglitz, J. E. (1970), 'A consumption-oriented theory of the demand for financial assets and the term structure of interest rates', *Review of Economic Studies*, **37**, pp. 321–51.

Stone, J. R. N. (1954), 'Linear expenditure systems and demand analysis: an application to the pattern of British demand', *Economic Journal*, **64**, pp. 511–27.

Stone, R. and D. A. Rowe (1957), 'The market demand for durable goods', *Econometrica*, **25**, pp. 423–43.

—— (1958), 'Dynamic demand functions: some econometric results', *Economic Journal*, **68**, pp. 256–70.

Theil, H. (1954), *Linear Aggregation of Economic Relations*, Amsterdam: North-Holland.

Tintner, G. (1938), 'The theoretical derivation of dynamic demand curves', *Econometrica*, **6**, pp. 375–80.

Tobin, J. (1958), 'Liquidity preference as behaviour towards risk', *Review of Economic Studies*, **25**, pp. 65–86.

Townend, J. C. (1976), 'The personal savings ratio', *Bank of England Quarterly Bulletin*, **16**, pp. 53–73.

Westin, R. B. (1975), 'Empirical implications of infrequent purchase behaviour in a stock-adjustment model', *American Economic Review*, **65**, pp. 384–96.

9 Liquidity and inflation effects on consumers' expenditure[1]

DAVID F. HENDRY
AND THOMAS VON UNGERN-STERNBERG

1 Introduction

In a recent study of the time-series behaviour of consumers' expenditure in the United Kingdom, Davidson *et al.* (1978) (denoted DHSY below), presented results for an equation in constant (1970) prices, relating consumers' expenditure on non-durables and services (C) to personal disposable income (Y) and the rate of change of prices (P):

$$\Delta_4 c_t = \alpha_1 \Delta_4 y_t + \alpha_2 \Delta_1 \Delta_4 y_t + \alpha_3 \Delta_4 p_t + \alpha_4 \Delta_1 \Delta_4 p_t + \alpha_5(c_{t-4} - y_{t-4}) + \alpha_6 \Delta_4 D_t + \varepsilon_t \tag{1}$$

In (1), lower case letters denote $\log_e$ of corresponding capital letters, P_t is the implicit deflator of C_t, $\Delta_j = (1 - \mathscr{L}^j)$ where $\mathscr{L}^k x_t = x_{t-k}$ and ε_t is assumed to be a white-noise error process. D_t is a dummy variable for 1968(i) and (ii) and for the introduction of VAT.

DHSY selected equation (1) using the criteria that it:
 (i) encompassed as special cases most previous empirical models relating C_t to Y_t;
 (ii) was consonant with many steady-state economic theories of non-durable consumption;
 (iii) explained the salient features of the available data;
 (iv) provided a simple dynamic model in terms of plausible decision variables of economic agents;
 (v) helped explain why previous investigators had selected their (presumed incorrect) models;
 (vi) exhibited an impressive degree of parameter constancy over twenty quarters after the end of the estimation sample (through a period of rapid change in P and C/Y).
Nevertheless, DHSY did *not* conclude that (1) represented a 'true' structural relationship and three issues merited immediate re-examination, namely, liquidity effects, the role of inflation, and the treatment of seasonality.

 Although DHSY obtained negative results when investigating liquid

237

asset effects in (1), Professor Sir Richard Stone established a significant influence for cumulated savings on consumers' expenditure using annual data (see, for example, Stone (1966) and (1973)). Moreover, the dynamic specification of (1) is logically incomplete as some latent asset stock must be altering when total expenditure is unequal to income. Alternatively expressed, in the terminology of Phillips (1954) and (1957), the formulation in (1) includes derivative and proportional control mechanisms but omits *integral* control, and the influence of liquid assets is considered below as an observable proxy for such an integral control. This interpretation is close to the spirit of Professor Stone's approach. Integral correction mechanisms are analysed in section 2, together with a pilot Monte Carlo study of the finite sample properties of least-squares estimators in such models.

Several theories have been offered to account for the direct influence of inflation on savings (see, for example, Deaton (1977), Bean (1978) and the references therein) and in section 3 we consider the model developed in Ungern-Sternberg (1978) based on the mis-measurement of real income in inflationary conditions. The resulting equation avoids the problem in (1) that, as inflation increases, C/Y falls without a positive lower bound.

The empirical evidence for the UK is re-examined in section 4 using an extension of (1) which allows for a seasonally varying average propensity to consume and thereby explains one of the 'paradoxes' noted by DHSY. Section 5 concludes and summarises the study.

Since (1) accounts for much previous empirical research relating C to Y in the UK, we commence from DHSY's model and supplant it by an equation which still satisfies the six criteria noted above. Although the resulting model remains parsimonious, is data coherent and exhibits a fair degree of parameter constancy, it is undoubtedly far from being the final resolution of this complex subject. It is offered as a further step in that scientific progression which has been a hallmark of Professor Stone's research.

2 Integral correction mechanisms

Simple dynamic models based on 'error correction' feedbacks as in (1) are important in linking equations formulated in *levels* with those formulated in *differences* of the original variables. Further, an error correction model (denoted ECM) has many interesting dynamic and econometric properties (see, for example, Sargan (1964), DHSY and Hendry (1980)) and, appropriately specified, can ensure that an estimated equation reproduces as its steady-state solution the economic theory from which it was derived, thus facilitating rigorous testing of theories. Consequently, (1) provides an example of a useful class of dynamic equations.

Nevertheless, (1) has a major flaw as a *complete* account of the dynamic behaviour of flow variables. Consider the simplest example of an ECM relating two variables denoted by w_t and x_t:

$$\Delta_1 w_t = \gamma_1 \Delta_1 x_t + \gamma_2 (x_{t-1} - w_{t-1}) + v_t \tag{2}$$

where $v_t \sim NI(0, \sigma_v^2)$ and $E(x_t v_s) = 0 \,\forall\, t, s$, with $1 > \gamma_1, \gamma_2 > 0$. The non-stochastic steady-state solution of (2) when $\Delta_1 x_t = g$ must have $\Delta_1 w_t = g$ and hence:

$$W = KX \quad \text{where} \quad K = \exp((\gamma_1 - 1)g/\gamma_2) \tag{3}$$

and (2) is stable provided $2 > \gamma_2 > 0$. However, the convergence of W_t to its steady-state growth path following any disturbance is monotonic and if $\gamma_1 < 1$ then w_t converges to $x_t + k$ from below (above) when x_t increases (decreases) (note that, in terms of stabilising W/X, $\Delta_1 x_t$ has the appropriate negative coefficient). Consequently, even when $K = 1$ ($k = 0$) there is a cumulative underadjustment if x_t is steadily increasing or decreasing. If w_t is an expenditure and x_t an accrual then some stock of assets is implicitly altering and for decreases in x_t is essential to finance the 'overspending'.

In the terminology of Phillips (1954 and 1957), (2) incorporates derivative ($\Delta_1 x_t$) and proportional ($x_{t-1} - w_{t-1}$) control mechanisms, but *no* integral control ($\Sigma_{j<t} (x_j - w_j)$). Such an integral can be interpreted most easily by introducing a state variable A_t (which may or may not be observable) defined by (using end-of-period definitions):

$$A_t \equiv A_{t-1} + X_t - W_t \tag{4}$$

In terms of the original variables, A_t is the integral of past discrepancies between X and W. Whether or not integral control mechanisms (denoted by ICMs) influence behaviour is, from this viewpoint, simply a matter of dynamic specification. Nevertheless, economic theory is far from being devoid of alternative interpretations (for example, Pissarides (1978) presents a theoretical analysis of the role of liquid assets in consumption which yields conclusions similar to those obtained below) and we record with interest that Phillips (1954, p. 310) considered the 'Pigou Effect' to be an integral regulating mechanism inherent in the economy.

Indeed, many previous researchers have incorporated integral variables in expenditure equations, including the explicit use of *cumulated savings* by Stone (1966) and (1973), *liquid assets* (see, inter alia, Zellner *et al.* (1965) and Townend (1976)) and *wealth* (see Ball and Drake (1964), Deaton (1972; 1976) and Modigliani (1975)). However, since there are many econometric relationships in which integral effects are potentially relevant but do not appear to have been used previously (such as wage–price equations) we develop the simplest form of model which extends (2) to allow for an ICM, following an approach similar to Deaton (1972) and Hendry and Anderson (1977).

To focus attention on the dynamic specification, we assume that a prior steady-state utility maximization exercise leads agents to seek to maintain constant ratios both between W and X as in (2) and between A and X (ceteris paribus), namely: $W^e = K^*X$ and $A^e = B^*X$ where ^{e} denotes 'dynamic equilibrium'. For consistency with (4) in steady state, $K^* = 1 - (g/(1 + g))B^*$. Either linear or log-linear decision rules could be formulated, but since we want the latter in order to generalize (2) (noting also that both DHSY and Salmon (1979) found Sargan's (1964) likelihood criterion favoured log-linear models for C_t), (4) has to be replaced by its steady-state approximation:

$$\Delta_1 a_t^e = H^*(x_t - w_t^e) \quad \text{where} \quad H^* = (1 + g)/B^* \tag{5}$$

The long-run targets can be written in logs as:

$$w_t^e = k^* + x_t \quad \text{and} \quad a_t^e = b^* + x_t \tag{6}$$

Since the actual outcomes are stochastic, and (4) rather than (5) holds for the observed data, disequilibria can occur. To model agents assigning priorities to removing these, a quadratic loss function is postulated where the first two terms are the relative costs attached to discrepancies occurring between planned values (w_t^p and a_t^p) and their respective steady-state outcomes. Further, to stabilize behaviour when the environment remains constant (i.e. to avoid 'bang-bang' control in response to *random* fluctuations), agents attach costs to changing w_t^p from w_{t-1}. However, when the primary objectives are to attain (6), it does not seem sensible to *quadratically* penalize changes in w_t^p when it is *known* that w_t^e has changed. Thus there is an offset term to allow *more adjustment at a given cost when w_t^e has changed than when it is constant*. By comparison, partial adjustment models enforce quadratic adjustment costs irrespective of how much the target is known to have changed.

Collecting together these four terms in a one-period loss function yields:

$$q_t = \lambda_1(a_t^p - x_t - b^*)^2 + \lambda_2(w_t^p - x_t - k^*)^2 \\ + \lambda_3(w_t^p - w_{t-1})^2 - 2\lambda_4(w_t^p - w_{t-1})(x_t - x_{t-1}) \tag{7}$$

where $\lambda_i \geq 0$ ($i = 1, ..., 4$). Allowing for the possibility that the current value of x_t might be uncertain, $E(q_t)$ has to be minimized with respect to w_t^p (or a_t^p), taking account of (5) holding for *planned* quantities. The deliberately myopic formulation in (7) naturally leads to a 'servomechanism' solution when x_t is known, or more generally on setting $(\partial E(q_t)/\partial w_t^p)$ to zero:

$$\Delta_1 w_t = \theta_0 + \theta_1 \Delta_1 \tilde{x}_t + \theta_2(x_{t-1} - w_{t-1}) + \theta_3(a_{t-1} - x_{t-1}) + u_t \tag{8}$$

where $\Delta_1 \tilde{x}_t = E(x_t) - x_{t-1}$, $w_t - w_t^p = u_t \sim NI(0, \sigma_u^2)$ independently of w_t^p and the $\theta_i \in (0, 1)$ are given by:

$$\theta_0 = (\lambda_2 k^* - \lambda_1 H^* b^*)/\psi, \quad \theta_1 = (H^*\lambda_1(H^* - 1) + \lambda_2 + \lambda_4)/\psi$$

$$\theta_2 = (H^{*2}\lambda_1 + \lambda_2)/\psi, \quad \theta_3 = H^*\lambda_1/\psi \quad \text{and} \quad \psi = (H^{*2}\lambda_1 + \lambda_2 + \lambda_3)$$

The three variables in (8) correspond respectively to derivative, proportional and integral control mechanisms as required; the equivalent partial adjustment cost function would constrain $\theta_1 + \theta_3$ to equal θ_2 (which, in the absence of an ICM, entails having prior information that $\theta_1 = \theta_2$, i.e. that x_{t-1} does *not* occur in the equation).

The planning rule for w_t given by the above approach is of the form advocated by Richard (1980), where agents' behaviour is described by conditional expectations functions, but agents have no control over the variability around the function. Indeed, the uncertain and highly variable nature of real income makes a feedback control model like (8) an attractive behavioural possibility for expenditure. Also, the inclusion of specific mechanisms for correcting past mistakes makes the white-noise assumption for u_t more tenable.

Let $x_t - \tilde{x}_t = \varepsilon_t \sim NI(0, \sigma_\varepsilon^2)$, then (8) holds with $\Delta_1 \tilde{x}_t$ replaced by $\Delta_1 x_t$ and u_t by $v_t = u_t - \theta_1 \varepsilon_t$ where $E(x_t v_t) = -\theta_1 \sigma_\varepsilon^2$. Conversely, time aggregation could introduce simultaneity between x and the equation error for the observation period even if x_t is weakly exogenous in the decision time period (see Richard, 1980); these two effects will be offsetting and are in principle testable, but, for the remainder of this paper, both are assumed to be absent.

Equation (8) seems to be the simplest generalization of (2) which incorporates an integral control and it yields a non-stochastic steady-state solution when $\Delta_1 x_t = g = \Delta_1 w_t = \Delta_1 a_t$ given by:

$$W/X = D(A/X)^\phi \tag{9}$$

where $\phi = \theta_3/\theta_2 > 0$ and $D = \exp\{(\theta_0 - (1 - \theta_1)g)/\theta_2\}$. Moreover, (5) (for planned magnitudes) and (8) imply that:

$$\Delta_1 a_t = H^*\{\theta_3(x_{t-1} - a_{t-1}) - \theta_0 + (1 - \theta_2)(x_{t-1} - w_{t-1}) + (1 - \theta_1)\Delta_1 x_t - u_t^0\} \tag{10}$$

(where u_t^0 deviates from u_t by a term involving the product of the disequilibria in the two endogenous variables). Consequently, in non-stochastic steady state:

$$A = BX \quad \text{or} \quad a = b + x \tag{11}$$

and hence

$$W = KX \quad \text{or} \quad w = k + x \tag{12}$$

where $k = -gB/(1 + g)$ (i.e. $K = 1 - gB/(1 + g)$, and

$$(b + MB) = (b^* + MB^*) + (\lambda_4 - \lambda_3)k^*/\lambda_1 \qquad (13)$$

when $M = \lambda_3 k^*/\lambda_1(1 + g)$. Expanding $(b + MB)$ in a first-order Taylor series around b^* yields $b = b^* + (\lambda_4 - \lambda_3)gk^*/(g\lambda_1 - \lambda_3 k^{*2}) = b^* + 0(g/(1 + g))$.

Equations (11) and (12) reproduce the forms of the 'desired' relationships in (6), and show that the long-run ratios depend on the agents' aims and on the losses attached to the various terms in the objective function (7). Since only two alternatives are allowed (e.g. spending W_t or saving $\Delta_1 A_t$), $W = X$ when $g = 0$, but in practice this restriction need not hold for a sub-category of expenditure.

The dynamic reaction of w_t to exogenous changes in x_t can be expressed in the form:

$$\Psi(\mathscr{L})w_t = \Phi(\mathscr{L})x_t \qquad (14)$$

and $\Psi(.)$ is the same for the autoregressive-distributed lag representation of a_t (using (5) and (10)), where:

$$\Psi(\mathscr{L}) = \{1 - (1 + (1 - \theta_2) - \theta_3 H^*)\mathscr{L} + (1 - \theta_2)\mathscr{L}^2\}$$

$$= \sum_{i=0}^{2} \psi_i \mathscr{L}^i \qquad (15)$$

(15) is identical to the lag polynomial of the simple multiplier–accelerator model and has stable roots since $0 < \theta_2, \theta_3 H^* < 1$, the roots being a complex conjugate pair if $(\theta_3 H^*)^{1/2} > \frac{1}{2}(\theta_2 + \theta_3 H^*)$, in which case the adjustment path is oscillatory with period of oscillation given by $2\pi/\delta$ where $\cos \delta = (-\psi_1/2(\psi_2)^{1/2})$ (for an exposition see Allen, 1963, ch. 7).

Changes in x_t have an impact elasticity of $\theta_1(1 - \theta_1)$ on $w_t(a_t)$, and for $\theta_1 \neq 1$, discrepancies are created between the actual values of A_t and W_t and their 'equilibrium' levels BX and KX respectively, *both* of which are partly corrected in the next period. In fact, even if $\theta_1 = 1$, the ECMs are *still* required to correct for stochastic variation (i.e. unless $u_t = 0 \; \forall \; t$) or for 'unanticipated' changes in x_t, when that variable is not known for certain till the end of the period.

Rather little is known about the finite sample properties of least-squares estimators of the θ_i in (8), both when the equation is correctly specified and when the lag structure has been wrongly formulated. The case $\theta_3 = 0$ was investigated by DHSY and here we consider the one set of parameter values: $(\theta_0, \theta_1, \theta_2, \theta_3) = (-0.1, 0.5, 0.3, 0.1)$ at sample sizes $T = (20, 40, 60, 80)$ when the model is: (i) correctly formulated; (ii) the ICM is omitted; (iii) both the ICM and the proportional ECM are omitted. $\sigma_u^2 = 1, \sigma_\varepsilon^2 = 0$ and x_t was generated by:

$$x_t = 0.8x_{t-1} + e_t \quad \text{with} \quad e_t \sim NI(0, 9)$$

The first 50 values of each data series were discarded in every replication, and each experiment was replicated 400 times, identical random numbers being used across the three sets of experiments. Normalizing on $\lambda_1 = 1$, the underlying parameter values are $(\gamma_2, \gamma_3, \gamma_4) = (0.97, 2.58, 1.10)$ with $g = 0$ and $h^* = -1$. These parameter values were selected to mimic the empirical results reported below; the chosen model has a static equilibrium solution given by:

$$w = x \quad \text{and} \quad a = 1 + x$$

with the roots of the $\Psi(\mathscr{L})$ polynomial being $0.8 \pm 0.245\,i$. To investigate the usefulness of autocorrelation diagnostic tests as indicators of the dynamic mis-specifications, rejection frequencies for Lagrange Multiplier (LM) based tests of first and (general) fourth order residual autocorrelation were computed (see Godfrey, 1978; and Breusch and Pagan, 1980). The results for $T = 80$ are recorded in table 1 (similar outcomes were obtained at the other sample sizes), and several features merit note.

Firstly, the simulation findings reveal no new problems for estimating correctly specified single equations involving integral control variables since, although a_t is generated by a cumulative process as in (4), $(a_t - x_t)$ is stationary as shown in equation (10). In case (i), the coefficient biases are small and $SD \simeq SE$ with the residual autocorrelation tests having approximately the right empirical significance levels as found more generally by Mizon and Hendry (1980). Dropping the ICM does *not* cause very large biases in $\hat{\theta}_1$ and $\hat{\theta}_2$ but *does* bias the intercept to zero; s^2 is biased up-

Table 1. *Simulation findings for (8) at T = 80*

		θ_1	θ_2	θ_3	θ_0	s^2	$z_4(1)$	$z_4(4)$
(i)	Bias*	0.00	0.01	0.01	−0.01	0.00	0.06	0.04
	SD	0.04	0.05	0.02	0.13			
	SE	0.04	0.05	0.02	0.12			
(ii)	Bias	−0.01	−0.03	—	0.10	0.29	0.11	0.11
	SD	0.04	0.04	—	0.04			
	SE	0.04	0.05	—	0.13			
(iii)	Bias	−0.04	—	—	0.10	0.76	0.16	0.06
	SD	0.05	—	—	0.05			
	SE	0.05	—	—	0.15			

* For coefficient estimates, this denotes the simulation estimate of $E(\hat{\theta}_1 - \theta_1)$, and for $z_4(i)$ (the LM test for ith order residual autocorrelation) shows the % rejection frequency of the null of no autocorrelation; SD denotes the sampling standard deviation and SE the average estimated coefficient standard error; — denotes that the parameter in question was not estimated (and hence has a bias of $(-\theta_j)$). The sampling standard error of the estimated bias is SD/20.

wards by almost 30% and the LM tests detect significant autocorrelation in the residuals only 11% of the time. Further, the equilibrium solution remains $w = x$ so that this mis-specification would seem to be very difficult to detect. Consequently, these findings are consistent with 'true' models like (8), generating data which are apparently well explained by equations like (2) (as reported by DHSY, for example). Except for a further large increase in s^2, the outcome is not much changed by also dropping the proportional ECM (note the results obtained by Wall *et al.* (1975)).

Thus, although $(a_t - x_t)$ is highly autoregressive, dropping $(a_{t-1} - x_{t-1})$ does *not* cause detectable autocorrelation in the residuals. This is important given that the derivation of equations like (12) is often ostensibly by *differencing* a stock–flow relationship (see, for example, DHSY, p. 669); such interpretations are not unique because of the two formulations of 'differencing' noted by DHSY (p. 673), and (2) can be obtained from a linear equation relating w_t to x_t and a_t *either* by filtering *or* by imposing invalid coefficient restrictions on the integral control, with very different implications for the error process. It should be noted that Mizon and Hendry (1980) found the LM autocorrelation tests to have reasonable rejection frequencies when the error was generated as an autoregressive scheme.

There are obviously a large number of steps from obtaining simple error correction models like (8) to empirical implementation, of which aggregation over agents and time, and the choice of a proxy for A_t, are perhaps the most important in the present context. A proper treatment of aggregation is beyond the scope of this paper, but (8) still provides a useful guide to equation formulation in terms of interpretable and relatively orthogonal variables.

For C_t, the stock of real net liquid assets of the personal sector (denoted by L_t) seems to play a role analogous to A_t (complicated by portfolio adjustments in response to changes in rates of return on other assets and durable expenditure, jointly denoted by N_t):[2]

$$L_t = (1 - \Delta_1 p_t)L_{t-1} + Y_t - C_t - N_t$$

Thus, in logs:

$$\Delta_1 l_t = -\Delta_1 p_t + H(y_t - c_t) - \eta_t \tag{16}$$

where $H = Y/L$, η_t depends on N_t (and changes in H) and the variability of η_t is assumed to be small relative to that of $\Delta_1 p_t$ and $(y_t - c_t)$. The data for $P_t L_t$ are taken from the various issues of *Financial Statistics* (see e.g. Table 10.3 in the June 1979 issue where $P_t L_t$ = total identified less bank advances). In fact, the form of equation (16) points directly to the issue examined in the next section.

3 Real income and inflation

The measure of personal disposable income used by DHSY is the 'conventional' series reported in *Economic Trends* and comprises wages, salaries, earnings of the self-employed, rents, net interest receipts, dividends and transfer payments less direct taxes, all revalued using the implicit deflator for total consumers' expenditure. Since the personal sector is a substantial net creditor (see *Economic Trends*, 1978, p. 291), interest receipts are a non-negligible fraction of Y; moreover, as inflation increases, nominal interest rates tend to rise, thereby increasing the interest component of Y. It seems inappropriate to measure 'real income' as increasing in such a situation, since the large nominal interest receipts are offset by capital losses on all monetary assets, which are *not* being deducted from the income variable used (Townend (1976) makes a related point, but does not estimate such an effect). It is easy to understand why the national income accounts should wish to calculate income as the sum of readily observable components, avoiding hard to measure and rather volatile changes in the real values of a spectrum of assets. However, if Y^*, the real income *perceived* by consumers, differs from Y, then consumption functions based on Y will manifest predictive failure when the correlation between Y and Y^* alters.

Hicks (1939, ch. 14) discusses the many difficulties involved in defining and measuring real income when interest rates and prices (and expectations about these) are changing. One improvement over Y might be 'that accrual which would leave real wealth intact', but despite recent improvements in the available statistical evidence we doubt our ability to construct such a quarterly time-series *relevant to consumers' expenditure*. Indeed, to the extent that Y^* differs from Y, it must do so by some easily observable magnitude.

Since most households are aware of their liquid asset position and since the personal sector's losses on liquid assets are a major component of its overall financial loss during inflationary periods, $\dot{p}L$ (where $\dot{p}$ denotes the rate of inflation) seems a prime candidate for relating perceived to measured income. Moreover, aggregate data on net liquid assets (which comprise, very roughly, 20% of wealth and 40% of financial assets) seem reasonably accurate and will occur in our models as the basis of the ICM in any case. Thus the simplest initial hypothesis is that $Y^* = Y - \beta \dot{p}L$ where β has been introduced to account for any scale effects due to wrongly choosing measures for $\dot{p}$ or L; note that if $\beta = 1$ (i.e. if the loss on our measure of net liquid assets is the variable which consumers perceive as negative income), then (16) could be rewritten as $\Delta_1 l_t = H^0(y_t^* - c_t) - \eta_t$ where $H^0 = Y^*/L$.

More or less inclusive measures proxying A_t could be chosen, and the validity of these is open to test on the data. For example, the choice of L entails that agents react asymmetrically to erosion of their deposits in Building Societies as against their mortgages from the same institutions, but, to the extent that such variables behave similarly, the scaling will be corrected by β (for example, Building Society Mortgages are about 40% of L and are very highly correlated with L). A two-year moving average of the quarterly inflation rate of the Retail Price Index (R) was selected for $\dot{p}$ (i.e. $\dot{p} = \Delta_8 \log_e R_t/8$).

To give some idea of the magnitude of the correction to real income involved in Y^*, if $\beta = 1$ and $\dot{p} = 0.05$ (per quarter) then, using $L/Y = 3$, $Y^* = Y(1 - \dot{p}(L/Y)) = 0.85\ Y$, inducing a dramatic reduction in the income measure. As $\dot{p}$ increases, L falls so that $\dot{p}L/Y$ does not increase without bound, unlike the linear term in $\Delta_4 \ln P_t$ in (1). Further, when $\dot{p}$ is small, Y^* and Y are very highly correlated and this breaks down only when inflation increases substantially; consequently, if $C = f(Y^*)$, but models attempted to explain C by Y, then such equations would fail only when $\dot{p}$ altered rapidly. Moreover, the increase in $\dot{p}$ in the 1970s in the UK is closely correlated with the fall in L/Y (see figures 1 and 2) and hence including $\dot{p}$ alone as a linear regressor (as DHSY do, for example) would

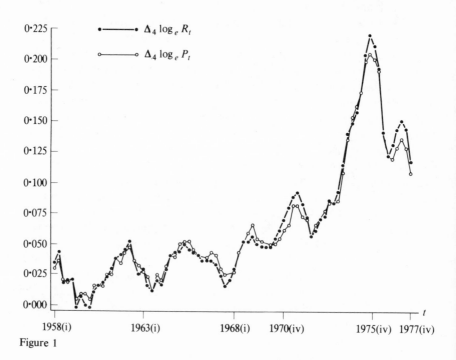

Figure 1

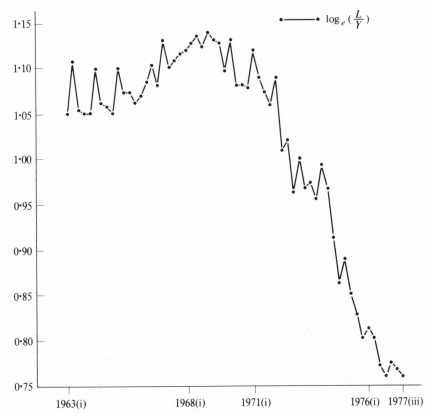

Figure 2

provide an excellent proxy for $\dot{p}L/Y$: i.e.

$$\log_e \left(Y \left(1 - \beta \dot{p} \frac{L}{Y} \right) \right) \simeq y - \left(\beta \frac{L}{Y} \right) \dot{p} \tag{17}$$

The converse also holds, of course, but our hypothesis seems potentially able to account for the existing evidence.

Alternatively expressed, assuming that the long-run income elasticity of consumption is unity, the apparent fall in C/Y during the 1970s must be due in large part to mis-measurement of the denominator; one simple check on the credibility of this hypothesis is the behaviour of C/Y^* (which should be more nearly constant than C/Y). Figure 4 shows the time series of $(c_t - y_t)$ and $(c_t - y_t^*)$ (for $\beta = 0.5$) and confirms that the use of Y_t^* has greatly stabilized the consumption/income ratio. The main test of the hypothesis is, of course, whether the resulting model performs as well as (1) on the six criteria of section 1, which includes satisfying all of the diagnostic tests in section 4 below.

It should be stressed that the use of Y^* is in principle complementary to the theory in Deaton (1977), although in practice the explanations are likely to be more nearly substitutes. Our model is also distinct from the hypothesis that the fall in C/Y is due *solely* to consumers rebuilding their real liquid assets; certainly an ICM (like a real balance effect) implies that C/Y will fall when L/Y has fallen, but this is a joint determinant together with the increase in $\dot{p}$. Since our model uses L/Y^* as the ICM, (which also falls less than L/Y) and since DHSY accounted fully for the fall in C/Y using $\dot{p}$, the correction to Y constitutes a major part of the explanation for the rise in the observed savings ratio. We note that the London Business School (1980) model also requires both inflation and integral effects, although their specification is rather different from equation (27) below.

4 Empirical evidence for the United Kingdom

For ease of comparability, we retained DHSY's data definitions, and, so far as possible, their actual data series, extending the sample to 1977(iv) (no further data being available in 1970 prices) but curtailing the early period to 1962(iv) due to the lack of observations on liquid assets prior to this date. Also, the implicit deflator of C (P) was replaced by R (the two data series are very highly correlated as shown in figure 1). Re-estimating equation (1) from 1963(i) and testing its predictions for 1973(i)–1977(iv) yields:

$$\widehat{\Delta_4 c_t} = \underset{(0.04)}{0.50}\, \Delta_4 y_t - \underset{(0.05)}{0.26}\, \Delta_1\Delta_4 y_t - \underset{(0.017)}{0.076}(c_{t-4} - y_{t-4}) + \underset{(0.004)}{0.01}\, \Delta_4 D_t$$

$$- \underset{(0.051)}{0.089}\dot{p}_t - \underset{(0.151)}{0.253}\, \Delta_1\dot{p}_t \tag{18}$$

$$T = 40 \quad R^2 = 0.785 \quad s = 0.0066 \quad d = 2.1 \quad z_1(20) = 49.8$$
$$z_3(20,34) = 1.3 \quad z_2(8) = 11 \quad z_4(6) = 3.1$$

In (18), $\dot{p}_t = \Delta_4 \log_e R_t$, T denotes the estimation sample size, s is the standard deviation of the residuals, $z_1(20)$ and $z_2(8)$ are the χ^2 predictive test and the Box–Pierce statistic as reported by DHSY, and $z_3(20,34)$ and $z_4(6)$ are the Chow test of parameter constancy and the Lagrange Multiplier test for residual autocorrelation respectively. Note that if $z_1(n) > n$ then the *numerical* values of parameter estimates provide inaccurate predictions, but z_3 could still be less than unity so that, with the best re-estimated parameter values, s will not increase.

While the greatly changed behaviour of $\dot{p}_t$ means that the last 20 observations on c_t are far from easy to predict, the predictive performance of

(18) is distinctly less impressive than that over the DHSY forecast period of 20 quarters (which included the first 12 observations of the present forecast set). Re-estimation over the entire sample yields:

$$\widehat{\Delta_4 c_t} = \underset{(0.03)}{0.51} \, \Delta_4 y_t - \underset{(0.05)}{0.25} \, \Delta_1 \Delta_4 y_t - \underset{(0.013)}{0.082}(c_{t-4} - y_{t-4}) + \underset{(0.003)}{0.01} \, \Delta_4 D_t$$

$$- \underset{(0.022)}{0.132} \dot{p}_t - \underset{(0.151)}{0.036} \, \Delta_1 \dot{p}_t \qquad\qquad (19)$$

$$T = 60 \quad R^2 = 0.866 \quad s = 0.0070 \quad d = 1.9 \quad z_2(8) = 11$$
$$z_4(6) = 1.8$$

confirming the change in parameter values (especially for $\Delta_1 \dot{p}_t$) and the increase in s. Although the values of z_2, z_3 *and* z_4 in (18) are not significant, the evidence in (19) suggests that it may be possible to improve on the DHSY specification using the ideas developed in sections 2 and 3.

One direct check (which could have been undertaken before proceeding but in fact was computed later) is to test the null hypothesis that $\beta = 0$ by applying to (19) the LM test proposed in Engle (1979). Engle's statistic (based on (17)) rejects the null at the 5% significance level, and while rejection cannot be taken as corroborating any given alternative hypothesis, it does confirm the potential for improvement and is consistent with the argument in section 3.

Firstly, DHSY's steady-state assumption that $C = KY$ seems questionable in view of the strong and persistent seasonal behaviour of C/Y (see figure (4)). A steady-state solution of the form $C = K_i Y$ (where K_i varies seasonally) is more plausible on the basis of their own analysis and suggests an error correction mechanism of the form $\log_e (C/K_i Y)_{t-4}$ which could be implemented either by geometrically 'seasonally adjusting' Y or adding seasonal dummies. Indeed, seasonal dummy variables are significant if added to (1) which thereby fits better than equation (44) of DHSY, resolving their conflict (p. 688) between goodness of fit and parameter constancy. In most results reported below, the K_i were estimated unrestrictedly as coefficients of seasonal dummies, although very similar results were obtained when C/Y was corrected using the quarterly sample means.

Secondly, DHSY's test for the significance of liquid assets by adding L to (1) is inappropriate as it forces the steady-state solution to be $C/Y = Kf(L)$ which is dimensionally incorrect (scale changes in L alter C/Y); it seems more reasonable to anticipate $C/Y = Kf(L/Y)$. Such a mistake would have been avoided had the authors estimated the least restricted model in their class (see table 2 below), but omitting the ICM did *not* induce autocorrelated residuals.

Thirdly, the analysis in section 3 requires recomputing real income

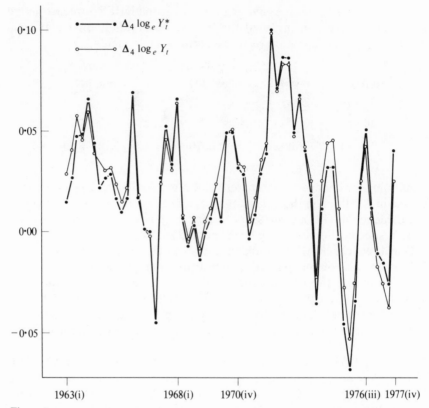

Figure 3

using $Y_t^* = Y_t - \beta \dot{p} L_{t-1}$ (with $\dot{p} = \frac{1}{8}(\dot{p}_t + \dot{p}_{t-4})$, henceforth denoted by $\bar{p}_t$). Since β enters non-linearly in y^*, initial estimates were obtained using a grid search over $0 \le \beta \le 1$ by steps of 0.1 for a specification similar to (18) but excluding $\dot{p}_t$ and $\Delta_1 \dot{p}_t$ and including $(\bar{l} - \bar{y}^*)_{t-1} = \log_e(\Sigma_{i=1}^4 L_{t-i}/\Sigma_{i=1}^4 Y_{t-i}^*)$. The minimum residual sum of squares for various sample periods lay in the interval [0.4, 0.6] and $\hat{\beta} = 0.5$ was selected for most of the subsequent regression analysis (see figure 3 for the time-series plots of $\Delta_4 y_t$ and $\Delta_4 y_t^*$).

Conditional on $\hat{\beta} = 0.5$, $(\dot{p}_t \dots \dot{p}_{t-4})$ were insignificant ($F_{25}^5 = 1.8$) if added to the otherwise unrestricted log-linear equation:

$$c_t = \sum_{i=0}^{n} (\alpha_i c_{t-i-1} + \gamma_i y_{t-i}^* + \delta_i l_{t-i-1} + \xi_i Q_{it})$$
$$+ \mu_1 D_t + \mu_2 D_{t-4} + \varepsilon_t \tag{20}$$

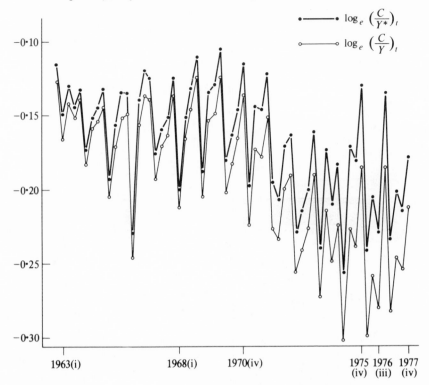

Figure 4

(where $n = 3$ for c, l and Q and 6 for y^*) and table 2 reports the estimates obtained for (20). The s value is substantially smaller than DHSY report for their unrestricted model, $\hat{\delta}_i$ and $\hat{\xi}_i$ being individually significantly different from zero at the 0.05 level. Because of the shorter sample period, only 6 observations have been retained for parameter constancy tests and, while both z_1 and z_3 are unimpressive, the parameterization is profligate (the equivalent z_3 value using Y in place of Y^* is 2.13).

The long-run solution of (20) derived from table 2 is:

$$c = k_i - 8.3g + 0.57y^* + 0.38l \quad \text{where } k_i \text{ varies seasonally,}$$
$$\quad (7.8) \quad (0.14) \quad (0.20)$$

g is the quarterly growth rate of y^* and l, and numerically computed asymptotic standard errors of the derived parameters are shown in parentheses. The sum of the coefficients of y^* and l is not significantly different from unity (1.06 (0.10)) but, as discussed by Currie (1979), the coefficient of g is badly determined and is not significantly different from zero.

Table 2. *Unrestricted estimates of (20) with $\dot{\beta} = 0.5$*

j	0	1	2	3	4	5	6
c_{t-j}	-1.0	$-0.04(0.12)$	$-0.05(0.09)$	$0.29(0.11)$	$0.61(0.13)$	—	—
t^*_{t-j}	$0.26(0.04)$	$0.19(0.06)$	$0.06(0.06)$	$-0.10(0.07)$	$-0.10(0.06)$	$-0.17(0.05)$	$-0.04(0.04)$
l_{t-j}	—	$0.29(0.10)$	$-0.39(0.17)$	$0.10(0.17)$	$0.07(0.11)$	—	—
Q_{tt}	$0.03(0.20)$	$-0.05(0.02)$	$-0.03(0.01)$	$-0.04(0.01)$	—	—	—
D_{t-j}	$0.01(0.004)$	—	—	—	$-0.01(0.003)$	—	—

$T = 51$ $R^2 = 0.9978$ $s = 0.0053$ $z_1(6) = 33.5$ $z_2(8) = 14.0$ $z_3(6,30) = 1.7$

The roots of $\alpha(\mathcal{L}) = 0$ are: $0.95, -0.78, -0.10, \pm 0.90i$

Such results are consistent with the theory developed in section 2, but a more parsimonious restricted specification facilitates interpreting the data. Firstly, for the derivative term, the results in DHSY and Bean (1978) suggest using a distributed lag in $\Delta_4 y_t^*$ and the simple Almon polynomial (see Sargan, 1980) $Ay_t^* = \Sigma_{i=0}^2 (3 - i) \Delta_4 y_{t-i}^*$ adequately captures this. Note that Ay_t^* is, in effect, 'self seasonally adjusted' and continuing this idea for the ICM suggests using $(\bar{l} - \bar{y}^*)_{t-1}$ as defined above: likewise, the proportional ECM takes the form $(c - k_i - y^*)_{t-4}$ discussed earlier. Finally, to strengthen derivative control and dampen any potential oscillatory behaviour generated by the ICM, $\Delta_1 l_{t-1}$ was also included as a regressor (see table 2). Thus, the restricted dynamic model to be estimated is of the general form:

$$\Delta_4 c_t = \alpha_1 Ay_t^* + \alpha_2(c - y^*)_{t-4} + \alpha_3(\bar{l} - \bar{y}^*)_{t-1} + \alpha_4 \Delta_1 l_{t-1}$$
$$+ \alpha_5 \Delta_4 D_t + \sum_{j=6}^{9} \alpha_j Q_{jt} + u_t \tag{21}$$

Estimation of this specification yielded equation (22):

$$\widehat{\Delta_4 c_t} = \underset{(0.005)}{0.082 Ay_t^*} - \underset{(0.05)}{0.20(c - y^*)_{t-4}} + \underset{(0.018)}{0.074(\bar{l} - \bar{y}^*)_{t-1}} + \underset{(0.07)}{0.24 \, \Delta_1 l_{t-1}}$$

$$+ \underset{(0.002)}{0.009 \, \Delta_4 D_t} - \underset{(0.025)}{0.098} - \underset{(0.004)}{0.017 Q_{1t}} - \underset{(0.003)}{0.007 Q_{2t}} - \underset{(0.003)}{0.003 Q_{3t}} \tag{22}$$

$$T = 47 \quad R^2 = 0.928 \quad s = 0.0052 \quad z_1(6) = 4.9 \quad z_3(6,38) = 0.6$$
$$z_2(8) = 19.5 \quad z_4(6) = 11.2$$

Since the $z_4(6)$ value indicated significant fourth order residual autocorrelation, the simple autoregressive form $u_t = \rho_4 u_{t-4} + \varepsilon_t$ was assumed and re-estimation provided equation (23):

$$\widehat{\Delta_4 c_t} = \underset{(0.004)}{0.083 Ay_t^*} - \underset{(0.05)}{0.18(c - y^*)_{t-4}} + \underset{(0.015)}{0.072(\bar{l} - \bar{y}^*)_{t-1}} + \underset{(0.06)}{0.22 \, \Delta_1 l_{t-1}}$$

$$+ \underset{(0.002)}{0.010 \, \Delta_4 D_t} - \underset{(0.021)}{0.094} - \underset{(0.004)}{0.016 Q_{1t}} - \underset{(0.002)}{0.007 Q_{2t}} - \underset{(0.002)}{0.003 Q_{3t}}$$

$$\hat{\rho}_4 = \underset{(0.15)}{-0.33} \tag{23}$$

$$T = 47 \quad s = 0.0050 \quad z_1(6) = 5.7 \quad z_5(5) = 4.0 \quad z_6(6,38) = 0.7$$

where z_6 is an approximate F-test of parameter constancy based on the change in s^2 when the sample size is increased. Figure 5 shows the plot of the actual data and the fit of (23), including the 6 'prediction' observations. Since $z_1(6) \simeq 6$ and $z_6 < 1$, parameter constancy is ensured when the sample is extended to include the last 6 observations and (in contrast

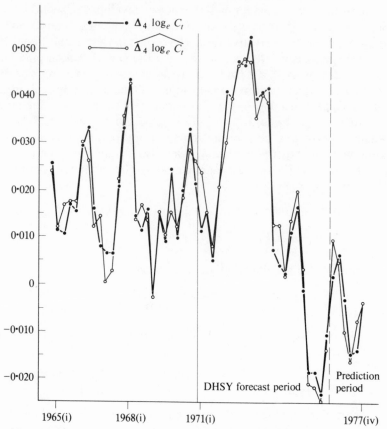

Figure 5

to (18)) s will fall; re-estimation yielded equation (24):

$$\widehat{\Delta_4 c_t} = \underset{(0.004)}{0.083 A y_t^*} - \underset{(0.04)}{0.16(c - y^*)_{t-4}} + \underset{(0.009)}{0.072(\bar{l} - \bar{y}^*)_{t-1}} + \underset{(0.06)}{0.19\,\Delta_1 l_{t-1}}$$

$$+ \underset{(0.002)}{0.009\,\Delta_4 D_t} - \underset{(0.013)}{0.091} - \underset{(0.003)}{0.015 Q_{1t}} - \underset{(0.002)}{0.007 Q_{2t}} - \underset{(0.002)}{0.004 Q_{3t}}$$

$$\hat{\rho} = \underset{(0.14)}{-0.30} \tag{24}$$

$$T = 53 \quad s = 0.0049 \quad z_5(5) = 5.2$$

In both (23) and (24), $z_5(5)$ denotes the likelihood ratio based χ^2-test of the autoregressive error 'common factor' restrictions (see Sargan, 1964; and Mizon and Hendry, 1980).

There are many interesting features of these results which deserve comment. Firstly, s is less than $\frac{1}{2}\%$ of C and even in terms of tracking the quarterly movements in the annual growth rate, the equation fits extremely well. Compared with (19) (the most comparable sample period), the s value is over 30% smaller. Further, the proportional ECM coefficient is nearly twice as large as in (19), reflecting the omitted seasonals bias of the latter, although the sum of the income change coefficients is almost identical. All of the individual coefficients are well determined and the diagnostic statistics (including the parameter constancy tests) are insignificant, yet the last 6 observations seem to 'break' a collinearity between $(\bar{l} - \bar{y}^*)_{t-1}$ and the intercept, judging by the fall in their standard errors (this could be due to the marked upturn in L_t which occurred during 1977).

Finally, given that the integral control is close to the cumulated real savings measure used in Stone (1973) and Deaton (1976) it is interesting that the R^2 of (24) (without the fourth order autoregressive error) is 0.934, similar to values previously obtained using *annual data* for changes in C_t.

Despite the many steps and approximations from the simple theory of section 2 to equations like (21), the results are readily interpretable in terms of the parameters of (5)–(7) above. The static solution of (24) (i.e. when $g = 0$) is:

$$(c - y^*) = -0.55 + 0.44(l - y^*) - 0.088Q_1 - 0.041Q_2 - 0.026Q_3$$
$$\quad\;\;(0.07)\;\;(0.08)\qquad\qquad(0.009)\qquad(0.011)\qquad(0.012)$$

$$(25)$$

Taking $b^* = 1.1$ (the mean of $(\bar{l} - \bar{y}^*)$ prior to 1970) and normalizing $\lambda_1 = 1$ yields $\lambda_2 = 0.65$ (from ϕ), $\lambda_3 = 3.9$ (from θ_3) and $\lambda_4 = 1.9$ (from θ_1); the overidentifying restrictions can be used as a consistency check and the λ_i and b^* imply $\theta_0/\theta_2 = -0.48$ as against -0.55 in (25). Note the efficiency gain in estimating ϕ relative to the solution from (20).

If the *annual* growth rate of Y is $g > 0$, the two values of θ_0/θ_2 match more closely and the term $2.7g$ must be subtracted from (25). The λ_i are hardly altered for $g = 0.025$ (the sample average was 0.022) and b^* differs from b by about 0.02%. Eliminating $(l - y^*)$ from (25) using $b^* = 1.1$ and $g = 0.025$ yields:

$$(c - y^*) = -0.22Q_1 - 0.17Q_2 - 0.16Q_3 - 0.13Q_4 \qquad (26)$$

which compares closely with the time-series shown in figure 4. If L/Y^* depended on any outside variables (such as interest rates) then these would enter (26) as a 'reduced form' effect.

The full long-run impact of $\dot{p}$ in (25) is hard to obtain, but neglecting any behavioural dependence of L/Y^* on $\dot{p}$, using $e^{b^*} = B^* = 3$ yields $c = y - 0.38\mu - \Sigma_1^4\, k_iQ_i$, where μ is the *annual* rate of inflation. This is a much smaller inflation effect than that obtained by DHSY, primarily due to the downward bias in their coefficient of $(c - y)_{t-4}$ and their omission of an ICM.

As a check on the choice of $\hat{\beta} = 0.5$, equation (24) was re-estimated using non-linear least squares to compute the optimal value of β, in an equation which set $\hat{\rho}_4$ to zero and used the quarterly sample means to compute $(C_t/K_iY_t^*)$ (denoted by $(c^a - y^{*a})_t$ below) to economize on parameters:

$$\widehat{\Delta_4 c_t} = \underset{(0.004)}{0.082 A y_t^*} - \underset{(0.04)}{0.21(c^a - y^{*a})_{t-4}} + \underset{(0.011)}{0.089(\bar{l} - \bar{y}^*)_{t-1}} + \underset{(0.05)}{0.15 \, \Delta_1 l_{t-1}}$$

$$+ \underset{(0.003)}{0.010 \, \Delta_4 D_t} - \underset{(0.018)}{0.123} \quad \underset{(0.12)}{\hat{\beta} = 0.44} \tag{27}$$

$$T = 52 \quad R^2 = 0.936 \quad s = 0.0049 \quad d = 2.04$$

(d is the Durbin–Watson statistic value). The results in (27) are consistent with the initial choice of $\hat{\beta}$ as 0.5 and suggest little bias in the quoted standard errors from conditioning on $\hat{\beta}$. Similar results were obtained when estimating equations like (27) over different sample periods (see Ungern-Sternberg, 1978) although point estimates of β were not well determined in smaller sample sizes.

Lastly, as a weak test of parameter constancy, equation (21) with $\hat{\beta} = 0.5$ was used to predict the 20 quarters on which (18) was tested:

$$\widehat{\Delta_4 c_t} = \underset{(0.009)}{0.085 A y_t^*} - \underset{(0.10)}{0.27(c - y^*)_{t-4}} + \underset{(0.043)}{0.099(\bar{l} - \bar{y}^*)_{t-1}} + \underset{(0.16)}{0.36 \, \Delta_1 l_{t-1}}$$

$$+ \underset{(0.003)}{0.010 \, \Delta_4 D_t} - \underset{(0.058)}{0.137} - \underset{(0.008)}{0.022 Q_{1t}} - \underset{(0.003)}{0.006 Q_{2t}} - \underset{(0.003)}{0.003 Q_{3t}}$$

$$\underset{(0.22)}{\hat{\rho}_4 = -0.36} \tag{28}$$

$$T = 33 \quad s = 0.0052 \quad z_1(20) = 44.4 \quad z_6(20,23) = 0.75 \quad z_5(5) = 2.1$$

In contrast to (19), there is no evidence of significant parameter changes although, as shown in table 3, the correlation structure of the main regressors altered radically between the estimation and prediction periods. Indeed, fitting (21) to *only* the last 20 observations provides the estimates (setting ρ_4 to zero given the sample size):

$$\Delta_4 c_t = \underset{(0.009)}{0.086 A y_t^*} - \underset{(0.07)}{0.17(c - y^*)_{t-4}} + \underset{(0.018)}{0.067(\bar{l} - \bar{y}^*)_{t-1}} + \underset{(0.07)}{0.12 \, \Delta_1 l_{t-1}}$$

$$+ \underset{(0.002)}{0.007 \, \Delta_4 D_t} - \underset{(0.016)}{0.085} - \underset{(0.007)}{0.017 Q_{1t}} - \underset{(0.004)}{0.010 Q_{2t}} - \underset{(0.005)}{0.009 Q_{3t}} \tag{29}$$

$$T = 20 \quad s = 0.0047 \quad R^2 = 0.97 \quad d = 1.74 \quad z_7(9,35) = 0.74$$
$$\hat{\phi} = 0.39(0.23)$$

Table 3. *Data correlations*

1964(iv)–1972(iv)	$\Delta_4 c_t$	Δy_t^*	$(c - y^*)_{t-4}$	$(\bar{l} - \bar{y}^*)_{t-1}$	$\Delta_1 l_{t-1}$
			1973(i)–1977(iv)		
$\Delta_4 c_t$		0.94	0.22	0.71	0.46
$A y_t^*$	0.85		0.25	0.56	0.41
$(c - y^*)_{t-4}$	0.18	0.22		−0.09	0.34
$(\bar{l} - \bar{y}^*)_{t-1}$	−0.25	−0.38	0.04		0.12
$\Delta_1 l_{t-1}$	0.19	0.07	−0.17	−0.15	

(where z_7 (9, 35) is the covariance F-test between $T = 53$ and the two sub-samples, all with $\rho_4 = 0$). The estimates in (28) and (29) are remarkably similar to those given in table 3 and strongly suggest that the relationship under study is *not* simply a conditional regression equation (see Richard, 1980). Supporting this contention, re-estimation of (23) using t, c_{t-1} and the lagged regressors as instrumental variables for $A y_t^*$ yielded almost identical results with $s = 0.0050$, $z_8(6) = 4.3$ (an asymptotically valid χ_6^2 test of the independence of the instruments and the error) $\hat{\phi} = 0.40$ (0.07) and $z_1(6) = 5.8$.

5 Summary and conclusions

Three extensions of the model presented by Davidson *et al.* (1978) are considered, namely integral correction mechanisms, a re-interpretation of the role of their inflation variable and a re-specification of the seasonal behaviour of consumers' expenditure on non-durables and services (C) in the UK. For the first of these, we adopt an approach similar to that of Stone (1966), (1973) (who used cumulated real savings in an annual model) which leads to the use of the liquid asset to income ratio (L/Y) in the empirical equation as a proxy for integral control. The second extension involves the recalculation of real income by subtracting a proportion of the losses on real liquid assets due to inflation ($\dot{p}$) and yields a ratio of consumption to perceived income (Y^*) which is substantially more stable than the ratio of the original series. Allowing for a seasonally varying average propensity to consume (K_i) produces a model with a steady-state solution given by:

$$C/Y^* = K_i(L/Y^*)^{0.44} \quad \text{where } Y^* = Y - \frac{1}{2}\dot{p}L \quad \text{and} \tag{30}$$

where K_i also depends on the growth rate of real income. The dynamic formulation of (30) satisfies the equation selection criteria proposed by DHSY and both simulation evidence and analysis are used to explain how they managed to choose an incorrect model (with mis-specifications not detectable by their diagnostic statistics) which nevertheless provided a reasonable approximation to (28) above over their sample period.

The results are consistent with Stone's findings and, like Deaton (1976) and Townend (1976), we confirm the importance of some cumulative measure in explaining C in the UK. In addition, the hypothesis that real income is seriously mis-measured in times of inflation is supported by the data and plays a major role in accounting for the sharp fall in C/Y during the 1970s (compare Siegel, 1979).

Strikingly similar results have also been obtained for equivalent equations using West German semi-annual data (see Ungern-Sternberg, 1978), providing strong additional support for our hypothesis concerning the negative income effects of inflation on consumers' expenditure.

Notes

1 This research was financed in part by a grant from the Social Science Research Council to the Quantitative Economics Programme at the London School of Economics. Valuable assistance from Frank Srba is gratefully acknowledged. We are indebted to Charles Bean, Angus Deaton, Robert Engle, George Hadjimatheou, Jean-Francois Richard, Tom Rothenberg, Mark Salmon and Pravin Trivedi for helpful comments on an earlier version of this paper, although we do not hold them responsible for the residual errors.

2 Strictly, the first term should be $(1 + \Delta_1 p_t)^{-1}$, the result quoted being accurate only for small values $\Delta_1 p_t$.

References

Allen, R. G. D. (1963) *Mathematical Economics*. 2nd edn. Macmillan, London.

Ball, R. J. and Drake, P. S. (1964) 'The Relationship Between Aggregate Consumption and Wealth'. *International Economic Review*, **5**, 63–81.

Bean, C. R. (1978) 'The Determination of Consumers' Expenditure in the UK'. Government Economic Service Working Paper No. 4, HM Treasury, London.

Breusch, T. S. and Pagan, A. R. (1980) 'The Lagrange Multiplier Test and its Applications to Model Specification in Econometrics', *The Review of Economic Studies*. **47**, 239–53.

Currie, D. (1979) 'Growth, Inflation and The Demand for Money : Some Features of Recent UK Money Demand Studies', Unpublished paper, Manchester University.

Davidson, J. E. H., Hendry, D. F., Srba, F. and Yeo, S. (1978) 'Econometric Modelling of the Aggregate Time-Series Relationship Between Consumers' Expenditure and Income in the United Kingdom'. *The Economic Journal*, **88**, 661–92.

Deaton, A. S. (1972) 'Wealth Effects on Consumption in a Modified Life-Cycle Model'. *The Review of Economic Studies*, **39**, 265–77.

(1976) 'Personal Consumption' in *Economic Structure and Policy*. ed. T. S. Barker, Chapman and Hall, London.

(1977) 'Involuntary Saving Through Unanticipated Inflation'. *American Economic Review*, **67**, 899–910.

Engle, R. F. (1979) 'A General Approach to the Construction of Model Diagnostics Based upon the Lagrange Multiplier Principle'. Discussion paper, London School of Economics.

Godfrey, L. C. (1978) 'Testing Against General Autoregressive and Moving Average Error Models when the Regressors Include Lagged Dependent Variables'. *Econometrica*, **46**, 1293–1301.

Hendry, D. F. (1980) 'Predictive Failure and Econometric Modelling in Macroeconomics: The Transactions Demand for Money'. Ch. 8 in *Economic Modelling*, ed. P. Ormerod, Heinemann Educational Books, London.

Hendry, D. F. and Anderson, G. J. (1977) 'Testing Dynamic Specification in Small Simultaneous Systems: An Application to a Model of Building Society Behaviour in the United Kingdom' in *Frontiers in Quantitative Economics*, vol. IIIA, ed. M.D. Intriligator, North-Holland Publishing Co., Amsterdam.

Hicks, J. R. (1939) *Value and Capital: An Enquiry into Some Fundamental Principles of Economic Theory*. 2nd edn (1950), Clarendon Press, Oxford.

London Business School (1980) 'The London Business School Quarterly Econometric Model of the United Kingdom Economy: Relationships in the Basic Model as of February, 1980. Econometric Forecasting Unit, London Business School.

Mizon, G. E. and Hendry, D. F. (1980) 'An Empirical Application and Monte Carlo Study of Tests of Dynamic Specification'. *The Review of Economic Studies*, **47**, 21–45.

Modigliani, F. (1975) 'The Life Cycle Hypothesis of Saving Twenty Years Later' in *Contemporary Issues in Economics*, ed. M. Parkin and A. R. Nobay, Manchester University Press, Manchester.

Phillips, A. W. (1954) 'Stabilisation Policy in a Closed Economy'. *The Economic Journal*, **64**, 290–323.

(1957) 'Stabilisation Policy and the Time-Forms of Lagged Responses'. *The Economic Journal*, **67**, 265–77.

Pissarides, C. A. (1978) 'Liquidity Considerations in the Theory of Consumption'. *Quarterly Journal of Economics*, **82**, 279–96.

Richard, J-F. (1980) 'Models with Several Regimes and Changes in Exogeneity'. *The Review of Economic Studies*, **47**, 1–20.

Salmon, M. (1979) 'Recursive Estimation, Parameter Variation and Misspecification : An Application to the UK Consumption Function'. Working paper, Warwick University.

Sargan, J. D. (1964) 'Wages and Prices in the United Kingdom: A Study in Econometric Methodology' in *Econometric Analysis for National Economic Planning*, ed. P. E. Hart, G. Mills and J. K. Whitaker, Butterworths Scientific Publications, London.

(1980) 'The Consumer Price Equation in the Post War British Economy: An Exercise in Equation Specification Testing'. *The Review of Economic Studies*, **47**, 113–35.

Siegel, J. J. (1979) 'Inflation Induced Distortions in Government and Private Saving Statistics'. *Review of Economics and Statistics*, **61**, 83–90.

Stone, R. (1966) 'Spending and Saving in Relation to Income and Wealth'. *L'industria*, **4**, 471–99.

(1973) 'Personal Spending and Saving in Postwar Britain' in *Economic Structure and Development* (essays in honour of Jan Tinbergen), ed. H. C. Bos, H. Linneman and P. de Wolff, North-Holland Publishing Co., Amsterdam.

Townend, J. C. (1976) 'The Personal Saving Ratio'. *Bank of England Quarterly Bulletin*, **16**, 53–61.

Ungern-Sternberg, T. von (1978) 'Real Balance Effects and Negative Income: The Rise in the Savings Ratio'. Unpublished paper, University of Bonn.

Wall, K. D., Preston, A. J., Bray, J. W. and Peston, M. H. (1975) 'Estimates of a Simple Control Model of the UK Economy' in *Modelling the Economy*, ed. G. A. Renton, Heinemann Educational Books, London.

Zellner, A., Huang, D. S. and Chau, L. C. (1965) 'Further Analysis of the Short-run Consumption Function with Emphasis on the Role of Liquid Assets'. *Econometrica*, **33**, 571–81.

Other aspects: fertility and labour supply

Introduction to part four

One of the most significant developments in economics over the past twenty years has been the increasing extent to which economists have been prepared to apply the basic tools of consumer theory to areas other than just the demand for goods. A particularly notable example is the analysis of labour supply, where utility theory has been successfully used in the empirical analysis of a wide range of phenomena, including the supply decisions of primary and secondary workers, the decision whether or not to participate, and the type of behaviour which results from the complex rules of modern tax and social security systems. For a discussion of this material see, e.g. Killingsworth (1981) or Deaton and Muellbauer (1980, chapter 11). More generally, the 'characteristics' or household production model has been applied to a wide variety of economic problems. Amongst the earliest examples is Gorman's famous 1956 paper on eggs, although it was Lancaster (1966a, b) whose work firmly established the methodology in the literature. In part one of this volume, the chapter by Theil and Laitinen can be interpreted as a characteristics model with the transformed goods as the characteristics, but much wider applications are possible. In particular, the model has been applied to the analysis of human capital formation, of fertility, of the use of time, of sexual and racial discrimination, of quality, and of health, to name only a few topics. The remarkable volume by Becker (1976) gives an excellent overview of this literature as well as providing some of its best examples. At its worst, this literature provides a laboured and artificial description of phenomena with seemingly better explanations, but, in the right hands, the approach is a powerful tool for generating fresh insights and new research problems. Particularly important is the aspect emphasized by Stigler and Becker (1977), that the household production approach explains differences between individuals by objective (and in principle observable) differences in the circumstances which they face, rather than by subjective and unobservable differences in tastes.

The two chapters in this section are both concerned with labour supply within the wider context of household production. The chapter by Anthony Atkinson and Nicholas Stern is particularly notable in that it is one of the first to use the microeconomic data provided by the British annual Family Expenditure Survey. This is one of the very few data sets in the world which combines labour supply and commodity demand data so that both phenomena can be studied simultaneously at the level of the

262

individual household. The model which Atkinson and Stern use is essentially that of Becker (1965) whereby leisure time has no value of its own but is required for the consumption of goods. Hence, work has no direct disutility but more work limits the opportunities for consumption. This can be incorporated into the standard model of demand for goods if to each price we add a quantity equal to the product of the wage rate and the time cost per unit of the good. The authors do this within the linear expenditure system and find, on their data, that significant time costs are estimated for alcohol and significant time *savings* for purchases of services. The labour supply curve implicit in the results is a complex one but has the unusual feature of being backward sloping for low wage rates and forward sloping for high wage rates. These results are no doubt provisional, but they illustrate some of the potential of a data set as rich as the Family Expenditure Survey.

The final chapter, by Marc Nerlove and Assaf Razin is an excellent example of the application of household production theory to the analysis of fertility. In particular, the authors analyse the determinants of child spacing, the average time between successive births, and its influence on the amount of time spent in the labour force by the mother. Once again, an extraordinarily rich data set is available, in this case a Canadian sample survey which obtained information not only on the usual socio-economic variables, but also on tastes, e.g. on religious attitudes and attitudes towards contraception. The theory which Nerlove and Razin develop predicts a negative association between time spent working outside the home and the average interval between the births of children. The data, as so often, are ambiguous, but there is at least some support for this and other aspects of the model.

One of the hallmarks of Sir Richard Stone's work has been his comprehensive vision of a complete interlocking set of economic, social and demographic accounts in which econometric models provide the driving mechanism. His own work has filled in many of the slots in this system, see [110], [112], [123], [129], [130], [131], [134], [135], [137], [138], [139], [142], [143], [146], [148] in particular for the social and demographic side. The economics and econometrics of fertility, as represented here, have an important part in further closing the system.

References for introduction to part four

Becker, G. S. (1965), 'A theory of the allocation of time', *Economic Journal*, **75**, pp. 493–517.

(1976). *The economic approach to human behavior*, University of Chicago Press.

Deaton, A. S. and J. Muellbauer (1980), *Economics and Consumer Behavior*, Cambridge University Press, New York.

Gorman, W. M. (1956), 'A possible procedure for analysing quality differentials in the egg market', London School of Economics, mimeo.

Killingsworth, M. R. (1981), *Neoclassical models of labor supply*, Cambridge University Press, New York forthcoming.

Lancaster, K. J. (1966a), 'A new approach to consumer theory', *Journal of Political Economy*, **74**, pp. 132–57.

　(1966b), 'Change and innovation in the technology of consumption', *American Economic Review*, **56**, pp. 14–23.

Stigler, G. J. and G. S. Becker (1977), 'De gustibus non est disputandum', *American Economic Review*, **67**, pp. 76–90.

10 On labour supply and commodity demands[1]

A. B. ATKINSON,
N. H. STERN,
IN CONJUNCTION WITH J. GOMULKA

1 Introduction

The study of labour supply and commodity demands has, for the most part, proceeded on separate lines. There has been an extensive literature, much of it inspired by the work of Sir Richard Stone (see, for example, Stone 1954), on the estimation of commodity demand systems; and there has been a recent growth of interest in labour supply equations. However, there have been relatively few attempts to estimate jointly labour supply and commodity demand relationships. At a theoretical level, the main contribution to linking these two aspects of household decision-making has been in the work on household production. The 'activities' approach, developed particularly in Becker's theory of the allocation of time (1965), provides considerable insight, but has not been widely adopted in empirical research. In this paper we build on Becker's theoretical work and develop the activities approach as the basis for an econometric investigation of the joint determination of labour supply and commodity demand in the United Kingdom.

We begin in section 2 by discussing the household allocation of income and time, and relating it to the theory of rationing. To illustrate the extension of the standard consumer demand model, we take in section 3 the case of the linear expenditure system. This provides the basis for the empirical work, which uses data on expenditure by commodity category, and hours of work, contained in the Family Expenditure Survey for the United Kingdom. This source is described briefly in section 4, where we also discuss the estimation procedure. The results of estimating a simple form of the household activity model, with a Stone–Geary utility function, are presented in section 5. Finally, section 6 contains concluding remarks.

The chapter owes a great deal to the earlier literature and consists, in large part, of assembling already existing building blocks. There are, however, three features which should be stressed. First, by developing the

265

household activity framework, we are able to throw light on a number of issues relevant both to labour supply and to other subjects, such as the treatment of quantity constraints discussed in recent macroeconomic models (e.g. Muellbauer and Portes, 1978). Secondly, we have explored how far the extension to incorporate activities allows greater flexibility to the linear expenditure system (LES), providing an alternative to the adoption of more general functional forms for the utility function. Thirdly, in contrast to earlier studies (e.g. Abbott and Ashenfelter, 1976) based on time series, we have employed cross-section data. This approach has evident disadvantages, in that inferences can be made about price effects only on the basis of a strong theoretical specification, such as that embodied in the linear expenditure system. On the other hand, the Family Expenditure Survey is a rich source of micro-data which has as yet been too little exploited.

2 Theoretical framework

2.1 Household production model

We begin by considering the model without explicit treatment of time, in order to bring out its relation with the literature. The basic insight of the household production function approach is that *goods* purchased on the market are desired not for their own sake but as inputs into the production of *commodities*. Thus a household maximises $u(c)$, where c denotes the m-dimensional vector of commodities, subject to the household production function. The demand for goods is then a derived demand, based on the underlying preferences regarding commodities.

The properties of the demand functions depend on those of the production function (see Gorman, 1976; and Pollak and Wachter, 1975), and a number of special cases have been studied. Since these have not always been clearly distinguished in the literature, it may be helpful to clarify their nature with the aid of the constant elasticity of substitution example used by Gorman. Household consumption of the jth commodity is given by:

$$c_j(z, \sigma) \equiv \left[\sum_i a_{ij}^{-1} z_i^{1-1/\sigma} \right]^{1/(1-1/\sigma)} \tag{2.1}$$

where z is an n-dimensional vector. The characteristics approach popularised by Lancaster (1971)[2] is the special case where σ tends to infinity. If x is an n-dimensional vector of goods, then

$$c_j = \sum_i a_{ij}^{-1} x_i \tag{2.2}$$

Each unit of good i generates a_{ij}^{-1} units of characteristic j, and the demand functions may be obtained directly by substituting from (2.2) into the utility function and maximising with respect to x_i. The second special case, and the one on which we concentrate in this paper, is $c_j(x_j, 0)$ where x_j is the vector of inputs into the jth commodity and $x = \Sigma_j\, x_j$:

$$c_j = \min_i\, [a_{ij}^{-1}\, x_{ij}] \tag{2.3}$$

In this case there is no joint production, in contrast to the 'complete jointness' of Lancaster, and the elasticity of substitution is zero rather than infinite. This case we refer to as the 'Becker' model, since it is employed by him when discussing the allocation of time (1965). (It is also discussed briefly in Lancaster (1971, pp. 47–9).)

The two special cases may in fact be seen to be polar opposites in the sense that with the characteristics model the commodities are determined by x and the prices must satisfy an inequality constraint:

$$c = B'x \quad \text{and} \quad p' \geq r'B' \tag{2.4}$$

where B denotes the $n \times m$ matrix $[a_{ij}^{-1}]$, p denotes the vector of goods prices, and r is the vector of shadow prices associated with the commodities. The relationship between the prices and shadow prices in (2.4) must hold at the optimum, with equality where the good is purchased. With the Becker model, we have the conditions

$$x \geq Ac \quad \text{and} \quad r' = p'A \tag{2.5}$$

where A denotes the $n \times m$ matrix $[a_{ij}]$. The inequality translates the production constraint into requirements of goods and at the optimum holds with equality where the good has a strictly positive price. The price relationship converts the goods prices into commodity prices in a natural way.[3]

In concentrating on the Becker version, we are not asserting its superiority over the characteristics approach or the more general formulation (2.1). The main function of this special case is to provide a simple framework within which we can explore the properties of the model. Nonetheless we do feel that the representation captures some important features of reality, particularly with regard to labour supply, to which we now turn.

2.2 Labour supply and leisure

We have defined m 'commodities', or, as we call them from this point, 'activities'. We now introduce the allocation of time. First, each consumption activity uses time, so that, in addition to the input of goods $a_{ij}c_j$ into activity j, we have a time requirement t_jc_j. For most activities it is natural to think of t_j being positive, but 'time-saving' activities are possible.

Secondly, we introduce an activity, $j = 0$, called 'work'. This involves a unit of time per unit of activity ($t_0 = 1$) and produces income. If we define work to be good 0 (as well as activity 0), then we have additional input coefficients: $a_{00} = 1$, $a_{i0} = a_{0j} = 0$ for $i = 1, ..., n, j = 1, ..., m$ (i.e. the other activities do not involve 'pure work'). The price associated with good 0 is minus the wage rate ($-w$). The level of the work activity is referred to interchangeably as c_0 and l, the former being compact, and the latter mnemonic, notation.

Finally, the household is assumed to be endowed with T units of time and M of unearned income. It behaves as though it were a single decision-maker maximising $u(c)$ subject to

$$r.c = p'Ac \le M$$

$$t.c \quad\quad \le T$$

$$c \quad\quad \ge 0 \tag{2.6}$$

This formulation is a fairly flexible one, and captures a relatively wide range of possibilities. For many types of consumption behaviour it appears a natural way to treat the problem. Thus the activity 'playing golf' requires golf clubs and balls, as well as a considerable amount of time. Pure 'leisure' would require time only and no other inputs, but, apart from sunbathing naked, it is hard to think of an activity which requires no complementary inputs. Finally, we do not allow the time spent on activities to enter the utility function independently (see Pollak and Wachter, 1975).

2.3 Where labour does not enter the utility function

The consumer's maximisation problem (2.6) is an example of the standard problem of rationing with two constraints, instead of the single budget constraint in usual consumer demand theory. Where, however, labour does not enter the utility function, the problem can be reduced to a single constraint, as Becker (1965) pointed out. Writing c_0 as l, the consumer maximises $u(c_1, ..., c_m)$ subject to

$$\sum_{j=1}^{m} r_j c_j \le M + wl \tag{2.7a}$$

$$\sum_{j=1}^{m} t_j c_j \le T - l \tag{2.7b}$$

We assume that $l, c_1, ..., c_m > 0$. Both constraints (2.7a) and 2.7b) bind at the optimum, provided that the consumer is not satiated and at least one of the r_i, $i = 1, ..., m$, is strictly positive. From (2.7a and b) we can derive the single constraint:

$$\sum_{j=1}^{m} q_j c_j \equiv \sum_{j=1}^{m} (r_j + wt_j)c_j = M + wT \tag{2.8}$$

where q_j denotes the total price of activity j, which we assume is strictly positive:

$$q_j \equiv r_j + wt_j = \sum_{i=1}^{n} a_{ij}p_i + wt_j \tag{2.9}$$

The maximisation of $u(c_1, \ldots, c_m)$ subject to (2.8) is the usual representation of the consumer problem, the only difference being in the definition of the total price, q_j. In a formal sense the model is no different, and we can apply the standard theory of demand, a fact which is worth emphasizing in view of the claims sometimes made to the contrary. That we can apply standard results is a considerable analytical convenience, and allows us to see more clearly how the *interpretation* of the results differs in the present case.

In order to illustrate this, we define the expenditure function $E(q, u)$, where q is the m vector $(q_1, \ldots, q_m)$. The compensated demand function for the jth activity is

$$c_j(q, u) = E_j(q, u) \tag{2.10}$$

where E_j denotes the derivative of E with respect to q_j. The properties of the compensated demand functions follow directly. In particular, since

$$l(q, u) = T - \sum_{j=1}^{m} t_j c_j(q, u) \tag{2.11}$$

the compensated derivative

$$\frac{\partial l(q, u)}{\partial w} = -\sum_{j=1}^{m} t_j \frac{\partial c_j}{\partial w}$$

$$= -\sum_{j=1}^{m} t_j \left(\sum_{k=1}^{m} \frac{\partial c_j}{\partial q_k} \frac{\partial q_k}{\partial w} \right) \tag{2.12}$$

From (2.9),

$$\frac{\partial q_k}{\partial w} = t_k \tag{2.13}$$

so that the compensated labour derivative is

$$\frac{\partial l(q, u)}{\partial w} = -\sum_{j=1}^{m} \sum_{k=1}^{m} t_j E_{jk} t_k \tag{2.14}$$

where E_{jk} is $\partial^2 E / \partial q_j \partial q_k$. Then, by the concavity of the expenditure function, the right-hand side is non-negative. A rise in w increases the price of activities where $t_j > 0$, but this indirect effect in favour of the less time-intensive activities cannot offset the direct effect. This illustrates the fact that the time allocation model is a less radical departure from the standard theory than Becker on occasion suggests.

2.4 Theory of rationing

The assumption that $\partial u/\partial c_0 \equiv 0$ is crucial to the Becker formulation, for only then does the substitution of the time constraint into the income constraint reduce the problem to a single constraint form. The role of this assumption is not taken into account in Becker's claim (1965, p. 497, n. 1) that the problem is not the same as that discussed in the theory of rationing. Outside the special case $\partial u/\partial c_0 \equiv 0$, we have a genuine example of the theory of rationing,[4] and we discuss below the interpretation of our model in terms of that theory. Note also that the introduction of the time constraint allows the possibility that $(\partial u/\partial c_0) > 0$, i.e. at the margin work gives utility. This could not happen if income were the only constraint, since an increase in labour would always be feasible, and hence, at the optimum, $\partial u/\partial c_0$ could not be positive.

We assume that both income and time constraints are binding at the consumer's optimum (otherwise we are back with the standard problem). The consumer maximises $u(c_0, \ldots, c_m)$ subject to

$$r.c = M$$
$$t.c = T \tag{2.15}$$

which may be written as

$$Rc = y \tag{2.15'}$$

where y is the vector (M, T), and R is the $2 \times (m + 1)$ matrix whose kjth element is the price of the jth activity in the kth constraint. This formulation is used by Diamond and Yaari (1972), who derive the basic results on compensated demand functions.

Where there is more than one constraint, we have to specify the constraint in which the compensation occurs. Let $|_{M-\text{comp}}$ denote a compensated derivative where utility is held constant by changing M, with a corresponding notation where compensation is through changes in T. Diamond and Yaari show that a change in a price in the M-constraint can be decomposed as in the standard Slutsky equations, where the compensated derivative is defined with respect to compensation in M. These substitution terms have the properties of symmetry, and non-positivity of the own-price terms. In particular, we have[5] $\partial l/\partial w \mid_{M-\text{comp}} \geq 0$, which is a generalisation of the result in the previous section. Moreover, with

$\partial u/\partial l > 0$, it is quite possible that the income effect on l of a rise in w is positive, which would mean that there is no ambiguity in the labour supply curve – a situation consistent with the observations of Scitovsky (1976, pp. 97–100) about the rising working hours and rising wages of professional and other workers.

Similar results hold for compensated demands in terms of the time constraint. Thus $\partial l/\partial t_0 \mid_{T-\text{comp}} < 0$ (where t_0 is the time input into a unit of work), in other words a time-compensated increase in the time required to perform labour results in less work. Moreover, if we define λ_M, λ_T as the Lagrange multipliers associated with the two constraints in the maximisation problem, then the relationship between the two forms of compensation is given by (Diamond and Yaari, equation (18)):

$$\frac{1}{\lambda_M} \frac{\partial c_j}{\partial r_k}\bigg|_{M-\text{comp}} = \frac{1}{\lambda_T} \frac{\partial c_j}{\partial t_k}\bigg|_{T-\text{comp}} \tag{2.16}$$

If goods are substitutes in one constraint, they are substitutes in all constraints. Results such as those concerning the effects of a rise in w on goods with different time intensities can be extended therefore to the effects of time-compensated changes in t_0, the time required for work, on the demand for the same goods.

From the Lagrangian for the problem we have the first-order condition (where we suppose $l > 0$ at the optimum):

$$\frac{\partial u}{\partial l} = \lambda_T\, t_o - \lambda_M\, w \tag{2.17}$$

In the case $\partial u/\partial l \equiv 0$, this gives the relationship between λ_T and λ_M which allows us to reduce the problem to a single constraint. More generally, the shadow price of time evaluated in terms of income is:

$$\hat{w} \equiv \frac{\lambda_T}{\lambda_M} = \frac{w}{t_0} + \frac{1}{t_0} \frac{1}{\lambda_M} \frac{\partial u}{\partial l} \tag{2.18}$$

Where work is intrinsically valued or disliked, this departs from the effective wage w/t_0. Differentiating the Lagrangian with respect to c_j yields the conditions

$$\frac{\partial u/\partial c_j}{\partial u/\partial c_k} = \frac{r_j + \hat{w}t_j}{r_k + \hat{w}t_k} \tag{2.19}$$

In other words the demand for activities is determined by the prices $r_j + \hat{w}t_j$, where the time input is valued at the 'virtual wage', $\hat{w}$. In contrast to the formulation of Becker this does not in general equal the wage where $\partial u/\partial l \neq 0$. We can interpret $\hat{w}$ as the wage rate which would induce the consumer voluntarily to satisfy the time constraint (the idea of using marginal rates of substitution at the optimum as 'virtual prices' was advanced by Rothbarth (1940–41) – for a recent discussion, see Neary and Roberts (1978)).

The formulation as a rationing problem provides a natural way to incorporate other constraints. The most important is probably that on the quantity of labour which can be supplied. Suppose that the constraint is written $l \leq \bar{L}$. This is equivalent to expanding the R matrix to take the form (with $t_0 = 1$):

$$
\begin{bmatrix}
-w & r_1 & \ldots & r_m \\
1 & t_1 & \ldots & t_m \\
1 & 0 & \ldots & 0
\end{bmatrix}
\tag{2.20}
$$

(with $y = M, T, \bar{L}$) and we can apply the analysis as before. In particular, the marginal rates of substitution are given by (2.19), where the virtual wage is now (with $t_0 = 1$):

$$
\hat{w} = \frac{\lambda_T}{\lambda_M} = w + \frac{\partial u}{\partial l} \frac{1}{\lambda_M} - \frac{\lambda_L}{\lambda_M}
\tag{2.21}
$$

where λ_L is the Lagrange multiplier associated with the constraint ($l \leq \bar{L}$). This then provides a further reason why the virtual wage may depart from w; even if $\partial u / \partial l \equiv 0$, where the labour constraint is binding, $\lambda_L > 0$ and $\hat{w} < w$. Where all three constraints are binding, we can solve by substituting $l = \bar{L}$. It should be noted that $\bar{L}$ enters both the income constraint ($M + w\bar{L}$) and the time constraint ($T - \bar{L}$).

3 Linear expenditure system

3.1 The Stone–Geary utility function

The Stone–Geary utility function provides a natural starting point for the empirical implementation of the model described in section 2. We begin by considering the situation where labour may enter the utility function and there are constraints on labour supply. The household maximizes

$$
u(c) = \sum_{j=0}^{m} \beta_j \log (c_j - \gamma_j)
\tag{3.1}
$$

subject to

$$
r.c \leq M
$$
$$
t.c \leq T
$$
$$
l \leq \bar{L}
\tag{3.2}
$$

The parameters β_j are assumed to be non-negative for $j = 1, \ldots, m$, but may be negative for activity zero (work). We normalize[6] by setting $\sum_0^m \beta_j = 1$. We assume that the variables c, l are all strictly positive at the optimum. Forming the Lagrangian

$$u(c) - \lambda_M(r.c - M) - \lambda_T(t.c - T) - \lambda_L(l - \bar{L}) \tag{3.3}$$

we have first-order conditions

$$\frac{\beta_j}{c_j - \gamma_j} = \lambda_M r_j + \lambda_T t_j \quad j = 1, \ldots, m \tag{3.4a}$$

$$\frac{\beta_0}{l - \gamma_0} = -\lambda_M w + \lambda_T + \lambda_L \tag{3.4b}$$

Throughout the discussion we assume that the income constraint is binding (and $\lambda_M > 0$), so that (3.4) may be written (where $\hat{w}$ is as defined in (2.21) with $t_0 = 1$)

$$c_j = \gamma_j + (1/\lambda_M) \left[\frac{\beta_j}{r_j + t_j\hat{w}} \right] \tag{3.5a}$$

$$l = \gamma_0 + (1/\lambda_M) \left[\frac{\beta_0}{\hat{w} - w + \lambda_L/\lambda_M} \right] \tag{3.5b}$$

Hence

$$r.c = r.\gamma + 1/\lambda_M \left[\sum_1^m \frac{\beta_j r_j}{r_j + t_j\hat{w}} - \frac{\beta_0 w}{\hat{w} - w + \lambda_L/\lambda_M} \right] = M \tag{3.6}$$

We now consider the form of the demand functions under the different regimes which arise depending on which constraints are binding:

Labour and time constraints binding. From (3.5a) and the income constraint

$$1/\lambda_M \left[\sum_1^m \frac{\beta_j r_j}{r_j + t_j\hat{w}} \right] = M + w\bar{L} - \sum_1^m r_j\gamma_j \tag{3.7}$$

We obtain a generalization of the standard expression for the linear expenditure system, with expenditures determined by

$$r_j c_j = r_j\gamma_j + \mu_j \left(M + w\bar{L} - \sum_{j=1}^m r_j\gamma_j \right) \tag{3.8}$$

where

$$\mu_j \equiv \frac{\beta_j r_j}{r_j + t_j\hat{w}} \bigg/ \left(\sum_1^m \frac{\beta_j r_j}{r_j + t_j\hat{w}} \right) \tag{3.8a}$$

The marginal propensities to consume out of 'supernumerary' income (μ_j)

are now functions of the prices (r_j) and the virtual wage ($\hat{w}$), rather than constants as in the standard case (obtained by setting $t_j = 0$, for all $j = 1, ..., m$). The virtual wage depends on the Lagrange multiplier on the time constraint; if this constraint is not binding, then $\hat{w} = 0$ and we again have the standard linear expenditure system.

Labour constraint not binding. We suppose now that $\lambda_L = 0$. If the time constraint is also slack, then we are again back to the standard problem. Where the time constraint is binding, then the expenditure equations can be solved using (3.6):

$$r_j c_j = r_j \gamma_j + \mu_j' \left(M + w\gamma_0 - \sum_{j=1}^{m} r_j \gamma_j \right) \tag{3.9}$$

where

$$\mu_j' = \frac{\beta_j r_j}{r_j + t_j \hat{w}} \Bigg/ \left(\sum_{1}^{m} \frac{\beta_j r_j}{r_j + t_j \hat{w}} - \frac{\beta_0 w}{\hat{w} - w} \right) \tag{3.9a}$$

The virtual wage depends again on the Lagrange multiplier associated with the time constraint.

Labour constraint not binding; labour does not enter utility function. In the 'Becker' case, where $\beta_0 = 0$, $\gamma_0 = 0$ (and the labour constraint is not binding), we can eliminate l between the constraints, and use the fact that the virtual wage is now equal to w. Writing $q_j = r_j + wt_j$, the budget constraint is (from (2.8))

$$\sum_{1}^{m} q_j c_j = M + wT \tag{3.10}$$

From (3.5a)

$$q_j c_j = q_j \gamma_j + \beta_j / \lambda_M \tag{3.11}$$

Hence

$$1/\lambda_M = M + wT - \sum_{1}^{m} q_j \gamma_j \tag{3.12}$$

and

$$r_j c_j = r_j \gamma_j + \mu_j''(M + wT - \sum_{1}^{m} q_j \gamma_j) \tag{3.13}$$

where

$$\mu_j'' = \frac{\beta_j r_j}{r_j + t_j w} \tag{3.13a}$$

The three forms of the demand functions given by equations (3.8), (3.9) and (3.13) provide an interesting comparison. In each case the demand system is more flexible than the standard linear expenditure system, in that the marginal propensities to consume depend on the ratio of the goods price (r_j) to the total price of each activity, rather than being constant. The relationship between r_j and w, or $\hat{w}$, is clearly important when using cross-section data. The comparison also brings out the considerable simplification provided by the Becker assumption, where the labour constraint is not binding. This effectively allows us to replace the unobserved virtual wage, $\hat{w}$, by the actual wage. For this reason we have concentrated in the empirical work on this formulation. We should, however, emphasize that this is not because we believe constraints to be unimportant; indeed a major aim of subsequent empirical work is to treat the constrained case.

3.2 The activity matrix

From this point we concentrate on the Becker formulation, with $\beta_0 = \gamma_0 = 0$ and labour not constrained. The observed evidence relates to purchases of goods, not to the consumption of activities. Following the formulation set out in section 2.1, the prices and quantities are related by (where the p_i are all positive)

$$x = Ac \quad \text{and} \quad r' = p'A$$

Thus

$$r_j = \sum_{i=1}^{n} p_i a_{ij} \tag{3.14}$$

and from (3.13) the implied demands for goods

$$x_i = \sum_{j=1}^{m} a_{ij}\gamma_j + \left(\sum_{j=1}^{m} \left[\frac{a_{ij}\beta_j}{\left(\sum_{k=1}^{n} p_k a_{kj} + t_j w\right)}\right]\right) \left(M + wT - \sum_{1}^{m} q_j\gamma_j\right)$$

$$i = 1, \ldots, n \tag{3.15}$$

This contains the following unknown parameters: a_{ij}, γ_j, β_j, t_j and T. Where m is of any sizeable order, there would be considerable difficulties in attempting to estimate all these parameters. We consider therefore special cases, starting from the standard model.

The standard model with variable labour supply (see Abbott and Ashenfelter (1976)) is given by the diagonal activity matrix ($m = n$, $a_{ij} = 0$ for $i \neq j$, $a_{ii} = 1$), and zero time requirements, $t_i = 0$ for $i = 1, \ldots, n - 1$, where we interpret the nth activity as pure leisure, requiring no goods and one unit of time ($a_{in} = a_{nj} = 0$, for all i, j, $t_n = 1$). This gives the conventional demand functions for goods (the dimensionality of which is reduced now to $n - 1$):

$$p_i x_i = p_i \gamma_i + \beta_i \left(M + wT' - \sum_{j=1}^{n-1} p_j \gamma_j \right) \quad \text{for} \quad i = 1, ..., n - 1 \tag{3.16}$$

where $T' = T - \gamma_n$, and the budget constraint implies the labour supply equation (using the fact that $\beta_n = 1 - \Sigma_1^{n-1} \beta_i$):

$$wl = (1 - \beta_n)wT' - \beta_n \left(M - \sum_{j=1}^{n-1} p_j \gamma_j \right) \tag{3.17}$$

With the cross-section data used here, where we assume no variation in prices, the model estimated is:

$$p_i x_i = h_{0i} + h_{1i}(M + wT') \quad \text{for} \quad i = 1, ..., n - 1 \tag{3.18}$$

The coefficients to be estimated are the h and T' and the exogenous variables are w and M. The coefficients h_{1i} allow us to determine β_i for all i (β_n being determined from the normalization). Similarly, the terms $p_i \gamma_i$ can be determined from:

$$\sum_{1}^{n-1} h_{0i} = \left(\sum_{1}^{n-1} p_j \gamma_j \right) \left(1 - \sum_{1}^{n-1} \beta_i \right) = \beta_n \sum_{1}^{n-1} p_j \gamma_j \tag{3.19a}$$

and

$$p_i \gamma_i = h_{0i} + \beta_i \left(\sum_{1}^{n-1} p_j \gamma_j \right) \tag{3.19b}$$

That one can estimate the price elasticities from cross-section data with no price variation is of course a product of the tight specification implied by the linear expenditure system. The restrictive nature of the assumptions which allow this are discussed in Deaton (1974).

In relaxing the strong assumptions of the standard model, the first step is to introduce the time requirements, allowing t_i to be non-zero for $i = 1$, ..., $n - 1$. This in itself makes the model considerably richer – and adds to the complexity of the estimation process. It seems necessary therefore to maintain, at least initially, some simplifying assumptions about the activity matrix. These could take the form of limiting the dimensionality of m, and it may be noted that the expenditure equations are ratios of polynomials of order m. Alternatively, and this is the approach adopted here, we can retain the diagonality assumption. Among other things, this has the advantage that the preceding model is directly obtainable as a special case.

With the introduction of the time requirement, and with diagonal A (for

$i = 1, ..., n - 1$), the demand functions are:

$$p_i x_i = p_i \gamma_i + \frac{\beta_i p_i}{p_i + t_i w} \left(M + wT'' - \sum_{j=1}^{n-1} p_j \gamma_j \right)$$

$$\text{for} \quad i = 1, 2, ..., (n - 1) \quad (3.20)$$

where $T'' = T - \gamma_n - \sum_{j=1}^{n-1} t_j \gamma_j$

Note that (3.16) is the special case of (3.20) where $t_i = 0$, $i = 1, 2, ...,$ $(n - 1)$. The labour supply equation is implied by the budget constraint:

$$wl = - \left(M + wT'' - \sum_{1}^{n-1} p_j \gamma_j \right) \left(\sum_{1}^{n-1} \frac{\beta_j w}{p_j/t_j + w} + \beta_n \right) + wT'' \quad (3.21)$$

where we have used the normalization $\sum_{i-1}^{n} \beta_i = 1$. With the cross-section data, the model estimated is:

$$p_i x_i = h_{2i} + \frac{h_{3i}(M + wT'' + h_4)}{1 + h_{5i}w} \quad \text{for} \quad i = 1, 2, ..., n - 1 \quad (3.22)$$

The coefficients to be estimated are the h and T'' and the exogenous variables are w and M. From h_{3i}, h_{5i} and h_{2i} we obtain estimates of β_i, t_i/p_i and $p_i \gamma_i$ respectively. Again, therefore, the key parameters are identified, although we have the additional constraint that

$$- \sum_{1}^{n-1} h_{2i} = h_4 \quad (3.22a)$$

As in the standard linear expenditure system, we can calculate a full set of price responses. In contrast to that case, however, we are observing variation (with w) in the 'full' price of activities.

3.3 Estimation of the LES/diagonal system

In what follows we concentrate on the estimation of system (3.22), based on the Stone–Geary utility function with the diagonal activity matrix, and on the comparison with the standard system (3.18).

In estimating the equations we assume that there is an additive stochastic term ε_i. In view of the budget constraint, for a given observation, the stochastic terms in the expenditure equations must sum to the stochastic term in the earnings equation. It follows that the variance–covariance matrix of the error terms for the full expenditure and earnings system is singular (Barten, 1969). Accordingly, we delete one equation from the system, and for this purpose the most convenient is the earnings equation.[7] The assumption made concerning the remaining equations is that ε_i is normally distributed with variance σ_i^2, and that cov $(\varepsilon_i, \varepsilon_j) = 0$ for $i \neq j$. This assumption implies that the errors are uncorrelated across expenditure equations but positively correlated with the error in earnings. Thus if a few hours more are worked than were anticipated, the extra earnings are spread across goods in the manner described by the co-variance terms. If one equation has to be singled out in this way, then la-bour supply may be the appropriate one; however, we plan to consider more general specifications of the covariance matrix in subsequent work.

More broadly, the mere addition of an error term is unsatisfactory, and we regard it solely as a preliminary step. The stochastic specification should be related to the underlying economic model. In particular, even if the model correctly portrays the behaviour of an individual household, we should expect there to be unobserved variation across households arising from (i) differences in tastes, (ii) differences in endowment of time, (iii) differential impact of constraints on labour supply, and (iv) transitory de-viations from desired purchases. It is also possible that observed house-hold characteristics may influence household consumption patterns. These are denoted by a vector K which is assumed to enter $p_j \gamma_j$ lin-early : e.g. the minimum consumption needs depend on family size.

The estimation of the equations (3.22) with the errors in different equa-tions distributed independently and normally is by maximum likelihood, taking account of the cross-equation constraints. The numerical proce-dure used is described in the next section, after a brief account of the data.

4 Data and estimation procedure

4.1 Family expenditure survey

The Family Expenditure Survey (FES) is a continuous sample survey carried out in the United Kingdom by the Office of Population Censuses and Surveys on behalf of the Department of Employment. The ef-fective sample in 1973 (the year used here) was around 10,500 households and the response rate was 68%. The main purpose of the survey is to col-lect information for the annual adjustment of the weights used in the Re-tail Price Index, but it contains a great deal of other data. (For a descrip-tion, see Kemsley (1969) and Stark (1978).) The information used here is of three main types:

Expenditure data. Evidence on expenditure is collected partly by inter-view and partly by records kept by individual members of the household (participants maintain a detailed 'diary' of all expenditure during a 14 day period). The data used are the total household expenditures from that diary[8] on nine broad commodity groups: (1) food, (2) alcoholic drink, (3) tobacco, (4) clothing and footwear, (5) durable household goods, (6) other goods, (7) transport and vehicles, (8) services, (9) 'composite' (see below). (We have not tried to explain directly expenditure on housing, fuel, light and power. Expenditure on these items goes into the 'composite' category (see below).)

Income data. Evidence on income from different sources and hours of work relates both to the most recent pay period and to 'normal' income and hours. Our wage variable is taken as the normal hourly wage of the head of household, calculated by dividing normal earnings per week by normal working hours.[9] Unearned income of the head is calculated as the net income of the household excluding the earnings of the head; it includes all unearned income, social security benefits and earnings of other family members. The household is assumed to act as if the head makes all the expenditure decisions and decides how much to work, taking the earnings of other household members as fixed. (A fuller treatment of household decision making is clearly necessary.)

Composite. The 'composite' expenditure category is defined as total unearned income of the head of household, plus 0.675 times gross earnings, plus the cash value of tax allowances less the sum of expenditure on the other eight categories. (The rationale is explained below.)

Household characteristics. The FES contains a great deal of information on household characteristics which seem likely to affect the pattern of expenditure.

4.2 Budget constraint and choice of sub-sample

In our empirical work here we have concentrated on the subsample of households with male heads (aged 18–64) in employment. These households are likely to pay income tax, are liable for National Insurance contributions, and may receive social security benefits in addition to their earnings. They may also be receiving income-related benefits in kind, such as rent rebates. As a result, the budget constraint is likely to depart considerably from textbook linearity. This is an aspect which has been studied by a number of authors (including Burtless and Hausman (1978), Wales and Woodland (1979) and Ashworth and Ulph (1977)), and it is one which we plan to examine further with the aid of the FES data.

At this stage, we decided to limit attention to a range of wage rates where the budget constraint is relatively straightforward.[10] We have therefore taken those households where the hourly wage rate (in 1973) fell in the range £0.85–£3.00; we have also restricted our attention to house-holds interviewed after 6 April 1973, when the unified tax system came into operation. By restricting the earnings range, we hoped to include relatively few families receiving means-tested benefits (although there may be some in receipt of rent rebates). Thus the maximum earnings at which the Family Income Supplement was paid at that time for a family with 5 children was £31.50 a week. At the other end, very few households were likely to be liable to higher rates of tax (which after April 1973 started at £5000 taxable income). The mean hourly earnings for adult males in April 1973 in the New Earnings Survey was £1.08.

The typical marginal tax rate for the sub-sample was therefore taken to be the basic rate of tax[11] of 30% plus National Insurance contributions of 4.75% (5% after 1 October 1973). The latter were payable up to £48 (£54 after 1 October 1973). For simplicity we averaged these, taking a figure of 32.5% (i.e. we did not treat the kink at £48). We used this tax rate to calcu-late the marginal net wage, and the fixed component of income, M, was taken as after tax. We are supposing, therefore, that there is a linear budget constraint which gives a disposable income equal to M, plus 0.675 times gross earnings, plus the cash value of tax allowances. We have sim-plified at this stage by not calculating the tax allowances for each house-hold; they will be reflected in the constant in the expression for full in-come and in the coefficients on household characteristics. (They are excluded from the 'composite' expenditure category.)

To summarize, the sub-sample of the 1973 FES used here consists of those meeting the following criteria:
(a) interviewed after 6 April 1973,
(b) with a male head aged 18–64 and in full-time employment,
(c) hourly earnings of head in range £0.85–£3.00.
The sub-sample consisted of 1617 households.

4.3 Sources of error

The FES is a long established survey, having been running con-tinuously since 1957, and the data appear to be of the highest quality attainable with sample survey methods. There remain nonetheless a number of problems with the use of this source. First, the non-response rate is around 30% and there is evidence of differential non-response by household characteristics (Kemsley, 1975). To some extent this problem is less for the sub-sample used here. Thus, we exclude the self-employed and those with high earnings. There remains, however, an unknown bias in the estimates. Second, the accuracy of reporting of expenditure on cer-tain items is known to be poor. For example, the estimated expenditure on alcoholic drink is (when 'grossed-up') about 60% of that indicated by the Customs and Excise statistics, and tobacco is also considerably under-reported. The implications of such under-recording clearly depend on whether it is correlated with the independent variables in the equations to be estimated.

A third problem concerns the relatively short period over which the records are kept. We have referred earlier to transitory variations as one source of error in the equations. Particular reference should be made to zero entries : for some expenditure categories there is a sizeable fraction of the sample with zero expenditure. In the case of tobacco, it is possible that this is the normal expenditure; for items such as durables, it is likely to reflect the periodic or irregular nature of such payments. In what follows we adopt the procedure of estimating the equations for those values where there is strictly positive expenditure. This may be seen as the simplest of the procedures to deal with missing observations, but should clearly be replaced by a more satisfactory approach. In particular, account should be taken of the fact that the probability of recording expenditure on an item in a given 14-day period may be a function of observed characteristics.

Finally, there are errors in the recording of the income and wage rate used as independent variables. Comparison of the FES with other sources suggests that there may be considerable under-reporting of investment and self-employment income, and of the earnings of women in part-time employment (Stark, 1978). This may lead to measurement error in the income variable, M, although again the choice of sub-sample (see below) should reduce the importance of such errors (e.g. by excluding the higher earnings groups, more likely to have investment income). In the case of earned income, 'data in the survey tend to be slightly deficient, though generally within a few per cent of those indicated by other sources' (FES Report, 1975, p. 3). There is however the further econometric problem introduced by the method used to calculate wage rates (the error in wage rates being correlated with that in hours of work.[12]

4.4 Estimating equations and numerical methods

The expenditure systems estimated are based on equations (3.18), the standard linear expenditure system with variable labour supply, and (3.22) the system which arises from adapting the linear expenditure system to the case where consumption takes time. We have included variables in each equation of the system to allow for differences in household characteristics, in particular : OWN which takes the value 1 if the household is an owner-occupier and 0 otherwise, $NEARN$ the number of earners in the household and NCH the number of children.[13]

For the standard linear expenditure system, the estimating equations can straightforwardly be modified to allow for household characteristics (vector $K = OWN, NEARN, NCH$) and for taxation:

$$p_i x_i = h'_{0i} + \sum_K h'_{Ki} K + h'_{1i}(M + \alpha'_1 W) + \varepsilon'_i$$

$$\text{for} \quad i = 1, ..., 9 \text{ (pure leisure is commodity 10)} \quad (4.1)$$

where M is the fixed component of income (see section 4.1), W is the gross-of-tax wage, $\alpha'_1 = 0.675T'$ (see eqn (3.10) and section 4.2), and ε'_i is a normally distributed random variable, $N(0, \sigma_i'^2)$, independent across observations and equations. (The coefficients of the characteristics represent the net effect, allowing for the term in $-\beta_i \sum p_j \gamma_j$.)

In the case of the extended model with time requirements, the position is more complicated. The form estimated is:

$$p_i x_i = h''_{2i} + \sum_K h''_{Ki} K + h''_{3i} \frac{(M + \alpha''_1 W + \alpha''_2)}{(1 + h''_{5i} W)} + \varepsilon''_i$$

$$\text{for} \quad i = 1, ..., 9 \quad (4.2)$$

where α''_1 is $0.675T''$ (see eqn (3.22) and section 4.2), and α''_2 is the value of personal tax allowances, A, less $\sum_1^{n-1} p_j \gamma_j$. If the personal characteristics are interpreted as influencing $p_j \gamma_j$, then they should enter α''_2; similarly, it is likely that the tax allowance depends on the vector K. For simplicity of estimation, we have at this stage assumed α''_2 independent of K; moreover, in the results presented here we have set α''_2 equal to zero. This means that the coefficients h''_{2i}, h''_{Ki} should satisfy the restrictions:[14]

$$\sum_{i=1}^{n-1} h''_{2i} = 0$$

$$\sum_{i=1}^{n-1} h''_{Ki} = 0 \quad \text{all } K \quad (4.3)$$

These constraints are not included in the estimation process, but we discuss them further in section 5.4.

Estimation of both (4.1) and (4.2) was by maximum likelihood. The system (4.2) raised some interesting computational problems. The technique developed to cope with them is the work of Joanna Gomulka and the brief description which follows is due to her. A full description is available in Gomulka (1980).

Given the data, the log-likelihood of the system can be calculated, as a function of the parameters to be estimated, in a straightforward manner using the assumption that the errors are normally distributed and independent both across observations and equations. We have

$$\mathcal{L}(\sigma, h^1, ..., h^i, ..., h^9, \alpha)$$

$$= B + \sum_{i=1}^{9} \left[N_i \log \sigma_i + \frac{1}{2\sigma_i^2} \mathcal{L}_i(h^i, \alpha) \right] \quad (4.4)$$

where $\mathscr{L}$ is minus the log-likelihood of the sample, σ is the vector of σ_i, h^i is the vector of parameters in the equation for the ith good, α is the vector of common parameters, N_i is the number of observations for equation i (this varies across equations – see end of section 4.3), B is a constant, and $\mathscr{L}_i$ is the sum of squares of residuals in equation i. We wish to choose the arguments of $\mathscr{L}(\ )$ to minimize its value. In the case of equations (4.1) there are 55 parameters; in equations (4.2) there are 65 parameters.

The computational procedure is based on the fact that at most 2 of the variables appear in all equations, whereas the remaining variables are specific to their own equations. For given α, $\mathscr{L}$ is the sum of 9 independent terms each involving its own set of variables (h^i, σ_i). Thus, if we fix α, the 65 variable problem in the case of equations (4.2) reduces to 9 separate problems with 7 variables each (and from (4.4) we can see that the 7 variable problem itself decomposes as we can choose h^i to minimize $\mathscr{L}_i$, given α, independently of σ_i).

One way of exploiting the structure of the problem just described is to first minimize with respect to $(\sigma, h^1, ..., h^9)$ holding α constant, and then to minimize with respect to α holding the $(\sigma, h^1, ..., h^9)$ constant at the values selected in the first step, and so on. This method proved inefficient since for small values of the gradient it was able to make very little progress. The alternative procedure proposed in Gomulka (1980) is to define

$$f(\alpha) = \min_{\sigma, h^1, ..., h^9} \mathscr{L}(\sigma, h^1, ..., h^9, \alpha) \tag{4.5}$$

The full minimum is then found by minimizing $f(\ )$ with respect to α. The first step of the procedure just described can be regarded as an evaluation of $f(\ )$ at α. First and second derivatives of $f(\ )$ can be calculated without difficulty, noting that, where σ, h^1, ..., h^9 have been chosen to minimise, $\nabla f = \left(\dfrac{\partial \mathscr{L}}{\partial \alpha_1''}, \dfrac{\partial \mathscr{L}}{\partial \alpha_2''} \right)$. Thus one makes use of the envelope property familiar from other contexts (see, for example, Deaton, 1975, ch. 4).

A version of the Newton–Raphson algorithm was used to minimize $f(\alpha)$.

$$\alpha^{k+1} = \alpha^k - \theta H^{-1} g \tag{4.6}$$

where $g = \nabla f$, H is based either on the Hessian matrix of f or, as an alternative, the covariance matrix of the gradient (Berndt *et al.*, 1974), and θ is a suitable step size. In practice, the use of the covariance matrix proved more efficient. The evaluation of $f(\ )$ involves the minimization of each $\mathscr{L}_i$ with respect to h^i and for this purpose a NAG library implementation of the Marquardt method was used. For further details of the procedure, see Gomulka (1980).[15] Standard errors of the estimators were calculated following a method similar to that described in Berndt *et al.* (1974).

5 Results and interpretation

5.1 Introduction

Three sets of results from the estimation of expenditure systems are presented here. In table 1 we give OLS estimates with explanatory variables, M, W, OWN, $NEARN$ and NCH. The underlying linear model is not based on any properly articulated theory of household behaviour. The results are presented as descriptions of the data and as a benchmark for comparisons with our estimates of equations (4.1) and (4.2). Table 2 contains our estimates of the standard linear expenditure system with variable labour supply. The model of (4.1) is the special case of the model of table 1 with the restriction that the ratio of the coefficients on M and W should be equal across equations – thus there are eight extra restrictions for the model of table 2 as compared to that of table 1. We present in table 3 our results from estimating the non-linear system (4.2) where consumption of commodities takes time, and where we have set α_2'' to zero. The model of table 2 is thus the special case of table 3 where all the h_{5i}'' are set to zero, so that there are nine extra restrictions.

The overall 'goodness-of-fit' in tables 1, 2, 3 may be compared by looking at the differences in likelihood values. We can compare tables 1 and 2, and tables 2 and 3, formally since the model of table 2 is a special case of those tables 1 and 3. We make use of the chi-square property of the difference in log-likelihood ratios for nested models : asymptotically, twice the difference in log-likelihoods is distributed as chi-square with degrees of freedom equal to the difference in the numbers of parameters in the two models.[16]

For table 1 versus table 2 we have a chi-square value of 21.2. The 5% significance level for a chi-square variate with 8 degrees of freedom (d.o.f.) is 15.5; hence one would reject the null hypothesis that the more restricted model of table 2 is correct. A similar calculation comparing tables 2 and 3 gives a chi-square value of 35.6. The 5% significance level for a chi-square variate with 9 d.o.f. is 16.9; hence one would again reject the null hypothesis of the model involved in table 2 in favour of the model of table 3. In interpreting this test one must bear in mind that the chi-square property is asymptotic (we have 1617 observations).

We now discuss the results in more detail. Means, standard deviations and a correlation matrix are presented in the appendix.

5.2 The OLS estimates

The OLS results do not represent a model which we should want to propose, but they are useful for understanding the data. We examine first the coefficients on M and W. In interpreting these, we must take ac-

Table 1. *Expenditure equations: simple linear form and ordinary least squares*

Commodity group (expenditure in £/week)	No. of non-zero cases	Standard deviation of expenditure	Constant	M (£/week)	W (£/hour)	OWN	NEARN	NCH	R^2
1. Food	1617	5.118	4.499 (0.524)	0.087 (0.011)	1.976 (0.291)	0.057 (0.242)	1.522 (0.271)	1.370 (0.092)	0.2586
2. Alcoholic drink	1408	3.540	0.639 (0.408)	0.051 (0.009)	0.554 (0.225)	-0.928 (0.191)	0.904 (0.209)	0.097 (0.075)	0.1566
3. Tobacco	1136	1.742	1.930 (0.225)	0.018 (0.005)	-0.141 (0.134)	-0.701 (0.102)	0.466 (0.113)	0.078 (0.040)	0.1605
4. Clothing and footwear	1499	6.062	0.310 (0.716)	0.089 (0.015)	1.619 (0.397)	0.285 (0.331)	0.536 (0.366)	0.345 (0.126)	0.0877
5. Durable household goods	1279	12.898	0.958 (1.709)	0.037 (0.036)	1.785 (0.913)	1.618 (0.812)	0.045 (0.859)	-0.519 (0.308)	0.0143
6. Other goods	1617	3.850	0.790 (0.439)	0.053 (0.009)	1.333 (0.244)	0.252 (0.202)	0.156 (0.227)	0.185 (0.077)	0.0802
7. Transport and vehicles	1590	5.224	1.284 (0.606)	0.062 (0.013)	1.014 (0.335)	0.344 (0.280)	0.410 (0.313)	-0.075 (0.107)	0.0620
8. Services	1598	9.794	-1.100 (1.148)	0.047 (0.024)	3.432 (0.636)	-0.230 (0.530)	0.592 (0.593)	-0.440 (0.203)	0.0372
9. Composite	1617	22.223	-3.905 (2.385)	0.564 (0.051)	14.381 (1.324)	-0.680 (1.100)	-4.953 (1.234)	-0.717 (0.421)	0.1846

Log-likelihood value = −23,634.31.

Notes: (i) Data base: Family Expenditure Survey, 1973.

(ii) The variable to be explained in each equation is the expenditure (£/per week) for the commodity group indicated).

(iii) Cases included are those households interviewed after 6 April where the head is in full-time employment at a wage between 0.85p and £3.00 per hour. For each commodity group, cases involving zero expenditure have been omitted. Maximum number of cases is 1617.

(iv) Standard errors in brackets.

(v) W: wage, gross of tax (£/hour); M: 'unearned' income (£/week); NCH: number of children; OWN: number of earners in household; OWN: 1 if owner-occupier, 0 otherwise.

(vi) The log-likelihood value displayed requires an extra additive term. However the relevant magnitudes are differences in log-likelihood values between tables 1, 2 and 3 and these are unaffected.

Table 2. *Linear expenditure system: maximum likelihood estimates*

Commodity group (expenditure in £/week)	Constant	h'_{1i}	OWN	NEARN	NCH	R^2
1. Food	4.481	0.087	0.056	1.529	1.370	0.2588
	(0.408)	(0.008)	(0.240)	(0.230)	(0.092)	
2. Alcoholic drink	0.118	0.039	−0.973	1.132	0.096	0.1545
	(0.305)	(0.006)	(0.189)	(0.172)	(0.075)	
3. Tobacco	1.447	0.0082	−0.748	0.657	0.080	0.1538
	(0.159)	(0.0034)	(0.101)	(0.094)	(0.040)	
4. Clothing and footwear	−0.054	0.081	0.253	0.696	0.344	0.0873
	(0.543)	(0.011)	(0.328)	(0.303)	(0.126)	
5. Durable household goods	1.753	0.056	1.687	−0.306	−0.521	0.0140
	(1.267)	(0.023)	(0.804)	(0.692)	(0.307)	
6. Other goods	0.888	0.055	0.260	0.114	0.186	0.0802
	(0.331)	(0.007)	(0.201)	(0.189)	(0.077)	
7. Transport and vehicles	0.937	0.054	0.316	0.562	−0.075	0.0616
	(0.447)	(0.009)	(0.277)	(0.256)	(0.107)	
8. Services	0.899	0.093	−0.064	−0.286	−0.437	0.0334
	(0.846)	(0.017)	(0.526)	(0.486)	(0.203)	
9. Composite	−2.675	0.592	−0.580	−5.491	−0.715	0.1843
	(2.026)	(0.042)	(1.094)	(1.104)	(0.420)	

$\alpha'_1 = 22.936(2.138)$; log-likelihood value $= -23,644.91$

Notes: (i) See notes (i)–(iii), (v) and (vi) to table 1.

(ii) See table 1 for number of cases and standard deviation of each expenditure variable.

(iii) h'_{1i} (see equation (4.1)) is the marginal propensity (out of full income) to spend on the commodity.

(iv) α'_1 is $0.675T'$ (see equation (4.1)). Recall that the wage here is gross of tax and $T' = T - \gamma_n$ where T is total time (hours/week) available and γ_n is the minimum requirement of leisure.

(v) Numbers in brackets are asymptotic standard errors.

(vi) R^2 is calculated 'as if' the equations were independent.

count of measurement errors, under which we include errors in the reporting and collection of the data and those introduced by our assumptions (e.g. about the tax system). In the case of commodities one to eight, they may well lead to the usual downward bias in the coefficients. In contrast, the bias for the composite (commodity 9) is likely to be in the opposite direction (see Atkinson and Stern, forthcoming).

The coefficient on M can be regarded as a marginal propensity to consume out of lump-sum income. It is significant in all cases except durable household goods and the values look fairly plausible as marginal propensities apart from the coefficient on the composite expenditure category. This category consists mainly of saving and expenditure on housing. These are very substantial items but it seems unlikely that the marginal propensity could be as high as 0.56. As just explained, there may be an 'errors-in-variables' bias which leads us to overestimate the coefficient.

Table 3. *Non-linear system where consumption involves time: maximum likelihood estimates*

Commodity group (expenditure in £/week)	Constant	h_{3i}''	h_{5i}''	OWN	NEARN	NCH	R^2
1. Food	4.009	0.107	0.123	0.057	1.390	1.366	0.2594
	(0.671)	(0.023)	(0.123)	(0.240)	(0.276)	(0.092)	
2. Alcoholic drink	−0.385	0.101	0.623	−0.924	0.755	0.090	0.1594
	(0.470)	(0.031)	(0.327)	(0.190)	(0.213)	(0.074)	
3. Tobacco	1.198	0.109	4.012	−0.710	0.440	0.075	0.1620
	(0.208)	(0.139)	(6.268)	(0.102)	(0.113)	(0.040)	
4. Clothing and footwear	−0.452	0.094	0.096	0.253	0.620	0.342	0.0872
	(0.751)	(0.029)	(0.150)	(0.329)	(0.374)	(0.126)	
5. Durable household goods	1.503	0.061	0.056	1.670	−0.329	−0.522	0.0141
	(1.419)	(0.062)	(0.403)	(0.806)	(0.875)	(0.307)	
6. Other goods	0.618	0.064	0.090	0.256	0.061	0.184	0.0807
	(0.475)	(0.018)	(0.137)	(0.201)	(0.231)	(0.077)	
7. Transport and vehicles	0.528	0.083	0.242	0.331	0.347	−0.079	0.0625
	(0.607)	(0.030)	(0.225)	(0.279)	(0.320)	(0.107)	
8. Services	1.080	0.042	−0.222	−0.161	0.435	−0.423	0.0405
	(0.884)	(0.017)	(0.058)	(0.527)	(0.508)	(0.202)	
9. Composite	−4.133	0.524	−0.020	−0.733	−4.412	−0.713	0.1846
	(3.467)	(0.080)	(0.073)	(1.098)	(1.243)	(0.420)	

$\alpha_1'' = 26.612(5.191)$; log-likelihood value $= -23,627.18$

Notes: (i) See notes (i), (ii), (v) and (vi) from table 2.

(ii) h_{3i}'' (see equation (4.2)), is the modified marginal propensity to spend on the commodity concerned.

(iii) h_{5i}'' (see equation (4.2)), is $0.675\, t_i/p_i$.
Thus, $(0.675 W t_i)/p_i$ is the time cost (in money terms) divided by the money cost. The average wage for the sample (see appendix) is £1.24 per hour.

(iv) α_1' is $0.675 T''$, see equation (4.2). Recall that the wage here is gross of tax and T'' is total time available less that associated with the minimum requirement of each commodity (including leisure).

The coefficient on W represents the only 'price' effect which our data allow us to treat. The coefficient is significant and positive in every case except tobacco, where the coefficient is negative but insignificant. The apparent peculiarity of tobacco may be associated with a distribution of preferences in the population which is not independent of the wage rate – it is known, for example, that working-class males smoke more than middle-class males.

We turn now to the household characteristics. The coefficient on OWN is significant and negative for alcohol and tobacco and significant and positive for durable household goods – elsewhere it is insignificant. Thus, those who do not own their homes drink and smoke more and buy fewer consumer durables. The coefficient on NCH is significant and positive for food, tobacco and clothing, significant and negative for services, and insignificant elsewhere. Thus, children require expenditure on food and clothing and (we hazard a guess) the wife's presence at home implies less services purchased outside the home. Note that children do not drive you to drink but they make you smoke. The coefficient on $NEARN$ is significant and positive for food, alcohol, tobacco, and the composite. (The results for household characteristics in tables 2 and 3 are fairly similar, and are not discussed further.)

The labour supply equation implicit in table 1 can be calculated from the budget constraint

$$0.675Wl = -M + 5.405 + 1.008\ M + 25.95\ W + 0.017\ OWN$$
$$- 0.322\ NEARN + 0.324\ NCH \tag{5.1}$$

where the coefficients on the right-hand side of (5.1) are the corresponding column sums in table 1. Note that M effectively vanishes – we return to this point in the next section. If we substitute the means[17] of the variables (apart from W), we obtain:

$$l = \frac{8.096}{W} + 38.450 \tag{5.2}$$

This gives a wage elasticity at the mean wage of the sample of -0.146. This value is within the range of estimates of labour supply elasticities typically found in empirical studies – see for example Ashenfelter and Heckman (1973) or Stern (1976). The estimated elasticity varies over the range of the sample from -0.19 (at W = £0.85) to -0.07 (at W = £3.0).

5.3 The standard linear expenditure system

The estimates reported in table 2 are of the model of equations (4.1). This differs from table 1 in that there is the additional restriction that the ratio of the coefficients of W and M must be the same across equations. This common ratio is α_1' which is estimated at 22.94 and is highly significant. The coefficients h_{1i}', the marginal propensity to spend out of full income, are all significant and positive and are similar to those on M in table 1. The biggest difference is for services where we have an increase from 4.7% to 9.3% on passing from table 1 to table 2.

The coefficient α_1' is to be interpreted as $0.675T'$ where T' is total available time in hours/week over and above the minimum requirement of leisure. Thus, our estimate of T' is $\frac{22.96}{0.675}$ = 34.0 hours/week. This is implausibly low given that the mean hours worked in the sample is 42.8. It may be that the tobacco equation is partially responsible here since it would exert an influence which pulls down α_1' (the coefficient on W was negative in table 1). Moreover, we must continue to take account of measurement error, the treatment of which is less simple in this context than in the previous section.

It is however also possible that the model itself is inappropriate. Further evidence of this is provided by the labour supply equation implicit in table 2:

$$0.675Wl = -M + 7.794 + 1.065(M + 22.936W) + 0.207\ OWN$$
$$- 1.393\ NEARN + 0.328\ NCH \qquad (5.3)$$

where the coefficients on the right-hand side of (5.3) are the corresponding column sums in table 2. The coefficient on M is $+0.065$, close to zero, as it was in (5.1), although now it is a little larger. From (3.17) we see that the implication is that there is a small negative weight β_n on leisure in excess of the minimum γ_n. Since a negative weight is inconsistent with the formulation, we should clearly impose the constraint that $\beta_n \geq 0$; and the results suggest that the model needs respecification. This could take the form of assuming that labour supply is constrained (the form of such constraints is discussed further in Atkinson and Stern (forthcoming); or we could allow labour to enter the utility function. Alternatively, we can use a specification which does not depend on leisure as such being valued – as with the activity analysis extension of the linear expenditure system.

5.4 Non-linear model where consumption involves time

Table 3 contains our estimates of the model (4.2). We have already explained that α_2'' in (4.2) is set to zero (effectively this assumes that the value of the tax allowances is just equal to the value of the minimum consumption levels). Our estimate of T'', total available time in excess of that required for the consumption of the minimum commodity requirements and minimum leisure, is calculated from α_1'' by dividing by 0.675 (see eqn (4.2)). Our estimate of α_1'' of 26.61 is highly significant and yields a T'' of 39.42 hours/week. Given that the mean hours worked are 42.8 this would indicate that our average individual works for more of his time than the 'committed minimum' would allow. A higher value of T'' would be more plausible, and it is possible that this is related to the behaviour of the coefficient on pure leisure. $(1 - \Sigma_1^{n-1}\ \beta_i)$ is equal to β_n, the weight on the logarithm of pure leisure above the minimum in the utility function. Thus, the weight on pure leisure is -0.185 (the sum of h_{3i}'' in table 3 is 1.185). This indicates that we should impose the constraint $\Sigma_1^9\ h_{3i}'' = 1$, and we intend to do this in further computations. (In contrast to the standard linear expenditure system, it is quite consistent with the model that $\beta_n = 0$; indeed we suggested earlier that pure leisure is likely to be of little importance.)

The coefficients h_{5i}'' represent the time price in hours (times 0.675) divided by the money price for commodity i. To convert to a pure ratio we may multiply by the gross of tax wage, W. The significant coefficients h''_{5i} are for alcohol and services. In the former case, for a person with the mean wage (£1.235), the time cost is 77% of its money cost. To illustrate what that would mean, a pint of beer costing 20p would take 0.20 times 0.623 divided by 0.675 or 0.185 hours to consume – a pint in 11 minutes. Remember that 'consuming beer' is the only beer-argument in the utility function; if there were enjoyment from the time itself that would lower the perceived time cost.

The purchase of services has a negative time cost, in other words an increase in expenditure on services increases the total amount of time available : an extra £1 on services saves 0.33 hours. The person with the mean wage would be prepared to pay the equivalent of 3.7 hours for an activity which involved the saving of an hour. This would be implausible if the only aspect of the purchase of services was the saving of time. However, the consumption of services may be of value for its own sake and difficult to perform by oneself in the equivalent amount of time.

Whilst the other coefficients h''_{5i} are not significantly different from zero their magnitudes do have some interesting features. That for tobacco is very large, the time cost being more than three times the money cost. A packet of 20 cigarettes would take over 2 hours to smoke. This might not be wildly unrealistic but it is complicated by the fact that people can do more than one thing at the same time. The high value for h''_{5i} in this case is, we presume, connected with the taste differences referred to earlier.

As before we can calculate the labour supply equation:

$$0.675 Wl = 26.612 W + 3.966 + 0.038 \, OWN - 0.692 \, NEARN$$
$$+ 0.320 \, NCH + (M + 26.612 W) \left(\sum_{i=1}^{9} \left(\frac{h''_{3i}}{1 + h''_{5i} \, W} \right) - 1 \right) \quad (5.4)$$

where the constant and coefficients on OWN, $NEARN$ and NCH are the relevant column sums in table 3, and h''_{3i} and h''_{5i} are as in table 3. Equation (5.4) is invalid where $1 + h''_{5i} \, W < 0$, and therefore does not apply to values of W greater than $(1/0.222) = £4.50$ per hour (see the h''_{5i} coefficient for services). We noted earlier that the constant and the sum of the coefficients on the characteristic terms should be zero (see eqn (4.3)). These are not, however, satisfied, and, evaluated at the mean, these terms tend to raise the right-hand side. When we replace the variables OWN, $NEARN$, NCH and M by their sample means, the elasticity of labour supply with respect to the wage rate, evaluated at the mean, is -0.230. This is substantially higher than that obtained with the OLS estimates. On the other hand, this simple comparison fails to bring out the full extent of backward-bending and then forward-bending – see figure 1 – which is the reverse

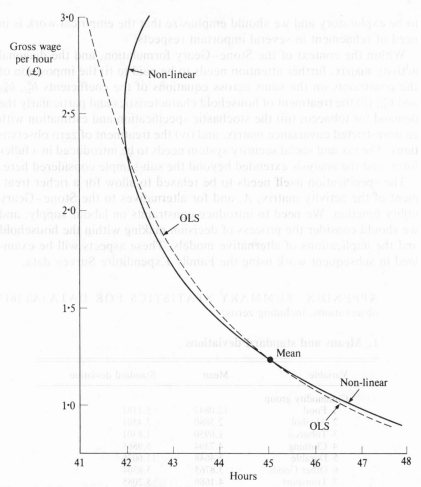

Figure 1. Labour supply as function of W

of the usual textbook shape. A person with a high wage may, in effect, choose to both work long hours and buy time-saving services.[18] The implications for taxation are explored further in Atkinson and Stern (1979), but it is clear that the change in specification has led to a rather different representation of the labour supply relationship.

6 Concluding remarks

The main aim of this paper has been to explore how far the household production model can be used to bridge the gap between systems of commodity demand equations and models of labour supply. As such, it is intended to be exploratory and we should emphasize that the empirical work is in need of refinement in several important respects.

Within the context of the Stone–Geary formulation, and the diagonal activity matrix, further attention needs to be paid to (i) the imposition of the constraints on the sums across equations of the coefficients h_{2i}'', h_{Ki}'' and h_{3i}'', (ii) the treatment of household characteristics and particularly the demand for tobacco, (iii) the stochastic specification and estimation with an unrestricted covariance matrix, and (iv) the treatment of zero observations. The tax and social security system needs to be introduced in a fuller form, and the analysis extended beyond the sub-sample considered here.

The specification itself needs to be relaxed to allow for a richer treatment of the activity matrix, A, and for alternatives to the Stone–Geary utility function. We need to introduce constraints on labour supply; and we should consider the process of decision making within the household and the implications of alternative models. These aspects will be examined in subsequent work using the Family Expenditure Survey data.

APPENDIX: SUMMARY STATISTICS FOR DATA (All 1617 observations, including zeros)

1. Means and standard deviations

Variable	Mean	Standard deviation
Commodity group		
1 Food	12.0847	5.1181
2 Alcohol	2.5880	3.4501
3 Tobacco	1.6950	1.8301
4 Clothing	4.7394	5.9865
5 Durable	3.4648	11.6076
6 Other Goods	3.8765	3.8504
7 Transport	4.1686	5.2085
8 Services	4.0206	9.7461
9 Composite	14.5099	22.2225
Gross earnings	52.3993	17.4270
M	15.7779	15.4535
W	1.2354	0.4014
NCH	1.1608	1.2167
$NEARN$	1.4088	0.6433
OWN	0.6531	0.4761
Hours worked	42.79	6.71

Notes

1 This research was supported by a Social Science Research Council programme grant on Taxation, Incentives and the Distribution of Income. The paper draws on a more extensive version, circulated as a discussion paper, Atkinson and Stern (forthcoming), which provides a fuller treatment of several aspects of the work. We are grateful for the advice of A. S. Deaton, M. A. King and K. F. Wallis. All errors are ours.

2 The idea is an old one, going back at least to Menger (cf. Lancaster (1971), p. ?), and is extensively discussed in Gorman (1956).

3 Where λ is assumed ≥ 0, and all prices are strictly positive, $c = A^{-1}x$, and total expenditure ... may be written as $c.c = (p'A^{-1}x) = p.x$. This transformation is discussed in Deaton (1967, pp. 155–8), who noted that proper-ties such as negativity ... and symmetry are preserved by such trans-formation.

4 It is of course possible to solve for c_i from the time ... ... where that is binding, this eliminates from the problem (as in Becker 1965); however the resulting reduced form utility function $w(c_i, \ldots)$ ... does not necessarily have the properties ...

5 Note that the ...

6 We suppose that these coefficients do not sum to zero so that the normalization is permissible.

7 For discussion of a ... generalized inverse ... which preserves symmetry between ... equation ... Rao (1973, ch. 4).

8 At this stage we ... excluded items for which expenditure is recorded elsewhere in the ...

9 This is unsatisfactory ... not allow for non-proportional wage schedules; in particular, we have in mind both overtime premia and unpaid overtime by salaried ...

10 This approach is not ... where there has been an extensive litera-ture on the question of sample selection (see for example Hausman and Wise (1977) and Heckman ...). The procedure adopted here avoids the diffi-culties associated with ... dependent variable, but we need to allow for the fact that the change in constant outside the range chosen is likely to lead to rather different behaviour.

11 The personal tax ... nearly all families in the sub-sample would have ... A married couple with 3 children (2 aged 11–16) they were some £37 per week.

12 It should also be noted that ... all households face the same prices, whereas there ... variation in the sample arising from variations across regions and over the sampling period.

13 These particular choices ... the basis of judgement as to which aspects of ... most important and ... make experi-ments with alternatives such as age of head of household.

14 Note that A has been ... for ... from the category ...

15 In practice, for our ... and ... to ... that with respect to x. This ... and we ... the relative prices of the expenditure equation for tobacco. We have more to say about tobacco equation in section 2 and we hope to investigate its peculiarities in later work. We decided for this ... to set at zero in our computation ...

16 The use of this procedure ... Rao et al. ... although general proofs are not cited.

2. Correlation matrix

	Commodity group									Gross earnings	M	W	NCH	NEARN	OWN
	1	2	3	4	5	6	7	8	9						
Commodity group															
1	1.0000														
2	0.3360	1.0000													
3	0.1585	0.3886	1.0000												
4	0.3160	0.1733	0.0973	1.0000											
5	0.0556	0.0378	0.0442	0.0440	1.0000										
6	0.0326	0.1978	0.0196	0.3135	0.0483	1.0000									
7	0.1705	0.0811	0.0317	0.1181	0.0247	0.1202	1.0000								
8	0.0770	0.0588	−0.0226	0.0818	0.0348	0.0943	0.0677	1.0000							
9	−0.1716	−0.1192	−0.0632	−0.2628	0.4719	−0.1974	−0.1630	−0.3723	1.0000						
Gross earnings	0.2183	0.0774	−0.1064	0.1367	0.1138	0.1892	0.1088	0.1413	0.3103	1.0000					
M	0.3652	0.3594	0.2537	0.2629	0.0668	0.2356	0.2351	0.1278	0.3157	0.0734	1.0000				
W	0.1652	0.0391	−0.1436	0.1211	0.0910	0.1653	0.1018	0.1430	0.3042	0.0810	0.0942	1.0000			
NCH	0.2398	−0.0637	−0.0232	0.0442	−0.0484	0.0156	−0.0591	−0.0762	−0.0776	0.0529	−0.1728	−0.0027	1.0000		
NEARN	0.3085	0.3525	0.3026	0.2033	−0.0379	0.1598	0.1872	0.0979	0.1419	−0.0801	0.7537	−0.0786	−0.2089	1.0000	
OWN	0.0164	−0.1235	−0.2802	0.0441	0.0805	0.0620	0.0419	0.0215	0.0689	0.2325	−0.0126	0.2690	−0.0094	−0.1266	1.0000

Notes

1 This research was supported by a Social Science Research council programme grant on Taxation, Incentives and the Distribution of Income. The paper draws on a more extensive version, circulated as a discussion paper, Atkinson and Stern (forthcoming), which provides a fuller treatment of several aspects of the work. We are grateful for the advice of A. S. Deaton, M. A. King and K. F. Wallis. All errors are ours.

2 The idea is an old one, going back at least to Menger (cf. Lancaster (1971), p. 7), and is extensively discussed in Gorman (1956).

3 Where A is square, det $A \neq 0$, and all prices are strictly positive, $c = A^{-1}x$, and total expenditure may be written as $r.c = (p'A)(A^{-1}x) = p.x$. This transformation is discussed by Samuelson (1947, pp. 135–8), who notes that properties such as negative definiteness and symmetry are preserved by such transformations.

4 It is of course possible to substitute for c_0 from the time constraint, where that is binding, thus eliminating it from the problem (as in Baumol, 1973); however the resulting reduced form utility function $u^*(c_1, ..., c_m)$ does not necessarily have the properties usually assumed.

5 Note that r_0, the price of l, is $-w$.

6 We suppose that the β coefficients do not sum to zero so that the normalization is permissible.

7 For discussion of an approach using a generalized inverse, which preserves symmetry between equations, see Deaton (1975, ch. 4).

8 At this stage we have not included items for which expenditure is recorded elsewhere in the enquiry.

9 This is unsatisfactory in that it does not allow for non-proportional wage schedules; in particular, we have in mind both overtime premia and unpaid overtime by salaried workers.

10 This approach is not without difficulties. There has been an extensive literature on the question of sample selection (see for example Hausman and Wise (1977) and Heckman (1979)). The procedure adopted here avoids the difficulties associated with truncation on the dependent variable, but we need to allow for the fact that the budget constraint outside the range chosen is likely to lead to rather different behaviour.

11 The personal tax allowances were such that nearly all families in the subsample would have been liable for tax : for a couple with 4 children (2 aged 11–16) they were some £32 per week.

12 It should also be noted that we have assumed that all households face the same prices, whereas there is likely to be some variation in the sample arising from variations across regions and over the sampling period.

13 These particular characteristics were selected on the basis of judgment as to which aspects of the household would be important and after early experiments with alternatives such as age of head of household.

14 Note that A has been excluded from the composite category.

15 In practice, for our data, the log-likelihood surface proved to be very flat with respect to α_2''. This seems, in part, to be associated with the peculiarities of the expenditure equation for tobacco. We have more to say about the tobacco equation in section 5.2 and we hope to investigate its peculiarities in later work. We decided for the present to fix α_2'' at zero in our computations.

16 The use of this property is standard practice (see Berndt et al., 1974) although general proofs are not cited.

17 We have used the means which involve all 1617 observations – see appendix.
18 An alternative explanation, which we are currently exploring, would involve the effects of overtime on the calculation of wage rates (see section 4.1).

References

Abbott, M. and Ashenfelter, O. (1976), 'Labour Supply, Commodity Demand and the Allocation of Time', *Review of Economic Studies*, **43**, 389–412.

Ashenfelter, O. and Heckman, J. (1973), 'Estimating Labour-Supply Functions', in G. G. Cain and H. W. Watts (eds.), *Income Maintenance and Labour Supply*, Rand McNally, Chicago.

Ashworth, J. and Ulph, D. T. (1977), 'On the Structure of Family Labour Supply Decisions', University of Stirling Discussion Paper.

Atkinson, A. B. and Stern, N. H. (forthcoming), 'On Labour Supply and Commodity Demands', SSRC Programme on Taxation, Incentives and the Distribution of Income, Discussion Paper.

(1979), 'Labour Supply, Commodity Demands and the Switch from Direct to Indirect Taxation', *Journal of Public Economics*, **18**, 195–224.

Barten, A. P. (1969), 'Maximum Likelihood Estimation of a Complete System of Demand Equations', *European Economic Review*, **1**, 7–73.

Baumol, W. J. (1973), 'Income and Substitution Effects in the Linder Theorem', *Quarterly Journal of Economics*, **87**, 629–33.

Becker, G. S. (1965), 'A Theory of the Allocation of Time', *Economic Journal*, **75**, 493–517.

Berndt, E. R., Hall, B. H., Hall, R. E. and Hausman, J. A. (1974), 'Estimation and Inference in Nonlinear Structural Models', *Annals of Economic and Social Measurement*, **3**, 653–65.

Burtless, G. and Hausman, J. A. (1978), 'The Effect of Taxation on Labour Supply : Evaluating the Gary Negative Income Tax Experiment', *Journal of Political Economy*, **86**, 1103–30.

Deaton, A. S. (1974), 'A Reconsideration of the Empirical Implications of Additive Preferences', *Economic Journal*, **84**, 338–48.

(1975), *Models and Projections of Demand in Post-War Britain*, Chapman and Hall, London.

Diamond, P. A. and Yaari, M. E. (1972), 'Implications of the Theory of Rationing for Consumer Choice under Uncertainty', *American Economic Review*, **62**, 333–43.

Gomulka, J. (1980), 'Decomposition Algorithm for Smooth Unconstrained Optimisation Problems', in L. C. W. Dixon and G. P. Szego (eds.), *Numerical Optimisation of Dynamic Systems*, North-Holland, Amsterdam.

Gorman, W. M. (1956), 'A Possible Procedure for Analysing Quality Differentials in the Egg Market', Journal Paper J-3129 of the Iowa Agricultural Experiment Station (circulated in January 1976 as Discussion Paper B4 of the LSE Econometrics Programme).

(1976), 'Tricks with Utility Functions', in M. J. Artis and A. R. Nobay (eds.), *Essays in Economic Analysis*, Cambridge University Press.

Hausman, J. A. and Wise, D. A. (1977), 'Social Experimentation, Truncated Distributions, and Efficient Estimation', *Econometrica*, **45**, 919–38.

Heckman, J. J. (1979), 'Sample Selection Bias as a Specification Error', *Econometrica*, **47**, 153–61.

Kemsley, W. F. F. (1969), *Family Expenditure Survey : Handbook on the Sample, Fieldwork and Coding Procedures,* HMSO, London.

——— (1975), 'Family Expenditure Survey : A Study of Differential Response based on a Comparison of the 1971 Sample with the Census', *Statistical News.*

Lancaster, K. (1971), *Consumer Demand,* Columbia University Press, New York.

Muellbauer, J. N. J. and Portes, R. (1978), 'Macroeconomic Models with Quantity Rationing', *Economic Journal,* **88,** 788–821.

Neary, J. P. and Roberts, K. W. (1978), 'The Theory of Household Behaviour under Rationing', Warwick Economic Research Papers, 132, *European Economic Review,* **13,** 25–42.

Pollak, R. A. and Wachter, M. L. (1975), 'The Relevance of the Household Production Function and its Implications for the Allocation of Time', *Journal of Political Economy,* **83,** 255–78.

Rothbarth, E. (1940–41), 'The Measurement of Changes in Real Income under Conditions of Rationing', *Review of Economic Studies,* **8,** 87–104.

Samuelson, P. A. (1947), *Foundations of Economic Analysis,* Harvard University Press, Cambridge, Mass.

Scitovsky, T. (1976), *The Joyless Economy,* Oxford University Press, Oxford.

Stark, T. (1978), 'Personal Incomes', in *Reviews of United Kingdom Statistical Sources,* vol. VI, Pergamon, Oxford.

Stone, J. R. N. (1954), 'Linear Expenditure Systems and Demand Analysis : An Application to the Pattern of British Demand', *Economic Journal,* **64,** 511–27.

Stern, N. H. (1976), 'Taxation and Labour Supply : A Partial Survey', in *Taxation and Incentives,* Institute for Fiscal Studies, London.

Wales, T. J. and Woodland, A. D. (1979), 'Labour Supply and Progressive Taxes', *Review of Economic Studies,* **46,** 83–95.

11 Child spacing and numbers: an empirical analysis[1]

MARC NERLOVE
AND ASSAF RAZIN
ASSISTED BY WAYNE JOERDING
AND EVELYN LEHRER

1 Introduction

The impetus for our work on the timing and spacing of children has come
from two surveys done by the University of Montreal in 1971 (Henripin
and Lapierre-Adamcyk, 1974 and 1975). These surveys are unusual in that
they contain questions on work experience before marriage, after marriage but before the birth of the first child, at the time of the interview, and
the number of years worked after marriage. The questions enable one to
reconstruct the proportion of a woman's time spent working during the
child-rearing period. The usual questions are asked concerning socio-
economic background and pregnancy history. Because the time of the
mother spent with her children is thought to be an important determinant
of child 'quality' – begging the question of just what that is – and because
female labour force participation is known to be greatly inhibited by the
presence of young children (Sweet, 1973), it was clear to us that we had an
almost unique opportunity to explore the joint relationship among the
timing and the spacing of children and female labour force participation.[2]
In addition, the surveys contained an impressive set of questions related
to the couple's preferences for children. These questions included not
only the usual inquiry concerning the ideal number of children and the
number of children wanted by the couple, but also more abstract questions concerning couples in general, and questions related to preferences
about the timing and spacing of children. These questions enable us, addi-
tionally, to test a hypothesis advanced by Nerlove (1974) about the relative educational levels of husband and wife and the couple's underlying
preference for children vis-à-vis the wife's market activity.

In what follows, we develop and estimate a model which relates the
timing and spacing of children to their number and a measure of the
couple's preferences for children as well as other socio-economic variables. Despite the fact that the timing and spacing of children is an in-

herently dynamic phenomenon, we, nonetheless, work entirely within a static theoretical framework assuming utility maximization under perfect certainty, although at various points we consider what effects uncertain fecundity, uncertain contraception, and infant and child mortality might have. The point is that, while these phenomena are clearly of great importance in reality, they are not central to our development, which concentrates on a few of the more manageable relationships. A key feature of our analysis is the identification of average spacing between successive children as an indicator of child quality, greater spacing being associated with higher quality, *ceteris paribus*. This has already been noted informally by Ross (1973), who assumed that, at least up to a maximum of six years, longer intervals between births enhance child survival, health, intelligence and verbal ability. It is also consistent with Zajonc's (1976) explanation of the relationship between family configuration and intelligence, particularly of why earlier-born children have, on the average, higher intelligence than their later-born siblings, holding family size and socioeconomic group constant. The identification of child-spacing with childquality permits us to verify, among other things, some of the results of Becker and Tomes (1976) concerning the interaction between the quantity and quality of children.

Our theory predicts the following principal propositions: (1) The higher the level of a mother's education, holding both the number of children and the average space between them constant, the greater the age of the mother at the first birth. (2) The proportion of a mother's time spent in market activity during the child rearing period is *negatively* related to the average interval between births. (3) Under mild restrictions, the proportion of a woman's time spent in market activity during the child-rearing period is negatively related to the household's permanent income. (4) Finally, if the income elasticity of child quality is, plausibly, positive, the average interval between births increases as household income increases, but the number of children may increase or decrease depending upon the elasticity of substitution between other goods on the one hand, and the number and quality of children on the other. When preferences are homothetic and the non-time (direct) costs of children are small in comparison with the cost in terms of mother's time, Razin (1980) shows that numbers decrease with an increase in household income.[3]

There is naturally a considerable gap between the variables and constructs of theory and what can be, let alone what is, measured in practice. Generally, it is only possible to interpret the father's educational attainment as a measure of the permanent income of the household, the mother's attainment as indicative of the opportunity costs of her time, and the location of the household, e.g. rural vs. urban, as reflecting differences in the direct costs of children. Unfortunately, even these rather standard interpretations are further complicated by the existence and possible effects of differences among couples' preferences for children. Given, however, the limitations of any empirical analysis, we nonetheless, find a substantial degree of confirmation for the theory in the Quebec surveys mentioned. The average interval between births is negatively related to a mother's market activity during the child-rearing period for the sub-sample of women born before 1936. Numbers and average interval are also negatively related, although this might have been predicted on purely biological grounds. The father's education is negatively related to numbers, although often not strongly so, and positively associated with average interval (except for the older Québécoises). It is markedly and negatively associated with the wife's market activity during the child-rearing years. Our measure of the couple's preference for children, in general, vis-à-vis market activity and, therefore, other goods, is positively associated with numbers of children, holding both average interval and age at first birth constant.

The plan of the paper is as follows: first, following Razin (1980), we outline a theory of the timing and spacing of children and female labour force participation. Next, we give the details of two sets of empirical analyses based on the theoretical model: these are, respectively, for women in the Quebec survey born before 1936 and for women born after 1936. We have estimated equations for numbers of children (born alive and/or expected), average birth interval, age at first birth, and fraction of time the mother worked during the child-rearing period. The data available and the construction of the variables used are described in some detail. We also include a discussion of why the residual from the regression of a wife's formal schooling on that of her husband may partially measure the couple's preferences for children. Some tests of this theory using additional questions from the Quebec survey have been presented elsewhere (Nerlove and Razin, 1979, appendix B). Finally, we draw some conclusions with respect to directions for further research and the general implications of our analysis.

2 A theory of the timing and spacing of children and of female labour force participation

In a recent paper, Razin (1980) has extended the work of Becker and Lewis (1973) and of Becker and Tomes (1976) to model the interrelations of fertility and the timing and spacing of births with the labour-force participation of mothers. Although it is natural to consider this problem within the context of a model of *dynamic* optimization which would consider explicitly the sequential nature of decisions regarding contraceptive practice and the uncertainty of contraception and fecundity, such a general approach has not as yet proved to yield sufficiently unambiguous results to serve as a guide for empirical research.

As is usual in investigations of this sort, we assume a single household utility function is maximized. Utility depends on the parents' consumption of goods and services other than children, Y, the number of children they have during their lifetime, N, and the average 'quality' per child, Q. We do not allow for differences in quality among children, although one could easily modify the analysis along the lines of Becker and Tomes (1976, section 3) to allow for the effects of differences in child endowments.

The variables of the basic model we use are as follows:

θ = the proportion of the mother's time spent working outside the home during the child-rearing period

We will sometimes substitute

$\rho = 1 - \theta$ = proportion of time at home during the child-rearing period for convenience in the mathematical derivations

S = the average interval between births

N = the number of children

Y = parent's consumption of goods other than child numbers or quality

T_F = the mother's age at first birth

T_L = the mother's age at last birth

$\quad = T_F + (N - 1) S$

W_L = the mother's wage in the post-child-rearing period which we assume to be an increasing function of her experience up to T_L:

$$W_L = \varphi(T_F - A + \theta NS), \quad \varphi' > 0 \tag{1}$$

where

A = the mother's age when she entered the labour force in the pre-child-rearing period

A may include a period of education, as well as work. We take it as given in the theoretical analysis, although, to the extent that it includes formal education and even work experience, it may reflect in part the woman's preferences for children (and, therefore, her husband's as well, assuming assortative mating with respect to preferences). We assume she can earn this wage until retirement age, which we take as given.

R = age of retirement

We take as given, as well, the following variables:

C = the non-time or direct costs per child, including expenditures on goods and services during the child-rearing period, which may also contribute to quality

W_F = the mother's wage rate in the pre-first-birth period

To the extent that formal education influences W_F, and to the extent that the formal education a woman seeks is influenced by her preferences for children, this variable may be jointly determined with child numbers, birth spacing, and labour force participation.

W_M = the mother's wage rate or potential wage rate during the child-rearing period

One might also make this a function of experience in the period prior to the first birth, but the analysis is simplified without losing anything essential if we take it to be exogenous.

I = other income, including the father's wage income

τ = the last age at which a healthy child can be born

We assume there is a minimum interval between children:

σ = the minimal average interval between children

Utility is assumed to depend on the consumption of 'other' goods, the number of children, N, and their total 'quality'.

In our basic formulation, 'quality' per child is assumed to be proportional to the amount of time spent by the mother during the child-rearing period. Moreover, we assume that only time between the birth of a child and his or her next younger sibling counts in quality production, so that there are no economies of scale as there would obviously be if mother's time at home could produce quality in more than one child at a time.[4] If we denote the average interval between births by S and the proportion of time during the child-rearing period spent at home by ρ, then the production function for child quality is simply

$$Q = \rho S \tag{2}$$

so that average quality per child only depends on how much time the mother spends at home during the child-rearing period. We assume that mother's time benefits the child only until his next sibling is born and that all children are treated equally including the last child. We assume that S cannot be less than some minimal level σ, which may be in part biologically determined. ρ, of course, must lie between zero and one. Indeed, if quality is essential in the utility function, it is clear from (2) that $\rho = 0$ can never be optimal.

Relaxation of the strict conditions on the production function for quality of children, implicit in (2), to permit economies of scale and purchased inputs is discussed in Nerlove and Razin (1979, Appendix B). We do not, at this point, however, allow purchased inputs, or inputs other than mother's time, to enter the production process.[5] Utility is thus

$$U(Y, N, \rho S)$$

which is to be maximized subject to the budget constraint to be determined.

We divide the work career of the mother into three periods:

(1) The period after entry into the labour force, age A, but before the first birth, age T_F. This period may include education which enhances market productivity; the important thing is that work or other experience in this period enhances the wage of the mother in the post-child-rearing period.

(2) The child-rearing period, which extends from the age at first birth, T_F, until the age at last birth, T_L, plus the average interval between births. It is assumed that whatever interval between births is chosen is applied equally to all children including the last; however, the mother may work during all or part of the child-rearing period.

(3) The post-child-rearing period, in which the mother is assumed to return to market work until the age of retirement, R. Thus, this period extends from $T_L + S$ until R.

During the pre-first-birth period, A to T_F, we assume the mother can earn a market wage, W_F. This is assumed to depend on her education prior to A and other endowments, so that we treat it exogenously to the problem of optimal timing and spacing of children and market work. During the period of child-rearing, we assume the mother can command a market wage of W_M, which, for simplicity, we take to be entirely determined exogenously by the same factors which determine W_F. The wage in the post-child-rearing period is, however, assumed to vary endogenously with the amount of prior work experience a woman has had. Let $\theta = 1 - \rho$ be the proportion of time during the child-rearing period in which a mother engages in market work, then the total work experience to the end of the child-rearing period is

$$T_F - A + \theta NS$$

since T_F, T_L, N and S satisfy the identity

$$T_L = T_F + (N - 1)S \tag{3}$$

and the post-child-rearing period commences at $T_L + S$. Thus, we assume

$$W_L = \varphi(T_F - A + \theta NS), \quad \varphi' > 0 \tag{4}$$

The wage rates W_F, W_M, and W_L should be thought of as the average values of the discounted wages per unit of time for the periods in question. We should also allow anticipated economic growth to affect these wages, which may then affect some of the effects of discounting. Otherwise, W_L will almost certainly be much lower than W_F.

Earnings of the father and other sources of income, I, are treated as exogenous.

Finally, we assume that no family will choose to have a child after the latest age, τ, at which a healthy child can be born.

Thus the budget constraint, subject to which utility is to be maximized, is

$$I + (T_L - (N - 1)S - A)W_F + \theta SNW_M$$
$$+ (R - T_L - S)\varphi(T_L - (N - 1)S - A + \theta NS) = Y + CN \quad (5)$$

Note that the identity $T_L = T_F + (N - 1)S$ has been used to substitute for T_F. This, in effect, makes T_L the choice variable. In this formulation, there is a slight asymmetry between making T_L or T_F the choice variable. Of course, both cases lead to the same optimal solution; it is only a question of how we characterize it.[6] The result obtained when T_F is the choice variable are given below. The term $T_L - (N - 1)S - A$ represents the mother's time between entry into the labour force and age at first birth, the term θSN represents the amount of time the mother spends in the labour force during the child-rearing period. Finally $R - T_L - S$ is the amount of time spent in the labour force at the end of the child-rearing period if we assume that this period extends only to $T_L + S$. While unrealistic, this is clearly innocuous, since any fixed interval could be added without affecting the results. But, note, the existence of such a period might well be cause for economies of scale. The function φ for the mother's wage post child-rearing is evaluated as the time worked before the first birth plus the amount of time worked during the child-rearing period.

The wage rates W_F, W_M and

$$W_L = \varphi(T_L - (N - 1)S - A + \theta NS)$$

may be thought of as average values of the discounted wages per unit time for the periods in question. We should also allow anticipated economic growth to affect these wages as well, and thus offset some of the effects of discounting.

The first-order conditions for T_L, the choice variable

Form the Lagrangian expression

$$\mathcal{L} = U(Y, N, \rho S) + \lambda\{I + (T_L - (N - 1)S - A)W_F + (1 - \rho)SNW_M$$
$$+ (R - T_L - S)\varphi(T_L + S - \rho NS - A) - Y - CN\} \quad (6)$$

Differentiating with respect to T_L, Y, N, ρ, S, and λ we obtain:

$$\lambda\{W_F + (R - T_L - S)\varphi' - W_L\} \geq 0 \tag{7}$$

according as $T_L = \tau$ or $T_L < \tau$.[7] Since, differentiating with respect to Y yields

$$U_Y - \lambda = 0 \tag{8}$$

The quantity λ is the marginal utility of other consumption and must be positive. Therefore, the interpretation of (7) depends on whether a boundary condition is attained for the age at last birth: when the age at last birth is less than the latest age at which a healthy child can be born, the gain to be made by moving the child-rearing period forward by one unit, W_F, is just equal to the net loss in the post-child-rearing period, which consists of one period's wages W_L less the amount gained over the whole post-child-rearing period by virtue of the additional experience prior to the first birth, $(R - T_L - S)\varphi'$. Clearly, when T_L is already at the maximum possible the gain must exceed the net loss (otherwise the family would have the incentive to shift the child-rearing period back).

Differentiating with respect to N:

$$U_N - \lambda\{SW_F - (1 - \rho)SW_M + (R - T_L - S)\rho S\varphi' + C\} = 0 \tag{9}$$

if $N > 0$.[8] We do not consider the boundary solution $N = 0$. Since λ is the marginal utility of other consumption, condition (7) states that the marginal rate of substitution between children and other goods

$$MRS_{NY} = U_N/U_Y$$

equals the 'price' of an additional child in terms of other goods as a numeraire. Holding the interval between children constant, this 'price' consists of two parts: first, the direct, non-time costs of an additional child, C; second, the lost wage in the first pre-child-rearing period, SW_F, plus the reduction in wage in the post-child-rearing period due to reduced experience, $(R - T_L - S)\rho S\varphi'$, net of the additional wage earned during the longer child-rearing period, $(1 - \rho)SW_M$. Note that with S fixed, a larger N implies a longer child-rearing period. Differentiating with respect to ρ:

$$SU_Q - \lambda\{SNW_M + SN(R - T_L - S)\varphi'\} \gtreqless 0$$

according as $\rho = 1$, $0 < \rho < 1$, or $\rho = 0$, where U_Q is the marginal utility of 'quality'. This condition may be more readily interpreted by dividing through by S and substituting $U_Y = \lambda$. Then

$$MRS_{QY} = U_Q/U_Y \gtreqless (W_M + (R - T_L - S)\varphi')N \tag{10}$$

according as $\rho = 1$, or $0 < \rho < 1$. That is, with an interior solution, an increase in the amount of time, holding the interval between children and the number of children fixed, amounts to an increase in child quality. This increase occurs at the expense of time which might be spent working in the child-rearing interval, NW_M, and at the expense of a higher wage in the post-child-rearing interval, $N(R - T_L - S)\varphi'$ due to lost experience. When the mother is full time at home, $\rho = 1$, quality cannot be increased, so that the marginal rate of substitution between quality of children and other goods must be greater than the cost of achieving such an increase through variation in ρ. On the other hand, when the mother works full time outside the home, the marginal rate of substitution between quality of children and other goods must be less than the opportunity cost. The boundary condition $\rho = 0$ is implausible if the couple has any children and quality is essential in the utility function.

Finally, differentiating with respect to S we obtain

$$\rho U_Q - \lambda\{(N - 1)W_F - (1 - \rho)NW_M$$
$$+ W_L - (R - T_L - S)(1 - \rho N)\varphi'\} \leqq 0$$

according as $S = \sigma$ or $S > \sigma$[9]

$$MRS_{QY} = U_Q/U_Y \leqq \frac{1}{\rho}\{(N - 1) - W_F - (1 - \rho)NW_M$$
$$+ W_L - (R - T_L - S)(1 - \rho N)\varphi'\} \quad (11)$$

according as $S = \sigma$ or $S > \sigma$[10]

The condition (11) may be interpreted as follows: Raising S when S is above the minimal interval σ will increase quality *per child* by ρ, since ρ is the fraction of that extra unit of time that will go into quality production. The extra quality, in turn, increases utility by ρMRS_{QY} in terms of other goods. The benefits of an increase in S must be compared with the costs. With N fixed, an increment of 1 unit in S increases the length of the child-rearing period $T_L + S - T_F$ by N units; when T_L is fixed this means T_F must fall by $N - 1$ units, reducing the pre-first-birth interval by $N - 1$ units and wages earned during that period by $(N - 1) W_F$. On the other hand, $1 - \rho = \theta$ fraction of the time during the child-rearing period is spent in market work, so this offsets the wage loss by $(1 - \rho)NW_M$. If T_L is fixed and the woman leaves the child-rearing period at $T_L + S$, an increase in S reduces wages in the post-child-rearing period by W_L. Prior to this time, she loses $1 - \rho N$ units of experience, so her wage in the post-child-rearing period is reduced by $(1 - \rho N) (R - T_L - S)\varphi'$. Clearly, when $S = \sigma$ is minimal, the costs of increasing S must exceed the gains.

Differentiating with respect to λ yields the constraint (3).

The first-order conditions for T_F the choice variable

The Lagrangian expression is

$$\mathcal{L} = U(Y, N, \rho S) + \lambda\{I + (T_F - A)W_F + (1 - \rho)SNW_M$$
$$+ (R - T_F - NS)\varphi(T_F + NS(1 - \rho) - A) - Y - CN\} \quad (6^*)$$

Differentiating with respect to T_F yields

$$W_F + (R - T_F - NS)\varphi' - W_L \gtreqless 0 \quad (7^*)$$

according as $T_L = \tau$, $A < T_F < \tau$, or $T_F = A$, since, as before, differentiating with respect to Y yields $U_Y = \lambda$, which must be positive. If we substitute T_L for T_F from the identity connecting them and N and S, exactly (7) is obtained from (7*).

Differentiating with respect to ρ and substituting $U_Y = \lambda$, we obtain

$$MRS_{QY} = \frac{U_Q}{U_Y} \gtreqless (W_M + (R - T_F - NS)\varphi')N \quad (10^*)$$

according as $\rho = 1$ or $0 < \rho < 1$. Equation (10*) is identical to (10) if we substitute T_L for T_F from $T_F = T_L - (N - 1)S$.

Differentiating with respect to S, and substituting $\lambda = U_Y$, we obtain

$$\rho MRS_{QY} = \rho\frac{U_Q}{U_Y} \lesseqgtr \{W_L N - (1 - \rho)NW_M - (R - T_F - NS)\varphi'N(1 - \rho)\}$$
$$(11^*)$$

according as $S = \sigma$ or $S > \sigma$. Even if we substitute for T_F, equation (11*) is not identical to (11), because (11) is based on the assumption that T_F is at a boundary. The two results are identical, however, if we have a strictly interior solution with respect to T_F and T_L, i.e. $A < T_F \leq T_L < \tau$, because then

$$W_F + (R - T_F - NS)\varphi' - W_L = 0$$

and

$$W_F + (R - T_L - S)\varphi' - W_L = 0$$

When we have a strictly interior solution with respect to T_F and T_L, this determines a relation between W_F and W_L which then enables one to demonstrate the equivalence of (11) and (11*) for a strictly interior solution.

Differentiating with respect to N and substituting $\lambda = U_Y$ we obtain

$$MRS_{NY} = \frac{U_N}{U_Y} = S\{- (1 - \rho)W_M - (R - T_F - NS)\varphi'(1 - \rho) + W_L\} + C$$
$$(9^*)$$

for $N > 0$. (9*) differs from (9) by the appearance of W_F in (9) in place of

$W_L - (R - T_F - NS)\varphi' = W_L - (R - T_L - S)\varphi'$. But, as can be seen from the first-order condition for T_L, the two are equal for a strictly interior solution $A < T_F \leq T_L < \tau$.

Conditions for an inverse relationship between S and θ

One of the important conclusions we seek to establish here is an inverse relationship between S and θ. That one of the two must be at a boundary provides us with a unique measure of child quality. We can then invoke the Becker–Lewis–Tomes analysis to deduce the remaining properties of the model. Unfortunately, the inverse relation of S and θ can only be demonstrated to be plausible and does not unambiguously follow from the assumptions of our model.

Suppose that $S > \sigma$ and $\rho < 1$; then it is possible to decrease S and increase ρ so as to keep $Q = \rho S$ constant. Decreasing S by one period and increasing ρ by a compensating amount without changing the number of children must either raise the age at first birth or lower the age at last birth, or both, if we have a strictly interior solution: with N fixed, a decrease of one unit in S decreases the length of the child-rearing period, $T_L + S - T_F$, by N units and income earned during that period by NW_M. So, if $T_F = A$ is fixed, T_L decreases by N units, increasing the post child-rearing period by N units and wages earned during that period by $W_L N$. The net effect of reducing the length of the child-rearing period by N units and decreasing the amount of time spent working is to reduce experience prior to the post-child-rearing period and to offset the added income by $(R - T_F - NS)\varphi' N$. Clearly, there is no income in the pre-child-rearing period and no change in this as long as $T_F = A$. On the other hand, when $T_L = \tau$ is fixed, T_F increases by $N - 1$ units, so that income in the pre-child-rearing period is increased by $(N - 1)W_F$. Clearly, the income lost during the child-rearing period is the same, NW_M, as when $T_F = A$. Now, however, the net effect of the increase in the post-child-rearing period by one unit and the experience lost during the child-rearing period and gained during the pre-child-rearing period is to increase income in the post-child-rearing period by $W_L - (R - T_L - S)\varphi'$. To summarize: decreasing S by one unit with a compensating increase in ρ (holding $Q = \rho S$ constant) leads to the following change in lifetime income:

$$-NW_M + NW_L - (R - T_F - NS)\varphi' N, \quad \text{when } T_F = A$$

$$(N - 1)W_F - NW_M + W_L - (R - T_L - S)\varphi', \quad \text{when } T_L = \tau$$

$$(12)$$

When $A < T_F < T_L < \tau$, these two changes can be shown to be identical. Clearly, if the family starts from a a position in which it is possible to decrease S and increase ρ, holding Q constant, and if, at the same time, income is thereby increased, the situation cannot be optimal, so it will clearly pay the family to continue changing ρ and S until either $\rho = 1$ with $S > \sigma$ or $S = \sigma$ with $\rho < 1$. Now, if the expected growth in wages is very high, the child-rearing period will be pushed to the earliest possible point so that $T_F = A$; then income increases if

$$W_L - W_M > (R - T_F - NS)\varphi' > 0 \qquad (13)$$

Provided prior experience does not effect W_L too greatly, this will surely be true in a situation in which wages are expected to grow a great deal over time. Moreover, since it is likely to be necessary to work part time or to accept certain kinds of employment consistent with child-rearing, there are other reasons to expect W_M to be substantially less than W_L. Conversely, suppose that no, or little, growth in wages is expected over time; in this case discounting of future wages leads the family to push the child-rearing period to the latest possible point, $T_L = \tau$. In this case, income increases with a decrease in S and compensating increase in $\rho(Q = \rho S = \text{constant})$ if

$$N(W_F - W_M) > W_F - W_L + (R - T_L - S)\varphi' \qquad (14)$$

When discounting predominates, W_F will be considerably larger than W_L; moreover, the term $(R - T_L - S)\varphi'$ is positive; hence, whether or not income will increase with a decrease in S and compensating increase in ρ becomes a question of how much W_F exceeds W_M. For example, if, considering discounted values, W_F is twice W_M and the family has three children, then, neglecting the term $(R - T_L - S)\varphi'$, W_F can be as much as six times W_L. A wage difference of this magnitude caused by discounting alone (i.e. assuming equal undiscounted wages) implies a discount of approximately 13% if the child-rearing period is 15 years. Since the likely rate of discount is less, we conclude that, irrespective of whether $T_F = A$ or $T_L = \tau$, if $S > \sigma$ and $\rho < 1$, decreasing S and increasing ρ so as to hold Q constant will increase income. This is especially true if institutional factors make W_M low relative to both W_F and W_L. When $A < T_F < T_L < \tau$, the condition becomes simply

$$W_F - W_M > 0 \qquad (15)$$

Thus, *in equilibrium* we have either

$$\rho = 1 \quad \text{and} \quad S > \sigma \qquad \text{(I)}$$

or

$$\rho < 1 \quad \text{and} \quad S = \sigma \qquad \text{(II)}$$

Thus, *in equilibrium* we have the positive relation shown in figure 1

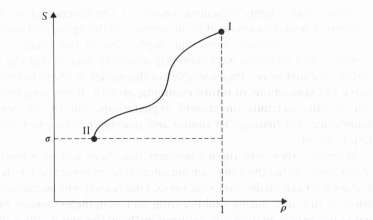

Figure 1. Relationship between interval between births and proportion of time spent at home

between S and ρ from I to II for any individual. This implies a negative relation between $\theta = 1 - \rho$ and S which we have sought to establish as plausible.

If no economic growth were expected, it is clear that W_F would in general exceed W_L so that the child-rearing period would, in this model, be postponed to the last possible moment. On the other hand, if very substantial economic growth is expected, W_L may exceed W_F by more than $(R - T_L - S)\varphi'$, in which case the first birth will be timed as early as possible. Neither type of behaviour is realistic in terms of our casual observation of what couples actually do. There are a number of reasons why the child-rearing period will not usually be pushed to either extreme and why, despite discounting of future earnings, the period will generally occur fairly early: first, fecundity is uncertain; couples do not know whether they will be able to have children, especially whether they will be able to have them near the end of the possible period. Moreover, child rearing may be more difficult and less enjoyable at an advanced age. In addition, if contraception is uncertain, couples may use a less-than-perfect method more-or-less continuously thus stretching out the entire child-rearing period and, on the average, having a first birth earlier than with perfect control. Finally, our assumption that the post-child-rearing period wage is simply a function of earlier experience omits the depreciation of skills and knowledge which may occur simply through the passage of time. If this is important, women with such skills may trade off experience early against a greater depreciation and bear children early in order to re-enter the labour force soon.

In any case, the implication which we wish to draw from the model is not that the child-rearing period will be pushed to one extreme or another, but rather that an exogenous increase in W_F, because for example the woman is more highly educated, should, in the absence of an important element of depreciation, lead to an increase in the age at first birth, *ceteris paribus*. An extremely important implication of the analysis, but one which cannot be tested with presently available data, is that the timing of births, and therefore other variables of the model, is likely to be very sensitive to expectations of future economic growth. It has long been argued that fertility depends on growth expectations, but to the best of our knowledge, the finding that timing and spacing may be even more sensitive is novel.

In general then, our theory predicts that there will be a tendency for much work during the child-rearing interval to be associated with short intervals between births, and vice versa. One reason why women may work part- or full-time during child-rearing and nonetheless space births out with relatively long intervals between births in the real world is that experience accumulated during this period has a more pronounced effect on wages in the post-child-rearing period than experience in the more distant pre-child-rearing period.

The argument so far suggests that, in investigating the comparative statics of our model, we may concentrate on two distinct situations: (1) wage growth over time is anticipated to be substantial and more than offsets the effects of discounting; and (2) wage growth does not offset the effects of discounting. In the first case, the child-rearing period will be as early as possible and birth intervals will be greater for women who do not work at all than for women who work:

$$\text{Case I:} \quad T_F = A \quad \text{and} \quad N > 0$$
$$S = \sigma \quad \text{and} \quad \rho < 1 \quad \text{or} \quad S > \sigma \quad \text{and} \quad \rho = 1$$

In the second case, the child-rearing period will be as late as possible, but the same conditions with respect to S and ρ apply:

$$\text{Case II:} \quad T_L = \tau \quad \text{and} \quad N > 0$$
$$S = \sigma \quad \text{and} \quad \rho < 1 \quad \text{or} \quad S > \sigma \quad \text{and} \quad \rho = 1$$

When the mother is completely specialized at home during the child-rearing period, the problem is identical to the problem considered by Becker and Lewis (1973) and extended by Becker and Tomes (1976). Quality is measured by average birth interval since $\rho = 1$. To paraphrase their results: if the 'true' income elasticity of S, holding constant the 'shadow' prices of S and N, is positive and larger than the true income elasticity of N, then the observed income elasticity of S, holding market prices of S and N constant, will also be positive if the elasticity of substitution between other consumption and the number of children is greater than or equal to the elasticity of substitution between other consumption and the quality of children. Under these circumstances birth intervals will increase with income at the same time that the number of children increases proportionately less or declines.

When the birth interval is minimal, the mother may or may not work outside the home, but, in any case, quality is determined by ρ since $Q = \rho\sigma$. Again, the Becker–Lewis analysis applies with quality interpreted as the fraction of time the mother spends at home. If the elasticity of substitution of child numbers for other consumption is greater than or equal to the elasticity of substitution between child quality and other consumption, and if the true income elasticity of child quality is larger than that of child numbers, then ρ will increase with income while N will either increase less than proportionately or decrease.[11]

The effect of changes in C, the autonomous direct cost per child, is relatively easy to analyse since C enters only the budget constraint and the first-order conditions (8) and (9*), which refer to MRS_{NY}. From the latter we conclude that, if the MRS_{NY} is diminishing, a compensated increase in C must cause N to fall. Moreover, this effect will not be altered if N is a normal good and/or if C is a relatively small part of the costs of a child, i.e. if the time costs bulk relatively large.

What can be said about changes in the timing and spacing of births as a result of exogenous changes in the mother's wage? As usual, changes in wage rates have both an income and a substitution effect, so we must consider compensated changes. We should also restrict ourselves to changes which leave the relation among W_F, W_M, and W_L unchanged, since for example, an increase in W_F unaccompanied by corresponding increases in the levels of W_M and W_L might have the abrupt, discontinuous effects of shifting the whole child-rearing period from the beginning of the life cycle to its end. A compensated change in the level of a mother's wage increases the cost of her time both within the child-rearing period and at either end. In *Case II*, this should lead to a reduction in the number of children and either an increase in the amount worked outside the child-rearing period or a decrease in the interval between children, depending on whether $S = \sigma$ and $\rho < 1$ or $S > \sigma$ and $\rho = 1$. This is because an increase in mother's wage is equivalent to a fall in the price of other consumption and if both child numbers and child quality are equally good substitutes for other consumption, one would expect a substitution away from both. However, one must be careful, because a change in numbers and a change in interval between births or proportion worked during the child-rearing period have different associated costs. In *Case II*, a reduction in numbers, *ceteris paribus*, augments income by SW_F, has no effect on income if the woman does not work during the child-rearing period, and augments income by $(R - T_L - S)S\varphi'$ during the post-child-rearing period. On the other hand, a reduction in interval, *ceteris paribus*, augments income by $(N - 1)(R - T_L - S)\varphi'$ in the final period. In addition, there is a saving of C due to a reduction in numbers of children. A careful analysis would require differentiation of the appropriate first-order constraints and would show the final result to be ambiguous.

3 Empirical results

In this section, we report the results of fitting relationships suggested by the foregoing model to data from the 1971 Étude de la Famille au Québec conducted by the University of Montreal. The Quebec survey contains reasonably detailed information on work history so it is possible to investigate whether or not the interval between births is negatively associated with both child numbers and the proportion of time the mother worked outside the home during the child-rearing period. Although numbers and spacing are strongly negatively associated, unfortunately the expected negative association between birth interval and labour force participation during the child-rearing period emerges only for the sub-sample of Quebec women born before 1936. The husband's education, which is the best indicator we have of the household's permanent income other than the mother's earnings, I, is negatively related to numbers of children in all samples, but sometimes positively related to birth interval and/or female labour force participation, contrary to theoretical expectations. The mother's level of formal schooling is negatively related to birth interval and positively related to labour force participation, as theory predicts. A detailed examination of the results follows.

Two surveys were conducted in 1971 by the University of Montreal. One was addressed to married women born before 1936, the other to married women born after that date.

The information common to both of these surveys is as follows:
(1) *Background variables:* the number of children in the wife's family, her father's level of schooling and occupation; husband's and wife's religion; national origin and birth dates; the area where the wife lived most of the time before marriage; wife's age on the date of marriage; income of the household other than husband's and wife's salaries.
(2) *Other information about the husband:* level of schooling; degree, if any; occupation at marriage and on the date of the survey; employment status on interview date; annual income at the time of the survey.
(3) *Female education and labour-force participation:* years of schooling; degree, if any; occupation, if any; whether she worked before marriage, between marriage and first birth, after the birth of her first child

and at the time of the interview; total number of years she worked after marriage; annual salary at the time of the interview, if applicable.

(4) *Pregnancy history:* the date of birth of each child, sex, and, if applicable, the date of death of the child.

(5) *Contraceptive history:* the contraceptive technique used before each pregnancy, whether it was interrupted in order to conceive; the method used at the time of the survey; knowledge of the various contraceptive methods; attitudes toward the use of contraception.

(6) *Subfecundity:* respondents were asked whether it ever happened that they wished to have a child and they could not, or whether it took them longer than they would have wished to have a child. If they experienced temporary sterility, there is information on when it occurred, whether they sought medical advice, and whether they received treatment.

(7) *Residence:* the area where husband and wife lived most of the time after marriage.

(8) *Preferences for children:* the attitudinal questions included in the survey are the following:

    (a) The more children a couple has, the happier the couple is.

    (b) It is essential for the happiness of a couple to have children.

    (c) In most cases a couple that prefers not to have children is a selfish couple that does not have a sense of responsibility.

    (d) In general those couples having few children are the happiest ones.

    (e) Those couples who decide not to have children are generally very happy.

    (f) People have too many children, and those couples who desire not to have any, help society.

Respondents were expected to express agreement, disagreement, neutrality or uncertainty about these statements.

The survey addressed to women born after 1936 includes *all* of the above information and also the following:

(1) *Female labour-force participation:* If the wife reported she was not working at the time of the interview, she was asked the reasons for this; whether she planned to work later on and at what age, and, also, how much she thought she could make if she were to work full-time in the market. If the wife reported that she was working at the time of the interview, she was asked whether this was on a part-time or full-time basis. If the former, she was asked how much she thought she could command in the market if she were to work full-time. Working women were also asked the reasons for participation, the date until which they expected to work, and whether they anticipated stopping definitely or temporarily at that time. They were also asked about their

child-care arrangements and the expense involved. In addition, each woman interviewed was asked the dates of beginning and end of each job held both before and after marriage, as well as the occupation involved on each occasion.

(2) *Expected fertility and spacing:* number of additional children expected and, if applicable, the dates at which the wife expects to have them.

(3) *Husband's background information:* number of siblings in his family, his father's level of schooling and occupation.

(4) *Wife's attitudes toward policy issues:* whether she feels it would be particularly useful for the government to build more child-care institutions, to engage help to take care of children after school and during vacations.

(5) *Wife's perception of adequacy of family income:* whether she feels that the income of her family is sufficient to fulfil its needs, whether she feels it is greater or smaller than that of most of their friends.

(6) *Aspirations for children's education:* schooling level the wife wishes her sons and daughters to attain.

Of the total of 1745 women interviewed we were able to obtain 404 to 464 (depending on the relation estimated) usable replies for women born in or after 1936 and 385 usable replies for women born before 1936. We call the first sample *Young Women,* and the second sample *Old Women,* with apologies to our readers born before 1936. Because the information collected is different in the two samples and because the Old Women could plausibly be assumed to have completed or very nearly completed their child bearing by the date of the survey, the definitions of the endogenous variables of the empirical counterpart of the model differ somewhat. They are as follows:

NUM *Old Women:* Number of children born alive. We excluded all cases in which no children were reported born alive.

Young Women: Number of children born alive to date of survey plus the additional number of children expected. We excluded all cases in which the woman had no children and did not expect to have any.

$SPAC$ *Old Women:* (Date of the last birth minus date of the first birth) / $(NUM - 1)$. If $NUM = 1$, we set $SPAC = 45 -$ mother's age at first birth. Less than 6% of these women had no child or only one.

Young Women: (Date, actual or expected of the last birth, minus date, actual or expected, of the first birth) / $(NUM - 1)$. As before, if $NUM = 1$, we set $SPAC = 45 -$ mother's age, actual or expected, at first birth. Since the survey only contains information on the expected dates of up to the next three births, if more than three additional children are expected we compute the average interval on the basis of children already born and the next three for whom expected dates of birth are reported.

AGEFB   *Old Women:* Mother's age at first birth.

Young Women: Mother's age at actual or expected first birth.

THETA   Percentage of time in market work during the child-rearing period (*CRP*).

Old Women: $(TOT - A - B)/CRP1$, where TOT = number of years worked after marriage, A = interval between marriage and first birth, B = period between the end of the *CRP* and the date of the survey or age 65, whichever is least, $CRP1$ = date of the last birth plus 6, if $NUM = 1$, or plus *SPAC*, if $NUM > 1$, minus date of first birth. A is subtracted only if the woman reports she worked between marriage and first birth. B is not subtracted if the woman is not working at the time of the survey and is younger than 65.

Young Women: $NUMER/CRP2$, where $NUMER$ = the sum of all work segments during the *CRP* according to the detailed work history, $CRP2$ = date of the last birth plus 6, if $NUM = 1$, or *SPAC*, if $NUM > 1$, minus the date of the first birth, if the date of the last birth plus 6 or *SPAC* is earlier than the date of the survey, otherwise = date of the survey minus the date of the first birth.

The exogenous or explanatory variables used in our study are defined as follows for both Old Women and Young Women:

HEDUC   Husband's education measured as number of years of formal schooling.

WEDUC   Wife's education measured as number of years of formal schooling.

RESID   Residuals of regression of the wife's education on the husband's.[12]

WEXPPD   Dummy variable which equals 1 if the wife had some work experience before marriage and is 0 otherwise.

WEXPAD   Dummy variable which is 1 if the wife had some work experience between marriage and the birth of the first child and is 0 otherwise.

SUBFD   Dummy variable which is 0 if the wife answered 'no' to the question: 'Has it ever happened to you that you wished to have a child and you could not, or that it took you longer than you would have wished to become pregnant?', and is 1 otherwise (i.e. if she answered 'yes', 'don't know', or if there was no response).

ACOND   Dummy variable for attitudes toward contraception, based on the question: 'Many couples try to avoid a pregnancy so as to have the number of children they wish, and have their children when they wish. Do you approve or disapprove of these couples?' *ACOND* is 1 if the answer is 'Approve absolutely', and 0 otherwise.

ARAF   Dummy variable which is 1 if the couple lived in a rural area most of the time after marriage, and 0 otherwise.

Our statistical results are summarized in a series of tables reporting *OLS* and *TOBIT* regressions of the dependent variables *NUM*, *SPAC*, *AGEFB*, and *THETA* on the exogenous variables. In a system of demand equations derived by utility maximization, the appropriate structural equations are also the reduced form equations. Thus, for example, if we argue that there is a negative association between the proportion of time spent working outside the home during the child-rearing period, *THETA*, and the average interval between children, *SPAC*, we would expect to find that the coefficients of the main exogenous variables differ in sign in the two reduced-form equations and that the residuals from the two equations are negatively correlated.

Some of the arguments for this approach have been advanced by M. Rosenzweig (1978, pp. 334–5). The current literature offers two basic econometric approaches. The first consists of formulating a 'structural' model; the dependent variables are treated as jointly determined, and, using simultaneous equations techniques, the direct relationship among them is quantified (see, e.g., DaVanzo, 1972). As noted by Rosenzweig (1978), this procedure leads to some problems. First, inappropriate restrictions may have to be imposed in order to obtain identification. Second, the information the resulting coefficients give us may be uninteresting. For example, if the coefficient of female work in a fertility equation is negative, this does not imply that, say, increasing employment opportunities for women will reduce family size. The negative coefficient may simply reflect the fact that the exogenous variables have influences of opposite signs on each of the dependent variables.

The second approach, used by Rosenzweig (1978) and others, consists of estimating 'reduced-form' equations, i.e. each dependent variable is regressed against all the exogenous variables in the system. Behind this procedure lies the notion that the household decision process is such that a common set of exogenous variables determines the values assumed by the dependent variables. Thus, what is important is to measure quantitatively the impact of each independent variable on each endogenous variable.

We follow the latter approach in this paper. But, in addition, we examine the correlations among the residuals of the reduced form equations. As explained below, this provides some information on the impact of *unobserved* exogenous variables on the dependent variables of interest.

As a very simple example, consider the following equations:

$$WORK = \alpha_0 + \alpha_1 X + \alpha_2 Y$$
$$FERTILITY = \beta_0 + \beta_1 X + \beta_2 Y$$

Let *WORK* represent the level of female labour supply in some given period, and let *FERTILITY* indicate complete family size. X is a vector of the exogenous variables on which we do have information. For simplicity, assume that there is only one independent variable on which we do not have information. Say it is Y, a dummy which equals one if the mother wished to work in the market in the given period, but was unable to find an acceptable job, and is zero otherwise. Thus, $\alpha_2 Y$ is the residual of the *WORK* equation, $\beta_2 Y$ is the residual of the *FERTILITY* equation. Suppose we compute the correlation coefficient between these residuals and obtain a significantly negative number. This would imply that Y influences *WORK* and *FERTILITY* in opposite directions: while Y has a negative influence on *WORK*, it has a positive impact on *FERTILITY*.

In reality, the residuals involve not one but many unobserved variables, ranging from preferences (to the extent these are not captured by the variables we do include) to sex and race discrimination in the labour market. The arguments above indicate that an analysis of the correlations among the residuals from the various regressions provides information as to whether these unobserved variables affect the dependent variables in the same or opposite direction, on average.

Reduced-form equations for *NUM, SPAC, AGEFB,* and *THETA* are presented in tables 1–4. In table 5 we present the simple correlations and the *p*-values of the residuals from the *OLS* estimates of the reduced-form equations and, in the case of *THETA,* from the *TOBIT* relationships.

As expected, the coefficients of husband's education, and other variables, for example, have opposite signs in the equation for *NUM* and those for *SPAC* and *AGEFB*. Unfortunately, this is not the case except for the old women as between the coefficient in either the *OLS* or *TOBIT* equation for *THETA*. Nor does the other important variable in the analysis, *RESID*, work especially well since it has a coefficient with the same sign in the equation for *THETA* and in the equation for *SPAC*. Moreover, the residuals from the two equations are negatively correlated as expected only for the old women. For the most part, however, these results are not significant.

In the equation for *NUM,* we find that husband's education has a significant negative effect on fertility for the older age group but not for the younger. In both cases, *RESID* has a strong negative effect as expected. Work experience before marriage has little effect but if the wife worked after marriage but before the birth of the first child, fertility is significantly

Table 1. Reduced Form OLS Regressions for NUM, Quebec, 1971. Figures in parentheses are standard errors. N = Sample size.

OLS Regression	Constant	HEDUC	RESID	WEXPPD	WEXPAD	ACOND	SUBFD	ARAF	R^2
1. Old women	5.6400	−0.09796	−0.1503	−0.2955	−0.7532	−0.7625	−1.3320	1.2651	0.2386
$N = 333$	(0.3955)	(0.03439)	(0.04974)	(0.2852)	(0.3824)	(0.2548)	(0.3624)	(0.2733)	
Elasticity at mean	—	−0.1993	—	—	—	—	—	—	
2. Young women	4.0987	−0.03734	−0.1191	−0.07053	−0.2934	−0.4572	−0.1618	0.4388	0.1649
$N = 385$	(0.2810)	(0.02000)	(0.02866)	(0.1860)	(0.1559)	(0.1413)	(0.1725)	(0.1431)	
Elasticity at mean	—	−0.1055	—	—	—	—	—	—	

Table 2. Reduced Form OLS Regressions for SPAC, Quebec, 1971. Figures in parentheses are standard errors. N = Sample size.

OLS Regression	Constant	HEDUC	RESID	WEXPPD	WEXPAD	ACOND	SUBFD	ARAF	R^2
1. Old women	2.6878	0.02234	0.003880	0.3796	0.1322	0.01421	0.1608	−0.2706	0.02814
$N = 333$	(0.3036)	(0.02640)	(0.03819)	(0.2189)	(0.2936)	(0.1956)	(0.2782)	(0.2098)	
Elasticity at mean	—	0.06299	—	—	—	—	—	—	
2. Young women	2.2072	0.01216	0.02246	0.2853	0.07917	0.005532	0.04778	−0.04065	0.01566
$N = 385$	(0.2848)	(0.02028)	(0.02905)	(0.1885)	(0.1580)	(0.1432)	(0.1748)	(0.1450)	
Elasticity at mean	—	0.04582	—	—	—	—	—	—	

Table 3. Reduced form OLS regression for AGEFB, Quebec, 1971. Figures in parentheses are standard errors. N = Sample size.

OLS Regression	Constant	HEDUC	RESID	WEXPPD	WEXPAD	ACOND	SUBFD	ARAF	R^2
1. Old women	23.3003	0.1592	0.2179	1.1991	-0.6108	-0.7519	1.9989	-0.4518	0.0771
$N = 333$	(0.8152)	(0.07089)	(0.1025)	(0.5878)	(0.7882)	(0.5252)	(0.7470)	(0.5634)	
Elasticity at mean	—	0.05543	—	—	—	—	—	—	
2. Young women	19.4161	0.1749	0.1351	1.8464	1.03867	-0.3125	0.7851	0.2666	0.1764
$N = 385$	(0.6229)	(0.04435)	(0.06355)	(0.4124)	(0.3456)	(0.3133)	(0.3824)	(0.3172)	
Elasticity at mean	—	0.07411	—	—	—	—	—	—	

Table 4. *Reduced Form OLS and TOBIT Equations for THETA, Quebec, 1971. Figures in parentheses are standard errors. N = Sample size.*

Equation	Constant	HEDUC	RESID	WEXPPD	WEXPAD	ACOND	SUBFD	ARAF	R^2
1. Old women OLS Regression N = 333	0.08864 (0.04472)	−0.006664 (0.003889)	0.004391 (0.005625)	0.06422 (0.03225)	0.3045 (0.04324)	0.01949 (0.02882)	0.06284 (0.04098)	−0.04515 (0.03091)	0.1810
Elasticity at mean	—	−0.4969	—	—	—	—	—	—	—
TOBIT equation	−0.8510 (0.1918)	−0.02012 (0.01478)	0.01916 (0.02091)	0.4178 (0.1522)	0.7241 (0.1413)	0.1641 (0.1144)	0.2887 (0.1490)	−0.2273 (0.1292)	—
N = 333 Elasticity at mean	—	−1.50	—	—	—	—	—	—	—
2. Young women OLS Regression N = 385	−0.004474 (0.08976)	0.003930 (0.006391)	0.03218 (0.009158)	0.02407 (0.05943)	0.4412 (0.04981)	0.02888 (0.04515)	0.005364 (0.05510)	0.006830 (0.04572)	0.2381
Elasticity at mean	—	0.2031	—	—	—	—	—	—	—
TOBIT equation	−1.4635 (0.3198)	0.01098 (0.02030)	0.1001 (0.02886)	0.3358 (0.2433)	1.2540 (0.1439)	0.03725 (0.1496)	0.08065 (0.1652)	−0.09282 (0.1535)	—
N = 385 Elasticity at mean	—	0.567	—	—	—	—	—	—	—

Table 5. *Correlation matrix, residuals from the OLS or TOBIT Reduced-Form Equations, Quebec 1971. Figures in parentheses are p-values.**

	NUM	*SPAC*	*AGEFB*	*THETA* (OLS)	*THETA* (TOBIT)
1. Old women, N = 333					
NUM	1.0000	−0.3249	−0.2921	−0.0467	0.0305
		(0.001)	(0.001)	(0.396)	(0.579)
SPAC		1.0000	−0.1408	−0.0979	−0.0640
			(0.010)	(0.074)	(0.244)
AGEFB			1.0000	−0.0007	−0.0005
				(0.990)	(0.993)
THETA (OLS)				1.0000	—
THETA (TOBIT)				—	1.0000
2. Young women, N = 385.					
NUM	1.0000	−0.3131	−0.2253	0.0514	0.0331
		(0.001)	(0.001)	(0.315)	(0.518)
SPAC		1.0000	0.0537	0.0638	0.0411
			(0.293)	(0.211)	(0.421)
AGEFB			1.0000	−0.0032	−0.0021
				(0.950)	(0.968)
THETA (OLS)				1.0000	—
THETA (TOBIT)				—	1.0000

* A p-value indicates the probability of obtaining a sample value as extreme as that actually observed, assuming the null hypothesis (that the coefficient is zero) is true. The reported p-values are based on two-sided tests.

lower. Attitudes toward contraception, subfecundity and rural residence have the expected signs.

As indicated, these variables have opposite signs in the equations for *SPAC* and *AGEFB* as predicted by the theory, but, unfortunately, our results for *THETA* do not strongly support the hypothesis of a negative association between *THETA* and *SPAC*. For the younger group, the results are the reverse although not significant. We believe that this is due largely to the difficulties in measuring *SPAC* and *THETA* for the younger women who have not completed their families.

Since most fertility surveys concentrate on women in the younger age groups and rarely contain information on work histories, it is likely to be difficult to obtain a definitive test of the hypothesis advanced in this paper. Additional, more detailed data, however, has recently become available for Malaysia and Guatemala. We hope to be able to explore further the hypothesis presented here and will report further results in subsequent papers.

Notes

1 The research on which this paper is based was carried out with the support of the Rand Corporation under Contract AID-otr-c-1432 and the Rockefeller Foundation under a grant to Northwestern University for the study of the Economics of Population and Family Decision Making. Some of the econometric analyses were supported by the National Science Foundation under Grant SOC 74–21194.

We are indebted to Gary Becker, Angus Deaton, Gilbert Ghez, Betsy Hoffman, T. Paul Schultz and Nigel Tomes for helpful suggestions on an earlier draft of part of this paper. Responsibility for any errors remains ours.

2 Lapierre-Adamcyk (1977) has also addressed herself to this question. She shows that female labour force activity, although associated with reduced fertility, cannot be considered a 'direct' cause of the reduction in the number of children. Moreover, the duration of employment both before and after marriage is not associated with fertility aspirations. Labour force activity, especially after marriage, is, however, associated with reduced fertility. In her analysis, Lapierre-Adamcyk relies almost entirely on bivariate cross-tabulations. Our multivariate simultaneous-equations model is intended to complement her research, and we have obtained rather different findings with respect to the relation between female labour force activity and fertility.

3 As Becker and Tomes (1976) show, however, the existence of sizeable innate quality endowments may result in a positive income elasticity of numbers at higher levels of income even though the elasticity is negative at lower levels.

4 Hill and Stafford (1971) have dealt with the question of how the amount of time spent on children by their parents varies with the age, spacing and number of children using data from the Michigan Survey Research Center, described in Morgan, et al. (1966). Their study suggests that the time spent on child care by parents increases with wider spacing. Lindert (1978, appendix C) summarizes existing studies of this problem and reports results using data from a Cornell University survey of 1296 Syracuse families in 1967–68. Lindert's results suggest that 'parental attention is a joint good shared by more than one sibling'. The impact of an infant on total time spent on child care is greater than for an older child, and the impact of a child of a given age tends to be lower the more children there are. His results imply that parents' time is not a perfect 'public good' but that there may be substantial increasing returns to scale.

5 The analysis may be modified to permit a more general production function: $QN = F(\rho SN, KN)$ where K represents inputs in the production of child quality other than mother's time, without any great modification in the implications of the model. In the present formulation, other inputs in the production of child quality are represented by an exogenously determined level per child, C, which represents a deduction from parents' consumption. We suppose that parents cannot affect this level per child nor the contribution of these inputs to child quality.

6 To treat the problem symmetrically, we introduce two Lagrangian multipliers, λ and μ. Then the Lagrangian is

$$\mathcal{L} = U(Y, N, \rho S) + \lambda\{I + (T_F - A)W_F + (1 - \rho)SNW_M \\ + (R - T_L - S)\varphi[T_F - A + (1 - \rho)(T_L - T_F + S)] - Y - CN\} \\ + \mu\{T_L - T_F - (N - 1)S\} \quad (*)$$

Differentiating with respect to N, S, T_F and T_L yields

$$\mathscr{L}_N = U_N + \lambda\{(1 - \rho)SW_M - C\} + \mu(-S) = 0$$

$$\mathscr{L}_S = U_Q\rho + \lambda\{(1 - \rho)NW_M - \varphi + (R - T_L - S)\varphi'(1 - \rho)\}$$
$$\qquad - \mu(N - 1) \leq 0 \qquad\qquad\qquad (**)$$

$$\mathscr{L}_{T_F} = \lambda\{W_F + (R - T_L - S)\varphi'\rho\} - \mu \leq 0$$

$$\mathscr{L}_{T_L} = \lambda\{-W_L + (R - T_L - S)\varphi'(1 - \rho)\} + \mu \geq 0$$

with the inequalities holding in either of the *last two* equations of (**) according as $T_F = A$ or $T_L = \tau$. The inequality in the second equation holds when $T_F = A$. When one equality holds, we may substitute for μ. In this way the two cases of the text are generated: The one we call 'T_L the choice variable' and the other we call 'T_F the choice variable'. Note that $\mathscr{L}_N$, $\mathscr{L}_S$, $\mathscr{L}_{T_F}$ and $\mathscr{L}_{T_L}$ are the only expressions involving μ so that all the other conditions derived in the text remain as stated.

7 Note, we must also have $A + (N - 1)S \leq T_L$ since $T_F \geq A$.

8 We must also have $N \leq \dfrac{T_L - A}{S} + 1$, which will normally hold for plausible values.

9, 10 We must also have $S < \dfrac{T_L - A}{N - 1}$.

11 Razin (1980) shows that if preferences are homothetic, numbers of children will unambiguously decrease with an increase in household income.

12 Elsewhere, Nerlove (1974), has advanced the hypothesis that the residuals of the regression of a wife's formal educational attainment on her husband's formal educational attainment reflect the couples' preferences for children. Thus, the coefficient of *WEDUC* in a regression explaining *NUM* and also including *HEDUC* will be a biased estimate of the effects of the opportunity costs of the wife's time. We have included both *HEDUC* and *RESID* in our regressions rather than *HEDUC* and *WEDUC* separately.

Since the residuals from the regression of a wife's education on that of her husband are simply linear combinations of the two education variables, a regression of a measure of fertility on the two education variables does not provide, of course, an independent test of the hypothesis, but rather a reinterpretation of the coefficients. It is only by comparing the residuals with alternative indicators of underlying preferences, as we do in Nerlove and Razin (1979), that an appropriate test may be obtained. The Quebec data appear to be almost unique in supplying several different alternative indicators of preferences for children.

The relation between the two forms of equation is as follows: Let $NUM = a + b \, HEDUC + c \, WEDUC$ be the regression of *NUM* on *HEDUC* and *WEDUC* separately. Let $RESID = WEDUC - \alpha - \beta \, HEDUC$ be the residuals from the regression of the wife's education on that of her husband. Then $NUM = d + e \, HEDUC + f \, RESID$ where $d = a + c\,\alpha$, $e = b + c\,\beta$, $f = c$. Thus the negative coefficient of *RESID* may simply indicate the usual strong negative relation between a woman's level of formal schooling and the number of children she has.

References

Becker, G. S., and Lewis, H. G. 1973. 'On the interaction between the quantity and quality of children', *Journal of Political Economy*, **81**: 279–88.

Becker, G. S., and Tomes, N. 1976. 'Child endowments and quantity and quality of children', *Journal of Political Economy*, **84**: S143–S162.

DaVanzo, J. 1972. *The Determinants of Family Formation in Chile, 1960: An Econometric Study of Female Labor Force Participation, Marriage and Fertility Decisions*. Santa Monica: Rand Corporation.

Featherman, D. L., Sobel, M., and Dickens, D. L. 1975. 'Manual for coding occupations and industries into detailed 1970 categories and a listing of the 1970 basis Duncan socio-economic and NOPC prestige scores'. Center for Demography and Ecology. *Working Paper 75–1*. University of Wisconsin.

Henripin, J., and Lapierre-Adamcyk, E. 1974. *La fin de la revanche des berceaux: qu'en pensent les Québécoises?* Montreal: Les Presses de l'Université de Montréal.

—— 1975. 'Fécondité et conditions de vie des familles au Québec'. Mimeographed. Université de Montreal.

Hill, C. R., and Stafford, F. P. 1971. 'The allocation of time to children and educational opportunity', Institute of Public Policy Studies Discussion Paper No. 32, University of Michigan.

Lapierre-Adamcyk, E. 1977. 'L'Activité feminine et son influence sur la fécondité'. Unpublished manuscript. Département de démographie, Université de Montreal.

Lindert, P. H. 1978. *Fertility and Scarcity in America*. Princeton: Princeton University Press.

Morgan, J. N., Sirageldin, I. A. and Baerwaldt, N. 1966. *Productive Americans*. Ann Arbor, Michigan: Institute for Social Research.

Nerlove, M. 1974. 'Toward a new theory of population and economic growth', *Journal of Political Economy*. **84**: S200–S219.

Nerlove, M. and Razin, A. (assisted by Wayne Joerding and Evelyn Lehrer). 1979. 'Child spacing and numbers: an empirical analysis'. Discussion Paper No. 371, Center for Mathematical Studies in Economics and Management Science. Northwestern University.

Razin, A. 1980. 'Number, birth spacing and quality of children: a microeconomic view', in Simon, J, and DaVanzo, J. (eds.) *Research in Population Economics*. **II.** Greenwich, Conn.: JAI Press.

Rosenzweig, M. 1978. 'The value of children's time, family size and non-household child activities in a developing country: evidence from household data', pp. 331–47 in Simon, J. L. (ed.) *Research in Population Economics*. **I.** Greenwich, Conn.: JAI Press.

Ross, S. G. 1973. *The Timing and Spacing of Births and Women's Labor Force Participation: An Economic Analysis*, Unpublished PhD dissertation, Columbia University.

Ryder, N. B., and Westoff, C. F. 1971. *Reproduction in the United States, 1965*. Princeton: Princeton University Press.

Sweet, J. A. 1973. *Women in the Labor Force*. New York: Seminar Press.

Tobin, J. 1958. 'Estimation of relationships for limited dependent variables'. *Econometrica*. **26**: 24–36.

Westoff, C. F., and Ryder, N. B. 1977. *The Contraceptive Revolution*. Princeton: Princeton University Press.

Zajonc, R. B. 1976. 'Family configuration and intelligence'. *Science*. **16**: 227–36.

Bibliography of Sir Richard Stone's works 1936–79

1936

[1] A study of costs (with W. A. Tweddle). *Econometrica*, vol. 4, no. 3, 1936, pp. 226–41.

1937

[2] 'Trends' (with W. M. Stone). Monthly articles in *Industry Illustrated*, June–December 1937.

1938

[3] The marginal propensity to consume and the multiplier (with W. M. Stone). *The Review of Economic Studies*, vol. VI, no. 1, 1938, pp. 1–24.
[4] 'Trends' (with W. M. Stone). Monthly articles in *Industry Illustrated*, January–December 1938.

1939

[5] Indices of industrial output (with W. M. Stone). *The Economic Journal*, vol. XLIX, no. 195, 1939, pp. 477–85.
[6] Pitfalls in assessing the state of trade (with W. M. Stone). In *British Management Yearbook 1939*, pp. 21–78.
[7] 'Trends' (with W. M. Stone). Monthly articles in *Industry Illustrated*, January–May 1939.

1941

[8] The construction of tables of national income, expenditure, savings and investment (with J. E. Meade). *The Economic Journal*, vol. LI, nos. 202–3, 1941, pp. 216–31. Reprinted in *Readings in the Concepts and Measurement of Income*, R. H. Parker and G. C. Harcourt (eds.), Cambridge University Press, 1969.

1942

[9] The national income, output and expenditure of the United States of America, 1929–41. *The Economic Journal*, vol. LII, nos. 206–7, 1942, pp. 154–75.

325

[10] The precision of national income estimates (with D. G. Champernowne and J. E. Meade). *The Review of Economic Studies*, vol. IX, no. 2, 1942, pp. 111–25.

1943

[11] National income in the United Kingdom and the United States of America. *The Review of Economic Studies*, vol. X, no. 1, 1943, pp. 1–27.
[12] The fortune teller. *Economica*, New Series, vol. X, no. 37, 1943, pp. 24–33.
[13] Two studies on income and expenditure in the United States. *The Economic Journal*, vol. LIII, no. 209, 1943, pp. 60–75.

1944

[14] Employment in US manufacturing. *The Economic Journal*, vol. LIV, no. 214, 1944, pp. 246–52.
[15] *National Income and Expenditure* (with J. E. Meade). Oxford University Press, 1944; second edition, Bowes and Bowes, Cambridge, 1948; third edition, Bowes and Bowes, Cambridge, 1952; fourth edition, Bowes and Bowes, London, 1957. (See also no. 74 below).

1945

[16] The analysis of market demand. *Journal of the Royal Statistical Society*, vol. 108, pts. 3 and 4, 1945, pp. 1–98.

1946

[17] John Maynard Keynes (obituary). *Economisch-Statische Berichten* (Amsterdam), 17 July 1946.
[18] The national income: a statistical account of the British economy. *The Times*, 27 May 1946.
[19] Economic models with special reference to Mr Kaldor's system (with E. F. Jackson). *The Economic Journal*, vol. LVI, no. 224, 1946, pp. 556–67.

1947

[20] Definition and measurement of the national income and related totals. Appendix to *Measurement of National Income and Construction of Social Accounts*, UN, Geneva, 1947.
[21] Social accounting: I. National income before and since the war; II. Consumption and the course of prices. *The Times*, 29 and 30 August 1947.
[22] On the interdependence of blocks of transactions. *Supplement to the Journal of the Royal Statistical Society*, vol. IX, nos. 1–2, 1947, pp. 1–45.
[23] Prediction from autoregressive schemes and linear stochastic difference systems. Paper presented at the ISC, Washington, 1947. In *Proceedings of the International Statistical Conferences, 1947*, Eka Press, Calcutta, 1951.
[24] The measurement of national income and expenditure: a review of the official estimates of five countries. *The Economic Journal*, vol. LVII, no. 227, 1947, pp. 272–98.

1948

[25] National accounting and national budgeting for economic policy. *National-ekonomiska Föreningens Förhandligar, 1947* (Stockholm), pt. 3, 1948, pp. 63–72.

[26] Social accounting, aggregation and invariance. *Cahiers du Congrès International de Comptabilité,* 1948. French translation: *Economie Appliqu*ée, vol. II, no. 1, 1949, pp. 26–54.

[27] The analysis of market demand: an outline of methods and results. *Review of the International Statistical Institute,* vol. 16, no. 1/4, 1948, pp. 23–35.

[28] *The Role of Measurement in Economics.* The Newmarch Lectures, 1948–49, Cambridge University Press, 1951.

[29] The theory of games. *The Economic Journal,* vol. LVIII, no. 230, 1948, pp. 185–201.

[30] The presentation of the central government accounts (with F. Sewell Bray). *Accounting Research,* vol. 1, no. 1, 1948, pp. 1–12.

[31] British output in 1946–47 (with C. F. Carter and W. B. Reddaway). *The Times,* 18 February 1948.

[32] National income: shift of purchasing power from rich to poor. *The Times,* 3 June 1948.

[33] *The Measurement of Production Movements* (with C. F. Carter and W. B. Reddaway). Cambridge University Press, 1948; reprinted, 1965.

[34] A new index of industrial production (with C. F. Carter, W. B. Reddaway and F. Winter). *Bulletin of the London and Cambridge Economic Service,* vol. XXVI, 1948.

[35] *The Distribution of Income and Saving.* W. F. L. 359, The National Savings Committee, London, 1949.

1949

[36] Functions and criteria of a system of social accounting. Paper presented at the IARIW conference, Cambridge, 1949. In *Income and Wealth, Series I,* Bowes and Bowes, Cambridge, 1951.

[37] The use of sampling methods in national income statistics and social accounting (with J. E. Utting and J. Durbin). Paper presented at the ISI conference, Berne, 1949. *Review of the International Statistical Institute,* vol. 18, no. 1/2, 1950, pp. 21–44; reprinted in *Accounting Research,* vol. 1, no. 4, 1950, pp. 333–56.

1950

[38] The relationship between input–output analysis and national accounting (with J. E. G. Utting). Paper presented at the first International Conference on Input–Output Techniques, Driebergen, 1950. In *Input–Output Relations,* H. E. Stenfert Kroese, Leiden, 1953.

1951

[39] Simple transaction models, information and computing. Paper presented at a conference on Automatic Control, Cranfield, 1951. *The Review of Economic Studies,* vol. XIX (2) no. 49, 1951–52, pp. 67–84.

[40] The demand for food in the United Kingdom before the war. *Metroeco-nomica*, vol. III, no. 1, 1951, pp. 8–27.
[41] The use and development of national income and expenditure estimates. In *Lessons of the British War Economy*, Cambridge University Press, 1951.
[42] Inter-country comparisons of the national accounts and the work of the national accounts research unit of the OEEC (with Kurt Hansen). Paper presented at the IARIW conference, Royaumont, 1951. In *Income and Wealth, Series III*, Bowes and Bowes, Cambridge, 1953.

1952

[43] Systems of aggregative index numbers and their compatibility (with S. J. Prais). *The Economic Journal*, vol. LXII, no. 247, 1952, pp. 565–83.

1953

[44] Model-building and the social accounts: a survey. Paper presented at the IARIW conference, Castelgandolfo, 1953. In *Income and Wealth, Series IV*, Bowes and Bowes, London, 1955.
[45] Recent developments in national income and social accounting (with Milton Gilbert). Paper presented at the ISI conference, Rome, 1953. *Bulletin de l'Institut International de Statistique*, vol. XXXIV, no. 2, 1954, pp. 367–97; reprinted in *Accounting Research*, vol. 5, no. 1, 1954, pp. 1–31.
[46] Forecasting from econometric equations: a further note on derationing (with S. J. Prais). *The Economic Journal*, vol. LXIII, no. 249, 1953, pp. 189–95.

1954

[47] Input–output and the social accounts. Paper presented at the second International Conference on Input–Output Techniques, Varenna, 1954. In *The Structural Interdependence of the Economy*, Wiley, New York: Giuffrè, Milan, 1955.
[48] Linear expenditure systems and demand analysis: an application to the pattern of British demand. Paper presented at the second International Conference on Input–Output Techniques, Varenna, 1954. *The Economic Journal*, vol. LXIV, no. 255, 1954, pp. 511–27. Also in *The Structural Interdependence of the Economy*, Wiley, New York; Giuffrè, Milan, 1955.
[49] Misery and bliss. Paper presented at the World Population Conference, Rome, 1954. *Proceedings of the World Population Conference, 1954*, vol. V, pp. 779–98, UN, New York, 1955. Also in *Economia Internazionale*, vol. VIII, no. 1, 1955, pp. 72–93.
[50] The way the money went. *The Times*, 25 and 26 February 1954.
[51] *The Measurement of Consumers' Expenditure and Behaviour in the United Kingdom, 1920–1938*, Vol. I (with D. A. Rowe and others). Cambridge University Press, 1954.

1955

[52] National income and national accounts: their construction and use in economic policy (in Greek). *Review of Economic and Political Sciences* (Athens), vol. X, no. 1–2, 1955, pp. 1–33.

[53] Transaction models with an example based on the British national accounts (in Spanish). *Boletin del Banco Central de Venezuela,* vol. XV, nos. 119–21, 1955, pp. 12–29. English version: *Accounting Research,* vol. VI, no. 3, 1955, pp. 202–26.

[54] Some estimation problems in demand analysis (with J. Aitchison and Alan Brown). *The Incorporated Statistician,* vol. 5, no. 4, 1955, pp. 165–77.

[55] Aggregate consumption and investment functions for the household sector considered in the light of British experience (with D. A. Rowe). Paper presented at the IARIW conference, Hindsgavl, 1955. *Nationaløkonomisk Tidsskrift* (Copenhagen), vol. 94, pts. 1 and 2, 1956, pp. 1–32.

1956

[56] *Quantity and Price Indexes in National Accounts.* OEEC, Paris, 1956.

[57] *Social Accounting and Economic Models* (in Turkish). Ajans-Türk Matbaasi, Ankara, 1956.

1957

[58] The market demand for durable goods (with D. A. Rowe). *Econometrica,* vol. 25, no. 3, 1957, pp. 423–43. Reprinted in *Consumer Behaviour,* A. S. C. Ehrenberg and F. G. Pyatt (eds.), Penguin Books, Middlesex, 1971.

1958

[59] Can economists help business? *The Accountant,* 22 March 1958, pp. 337–40.

[60] Dynamic demand functions: some econometric results (with D. A. Rowe). *The Economic Journal,* vol. LXVIII, no. 270, 1958, pp. 256–70.

1959

[61] Market forecasting and the family income. *The Times Review of Industry,* vol. 13, no. 153 (new series), 1959, pp. 6 and 9.

[62] *Social Accounting and Economic Models* (with Giovanna Croft-Murray). Bowes and Bowes, London, 1959. Japanese translation (with additions): Tōyō Keisai Shinposha, (New Publishing Co. of the Eastern Economist), 1964. Spanish translation (with no. 74 below): Ediciones Oikos-tau, Barcelona, 1965.

1960

[63] A comparison of the economic structure of regions based on the concept of distance. *Journal of Regional Science,* vol. 2, no. 2, 1960, pp. 1–20.

[64] A dynamic model of demand (in Polish). *Przeglad Statystyczny* (Warsaw), vol. VII, no. 3, 1960, pp. 255–70. English version in 113 below.

[65] Social accounts at the regional level: a survey. Paper presented at the OEEC conference on Regional Economic Planning, Bellagio, 1960. In *Regional Economic Planning: Techniques of Analysis,* OEEC, Paris, 1961.

[66] Three models of economic growth. Paper presented at the International Congress for Logic, Methodology and Philosophy of Science, Stanford, 1960. In *Logic, Methodology and Philosophy of Science*, Stanford University Press, 1962.

[67] The durability of consumers' durable goods (with D. A. Rowe). *Econometrica*, vol. 28, no. 2, 1960, pp. 407–16. Reprinted in *Readings in Economic Statistics and Econometrics*, Ed. Arnold Zellner, Little, Brown and Co., Boston, 1968.

1961

[68] An econometric model of growth: the British economy in ten years time. *Discovery*, vol. XXII, no. 5, 1961, pp. 216–19.

[69] Consumers' wants and expenditures: a survey of British studies since 1945. Paper presented at the CNRS conference, Grenoble, 1961. In *L'évaluation et le rôle des besoins de biens de consommation dans les divers régimes économiques*, Centre National de la Recherche Scientifique, Paris, 1963.

[70] How fast can Britain grow? *The Director*, vol. 13, no. 11, 1961, pp. 286–8.

[71] *Input–Output and National Accounts*. OEEC, Paris, 1961. Russian translation: Statistica Publishing House, Moscow, 1964.

[72] Multiple classifications in social accounting. Paper presented at the ISI conference, Paris, 1961. *Bulletin de l'Institut International de Statistique*, vol. XXXIX, no. 3, 1962, pp. 215–33.

[73] Population mathematics, demand analysis and investment planning (in Polish). *Przegląd Statystyczny* (Warsaw), vol. VIII, no. 2, 1961, pp. 127–36. English version in 113 below.

[74] *National Income and Expenditure* (with Giovanna Stone). Fifth edition, rewritten, 1961; sixth edition, 1962; seventh edition 1964; eighth edition, 1966; ninth edition, 1972; tenth edition, 1977; all Bowes and Bowes, London. Spanish translation (with no. 62 above): Ediciones Oikos-tau, Barcelona, 1965. Japanese translation, 1969.

[75] A long-term growth model for the British economy (with Alan Brown). Paper presented at the IARIW conference, Tutzing, 1961. In *Europe's Future in Figures*, North-Holland Publishing Co., Amsterdam, 1962.

1962

[76] A demonstration model for economic growth. *The Manchester School of Economic and Social Studies*, vol. XXX, no. 1, 1962, pp. 1–14.

[77] Some aggregation problems in input–output analysis (in Polish). *Przegląd Statystyczny* (Warsaw), vol. IX, no. 1, 1962, pp. 25–8.

[78] Models for seasonal adjustment (in Polish). *Przegląd Statystyczny* (Warsaw), vol. IX, no. 2, 1962, pp. 119–34. English version in 132 below.

[79] The housekeeper and the steersman. *L'industria*, no. 4, 1962, pp. 417–26.

[80] *A Computable Model of Economic Growth* (with Alan Brown). No. 1 in *A Programme for Growth*, Chapman and Hall, London, 1962. Czech translation: The Economico-Mathematical Laboratory of the Czechoslovakian Academy of Sciences, Prague, 1965.

[81] *A Social Accounting Matrix for 1960* (with Alan Brown and others). No. 2 in *A Programme for Growth*, Chapman and Hall, London, 1962.

[82] Behavioural and technical change in economic models (with Alan Brown). Paper presented at the IEA conference, Vienna, 1962. In *Problems in Economic Development,* Macmillan, London, 1965.

[83] Output and investment for exponential growth in consumption (with Alan Brown). *The Review of Economic Studies,* vol. XXIX, no. 80, 1962, pp. 241–5.

[84] A post-war expenditure function (with D. A. Rowe). *The Manchester School of Economic and Social Studies,* vol. XXX, no. 2, 1962, pp. 187–201.

[85] A generalisation of the theorem of Frisch and Waugh (in Polish). *Przeglad Statystyczny* (Warsaw), vol. IX, no. 4, 1962, pp. 401–3. English version in 132 below.

1963

[86] Computational analogue of economic growth (in Ukrainian). *Automatika* (Kiev), no. 5, 1963, pp. 39–45.

[87] Consistent projections in multi-sector models. Paper presented at the IEA conference, Cambridge, 1963. In *Activity Analysis in the Theory of Growth and Planning,* Macmillan, London, 1967.

[88] Models of the national economy for planning purposes. *Operational Research Quarterly,* vol. 14, no. 1, 1963, pp. 51–9.

[89] Possible worlds. *The Investment Analyst,* no. 6, 1963, pp. 10–14.

[90] Social accounting and standardised national accounts (in Spanish). *Informacion Comercial Española* (Madrid), no. 356, 1963, pp. 31–9. English version in 132 below.

[91] The *a priori* and the empirical in economics. *L'industria,* no. 4, 1963, pp. 467–86.

[92] The analysis of economic systems. Paper presented at the seventh study week of the Pontifical Academy of Sciences, Rome, 1963. In *Pontificiae Academiae Scientiarum Scripta Varia,* no. 28 (2 vols.), 1965. Also in *The Econometric Approach to Development Planning,* North-Holland Publishing Co., Amsterdam, 1965.

[93] A programme for economic growth (with Alan Brown). *Data Processing,* vol. 5, no. 2, 1963, pp. 70–7.

[94] *Economic Growth and Manpower* (with Alan Brown, Graham Pyatt and Colin Leicester). Report of the BACIE spring conference, 1963. British Association for Commercial and Industrial Education, London, 1963.

1964

[95] A framework for economic decisions. *Moorgate and Wall Street,* Spring 1964, pp. 5–24; reprinted in *Models for Decision,* English Universities Press, London, 1965.

[96] British economic balances in 1970: a trial run on Rocket. Paper presented at the sixteenth symposium of the Colston Research Society, Bristol, 1964. In *Econometric Analysis for National Economic Planning,* Butterworths, London, 1964.

[97] Computer models of the economy. *New Scientist,* vol. 21, no. 381, 1964, pp. 604–5; reprinted in *The World of 1984,* vol. 2, Penguin, 1965.

[98] Mathematics in the social sciences. *Scientific American,* vol. 211, no. 3, 1964, pp. 168–82. Reprinted in *Mathematics in the Modern World,* Freeman, San Francisco and London, 1968. Polish translation: *Matematyka w Swiecie Wsopołczesnym,* Polish Scientific Publishers (PWN), Warsaw, 1966.

[99] Private saving in Britain, past, present and future. *The Manchester School of Economic and Social Studies,* vol. XXXII, no. 2, 1964, pp. 79–112.

[100] The changing pattern of consumption. In *Problems of Economic Dynamics and Planning* (essays in honour of Michal Kalecki), Polish Scientific Publishers (PWN), Warsaw, 1964.

[101] *The Model in its Environment* (expanded version of no. 92 above). No. 5 in *A Programme for Growth,* Chapman and Hall, London, 1964.

[102] Transitional planning. In *On Political Economy and Econometrics* (essays in honour of Oskar Lange), Polish Scientific Publishers (PWN), Warsaw, 1964. Italian translation: *L'industria,* no. 3, 1966, pp. 327–46.

[103] Demand analysis and projections for Britain: 1900–1970: a study in method (with Alan Brown and D. A. Rowe). In *Europe's Future Consumption,* North-Holland Publishing Co., Amsterdam, 1964. Reprinted in shortened form in *Consumer Behaviour,* Eds. A. S. C. Ehrenberg and F. G. Pyatt, Penguin, Middlesex, 1971.

[104] The methodology of planning models (with Colin Leicester). Paper presented at the NBER conference, Princeton, 1964. In *National Economic Planning,* National Bureau of Economic Research, New York, 1967.

[105] Models for demand projections. In *Essays on Econometrics and Planning* (in honour of P. C. Mahalanobis), Pergamon Press, Oxford; Statistical Publishing Society, Calcutta, 1964.

1965

[106] A model of the educational system. *Minerva,* vol. III, no. 2, 1965, pp. 172–86.

[107] Modelling economic systems (in Russian). *Economics and Mathematical Methods* (Moscow), vol. I, pt. 3, pp. 363–90, and pt. 4, pp. 502–14, 1965.

[108] The Cambridge Growth Project. *Cambridge Research,* October 1965, pp. 9–15.

[109] The social accounts from a consumer's point of view. Paper presented at the IARIW conference, Lom, 1965. *The Review of Income and Wealth, Series 12,* no. 1, 1966, pp. 1–33.

1966

[110] Input–output and demographic accounting: a tool for educational planning. *Minerva,* vol. IV, no. 3, 1966, pp. 365–80. Russian translation: *Economics and Mathematical Methods,* vol. III, no. 3, 1967, pp. 355–69.

[111] Mathematical models in educational planning: a view of the conference. Introduction to the proceedings of a meeting held by the OECD, Paris, 1966. In *Mathematical Models in Educational Planning,* OECD, Paris, 1967.

[112] Mathematical models of the economy. *Bulletin of the Institute of Mathematics and its Applications,* vol. 2, no. 3, 1966, pp. 77–87.

[113] *Mathematics in the Social Sciences and Other Essays* (containing nos. 49, 63, 64, 65, 66, 72, 73, 76, 79, 88, 91, 96, 99, 100, 101, 102 and 106 above). Chapman and Hall, London, 1966. Polish translation, *Matematyka w Naukach Społecznych,* Polish Economic Publishers (PWE), Warsaw, 1970.

[114] National income. In *Chambers' Encyclopaedia,* fourth edition, 1966.

[115] Official statistics: a golden treasury or a working tool? Memorandum submitted to the Sub-Committee on Economic Affairs. In *Fourth Report from the Estimates Committee,* HMSO, London, 1966.

[116] Our unstable economy: can planning succeed? Sixth annual lecture of the UK Automation Council, December 1966. Reproduced in *Electronics and Power,* vol. 13, 1967, pp. 40 *et seq.,* and in *Control,* vol. II, no. 104, 1967, pp. 64–6. Italian translation: *L'industria,* no. 3, 1967, pp. 350–61.

[117] Spending and saving in relation to income and wealth. *L'industria,* no. 4, 1966, pp. 471–99.

[118] *The Measurement of Consumers' Expenditure and Behaviour in the United Kingdom, 1920–1938,* Vol. II (with D. A. Rowe). Cambridge University Press, 1966.

1967

[119] Economic and social modelling. Paper presented at a CEIR conference, London, 1967. In *Mathematical Model Building in Economics and Industry,* Griffin, London, 1968.

[120] The generation, distribution and use of income. Paper presented at the ISI conference, Sydney, 1967. *Review of the International Statistical Institute,* vol. 36, no. 2, 1968, pp. 148–57.

[121] The use of social accounting matrices in building planning models. Paper presented at the IARIW conference, Maynooth, 1967. In 132 below.

[122] An example of demographic accounting: the school ages (with Giovanna Stone and Jane Gunton). Paper presented at the IARIW conference, Maynooth, 1967. *Minerva,* vol. VI, no. 2, 1968, pp. 185–212.

1968

[123] Demographic input–output: an extension of social accounting. Paper presented at the fourth International Conference on Input–Output Techniques, Geneva, 1968. In *Contributions to Input–Output Analysis,* vol. 1, North-Holland, Amsterdam, 1970.

[124] A comparison of the SNA and the MPS. Paper presented at the Symposium on National Accounts and Balances, Warsaw, 1968. Polish translation in *Bilanse Gospodarki Narodowej,* Warsaw, 1968. English version in 132 below.

[125] The revision of the SNA: an outline of the new structure. Paper presented at the Symposium on National Accounts and Balances, Warsaw, 1968. Polish translation in *Bilanse Gospodarki Narodowej,* Warsaw, 1968. English version in 132 below.

[126] Input–output projections: consistent prices and quantity structures. *L'industria,* no. 2, 1968, pp. 212–24.

[127] Control of an economic system. In *Encyclopaedia of Linguistics, Information and Control,* Pergamon Press, 1969.

1969

[128] Foreign trade and full employment: an input–output analysis. *L'industria,* no. 4, 1969, pp. 431–43.
[129] *Demographic Accounting and Model Building.* OECD, Paris, 1971.
[130] Economic and demographic accounts and the distribution of income. Paper presented at the Symposium on National Economic Modelling, Novosibirsk, 1970. Russian translation: *Economics and Mathematical Methods,* vol. VII, no. 5, 1971, pp. 658–66. English version: *Acta Oeconomica,* vol. 11, no. 2/3, 1973, pp. 165–76.

1970

[131] An integrated system of demographic, manpower and social statistics and its links with the system of national economic accounts. Report discussed by an expert group convened by the Statistical Office of the UN, Geneva, 1970. *Sankhyā, Series B,* vol. 33, pts. 1 and 2, 1971, pp. 1–184.
[132] *Mathematical Models of the Economy and Other Essays* (containing 69, 78, 85, 87, 90, 105, 109, 110, 111, 112, 116, 117, 120, 121, 122, 124, 125, 126 and 128 above). Chapman and Hall, London, 1970.
[133] Process, capacity and control in an input–output system. *L'industria,* no. 1/2, 1973, pp. 3–17.
[134] The fundamental matrix of the active sequence. Paper presented at the Fifth International Conference on Input–Output Techniques, Geneva, 1971. In *Input–Output Techniques,* North-Holland, Amsterdam, 1972. French translation: *Cahiers du Séminaire d'Econométrie,* no. 14, 1972, pp. 9–23.

1971

[135] A system of social matrices. Paper presented at the IARIW Conference, Ronneby, 1971. *The Review of Income and Wealth,* series 19, no. 2, 1973, pp. 143–66. Spanish translation: *Desarrollo Económico* (Buenos Aires), vol. 13, no. 49, 1973, pp. 169–97.
[136] The evaluation of pollution: balancing gains and losses. *Minerva,* vol. X, no. 3, 1972, pp. 412–25.

1972

[137] A Markovian education model and other examples linking social behaviour to the economy. *Journal of the Royal Statistical Society, Series A (General),* vol. 135, pt. 4, 1972, pp. 511–43.
[138] Transition and admission models in social demography. Paper presented at a Conference on quantitative Social Theory and the Study of Formal Organizations, Virginia, 1972. *Social Science Research,* vol. 2, no. 2, 1973, pp. 185–230; also in *Social Indicator Models,* Russell Sage Foundation, New York, 1975.
[139] Demographic growth and the cost of education. In *Population Growth and Economic Development in the Third World,* 2 vols., International Union for the Scientific Study of Population, Ordina Editions, 1976.

1973

[140] Personal spending and saving in postwar Britain. In *Economic Structure and Development* (essays in honour of Jan Tinbergen), North-Holland, Amsterdam, 1973.
[141] Statistics. To be published in *Enciclopedia del Novecento*, Istituto della Enciclopedia Italiana, forthcoming.
[142] Demographic variables in the economics of education. Paper presented at an International Economic Association conference held at Valescure, 1973, and published in *Economic Factors in Population Growth*, Macmillan, London, 1976. Hungarian translation of a preliminary version: *Demográfia*, vol. XVII, no. 1, 1974, pp. 11–41.

1974

[143] Random walks through the social sciences. Paper presented at the Sixth International conference on Input–Output Techniques, Vienna, 1974.
[144] What is wrong with the national accounts? Paper prepared for the Statistical Office of the United Nations for submission to the Statistical Commission.
[145] Towards a model of inflation, 1: a survey of some recent findings on the determinants of changes in wages and prices.

1975

[146] Social statistics and social policy. Paper presented at the 40th Session of the International Statistical Institute, Warsaw, 1975. *Bulletin de l'Institut International de Statistique*, vol. XLVI, no. 1, 1975, pp. 498–510. Reproduced in *Statistical Policy in Less Developed Countries*, IDS Communication 114, 1975. French version: *Economie et Statistique*, no. 75, 1976, pp. 21–6. Hungarian translation: *Demográfia*, vol. XVIII, no. 4, 1975, pp. 467–78.
[147] The expanding frontiers of input–output analysis. Paper presented at the 40th Session of the International Statistical Institute, Warsaw, 1975. *Bulletin de l'Institut International de Statistique*, vol. XLVI, no. 1, 1975, pp. 306–21.
[148] Modelling the educational system. Paper presented at a Research Planning Conference on the Demography of Educational Organizations, Cambridge, Mass., 1975.
[149] Introduction to *Social Accounting for Development Planning: With Special Reference to Sri Lanka* by Graham Pyatt, Alan R. Roe and associates. Cambridge University Press, 1977.
[150] Direct and indirect constraints in the adjustment of observations. In *Nasjonalregnskap, Modeller og Analyse* (essays in honour of Odd Aukrust), Statistisk Sentralbyrå, Oslo, 1975.

1976

[151] Major accounting problems for a world model. Paper presented at a working seminar on Global Opportunities and Constraints for Regional Development,

Harvard University, Cambridge, Mass., 1976. In *Problems of World Modeling*, Ballinger, Cambridge, Mass., 1977. Hungarian translation: *Demográfia*, vol. XX, no. 1, 1977, pp. 23–55.
[152] Michael James Farrell (obituary). *Annual Report of the Council of King's College, Cambridge*, 1976, pp. 34–6.
[153] Abraham Aidenoff, 1913–1975 (obituary). *International Statistical Review*, vol. 44, no. 3, 1976, pp. 383–4.

1977

[154] The evolution of the Cambridge Growth Project. Lecture given at the Institut für Siedlungs-und Wohnungswesen der Westfälischen Wilhelms-Universität Münster. In *Beiträge zur Strukturpolitik*, Materialien zum Siedlungs-und Wohnungswesen und zur Raumplanung, no. 18, Münster, 1977. Hungarian translation: *Statistikai Szemle*, vol. 56, no. 3, 1978, pp. 236–49.
[155] Introduction to *Inland Revenue Report on National Income, 1929*. Department of Applied Economics, University of Cambridge, 1977.
[156] Introduction to *Econometric Contributions to Public Policy*, the proceedings of a conference held by the International Economic Association, Urbino, 1976, Macmillan, London, 1978.
[157] Harry Gordon Johnson (obituary). *Annual Report of the Council of King's College, Cambridge*, 1977, pp. 24–6.
[158] Discussion of Professor Abramovitz's paper on Rapid Growth Potential and its Realisation: The Experience of Capitalist Economies in the Postwar Period. Presented at the Fifth World Congress of the International Economic Association, Tokyo, 1977. In *Economic Growth and Resources. Vol. 1 The Major Issues*. Macmillan, 1979, pp. 34–44.

1978

[159] Introduction to *Towards a Methodology for Projecting Rates of Literacy and Educational Attainment*. UNESCO, Paris, 1978.
[160] The disaggregation of the household sector in the national accounts. Paper presented to the World Bank SAM Conference, Cambridge, England, 1978. To be published.
[161] Multipliers for Quesnay's tableau. To be published.
[162] Keynes, political arithmetic and econometrics. British Academy, Seventh Keynes Lecture in Economics, 1978. To be published.
[163] Input–output analysis and economic planning: a survey. Paper presented to an International Symposium on Mathematical Programming and Its Applications in Economics, Venice, 1978. To be published.
[164] Jacob Marschak, 1898–1977 (obituary). *Journal of the Royal Statistical Society, Series A (General)*, vol. 142, pt. 1, 1979, pp. 80–1.
[165] Tribute to Luigi Solari. Address presented to the European Meeting of the Econometric Society, Geneva, 1978. To be published.

1979

[166] Where are we now? A short account of the development of input–output studies and their present trends. Paper presented at the Seventh International Conference on Input–Output Techniques, Innsbruck, 1979.
[167] Sigmoids. Opening address to the Royal Statistical Society Conference, Oxford, 1979.
[168] Aspects of economic and social modelling. Lectures delivered at the University of Geneva, 1979.
[169] A simple stable model of economic growth.

Index of names

Subject index